CW01262752

TEXTUAL TRADITIONS AND MEDIEVAL LITERARY CULTURE

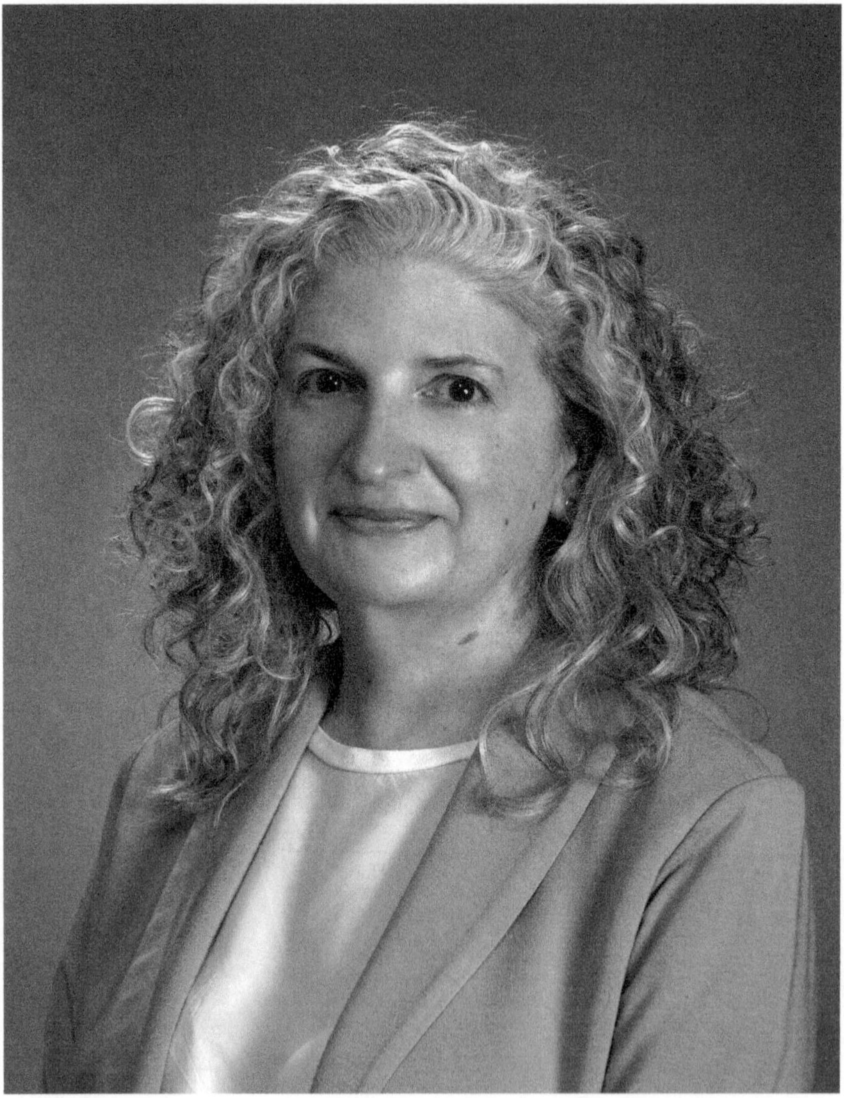

TEXTUAL TRADITIONS AND MEDIEVAL LITERARY CULTURE

ESSAYS IN HONOUR OF SIÂN ECHARD

Edited by

William Green, Daniel Helbert, and Noëlle Phillips

D. S. BREWER

© Contributors 2025

All Rights Reserved. Except as permitted under current legislation no part of this work may be photocopied, stored in a retrieval system, published, performed in public, adapted, broadcast, transmitted, recorded or reproduced in any form or by any means, without the prior permission of the copyright owner

First published 2025
D. S. Brewer, Cambridge

ISBN 978 1 84384 698 7

D. S. Brewer is an imprint of Boydell & Brewer Ltd
PO Box 9, Woodbridge, Suffolk IP12 3DF, UK
and of Boydell & Brewer Inc.
668 Mt Hope Avenue, Rochester, NY 14620–2731, USA
website: www.boydellandbrewer.com

A CIP catalogue record for this book is available
from the British Library

The publisher has no responsibility for the continued existence or accuracy of URLs for external or third-party internet websites referred to in this book, and does not guarantee that any content on such websites is, or will remain, accurate or appropriate

Please note that some of the discussion in this book addresses sensitive issues including sexual violence

This volume is dedicated to Siân Echard: a brilliant scholar, a wise mentor, and a kind colleague.

⊰ CONTENTS ⊱

List of Illustrations	ix
List of Contributors	x
List of Abbreviations	xii
Acknowledgements	xiii

Introduction   1
    WILLIAM GREEN, DANIEL HELBERT, AND NOËLLE PHILLIPS

PART I: NAVIGATING MULTILINGUALISM: MEDIEVAL BRITISH LANGUAGES IN CONTACT

1. *Gormes* and *Ysgymun* in the Dingestow *Brut*   9
   JOSHUA BYRON SMITH

2. *Melioratum ... et emendatum*: Rewriting, Polishing, and Textual Fluidity among Twelfth- and Thirteenth-Century Latin and Welsh Writers in Britain   25
   PAUL RUSSELL

3. Precarious Reimaginings of the British History in the English *Brut* Tradition   42
   JOHN J. THOMPSON

4. The Weight that English Carries: Vernacularity from *Hali Meiðhad* to Chaucer's *House of Fame*   59
   ANDREW GALLOWAY

PART II: GOWER'S BOOKS AND BOOKS OF GOWER

5. Gower's Ovidian Aesthetic and Its Discontents   89
   R. F. YEAGER

6. Gower's Allusive Forms: Anaphora and Political Desire in the *Visio Anglie*   108
   STEPHANIE L. BATKIE

7. Gower and the Heavens: The 'Dull' and the Divine in *Confessio Amantis*   133
   WILLIAM GREEN

8. A Knight at the Roxburghe (Club): George Granville Sutherland-Leveson-Gower and the Textual Transmission of *Balades and Other Poems by John Gower*   152
   DAVID WATT

PART III: HEROES AND THEIR AFTERLIVES

9. The Idea of *Beowulf* and 'The Book Beautiful'   169
   ELAINE TREHARNE

10. Trojan Ghosts in Arthurian Romance   193
    ELIZABETH ARCHIBALD

11. In Defence of British History: Sir John Prise, King Arthur, and the Tudors   212
    HELEN FULTON

12. Boys Gone Wild: Britain's Mythic Tradition in America's Boys' Clubs   229
    MARTIN B. SHICHTMAN AND LAURIE A. FINKE

Annotated Bibliography of Siân Echard's Publications   247
   KELSEY MOSKAL AND MAIRI STIRLING HILL

Index   260
Tabula Gratulatoria   267

ILLUSTRATIONS

9.1	William Morris's *Beowulf*.	187
9.2	Two *Beowulf* facsimiles, Zupitza's edition and Davis' re-edition.	190
9.3	Stanford's copy of the EETS edition of *Beowulf* edited by Julius Zupitza.	191
12.1	A boys' club engaging in chivalric rituals.	231
12.2	A depiction of a knight being armed.	245

⊰ CONTRIBUTORS ⊱

Elizabeth Archibald is Emeritus Professor of English Studies at Durham University

Stephanie L. Batkie is Teaching Professor of English at The University of the South

Laurie Finke is Professor Emerita of Women's and Gender Studies at Kenyon College

Helen Fulton is Chair in Medieval Literature in the Department of English at the University of Bristol

Andrew Galloway is James John Professor of Medieval Studies at Cornell University

William Green is Instructor of English at the University of Northern British Columbia

Daniel Helbert is Assistant Professor of English in the Department of Literature and Languages at Young Harris College

Mairi Stirling Hill was a PhD candidate under Siân Echard in the Department of English Language and Literatures at the University of British Columbia and defended her dissertation while this volume was being completed.

Kelsey Moskal is a PhD candidate under Siân Echard in the Department of English Language and Literatures at the University of British Columbia

Noëlle Phillips is Instructor of English at Douglas College and Honorary Affiliate Lecturer at the University of British Columbia

Paul Russell is Emeritus Professor of Celtic in the Department of Anglo-Saxon, Norse & Celtic at the University of Cambridge

Martin B. Shichtman is Professor Emeritus of English Language and Literature and was founding Director of Eastern Michigan University's Center for Jewish Studies

Joshua Byron Smith is Associate Professor of English at the University of Arkansas

John Thompson is Emeritus Professor of English in the School of Arts, English and Languages at Queen's University Belfast

Elaine Treharne is Roberta Bowman Denning Professor of Humanities and Professor of English at Stanford University

David Watt is Professor in the Department of English, Theatre, Film & Media at the University of Manitoba

R. F. Yeager is Professor of English Literature and Language, Emeritus, at the University of West Florida.

ABBREVIATIONS

BD	*Brut Dingestow*
BL	British Library
BN	Bibliothèque nationale de France
CA	John Gower, *Confessio amantis*
DGB	Geoffrey of Monmouth, *De gestis Britonum*
DOE	*The Dictionary of Old English*
EEMF	Early English Manuscripts in Facsimile
EETS	Early English Text Society
o.s.	Original series
e.s.	Extra series
MED	*Middle English Dictionary*
MO	John Gower, *Mirour de l'Omme*
OED	*Oxford English Dictionary*
SATF	*Société des anciens textes français*
SGGK	*Sir Gawain and the Green Knight*
STC	A. W. Pollard and G. R. Redgrave, *A Short Title Catalogue of Books Printed in England, Scotland, and Ireland and of English Books Printed Abroad, 1475–1640*
TEAMS	Teaching Association for Medieval Studies
TLF	*Texts littéraires français*
VC	John Gower, *Vox clamantis*

ACKNOWLEDGEMENTS

We would like to thank our stellar list of contributors for giving their time, energy, and expertise to this project. It has been a privilege to usher such brilliant work into publication. We also, of course, thank our honoree, whose prolific scholarly output has continued for decades even while she taught classes, raised children, and enjoyed her hobbies. Siân is truly a model of the academic life well-lived (#goals!). We are grateful to the Boydell editorial team and to the anonymous readers who provided helpful guidance as this project developed. Finally, the three of us each owe a debt of gratitude to our respective spouses and children, who often had to deal with our late nights and our exhaustion as we completed this mammoth project. We are grateful for your patience as we worked on this labour of love.

Introduction

WILLIAM GREEN, DANIEL HELBERT, AND NOËLLE PHILLIPS

For over three decades, Siân Echard has made a multitude of important scholarly contributions to a diverse range of fields relating to the study of the Middle Ages. From work on the poems of John Gower, to Arthurian matter and early British historiography, to the study of early printings of medieval texts, to nineteenth-century medievalism, Echard's interventions across the field of medieval studies have always been marked by her ability to draw connections. Indeed, the beauty of Echard's scholarship is the way it reveals so many meaningful connections between what appear to be separate areas of study. Echard's contributions have demonstrated, among other things, how Latin literature has been underappreciated in the Arthurian tradition, how Gower's multilingual literary output is undervalued in comparison to his contemporaries, and how printing practices in modernity shaped both popular and academic perceptions of the Middle Ages. In this volume, we have attempted to honour both the breadth and quality of her research and the positive effect she has had on so many other scholars.

Echard's endless intellectual pursuits may have been influenced by those of her late advisor, George Rigg, who was known for wide-ranging scholarly interests himself. When she began her academic career at the University of Toronto's Centre for Medieval Studies, where she completed her master's and doctoral work under Rigg's tutelage, she had the opportunity to learn from a scholar whose research covered an impressive range of fields, from manuscript miscellanies to medieval Latin texts to *Piers Plowman*. In the Festschrift she edited to honour her mentor, Echard spoke to Rigg's influence upon medieval studies when she described the challenges of trying to capture his body of work: 'It took more than a dozen people to put together a tribute whose range suggests what George encompasses in a single person.'[1] Given Rigg's own prolific output and generous spirit, it is perhaps not surprising that his advisee engaged in a similarly diverse array of research interests – and galvanised a similarly devoted following of students. Inspired and encouraged by Rigg, Echard began establishing a name for herself as an Anglo-Latinist, a

---

[1] Siân Echard and Gernot Wieland, eds, *Anglo-Latin and Its Heritage: Essays in Honour of A. G. Rigg on his 64th Birthday* (Turnhout, 2001), xiv.

field that ultimately drew her to the multilingual work of John Gower. Soon she was branching off into Arthuriana, Geoffrey of Monmouth, manuscript transmission, medievalism, and the post-medieval life of medieval books (and we are all interested to see what field she will break into next). At the end of this volume, readers can peruse an annotated bibliography of Echard's work thus far, a collection assembled by two of her recent doctoral advisees.

As three of Echard's former doctoral students, we feel honoured to be able to take this opportunity to reflect upon what medievalists have learned from her, and to celebrate her innovative and insightful scholarship alongside this volume's esteemed contributors. The collection of essays we have gathered together may cause consternation among those hoping to confine it within easily definable parameters: we present essays on Welsh literature alongside studies of Gower; we group Arthurian studies together with book history; and we align Anglo-Latin historiography and medievalism. To future bibliographers and librarians, we offer our sympathies, but the organising principle behind our work here necessarily reflects the diversity of Echard's extensive scholarship.

To be able to contribute meaningfully to such diverse fields is an impressive enough accomplishment, but Echard has never contented herself with merely being a contributor; she is a compelling and compassionate leader. She is frequently sought out to edit major companion collections and to provide definitive treatments of the state of her various fields of study, as her recent publication history attests, as well as to deliver keynote addresses and tutor rising scholars. Our academic community has consistently relied on Echard to guide and develop us, to inform and educate us, to surprise and captivate us over and again with her forays into medieval culture, always with wisdom, encouragement, and no small amount of razor-sharp wit. And most importantly, we have relied on Echard to *connect* us, to lure us out of our disciplinary silos in order to engage with one another in meaningful ways. Echard has long been interdisciplinary in her scholarship, her teaching, and her collaborations – regardless of whether 'interdisciplinarity' was in style at a given time.

Echard's ability to make meaningful connections in unexpected places has also been a cornerstone in her teaching duties, duties that, frankly, she has taken far more seriously and personally than many scholars of her merit are apt to do. She is universally beloved by her students, at all levels, because it is obvious she has poured just as much effort into designing and executing her classes as she does the books she has written. This dedication to her students is readily apparent in the large amount of teaching material that Echard painstakingly creates for each of her classes and then generously distributes to the world, making better teachers of medieval literature everywhere. Her excellence in teaching has long been recognised by her university, which awarded her its highest prize for teaching in 2001. She leads the classroom with commanding confidence, infectious curiosity, and a sense of humour that will leave even the surliest of pedants in stitches.

As Echard's former students, we feel we would be remiss were we not also to mention how much we, and her many other advisees at all levels, value the lessons we have learned, and continue to learn, under her mentorship. These lessons are, of course, not only about medieval literature. Siân is a role model for those in the early stage of their academic career: she understands the flexibility needed for students with growing families, those who are displaced, and those with diverse backgrounds. She has given valuable input on expected academic challenges such as getting past a cutting reader report or learning how to make one's scholarly work both rigorous and generous (a true skill, and one that Echard has repeatedly shown in her own publications). However, she has also provided guidance in more personal ways: she has been sought out for advice on navigating academia as a woman, on immigration conundrums, on non-academic job prospects for spouses and partners, and on choosing baby names with Welsh puns. As in her scholarship and her teaching, Echard is an exemplary role model; we were, and are, fortunate to have her.

In honour of Siân Echard's contributions as a scholar, teacher, and mentor, this group of seasoned veterans and rising stars have offered essays that span an impressive breadth of topics and, yet, are still intimately connected by many of the same impulses and worldviews. These essays collectively illuminate how medieval culture and identity has actively shaped, even as it has been shaped by, later authors, texts, and communities. As Echard has repeatedly demonstrated in her scholarship, the past is rarely, if ever, represented at face value by the cultural products that lay claim to it; our notion of the medieval past and its products is ever being reworked in another's image, shaped and contended with to frame an altered image for future generations. How did Britain confront its Welsh origins in Anglo-Latin and English literature? How did Gower grapple with his classical inheritance in Ricardian England? How has modernity contended with the lucid material evidence of the Middle Ages, connecting us with our medieval predecessors while also interpolating them? These essays emphasise that the medieval past, even within the Middle Ages, is an idea to be engaged with and adapted rather than passively accepted.

The first section of this book, 'Navigating Multilingualism: Medieval British Languages in Contact', is a testament to Echard's longstanding investments in the metamorphic potential of linguistic and cultural exchange. The essays in this section explore the movement of medieval texts through a linguistic landscape of impressive diversity. Joshua Byron Smith offers a close reading of a Welsh translation and adaptation of Geoffrey of Monmouth's *De gestis Britonum*, revealing the subtle but meticulous and thorough revisions the translator has made to demonise the pagan English and lionise the Christian Welsh. Revising and reframing the past is also a key concern in Paul Russell's essay, which examines the deliberate revisions made by Gerald of Wales to his own writings as a means of speculating on the motivations of those who revised and redacted the *De gestis Britonum* into its various recensions.

Further translations and revisions to Geoffrey's core conception of British history were made well into the Tudor era, as John Thompson's contribution to this collection describes in detail. Andrew Galloway then pans back out to reflect on medieval British languages from a wide and diachronic lens, tracing literary vernaculars from Early Middle English through Chaucer. Galloway yokes the concept and function of 'vernacularity' – especially as it is related to the polylingual state of the medieval English language – with conversations about language in African postcolonial writing. Galloway grounds these concepts in a reinterpretation of the widely documented changes in the status of the English language during the late medieval period, bringing Chaucer and the author of the Katherine Group into discussion with Chinua Achebe and Obiajunwa Wali.

The second section of our Festschrift focuses on the work of Gower, one of the poets to whom Echard's scholarship frequently returns. Echard's work, from the beginning of her career, has contributed richly to our understanding of Gower's poetry, his use of classical sources, and the post-medieval printing and reception of his works. Our contributors to this section continue these discussions in conversation with and appreciation of her interventions in Gowerian scholarship. In his essay, R. F. Yeager discusses the evolution of Gower's relationship with Ovid, the classical author who looms largest in his work, asking us to consider what it means for our perception of both of these complicated poets to try to identify *which* Ovid was 'Gower's Ovid'. Stephanie Batkie provides a compelling reading of Gower's use of classical rhetorical devices in his dream-vision warning of his fears of fourteenth-century England's potential for social breakdown in the wake of the peasants' revolt of 1381, arguing that Gower looks to Ovid in seeking to produce a recounting of the events that 'escapes the limits of the chronicle and coercion of the propagandistic'. In his essay examining the astronomical section of Book VII of Gower's *Confessio Amantis* and its critical reception, William Green asks us to reconsider our relationship with the extant products of medieval literary culture that we often consider ordinary and potentially dull. He argues that the texts that provoke these reactions should more often be recognised as the most potentially interesting, because they speak to the epistemological gulf between ourselves and the people who produced and used them. Finally, David Watt details the editorial history of an 1818 edition of Gower produced by the Second Earl Gower in arguing for a reconsideration of the editorial activities of the Roxburghe Club. Watt makes the case that Earl Gower, in using both an eighteenth-century transcription and the original manuscript to create his edition of the Trentham Manuscript, revealed something of the unexpressed editorial philosophies of Roxburghe Club members. Earl Gower's commitment to conveying and preserving what Jerome McGann calls the linguistic and bibliographic codes of the original medieval text is a prototype of later, more formalised, editorial philosophies. Watt's discussion reveals how Earl Gower's editorial practice anticipates our current debates about the use of digitised manuscripts and what truly counts as 'original'.

The final section of this volume, 'Heroes and Their Afterlives', captures the chronological and generic diversity of Echard's work, with essays that move from Old English poetry to modern libraries to American boys' organisations. Much of Echard's scholarship has explored the extended lives of manuscripts, the stories they house, and how history is made; as such, the essays in this final section honour the broad scope of her work and the insights it offers into modern society. Elaine Treharne takes readers from early English to the modern moment with her exploration of the full 'plenitextuality' of *Beowulf* in all its forms. Treharne's theorisation of plenitextuality – the 'wholeness' of a book – employs the analytic structure of Intentionality + Materiality + Functionality +/- Cultural Value, a formula that expands upon the more traditional 'Production, Transmission, Reception'. The plenitextual life of *Beowulf*, in its various editions, transcriptions, translations, and adaptations, as well as its existence in a composite manuscript, offers a multiplicity of 'whole' books – many different *Beowulf*s, in 'its thousands of edifices'. Moving from one famous medieval king to another, Elizabeth Archibald's essay considers the role of the ancient Trojan heroes in medieval tales of King Arthur. Archibald traces out the remnants of Troy, or its 'ghosts', in French and English romances and demonstrates how transient, deeply ambiguous, and, in her words, 'unsettling' the use of Trojan precedent in Arthurian legends is. Continuing on the path of Arthurian histories, Helen Fulton explores how the early modern writer Sir John Prise connected the medieval King Arthur to British historiography – and more specifically, Welsh historiography and a revised sense of true 'Britishness'. After outlining centuries of medieval and early modern British historiography, Fulton shows how Prise not only redeemed Geoffrey of Monmouth's account of Arthur but ostensibly documented Arthur's historical existence as a king of Welsh origin – a British king, rather than an English one. The final chapter jumps from the sixteenth to the late nineteenth century, with Martin Shichtman and Laurie Finke's account of Arthuriana in the United States. They explore how clergyman William Byron Forbush responded to contemporary anxieties about young boys 'gone wild' by creating a boys' club modelled upon King Arthur and his knights. Shichtman and Finke describe how, in these clubs, the medieval figure of Arthur functioned as a heroic model of white masculinity that shaped the American sense of manhood.

Many of the essays in this volume engage with a recurring theme of Echard's scholarship: the intersection of past and present, and of ideology and materiality, in the creation of meaning. In *Printing the Middle Ages*, Echard contends that 'any reading of a medieval text, past or present, amateur or professional, floats on the surface of a complex sea of expectations and desires which both governs, and is governed by, the books that mediate those readings'.[2] Her analytical approach never restricts our perspective of a given text; it only expands it and makes us consider elements other than the

---

[2] Siân Echard, *Printing the Middle Ages* (Philadelphia, 2008), 2.

immediately obvious. Complexity and nuance have always characterised her work, and we can only hope that our volume will reflect this in some way. To conclude this introduction, then, we hope that our collection will honour the manifold valuable contributions Siân has made to our discipline to this point, and to provide the opportunity to recognise her current, upcoming, and ongoing research. More than once during the completion of this volume, we have had to revise material to account for new work that Echard had completed. Had we waited any longer to organise this Festschrift, we are certain it would have been impossible to assemble only one volume that has the potential to speak to all of the fields upon which she has left her mark. We look forward to more brilliant and ground-breaking work to come from our honoree.

PART I

NAVIGATING MULTILINGUALISM: MEDIEVAL BRITISH LANGUAGES IN CONTACT

1

Gormes and *Ysgymun* in the Dingestow *Brut*

JOSHUA BYRON SMITH

A ghastly King Arthur, newly arisen from over a millennium of slumber, breaks into a remote Welsh farmhouse in Ifan Morgan Jones's 2008 novel *Igam Ogam*. A group of modern-day druids – the sort that frequent Eisteddfodau, not Stonehenge – had awaited his return in the prophesied location, lured there by information in a newly discovered manuscript, but they leave too soon, dejected and embarrassed at their apparent naivete, and so instead of a majestic druidic welcome, Arthur receives the frightened looks of two recent university graduates after stumbling into the nearby ramshackle farmhouse kitchen. Arthur then addresses them, quite naturally for a man of antiquity, in Latin: '"An vides quid factus sim?" *gofynnodd, gan hercio atynt a'i freichiau ar led.* "Paene mille annos nihil edi ..."' ('Do you see what I have become?' he asked, hobbling toward them with his arms outstretched. 'I have eaten nothing for almost a thousand years ...').[1]

The mix of elements in this scene – Arthur, Latin, medievalism, a mysterious manuscript – creates a heady narrative hook for the novel, but it also reminds me of the enviable breadth of Siân Echard's scholarship, which encompasses medievalism, Anglo-Latin literature, Arthurian studies, and the reception of medieval manuscripts, as well as fields that this already stretched comparison cannot accommodate (be thankful I found no reference to John Gower or Chaucer in the novel). As it happens, the resurrected Arthur in *Igam Ogam* also provides a good overview of this chapter's themes. Arthur, surprised that Welsh is still spoken, wonders that Latin has not become the language of the Britons. In return, one of the astonished onlookers replies that she only speaks Welsh and English, which irritates Arthur: '"Saesneg?" poerodd y creadur. "Felly mi wnaeth paganiaid anwaraidd y dwyrain lwyddo i drechu'n byddinoedd ..."' ('English?' spat the creature. 'So the savage pagans of the East succeeded in vanquishing our armies ...'). Bewildered, the two then ask Arthur who he is: 'I

---

[1] Ifan Morgan Jones, *Igam Ogam* (Talybont, 2008), 37.

am Britain (*Prydain*), as it is now', he proclaims, 'rotten and weak, conquered by foreign ravagers (*rheibwyr estron*).'[2] From these few lines, it is clear that the author, Ifan Morgan Jones, has read his medieval sources well, because here Arthur succinctly recounts key concepts from early Welsh historiography: the Island of Britain, once the sole dominion of the Welsh, has been overrun by foreign oppressors whose heathen religious practices are detestable. This chapter, in turn, shows how one of the early Welsh translators of Geoffrey of Monmouth's *De gestis Britonum (DGB)* enacted a series of small but resonant changes to his Latin source that amplify these same historiographical themes. The translator, as I hope to show, shares with the resurrected Arthur an ingrained tendency to view the history of Britain as a struggle against a series of pagan invaders.

Geoffrey of Monmouth's *DGB* chronicles the ancient history of Britain, including the reign of Arthur and the English invasion that drove the native Britons to the west of the island.[3] Attracting immediate acclaim and controversy after its dissemination in c. 1138, the *DGB* was translated into English, French, and Welsh within the next century. Three Middle Welsh translations of Geoffrey's history appeared in the thirteenth century.[4] As a whole, these

---

[2] Jones, *Igam Ogam*, 37: 'Fi yw Prydain, fel y mae hi nawr ... Yn bydredig a gwan, wedi'i goresgyn gan reibwyr estron.'

[3] Geoffrey of Monmouth, *The History of the Kings of Britain: An Edition and Translation of the De gestis Britonum*, trans. Neil Wright, ed. Michael D. Reeve (Woodbridge, 2007), hereafter cited as *DGB*. All translations are taken from this edition, though on many occasions I have slightly altered them to make the relationship between the Latin and Middle Welsh clearer.

[4] The three early versions are: Llanstephan 1, Peniarth 44, and the Dingestow version. For studies on these early Welsh translations, see: Brynley F. Roberts, 'Astudiaeth Destunol o'r Tri Chyfieithiad Cymraeg Cynharaf o *Historia Regum Britanniae* Sieffre o Fynwy' (PhD diss., University of Wales, Aberystwyth, 1969); Roberts, 'Fersiwn Dingestow o Brut y Brenhinedd', *Bulletin of the Board of Celtic Studies* 27 (1976–78): 331–61; *Brut y Brenhinedd: Llanstephan MS. 1 Version*, ed. Brynley F. Roberts (Dublin, 1971); Patrick Sims-Williams, *Rhai Addasiadau Cymraeg Canol o Sieffre o Fynwy* (Aberystwyth, 2011); Brynley Roberts, '*Brut y Brenhinedd* ms. National Library of Wales, Llanstephan 1 Version', in *L'Historia regum Britannie et les 'Bruts' en Europe, Tome I, Traductions, adaptations, réappropriations (xiie–xvie siècle)*, ed. H. Tétrel and G. Veysseyre (Paris, 2015), 71–80; Roberts, 'A Web of Welsh Bruts', in *Historia regum Britannie et les 'Bruts' en Europe, Tome II: Production, circulation et réception (XII e–XVI e siècle)*, ed. H. Tétrel and G. Veysseyre (Paris, 2018), 147–68; Ben Guy, 'The Reception of Geoffrey of Monmouth in Wales', in *A Companion to Geoffrey of Monmouth*, ed. Georgia Henley and Joshua Byron Smith (Leiden, 2020), 494–97; Nia Jones, 'The Most Excellent Princes: Geoffrey of Monmouth and Medieval Welsh Historical Writing', in *A Companion to Geoffrey of Monmouth*, ed. Henley and Smith, 257–90, esp. 273–82. For a late thirteenth- or early fourteenth-century translation, see *Liber Coronacionis Britanorum*, ed. P.

early Welsh translations suffer from comparable critical neglect, especially when considered alongside Wace's French and Layamon's English translations. Of these early Welsh translations, only one has a modern critical edition, the Dingestow *Brut*, so-called because its earliest surviving manuscript witness came to the National Library of Wales as part of the Dingestow Court purchase in 1916.[5] Brynley Roberts has done a great deal to throw light on the relationship of the eight surviving Dingestow *Brut* manuscripts while offering many insightful observations about the translator's style. He has characterised the Dingestow translator as having the 'gift of effectively and intelligently summarizing the words of his source'.[6] 'The translator', he continues, 'was a man who liked a sentence's form and movement, and occasionally his descriptions are livelier than Geoffrey's.'[7] His translation is fluid and has 'a good deal of the energy and bounce of the original'.[8] The Dingestow translator, while generally following the meaning of the Latin, nevertheless redacted and tweaked his source when he felt the need.

This chapter traces the translator's innovative use of two key terms, *gormes* and *ysgymun*, in the Dingestow *Brut*. An analysis of these two terms shows that the Dingestow translator sought to bring Geoffrey's narrative into a closer relationship with Welsh historical tradition by portraying the Island of Britain as overrun by foreign, pagan invaders.[9]

Geoffrey's *DGB* had already adapted major themes from the Welsh historical tradition to create his history, and his Welsh translators recognised and sometimes enhanced these themes.[10] In his Welsh sources, Geoffrey

---

Sims-Williams, 2 vols (Aberystwyth, 2016). The Dingestow *Brut* is edited in *Brut Dingestow*, ed. Henry Lewis (Cardiff, 1942), cited hereafter as *BD*. *Brut y Brenhinedd: Llanstephan MS. 1 Version*, ed. Roberts only presents selections of the Llanstephan 1 version. However, a full preliminary edition of Peniarth 44 can be found in Roberts, 'Astudiaeth Destunol'.

[5] For the earliest manuscript of the Dingestow *Brut*, which is dated to the second half of the thirteenth century, see Daniel Huws, *A Repertory of Welsh Manuscripts and Scribes c. 800–c. 1800*, vol. 1 (Aberystwyth, 2022), 211.

[6] Roberts, 'Fersiwn Dingestow', 356: 'Un o nodweddion amlycaf cyfieithydd fersiwn Dingestow yw'r ddawn sydd ganddo i grynhoi geiriau ei ffynhonnell yn effeithiol ac yn ddeallus.'

[7] Roberts, 'Fersiwn Dingestow', 357: 'Yr oedd y cyfieithydd yn ŵr a hoffai liw a symudiad brawddeg ac ar dro y mae ei ddisgrifiadau ef yn fwy bywiog na rhai Sieffre.'

[8] Roberts, 'Fersiwn Dingestow', 358: 'cryn dipyn o egni a sbonc y gwreiddiol'.

[9] It should be noted that few manuscripts of Geoffrey's Latin text survive from Wales, and so it is possible that the changes discussed in this chapter are the result not of a Welsh translator but of an intermediary Latin copy that is now lost.

[10] Brynley F. Roberts, 'Geoffrey of Monmouth and Welsh Historical Tradition', *Nottingham Mediaeval Studies* 20 (1976): 29–40; Patrick Sims-Williams, 'Some Functions of Origin Stories in Early Medieval Wales', in *History and Heroic Tale: A*

found an important concept: the sovereign unity of the Island of Britain, ruled over by a crowned monarch in London, had been broken by a series of invasions.[11] In Welsh-language sources, these invasions are called *gormes* (pl. *gormesoedd*), a word that in the earliest texts means 'oppression by an alien race or conqueror' but that also came to mean 'tyranny', 'plague', 'invasion'.[12] For those unfamiliar with the concept of *gormesoedd*, Triad 36 provides the most succinct introduction to this term and its implications:

> Three *gormesoedd* that came to this island, and not one of them went back:
> One of them was the people of the Coraniaid, who came here in the time of Caswallawn son of Beli: and not one of them went back. And they came from Arabia.
> The second *gormes*: the Gwyddyl Ffichti. And not one of them went back.
> The third *gormes*: the Saxons, with Horsa and Hengist as their leader.[13]

The *gormesoedd* can be historical – the Saxons (*y Saesson*) and the Picts (*Gwyddyl Ffichti*) – or even mythical: the short Welsh tale *Cyfranc Lludd a Llefelys*, for example, describes the mysterious Coraniaid as a separate race with supernatural hearing ability.[14] The concept of a series of *gormes* disrupting the initial unity of the island was familiar to the Dingestow translator, and he introduces it into his translation at the outset.[15] Compare the original Latin on the left to the Middle Welsh translation on the right, in which I have bolded the additions:

Symposium, ed. Tore Nyberg et al. (Odense, 1985), 97–131, esp. 105–6 for the following discussion.

[11] For a good summary of this theme already in Geoffrey, see Cadualadrus's lamentation at the end of the history: *DGB*, §203.532–44.

[12] *Geiriadur Prifysgol Cymru/A Dictionary of the Welsh Language*, ed. R. J. Thomas and Gareth A. Bevan (Cardiff, 1950–), s.v. *gormes*. See also *Trioedd Ynys Prydein/The Triads of the Island of Britain*, ed. Rachel Bromwich, 4th edn (Aberystwyth, 2014), 90–92. For the connection between *gormes* and the *Ormesta* of Orosius, see Cameron Wachowich, 'On *Ormesta*', in *Quaestio Insularis: Selected Proceedings of the Cambridge Colloquium in Anglo-Saxon Norse and Celtic* 22 (2021): 107–62, esp. 135–39.

[13] *Trioedd*, ed. Bromwich, no. 36, p. 90: 'Teir Gormes a doeth y'r Enys Hon, ac nyt aeth vrun dracheuyn: 6n o nadunt Kywda6t y Corryanyeit, a doethant eman yn oes Caswallawn mab Beli, ac nyt aeth 6r un onadunt dracheuyn. Ac or Auia pan hanoedynt. Eil, Gormes y Gwydyl Fychti. Ac nyt aeth 6r un onadunt dracheuyn.Tryded, Gormes y Saesson, a Hors a Hengyst yn benaduryeit arnadunt.' I have slightly altered the translation and have retained *gormes* instead of Bromwich's English translation 'oppression'.

[14] *Cyfranc Lludd a Llefelys*, ed. Brynley F. Roberts (Dublin, 1975).

[15] *Trioedd*, ed. Bromwich, 36.

It is finally inhabited by five peoples, the Normans, the Britons, the Saxons, and Picts and the Scots; of these the Britons once occupied it from shore to shore before the others, until their pride brought divine retribution down upon them and they gave way to the Picts and the Saxons.[16]	Finally, five peoples inhabit it, namely, Normans, and Britons, Saxons, and Picts, and Scots. **And none of those have the right to it**, except the Britons, since they had inhabited it from sea to sea **before any of the other peoples came as a** *gormes* **upon them**. And then to avenge their sin and their pride God gave the Saxons, and the Picts, **and the Irish**, as a *gormes* upon them.[17]

These additions suggest that the Dingestow translator could be directly referencing Triad 36 here, but, regardless of whether he knew this particular triad or one like it, his expansions and diction explicitly invoke the theme of *gormesoedd*.[18] He first adds *gormes* where no Latin equivalent exists and immediately thereafter translates 'divine retribution' (*ultione divina*), quite nicely, as God (*Dvw*) sending a *gormes* upon the Britons. Notice, too, how the translator adds the Irish (*Yscoteyt*) to the list of *gormesoedd*, creating a triadic structure beloved by Welsh readers. The translator therefore directs medieval Welsh readers to approach Geoffrey's history as a story of national

---

[16] *DGB, Description Insula* §5.42: 'Postremo quinque inhabitatur populis, Normannis uidelicet atque Britannis, Saxonibus, Pictis, et Scotis; ex quibus Britones olim ante ceteros a mari usque ad mare insederunt donec ultione diuina propter ipsorum superbiam superueniente Pictis et Saxonibus cesserunt. Qualiter uero et unde applicuerunt restat nunc perarare ut in subsequentibus explicabitur.'

[17] *BD*, i.2, pp. 2–3: 'Ac o'r dywed pvmp kenedyl ysyd yn y chyuanhedu, nyd amgen, Nordmannyeyt, a Brytannyeyt a Saesson, a Gvydyl Fychti ac Yscoteyt. Ac o'r rei hynny nyd dyledavc neb arnei namyn y Brytannyeyt, canys vynt a'e kyuanhedassant o'r mor bwy gylyd kyn dyuod neb o'r kenedloed ereyll yn ormes arnadunt. A hynny y dyal eu kamwed ac eu syberwyt arnadunt y rodes Dvw y Saesson a'r Gvydyl Fychty a'r Yscoteyt yn ormes arndadunt.' The Llanstephan 1 version seems to have included the description of the island, though the loss of these pages makes it difficult to see whether the Dingestow translator took inspiration from the Llanstephan 1 translator here, or if this passage is due solely to him. See Roberts, 'Brut y Brenhinedd: Llanstephan 1', 77; Roberts, 'A Web of Welsh *Bruts*', 151. All translations from the *DB* are my own.

[18] *Trioedd*, ed. Bromwich, 91. Bromwich observes that these additions 'seem to be an echo' of Triad 36. Interestingly, the scribe of MS Aberystwyth, National Library of Wales 5266b, which contains the earliest surviving version of the *DB*, also copied MS Aberystwyth, National Library of Wales, Peniarth 16(vi), which contains a version of *Trioedd Ynys Prydain* that includes Triad 36. See Huws, *Repertory*, 211, 340–41. More investigation of this relationship could prove fruitful. My thanks to Celeste Andrews for pointing this out to me.

oppression by foreign invaders from the beginning of the narrative, and he continues to heighten this rhetoric at key moments. With these alterations, the Dingestow *Brut* can be read as an extravagantly expanded triad that recounts the invasion of the Island of Britain by three successive waves of *gormesoedd*.

With only a few exceptions, the Dingestow translator follows his initial template, using the term *gormes* to reference the Picts, the Irish, and the Saxons – the *gormesoedd* explicitly identified in this opening section. After the introduction, the first occurrence of *gormes* is found in a flourish added to the end of Geoffrey's origin story for the Picts.[19] The Picts, mercenaries from Scythia in the *DGB*'s account, request wives from the British. Having been rebuffed by the Britons, the Picts ask for and receive wives from the Irish, whereupon their numbers grow.[20] To this short etiological anecdote, the translator adds: 'And the Picts are that people, and that is how they came and the reason they had ever been permitted in this island. And from then until today they are a *gormes* that has not gone from it.'[21] This last phrase is another clue that the translator has read Triad 36 or something closely related to it, as it echoes the title of Triad 36, which describes the *gormesoedd* as a permanent presence – 'and not one of them went back'.[22] The Picts are again described as a *gormes* a little later when the treacherous Carausius tells the Britons that if they crown him king, he will both expel the Romans and free the island from the 'barbarous people' (*barbara gente*), that is, the Picts.[23] In Welsh, this sentence becomes: 'He would defend [the island] from foreign people and from each *gormes* that came to it.'[24] Here, the translator carefully maintains a distinction between the Picts and their like – merely a 'barbarous people' (*gens barbara*) in Latin but a *gormes* in the Welsh – and the Romans, a 'foreign people' (*estravn genedyl*), who are tellingly not a *gormes*. As will be discussed below, the Dingestow translator never calls the Romans as a whole a *gormes*. The Picts, however, are simply classified as *gormes* with no equivocation.

The Irish are the next *gormes* to appear in the Dingestow *Brut*. At the beginning of Book 6, the British find themselves overrun by foreign invaders who have gathered in Ireland. Their force consists of 'the Irish (*Gwydyl*) and the Irish living in Britain (*Yscoteit*) and men of Denmark and Norway together

---

[19] For Geoffrey's Pictish history, see Alex Woolf, 'Geoffrey of Monmouth and the Picts', in *Bile ós Chrannaibh: A Festschrift for William Gillies*, ed. Wilson McLeod et al. (Ceann Drochaid, Perthshire, 2010), 439–50. See also *Trioedd*, ed. Bromwich, 93.

[20] *DGB*, §70.381–88.

[21] *BD*, iv.17, p. 60: 'A'r bobyl honno yv Gvydyl Ffichti, a llyna megys y doethant a'r achavs y kynvyssvt yn gyntaf eyroet yn yr enys hon. Ac yr hynny hyt hediw y maent yn ormes heb uynet ohonei.'

[22] *Trioedd*, ed. Bromwich, no. 36, p. 90: 'ac nyt aeth vrun dracheuyn'.

[23] *DGB*, §75.53–54: 'atque exterminatis Romanis totam insulam a barbara gente liberaret' (and after the Romans had been killed, he would free the island from the barbarous people).

[24] *BD*, v.4, p. 66: 'y hamdiffynei rac estravn genedyl a rac pob gormes o'r a delhei idi'.

with them'.[25] The Britons seek help from the Roman emperor, who sends a legion that defeats the Britons' enemies and 'free[s] the oppressed population from their terrible depredations (*a tam atroci dilaceratione*)'.[26] This last phrase becomes 'that pitiful, oppressive (*gormessavl*) captivity', with *gormessavl*, the adjectival form of *gormes*, added for extra emphasis.[27] But the translator does not stop there. Immediately after this victory, the emperor orders the men to construct a wall between Scotland and the northern Brittonic kingdom of Deira to prevent future incursions:

And he ordered them to build a wall from coast to coast between Scotland and Deira, which, when garrisoned by the crowd, would overawe such enemies as needed to be kept away and would protect the Britons. For Scotland had been completely devastated by barbarian occupation, and provided a useful base for any enemies who arrived there.[28]	And in order to oppose **gormesoedd** and enemies, Emperor Severus first ordered a wall be built between Deira and Scotland from sea to sea, since each **gormes** that came to **the Island of Britain** was accustomed to come to Scotland first.[29]

These invaders have come from Ireland, and the translator, while abbreviating his Latin source, nonetheless inserts the words *gormes* twice in quick succession. Moreover, the translator also adds the phrase 'the Island of Britain' (*enys Prydein*), reinforcing at this key moment both the geographical unity of Britain and the danger posed to it by these invaders. A few sentences later, the Romans reply to the British with contemptuous indifference, stating that they do not wish to be troubled 'on account of weak, wandering bands of robbers'.[30] Again, the translator takes this opportunity to add *gormesoedd* where no Latin equivalent exists, calling the barbarians 'wandering robbers and *gormesoedd*', and, perhaps in attempt to lessen the embarrassment of being harried by feeble enemies, the translator altogether removes the Latin

---

[25] *DB*, vi., p. 80: 'y Gvydyl a'r Yscoteit a guyr Denmarc a'r Llychlynwyr y gyt ac vywnt'.

[26] *DGB*, §89.12–13: 'oppressam plebem a tam atroci dilaceratione liberauit'.

[27] *BD*, vi.1, p. 81: 'a rydhau y gywarsaghedic bobyl o'r truan geithiwet ormessavl honno' (and freed the beaten-down people from that pitiful, oppressive captivity).

[28] *DGB*, §89.13–17: 'Ad quos iussit construere murum inter Albaniam et Deiram a mari usque ad mare ut esset arcendis hostibus a turba instructus terrori, ciuibus uero tutamini. Erat autem Albania penitus frequentatione barbarorum uastata, et quicumque hostes superueniebant oportunum infra illam habebant receptaculum.'

[29] *BD*, vi.1, p. 81: 'Ac yr gvrthlad gormessoed a gelynyon yd archassei Seuerus amheravdyr gynt guneuthur mur y rvng Deiuyr a'r Alban o'r mor bvy gylyd, canys y'r Alban y gnotaei dyuot yn gyntaf pob gormes o'r a delhei enys Prydein.' Cf. Roberts, 'Fersiwn Dingestow', 360.

[30] *DGB*, §89.20–21: 'ob imbelles et erraticos latrunculos'.

'*imbelles*' (weak).³¹ In the Welsh translation, the events that set Book 6 into motion are to be understood as a national calamity, of the like found in Triad 36, in which *gormesoedd* threaten the unity of the Island of Britain.

Later in the narrative, at the beginning of Book 8, the same tactic again appears in another important moment. The book opens with two speeches, one by Merlin closely followed by another, in which Aurelius Ambrosius urges an attack on the treacherous Vortigern. In Geoffrey's text, Aurelius's speech already has powerful rhetorical devices – illustrations of betrayal, an appeal to a better past, the destruction of churches. To these, the translator adds two more instances of *gormesoedd*. When Aurelius recalls how his father Constantinus 'had saved [Vortigern] and our country from the invasion of the Picts (*Pictorum irruptione*)', the Welsh version renders 'irruptio' (invasion) as *gormes*, again linking the previous invasion with this important concept and again reinforcing the introductory description of the Picts as one of the three *gormes* to threaten the Island of Britain.³² Aurelius's speech builds to a simple but effective conclusion: 'Let us free our country from their [i.e. the Saxons'] rapacity (*ingluuie*).'³³ In Welsh, *ingluuies* (rapacity) becomes *gormes*, categorising the Saxons as the final *gormes* in a succession of national invasions.³⁴ Indeed, this speech, already one of Geoffrey's finest, ends in the Welsh translation with the word *gormes*, a fitting crescendo for a rousing call to the British to attack Vortigern and the Saxons.

The Saxons, the final and fiercest enemy the Britons face in Geoffrey's history, are explicitly termed a *gormes* three more times. In Book 9, the Britons send messengers to King Hoelus to 'inform him of Britain's peril (*calamitatem Britanniae*)'.³⁵ But in Welsh, the messengers go 'to tell him of the *gormes* that the British had from the race of the pagan Saxons'.³⁶ The paganism of the Saxons triggers the translator to make another slight alteration during the passage describing how Augustine of Canterbury entreated the Britons to evangelise the Saxons. Geoffrey defends the lack of British missionary activity by simply noting that the British have their own church structure, and the 'race of the Saxons persisted in depriving them of their own country'.³⁷ They will therefore not help the souls of their enemies. The Welsh translator,

---

31 *BD*, vi.2, p. 81: 'crvydredigyon ladron a gormessoed'.

32 *DGB*, §119.40–41: 'qui ipsum et patriam a Pictorum irruptione liberauerat'; *BD*, viii.2, 118: 'y gvr a rydhavs y wlat ac ynteu y gan ormes y Fyichteit' (the man who freed the country and him [i.e. Vortigern] from the *gormes* of the Picts).

33 *DGB*, §119.52: 'et patriam ab eorum ingluuie liberemus'.

34 *BD*, viii.2, p. 118: 'a rydhavn y wlat y gan eu gormes' (and let us free the country from their *gormes*).

35 *DGB*, §144.51–52: 'qui ei calamitatem Britanniae notificarent'.

36 *BD*, ix.2, p. 146: 'y uenegi idav yr ormes oed ar y Brytanyeit gan genedyl Saesson paganyeit'.

37 *DGB*, §188.192: 'et gens Saxonum patriam propriam eisdem auferre perstarent'.

evidently pleased at Geoffrey's explanation, keeps the passage but adds a meaningful, and now familiar, phrase: 'The British have their own church structure, and the "race of the Saxons persisted in depriving them of their patrimony".'[38] Here, it is also worth noting that Dinoot, the British abbot replying to Augustine, is given another reason for refusing to preach to the Saxons. In only the Welsh version does Dinoot defend the British 'through various authoritative quotes from Holy Scripture'.[39] No such line exists in the Latin, which merely has Dinoot claiming 'various objections'.[40] Finally, at the close of the history, the Saxons are victorious because, as Geoffrey explains, a plague and various moral failings afflicted the British, making it impossible for them 'to hold off their foes (*hostes*) any longer'.[41] In Welsh, these foes become the *gormes* of a foreign race (*gormes estravn genedyl*), and so the Dingestow translator ends his work as he had begun, by invoking the *gormes* framework and bringing Geoffrey's history into even closer alignment with medieval Welsh tradition.[42]

With only three exceptions, the Dingestow translator applies *gormes* to the Picts, Irish, and Saxons. The first exception is the only generic application of the term and comes when the cruel British emperor Maximianus assaults France, bringing with him a host of British soldiers 'to protect them from hostile attack (*ab hostile irruptione*) in the country they were to inhabit'.[43] It is not uncommon for Welsh translators of Latin texts to render one Latin term with a doublet, and the translator does just that here, rendering this phrase as 'to defend them from *gormesoedd* and from their enemies'.[44] The final two exceptions both describe a particularly rapacious person, a later development of the term *gormes*, but one that is well attested in Middle Welsh. One describes the tyrant Maxentius as he afflicts the Roman nobility, who in turn flee to Britain and beg Constantine to attack Rome and depose Maxentius. The Dingestow translator changes the nobles' speech to indirect discourse and reduces it somewhat, but he does add a few details, including calling Maxentius 'a *gormes* from Rome'.[45] This moment is as close as the translator

---

[38] *BD*, xi.12, p. 191: 'a chenedyl y Saesson ynteu yn ormes arnadunt ac yn dwyn eu guir tref tat y arnadunt'.

[39] *BD*, xi.12, p. 191: 'tryv amrauael avdurdodeu yr Ysgrythur Glan'.

[40] *DGB*, §188.190: 'diuersis monstrauit argumentationibus'.

[41] *DGB*, §207.591: 'quod hostes longius arcere nequiuerant'.

[42] *BD*, xii. 19, p. 208: 'hyt na ellynt gvrthlad gormes estravn genedyl y vrthunt' (so that they could not fight off the *gormes* of a foreign race).

[43] *DGB*, §86.352: 'infra patriam qua mansuri erant ab hostile irruptione tuerentur'.

[44] *BD*, v.14, p. 78: 'y eu hamdiffyn rac gormessoed a rac eu gelynyon'. For the tendency of Welsh translators to use two words for one Latin word in order to better capture the semantic range of the Latin, see *Brut y Brenhinedd*, ed. Roberts, xxxii.

[45] *BD*, v.7, p. 70: 'Ac vrth hynny adolvyn idav ... y waret gormes o Ruuein' (And therefore they beseeched him to remove the *gormes* from Rome); cf. *DGB* §79.156–62.

comes to calling the Romans as a whole a *gormes*, but he studiously avoids doing so, reserving the term for the oppressive emperor alone.[46] Perhaps he felt compelled to stay close to the triadic framework given in the introduction, or he might have done so because in Geoffrey's history the Romans are more than a *gormes*. Their vast, prestigious empire is the one against which the Britons prove their own worth when they conquer it on multiple occasions. The last use of *gormes* is also used to reference a single individual, the giant of Mont Saint-Michel. After Arthur defeats the giant, a crowd gathers around to see the man 'who had freed the land from such a pest *(tanta ingluuie)*'.[47] Large threatening monsters can be described as a *gormes* in Middle Welsh, and so it is no surprise that the translator uses *gormes* here to describe the giant.[48] These three uses of *gormes* all fall within the normal semantic range of the term in Middle Welsh, but they are not used with the same specificity as the other instances, all of which describe one of the three foreign peoples that imperil the unity of the Island of Britain.

To recap, the Dingestow *Brut* begins with a triadic formula that describes the Picts, Irish, and Saxons as *gormesoedd* that will threaten the island, and the translator reinforces this framework at several crucial moments throughout the text. Often, the translator simply adds the word *gormes* when no Latin equivalent exists. At other times, various Latin terms *(ingluuies, irruptio, calamitas, hostes, gens barbara, ultio divina)* are translated *gormes*, sharpening a theme that is already present, though less explicit, in Geoffrey's history.

The translator's changes become more pronounced when examined side-by-side with the two other early Welsh translations of Geoffrey's history. Peniarth 44 only uses the term *gormes* twice, once to describe the Trojan refugees led by Brutus and Corineus who had landed in Aquitaine, and once to describe the Picts.[49] The other early Welsh translation, Llanstephan 1, also takes an interest in the theme of *gormes*, though this interest appears mainly in the form of a large interpolation, rather than in general translation practice. The Llanstephan 1 translation inserts into Geoffrey's history the *Cyfranc*

---

[46] For associations of the Romans with *gormesoedd* in the triadic tradition, see *Trioedd*, ed. Bromwich, 92–93.

[47] *DGB*, §165.106–7: 'qui patriam a tanta ingluuie liberauerat'.

[48] *BD*, x.3, p. 171: 'y gvr a rydhaassei y wlat o'r ryv ormes honno' (the man who had freed the country from such a *gormes* as that).

[49] MS Aberystwyth, National Library of Wales, Peniarth 44, p. 13: 'y wrthlad gormes estraőn kenedyl y wrth y gwlat' (to expel the *gormes* of a foreign race from the land); cf. *DGB*, §18.387: 'promittunt sese unanimiter expulsuros ex finibus Aequitaniae externam gentem quae aduenerat' (they promised to unite to drive off the foreigners who had landed in Aquitaine); Peniarth 44, p. 66: 'gormes estraőn kenedloed' (a *gormes* of foreign races); cf. *DGB*, §75.53: 'barbara gente' (barbarous people). For my search of Peniarth 44, I have used the dataset from 13th-Century Middle Welsh Prose Manuscripts, DOI: 10.20391/3abf4ef1-e364-4cce-859d-92bf4035b303.

Lludd a Llefelys, a short tale in which two brothers fight off a series of three *gormesoedd* that plague the Island of Britain.[50] Other than this interpolated episode, the Llanstephan 1 translator uses *gormes* only five times, and all but one of these reference the Saxons.[51] While attentive to the term and the theme, the Llanstephan 1 translator does not apply it in a systematic way, as does the Dingestow translator, whose use of *gormes* makes him an outlier among the three early translators.

Not only do *gormesoedd* threaten the political stability of the Island of Britain; they also imperil its Christianity. Geoffrey's *DGB* has in the past been characterised as a text that, relatively speaking, shies away from religious topics, although this view has been recently challenged.[52] Be that as it may, the *DGB* itself explicitly pits the Christianity of the British against the paganism of the invading Saxons. Recognising this contrast in his Latin source, the Dingestow translator proceeds to make it even sharper. Along with *paganiaid* (pagans), one of his favourite words for describing the Saxons is *ysgymun* (< Latin *excommunis*), which has a wide variety of meanings, all highly negative: excommunicated, expelled, rejected, accursed; execrable, detestable,

---

[50] For the interpolation, see *Cyfranc Lludd a Llefelys*, ed. Roberts, esp. xv and Roberts, 'Brut y Brenhinedd: Llanstephan 1', 76–77.

[51] MS Aberystwyth, National Library of Wales, Llanstephan 1. For my search of Llanstephan 1, I have used the dataset from 13th-Century Middle Welsh Prose Manuscripts, DOI: 10.20391/3abf4ef1-e364-4cce-859d-92bf4035b303. As in the Dingestow *Brut*, the enemies that threaten the Britons at the beginning of Book 5 are also called a *gormes*: Llanstephan 1, p. 90: 'gormessoed y gan estronolyon kenedloed' (the *gormesoedd* from foreign peoples); cf. *DGB* §75.41: 'ab incursione barbarica' (against a barbarian attack). The other uses of *gormes* all describe the Saxons. Llanstephan 1, p. 147: 'y vynegy ydav entev er ormes ar trveny ar ryvel oed gan e paganyeyt ar enys prydeyn' (to tell him of the *gormes* and the suffering and the war that the Island of Britain had from the pagans); cf. *DGB*, §144.51–52: 'qui ei calamitatem Britanniae notificarent' (who would inform him of Britain's peril); Llanstephan 1, p. 154: 'A chyn dyvot gormes e saysson' (And before the *gormes* of the Saxons had arrived); cf. *DGB*: §152.202: 'antequam Saxones praeualuissent' (before the Saxons took control); Llanstephan 1, p. 191: 'tewyssa6c a alley gwrthlad gormes estra6n kenedyl' (a prince who could oppose the *gormes* of a foreign race); cf. *DGB*: §191.259–60: 'principem qui eam ad pristinam dignitatem reduceret' (a leader who would restore their former glory); Llanstephan 1, p. 202: 'namyn en eska6yn ennyll en gwlat arnad6nt yr a delhey o ormessoed' (but vainly we have won our land from them, despite all the *gormesoedd* that came); cf. *DGB*, §203.536–7: 'Sed in uanum patriam super illos totiens recuperauimus' (In vain have we so often recovered our native land from them). Note that pp. 102–45 of Llanstephan 1 are taken from Peniarth 44, so the above should be regarded as a partial survey: see *Brut y Brenhinedd*, ed. Roberts, xxxvii; Huws, *Repertory*, 60, 355. Translations of Llanstephan 1 are my own.

[52] See Barry Lewis, 'Religion and the Church in Geoffrey of Monmouth', in *A Companion to Geoffrey of Monmouth*, ed. Henley and Smith, 397–424.

abhorrent, terrible, evil, wicked, villainous, heinous, contemptible, despicable.[53] The Dingestow *Brut* consistently uses *ysgymun* in reference to the Saxons' paganism, and, as with *gormes*, the translator often adds *ysgymun* even when there is no corresponding word in Latin.[54] For example, when Vortigern desires Hengest's daughter Ronwein, the devil is said to have 'jumped into him and caused him to consent to the wicked (*ysgymun*) pagan who had not been baptised',[55] whereas the Latin simply reports that Satan 'had entered into his heart, for despite being a Christian he wanted to sleep with a pagan woman'.[56] Not only does the Welsh version put more responsibility on the devil but it also further highlights Ronwein's faithlessness. Once merely a pagan, she is now a wicked, unbaptised pagan – a subtle but important escalation in rhetoric.

Another unprompted use of *ysgymun* occurs when the unarmed British noblemen die after being deceived by Hengest: 'And many from both sides fell there, yet the Saxons received that wicked (*ysgymun*) victory.'[57] In contrast, Geoffrey's Latin has only an unmodified 'victory'.[58] Moreover, after the Saxons butcher the British nobles and force Vortigern to surrender large swathes of the kingdom to them, Vortigern, 'in the face of such slaughter', retreats into Wales.[59] The Dingestow translator lets it be known exactly who has committed such a crime and who the victims are, writing of 'that pitiful slaughter of the natives by the wicked (*ysgymun*) people'.[60] Small, poignant moments like these are hallmarks of the Dingestow translator's style.

Of the twenty-three times that *ygymun* or *ysgymunedig* occurs in the Dingestow *Brut*, all but four uses refer to the Saxons or their allies.[61] In this

---

[53] *Geriadur Prifysgol Cymru*, s.v. 'ysgymun'.

[54] As Roberts notes, a tendency to add 'some pejorative adjectives' to the Saxons is also shared by the Llanstephan 1 translator. See Roberts, 'Brut y Brenhinedd: Llanstephan 1', 76. See also Roberts, 'Fersiwn Dingestow', 350.

[55] *BD*, vi.12, p. 95: 'neidyv a wnaeth diawul yndav a pheri idav gytsynhyav a'r paganes ysgymun heb uedyd arnei'.

[56] *DGB* §100.358–60: 'Intrauerat, inquam, Sathanas in corde suo quia cum Christianus esset cum pagana coire desiderabat.'

[57] 60*BD* v.16., p. 100: 'Ac llawer a syrthvs yna o pob parth, ac eissyoes yr ysgymun uudugolyaeth honno a gauas y Saesson.'

[58] *DGB* §105.487–88: 'Multi hinc et inde ceciderunt, sed uictoriam habuerunt Saxones.'

[59] *DGB* §105.497–98: 'Cum ergo tantam cladem inspexisset Vortegirnus, secessit in partibus Kambriae ...'

[60] *BD*, vi.16, p. 100: 'A guedy guelet o Ortheyrn y truan aerua honno ar y pryodoryon y gan yr ysgymun pobyl ...'

[61] My count is based on the data from 13th-Century Middle Welsh Prose Manuscripts, DOI: 10.20391/3abf4ef1-e364-4cce-859d-92bf4035b303. The first exception occurs when the Roman Hamo disguises himself as a Briton and kills Guider. See *BD*, iv.13, p. 56: 'yr ysgymun uudugolyaeth honno' (that wicked victory); cf. *DGB*, §66.297: 'nefanda uictoria' (wicked victory). The second occurs when Wanius, the king of the Huns, and Melga, the king of the Picts, lust after British women. See *BD*, v.16, p. 80: 'A guedy ymgyuaruot o'r morynyon a'r ysgymunedic pobyl honno' (And after

respect, the Dingestow *Brut* differs from Peniarth 44, whose exacting translator uses *ysgymun* only to render the Latin *nefandus* (wicked, abominable) and, once, *paganus*.[62] The Llanstephan 1 translator, on the other hand, does not seem overfond of the word, using *ysgymun* or its derivatives a mere four times, two of which translate *nefandus*.[63] The Dingestow translator does, in fact, translate *nefandus* as *ysgymun*, but only eight times – most of his uses are unprompted by the Latin.[64] The similarity between the Dingestow and

---

the maidens met that wicked people); cf. *DGB* §88.392–3: 'obuiauerunt praedictis puellis in partes illas appulsis' (they came upon the girls who had been driven there). The giant of Mt Saint-Michel is likewise called *ysgymun*. See *BD*, x.3, p. 169: 'yr ysgymunedic aghyghel' (the accursed giant); cf. *DGB*, §165.58: 'sceleratissimus ille inuisi nominis gigas' (that wicked giant of accursed name). The last example occurs at the end of the work and describes the Britons themselves as they fall into sin and strife. See *BD*, xii.15, p. 204: 'oc eu hysgymun teruysc' (from their wicked discord); cf. *DGB*, §203.521: 'detestabili discidio' (in contemptible strife).

[62] For *ysgymun* translating *nefandus* in Peniarth 44 (part of which is present in Llanstephan 1), see Peniarth 44, p. 57: 'a'r escymỽn ỽudỽgolyaeth honno' (and that wicked victory); cf. *DGB*, §66.297: 'nefanda uictoria' (wicked victory); Llanstephan 1, p. 107: 'escymỽn lw Gwynwas a Melwas' (the wicked host of Waniius and Melga); cf. *DGB* §88.388: 'nefandum exercitum Wanii et Melgae' (the wicked army of Wanius and Melga); Llanstephan 1, p. 107: 'er escymmỽnedygyon tewyssogyon henny' (those wicked princes); cf. *DGB*, §88.395–96: 'nefandi Pictorum et Hunorum duces' (the wicked leaders of the Picts and Huns); Llanstephan 1, p. 120: 'ar ỽorwyn escymyn honno' (and that wicked maiden); cf. *DGB*, §100.365: 'paganae' (pagan); Llanstephan 1, p. 125: 'er escymỽn wudỽgolyaeth honno' (that wicked victory); cf. *DGB*, §105.489: 'nefandum inceptum' (wicked plot); Llanstephan 1, p. 126: 'e pobyl escymỽn honn' (that wicked people); cf. *DGB*, §105.498: 'nefandam gentem' (wicked people); Llanstephan 1, p. 129: 'er escymỽn pobyl' (the wicked people); cf. *DGB* §118.10: 'nefandum populum' (wicked people); Llanstephan 1, p. 135: 'heyngyst escymỽn' (wicked Hengist); cf. *DGB*, §127.206: 'nefandus Hengistus' (wicked Hengist).

[63] Llanstephan 1, p. 80: 'er eskymỽn wudỽgolyaeth honno' (that wicked victory); cf. *DGB*, §66.297: 'nefanda uictoria' (wicked victory); Llanstephan 1, p. 182: 'e lladron twyllwyr eskymỽn' (the thieving, wicked betrayers); cf. *DGB*, §178.58: 'periuros et latrones' (disloyal thieves); Llanstephan 1, p. 186: 'yr eskymỽnedyc creỽlaỽn hỽnnỽ' (that wicked cruel one); cf. *DGB*, §186.155: 'infaustus tyrannus' (ill-omened usurper); Llanstephan 1, p. 183: 'er eskymỽnhaf ỽradỽr hỽnnỽ medraỽt' (that wickedest betrayer Mordred); cf. *DGB*, §178.71–2: 'proditor ille nefandus' (that wicked betrayer). It should be noted again that this survey likely omits other uses of *ysgymyn* in Llanstephan 1 because a significant chunk of the middle portion of the manuscript is lacking.

[64] *BD*, vi.13, p. 56: 'ysgymun uudugolyaeth' (wicked victory); cf. *DGB*, §66.297: 'nefanda uictoria' (wicked victory); *BD*, vi.16, p. 100: 'yr ysgymun uudugolyaeth honno a gauas y Saesson' (the wicked victory that the Saxons had); cf. *DGB*, §105.487–88: 'sed uictoriam habuerunt Saxones ... nefandum inceptum peregerunt' (the translator has conflated two Latin sentences here); *BD*, vii.4, p. 110: 'eu hysgymun sein' (their wicked sound); cf. *DGB*, §116.164: 'nefando sonitu' (wicked sound); *BD*, viii.1, p. 117: 'y genedyl ysgymun' (the wicked people); cf. *DGB*, §118.10: 'nefandum populum'

Llanstephan translations has been noted previously, so it is no surprise that on a handful of occasions the two agree in their use of *ysgymun* as a translation of *nefandus*.[65] Nonetheless, with his liberal but pointed use of the term *ysgymun*, the Dingestow translator is the outlier in these three early translations.

The use of *ysgymun*, however, is merely part of a series of slight changes that the Dingestow translator enacts in order to underscore the paganism of the Saxons. A few examples of this tendency should suffice. The Dingestow *Brut* adds a religious dimension to the slaughter of the 460 British noblemen betrayed by Hengest in the treachery of the long knives. A religious element already exists in Geoffrey's text, where their bodies are gathered up and given a Christian burial in the vicinity of Salisbury by Bishop Eldadus. After the Britons defeat Hengest, so great is the desire to commemorate these men that it leads Aurelius on a quest to steal the Giants' Ring from Ireland. With this episode, Geoffrey explains the origin of the structure that would later be known as Stonehenge, and, in celebrating the slaughtered men, the translator of the Dingestow *Brut* makes explicit what the Latin only implies. He proclaims the fallen noblemen martyrs: 'And then blessed bishop Eldadus took the corpses of the noblemen as martyrs, and buried them according to Christian law.'[66] Also of note here is that the Welsh translation explicitly names Eldadus as a bishop, which is not specified in the Latin text until Book 8.[67] What is more, Eldol, the one British noble to survive the slaughter, fiercely defends himself with a staff, killing seventy Saxons and sending them to hell (*ad Tartara*)

(wicked race); *BD*, viii.2, p. 118: 'ysgymun a ohodes pobyl ysgymun atav' (a wicked man who summoned wicked people to him); cf. *DGB* 119.47–48: 'nefandus populus quem nefandus ille inuitauit' (a wicked people whom that wicked one summoned); *BD*, viii.9, p. 125: 'yr ysgymun Heingyst' (wicked Hengest); cf. *DGB*, §127.206: 'nefandus Hengistus' (wicked Hengest); *BD*, viii.24, p. 143: 'yr ysgymunedigyon uratwyr' (the wicked betrayers); cf. *DGB*, §142.606: 'nefandi proditores' (wicked betrayers).

[65] Perhaps even more telling is that both translate *infaustus* as *ysgymun*. See *BD*, xi.10, p. 189: 'yr creulavn ysgymunedic hvnnv', compared to Llanstephan 1, p. 186: 'yr eskymónedyc creólaón hónnó', cf. *DGB*, §186.155: 'infaustus tyrannus'. For the use of Llanstephan 1 by the Dingestow translator, see Robert's, 'A Web of Welsh *Bruts*', 158; Roberts, 'Fersiwn Dingestow', 352–56.

[66] *BD*, vi. 15, p. 99: 'Ac yna y kymyrth Eidal escob guynuydedic corfforoed y guyrda hynny [megys] merthyri, ac y cladvs herwyd dedyf cristonogyaeth'; cf. *DGB*, §104.470–72: 'Quorum corpora beatus Eldadus postmodum sepeliuit atque Christiano more humauit.' A similar moment occurs in Peniarth 44 (witnessed in Llanstephan 1, p. 107), when the British women refuse to have sex with the hosts of Wanius and Melga, 'those traitors martyr them completely' ('eó merthyró en kóbyl. or bradwyr henny'); cf. *DGB*, §88.394–5: 'irruerunt in eas ambrones maximamque partem sine more trucidauerunt' (the villains fell on them and most of the Britons were quickly killed); and cf. *BD*, v.16, p. 80: 'eu llad y ran wuyhaf onadunt' (they killed the greatest part of them).

[67] *DGB*, §125.158.

before he is forced to flee.⁶⁸ The Dingestow translator adds a few nice touches to Eldol's heroic resistance.⁶⁹ Instead of a 'staff' (*palus*), Eldol wields a 'good, hard staff' (*pavl da cadarn*), and instead of sending Saxons to hell 'with it' (*cum illo*), he employs 'that blessed staff' ([y]*pavl bendigeit hvnnv*).⁷⁰ These small changes all heighten the religious implications in the slaughter of the 460 British nobles.

In the Dingestow *Brut*, moreover, God sometimes shows more favour to the British, and their Christianity remains slightly less adulterated than in the *DGB*. When Vortimer, in accordance with British discontent, rebels against the Saxons and his father Vortigern, Geoffrey relates that 'he ... began to drive out the barbarians, fighting them and launching sharp attacks'.⁷¹ To this sentence, the Dingestow translator adds the divine blessing 'as God was glad for them to do'.⁷² Moreover, God intervenes in another battle in the Dingestow *Brut*. As Aurelius prepares to meet Hengest in battle, the deceptive Saxon tries to catch the Britons off guard with a surprise attack. The *DGB* baldly states: 'But he did not deceive Aurelius.'⁷³ The Dingestow *Brut*, however, gives credit to God for revealing the plot: 'But through the strength of God, that was not concealed from Aurelius.'⁷⁴ The translator also omits some information that calls into question the Britons' religious devotion or purity. For instance, he ignores the disparaging remark about the Britons suffering from the Pelagian heresy, which in effect places the responsibility for the Britons' corrupted religion squarely on the Saxons. Geoffrey, however, had included both explanations: 'For their faith had fallen into decline, both because of the pagans whom the king had brought among them and through the heresy of Pelagius, which had already been poisoning it for a long time.'⁷⁵ The Dingestow *Brut* also elides the explanation for why the British find it difficult to tell a pagan from a Christian. The Latin points out that 'the pagans had married [the Britons'] daughters and relatives'.⁷⁶ But, in a moment that displays some anxiety about

---

⁶⁸ *DGB*, §105.483.

⁶⁹ See Roberts, 'Fersiwn Dingestow', 361.

⁷⁰ Cf. *BD*, vi. 16, p. 99 and *DGB*, §105.481, 482.

⁷¹ *DGB*, §101.400–1: 'Qui ... incepit expellere barbaros atque oppugnare et diris irruptionibus afficere.'

⁷² *BD*, vi.13, p. 96: 'A dechreu ymlad a'r Saesson a gneuthur aeruaeu mavr creulavn onadunt megys yd oed da gan Duw y wneuthur onadunt.'

⁷³ *DGB*, §121.88–90: 'Quod tamen non latuit Aurelium ...'

⁷⁴ *BD*, vii.4, p. 120: 'Ac eissyoes drvy nerth Duv nyd ymgelvs hynny rac Emreis ...'

⁷⁵ *DGB*, §101.370–73: 'Corrupta namque fuerat Christianitas eorum tum propter paganos quos rex in societatem eorum posuerat, tum propter Pelagianam haeresim, cuius uenenum ipsos multis diebus affecerat'; cf. *BD*, vi.2, 93–96: 'Canys llygredic oed eu cristonogyaeth yr pan dothoed y paganyeit yn eu plith' (Since their Christianity was polluted when the pagans came into their midst).

⁷⁶ *DGB*, §101.392–95: 'insuper tanta multitudo aduenerat ita ut ciuibus terrori

ethnic and religious intermingling, the Dingestow *Brut* simply attributes the confusion to the sheer number of the pagans.[77] When it comes to religious matters, the Dingestow translator is happy to move the needle in the Britons' favour, even ever so slightly.

Religious matters and the politics of the *adventus Saxonum* are common points of contention for later adapters of Geoffrey's *DGB*, including the author of the First Variant Version, Wace, Layamon, and the many anonymous Bruts of the thirteenth century. The Dingestow translator, whom Roberts considers 'perhaps the most fluent' among the early Welsh translators, willing to give 'the gist of his original' but 'not bound to the letter of it', participates in this widespread tendency to tweak salient elements of Geoffrey's narrative.[78] Indeed, as this chapter has shown, he makes several small changes that concern the concept of *gormes* and religious matters, and although these changes may seem minor in themselves, when taken together, a pattern is discernible. With the theme of *gormes*, the Dingestow translator makes explicit what Geoffrey's Latin only implies, making the *DGB* a history that shows how a series of three *gormesoedd* endangers and ultimately destroys British control over the island. Relatedly, the Welsh translator of the Dingestow *Brut* clearly gives in to the occasional temptation to heighten the Saxons' wickedness and stress the Christianity of the British. He is also mindful to police the ethnic boundary between the British and the Saxons, refusing to acknowledge the intermarriage that the *DGB* describes. These changes, however, are not always systematic. Rather, he prefers to tweak Geoffrey's text by adding a word or phrase in one place while omitting a clause or sentence at another. His small modifications mark him as a man who respects Geoffrey's Latin text but who on occasion allows his biases and partialities to move his pen.

---

essent; iam nesciebatur quis paganus esset, quis Christianus, quia pagani filias et consanguineas eorum sibi associauerant'.

[77] *BD*, vi.13, p. 96: 'Ac y gyt a hynny, kymeint oed eu niuer ac nat oed havd adnabot pvy a uei cristyavn, pvy a vei pagan' (Consequently, their number was so great that it was not easy to recognise who was a Christian and who was a pagan).

[78] *Brut y Brenhinedd*, ed. Roberts, xxix.

2

Melioratum ... et emendatum: Rewriting, Polishing, and Textual Fluidity among Twelfth- and Thirteenth-Century Latin and Welsh Writers in Britain

PAUL RUSSELL

Rogo itaque quatinus librum nostrum, sc. *Ecclesie Speculum*, beato Aethelberto anno iam fere preterito datum, mihi per hunc clericum presentium latorem, ad corrigendum adhuc plenius et utilia quedam locis competentibus adiciendum, remittere uelitis. Memorialem enim interim uobis *Topographiam Hybernicam*, et *Uaticinalem Hybernicae expugnationis Hystoriam*, opera duo sc. et diuersa, sed uno uolumine conserta, per eundem destinaui, quem cum melioratum susceperitis, quod in proximo fiet, et emendatum, alium, si placet, remittetis.[1]

[And so I ask that you kindly return my book to me, namely *Speculum ecclesiae*, which I donated to the shrine of blessed Æthelbert about a year ago, by this cleric who is delivering the present books, so that it may be corrected even more fully and supplemented by some useful material in the appropriate places. In the meantime, I have sent you by the same person my

---

[1] The text has been transcribed from the single-surviving manuscript, London, Lambeth Palace Library 236, fol. 160, with my punctuation and my translation. A classicised text was printed by J. S. Brewer, ed., *Giraldi Cambrensis Opera*, vol. 1, Rolls Series 21 (London, 1861), 409. The letter addressed to the chapter at Hereford (*Epistula ad capitulum Herefordense de libris a se scriptis*) is dated to after 1218. The underpinning of the thinking for this work has been supported by two funded projects: 'Vitae Sanctorum Cambriae' (AHRC-funded and held in the Department of Anglo-Saxon, Norse and Celtic in Cambridge), and 'The Writings of Gerald of Wales' (funded by the Leverhulme Trust and held in the Faculty of History in Oxford). I am grateful to Joshua Byron Smith for his extremely helpful comments on an early draft of this chapter, and to the editors for their detailed reading and useful comments. All translations are my own except where otherwise indicated.

remarkable[2] *Topographia Hibernica* and *Expugnatio Hiberniae*, two very different works but bound together in one volume that has been improved and reworked, and when you receive it, which will be soon, please send back the other one.][3]

In the last few years of his life, Gerald of Wales wrote to the canons of Hereford offering them revised versions of his *Topographia* and *Expugnatio*. At the same time, he asked that they return their copy of *Speculum ecclesiae* so that he could correct it and make some additions, the implication being that he would return the improved copy but not make a fair copy of it for them; what we do not know is whether the single surviving copy of *Speculum ecclesiae* represents the older version or the later.[4] We witness here the practical working out of Gerald's well-known propensity for rewriting himself and, at least in his own eyes, improving himself. His request for the return of the older versions also illustrates the control he tried to maintain over the circulation of his own

---

[2] *Memorialem* has been taken as 'pledge' (Nóirín Ní Bheaglaoi, '*Libri corrigendi*: Revising the *Topographia Hibernica*', in *Text, Transmission and Transformation in the European Middle Ages, 1000–1500*, ed. Carrie Griffin and Emer Purcell (Turnhout, 2018), 158–59; and as a possible alternative by Catherine Rooney, 'The Early Manuscripts of Gerald of Wales', in *Gerald of Wales: New Perspectives on a Medieval Writer and Critic*, ed. Georgia Henley and A. Joseph McMullen (Cardiff, 2018), 97–110, at 104, but the only example of *memorialis* in this sense given in *Dictionary of Medieval Latin from British Sources*, ed. R. E. Latham et al. (Turnhout, 2015) dates from the 1290s, and it is not clear that is what is meant here. Rooney's preferred translation is 'rough copy', which would be an odd way to refer to the *Topographia* at such a late stage. Accordingly, I take it to be used adjectivally and as reflecting the positive view Gerald had of his own work.

[3] While the final clause (*quem cum* ...) of the passage has usually been taken to refer to the Irish works mentioned in the preceding sentence, it is not easy to see how *quem* of the single-surviving manuscript (written *plene*) in the final sentence can refer to those works; it would need to be either feminine plural or neuter singular (referring to *uolumen*) for that to be the case. However, Ní Bheaglaoi, '*Libri corrigenda*', 158–59, cannot be right that *quem* in the final sentence refers to *Speculum ecclesie*, which earlier is referred to as *liber noster*. There are two distinct requests being made here for the return of books: first, the prompt return of the older recension of *Speculum ecclesie* by the messenger (*lator*) so that it can be improved; and, second, the return of the older recension of the Irish works at some point in the future, and only *si placet*. The last clause of this passage must refer to the latter request. For this to work grammatically, I take *quem* to be an error for *quod* (referring to the *uolumen*), presumably through a confusion of abbreviations in an earlier copy. I am grateful to Thomas Charles-Edwards for discussing this passage with me.

[4] The text is printed in Brewer, ed., *Giraldi Cambrensis Opera*, vol. 4 (London, 1873); the text survives uniquely in British Library, Cotton MS, Tiberius B. xiii, fols 1–153v; the earlier folios are damaged, and the latter part lacks rubrication.

works. We must assume that Gerald would have preferred that the earlier versions, 'recensions' as they have come to be termed, never saw the light of day again but were rather replaced by the second, third, and sometimes fourth and indeed fifth thoughts. As the surviving manuscripts of Gerald's works show, he was not entirely successful in this, for we have evidence of multiple recensions of his Irish and Welsh works and also some indications of reworking in some of his other works, in particular his version of the Life of St David (and others may come to light in the course of re-editing his writings). In some cases, such as *Descriptio Kambrie*, it is striking that the first recension is preserved in two closely related late fourteenth-/early fifteenth-century manuscripts and then only in a closely related group of sixteenth-century manuscripts, perhaps suggesting that only a few medieval copies escaped Gerald's clutches.[5] The case of Gerald's Life of St David is also interesting in another way: it shows that, in addition to his own works, Gerald also reworked the writings of others.[6]

We began with Gerald, but for the purposes of this discussion we take his works as marking an endpoint. The starting point is the textual fluidity evident in a range of mid- to late twelfth-century texts associated with Geoffrey of Monmouth. The chronological range between Geoffrey and Gerald encompasses a field of scholarship where Siân Echard established herself and has made numerous notable contributions.

The circumlocution used above, 'texts associated with', is deliberate as there is so much variation at all levels in both Geoffrey's versions of *De gestis Britonum* (*Historia Regum Britanniae*) (*DGB*)[7] and in their Welsh descendants, *Brut y Brenhinedd*,[8] that it is difficult to talk of a single text. Modern scholars, in a desire to fix clean texts of the different versions, have not unreasonably attempted to make sense of, and bring order to, this complicated

---

[5] Catherine Rooney, 'The Manuscripts of the Works of Gerald of Wales' (PhD diss., University of Cambridge, 2015), 87–101.

[6] We return to this below, 37–9.

[7] The standard Latin edition is now Michael Reeve and Neil Wright, eds and trans, *Geoffrey of Monmouth, The History of the Kings of Britain: An Edition and Translation of the* De gestis Britonum (Woodbridge, 2007) hereafter cited as *DGB*. Earlier editions include a single manuscript edition by Neil Wright, ed., *The* Historia Regum Britanniae *of Geoffrey of Monmouth, Vol. I: Bern, Burgerbibliothek, MS. 568* (Cambridge, 1985); and Acton Griscom, ed., *The* Historia Regum Britanniae *of Geoffrey of Monmouth, with Contributions to the Study of Its Place in Early British History* (London, 1929).

[8] Translations into other languages are not discussed here; for an overview of the broader reception of Geoffrey, see the contributions in Part 4, 'Reception', of Georgia Henley and Joshua Byron Smith, eds, *A Companion to Geoffrey of Monmouth* (Leiden, 2020), 425–97.

mass of textual disorder.[9] Useful though such editions are, they necessarily sideline questions of variation and fluidity. But so pervasive is this variation that in attempting to reduce it to some kind of order there is a risk of throwing the baby out with the bathwater, certainly for those interested in the more general issue of Latin prose writing in the twelfth and thirteenth centuries. A primary contention here is that perhaps we ought to think of ways to embrace the variation rather than to argue and edit it away. If this sounds like a paean to *mouvance* or *variance*, what follows takes them as its starting point for a discussion of the written transmission of Latin texts in twelfth-century Britain and then sets out to complicate our thinking about them.[10]

A striking feature of twelfth-century Latin prose writing in Britain is the fluidity of the texts. This discussion is primarily concerned with the deliberate changes, both small and larger scale, made to the texts as opposed to the accumulation of errors that inevitably crept in, though it is often difficult to distinguish them. One problem with such texts is that we have very little understanding of the rationale for rewriting them and how the choices were being made if or when competing versions were available – whether in Latin or Welsh – a scenario that may have been more common than we realise. Some help in understanding why such texts were reworked may be gained from two sources: not only the works of Gerald, with which we started and to which we shall return, but also from a wider range of hagiographical works from Wales where we can see texts being reworked in different ways.

What follows deliberately steps back from the detail – there is plenty of scholarship that engages with that, as the copious references below indicate – and instead considers the broad patterns of this variation; it is at times speculative but aims to ask questions that are less often asked. One of the problems is that only very rarely in the different versions of Geoffrey's *DGB* are we told why the texts vary so much: are we to imagine that a later version is thought to be an improvement on an earlier one, or were the different versions simply expressing the varying preferences of later compilers and redactors? It is suggested here that both may be in play.

Geoffrey's *DGB* has come down to us in a so-called 'vulgate' version and in at least two 'variant versions', if not more;[11] and even within each version

---

[9] Cf. the discussion by Brynley F. Roberts, 'A Web of Welsh *Bruts*', in *L'Historia regum Britannie et les 'Bruts' en Europe, Tome II: Production, circulation et reception (xiie–xvie siècle)*, ed. Hélène Tétrel and Geraldine Veysseyre (Paris, 2015), 147–68.

[10] For *mouvance*, see Paul Zumthor, *Essai de poétique médiévale* (Paris, 1972), and for variance, Bernard Cerquiglini, *Éloge de la variante; histoire critique de la philologie* (Paris, 1989).

[11] David Dumville, 'The Manuscripts of *Historia Regum Britanniae*', *Arthurian Literature* 3 (1983): 113–28, at 128, proposed a third variant version, though the idea has not gained traction; see Julia C. Crick, *The* Historia Regum Britanniae *of Geoffrey*

there is significant variation. The two variant versions are preserved in some twenty-six manuscripts (beside some two hundred vulgate copies, though many are mixed) and seem to have regional affiliations, but they are important for understanding the possible range of variation in the tradition. In general terms, the transmission of *DGB* seems to work within the following structure: §1–5, Preface; §§6–108, Books I–VI; §§ 109–10, Preface to the Prophecies; §§111–17, Prophecies; §§118–208, Books VIII–XI).[12] The main fault lines thus fall at §108 and §118, forming three textual units: the first half (history of the kings); the Prophecies of Merlin; and the second half (Arthur and the arrival of the English).

The first variant version, which has been well edited by Neil Wright, is in many respects a shorter, tighter, and more focused narrative;[13] it is less allusive and more explicit in its references, thus allowing a reader to work less hard. In what follows, I follow Wright in thinking that the first variant version is secondary to the vulgate, though a case has been made for the converse, for example by Robert Caldwell and followed by David Burchmore and others.[14] A significant contribution to our understanding of this version has recently

---

of Monmouth, IV: Dissemination and Reception in the Later Middle Ages (Cambridge, 1991), 98–99.

[12] See *DGB*, xi–xxxi; the prefaces are more fluid, being naturally determined more by the circumstances of the copying of that particular manuscript in that dedicatees change over time and are not considered further here.

[13] Neil Wright, ed., *The* Historia Regum Britanniae *of Geoffrey of Monmouth II: The First Variant Version; A Critical Edition* (Cambridge, 1988), summarised at liii–liv. An earlier edition is Jacob Hammer, ed., *Historia Regum Britanniae: A Variant Version*, Medieval Academy of America Publication 57 (Cambridge, MA, 1951); a more recent but far less satisfactory edition is David W. Burchmore, ed. and trans., *History of the Kings of Britain: The First Variant Version*, Dumbarton Oaks Medieval Library 57 (Cambridge, MA, 2019); see the review by Paul Russell, *North American Journal of Celtic Studies* 4, no. 2 (2020): 237–41.

[14] Robert A. Caldwell, 'Wace's *Roman de Brut* and the Variant Version of Geoffrey of Monmouth's *Historia Regum Britanniae*', *Speculum* 31 (1956): 675–82. His other work has for some time only been accessible through abstracts of his papers, but the original versions are now available: Caldwell, 'The Use of Sources in the Variant and Vulgate Versions of the *Historia Regum Britanniae*', *Bulletin bibliographique de la Société International Arthurienne* 9 (1957): 123–24; Caldwell, 'On the Order of the Variant and Vulgate Versions of the *Historia Regum Britanniae*'; Caldwell, 'The Order of the Variant and Vulgate Versions of the *Historia Regum Britanniae*', *Proceedings of the Linguistic Circle of Manitoba and North Dakota* 1, no. 2 (1959): 15–16. For Wright's arguments against, see Wright, ed., *The* Historia Regum Britanniae *of Geoffrey of Monmouth II*, liv–lxx.

been made in Georgia Henley's discussion of Dublin, Trinity College 11500, which has recently come to light, and in her work on this variant in Wales.[15]

A smaller group of manuscripts contains what is termed the less familiar 'second variant version'. Rather than a reworking of the whole text, the principal changes involve the Arthurian sections, Books VI and VIII–XI, which are significantly shortened with the effect that Arthur looms larger in this narrative than in other versions. The second variant version is less well known than the others as no edited text has been published.[16] Jacob Hammer prepared a draft edition before he died that was handed over to Thomas Jones for completion; being unable to finish it himself, he passed it on to Hywel Emanuel, who died before he completed it. Emanuel did at least publish a very useful article on the text suggesting how it might be edited.[17] Hammer identified fifteen manuscripts containing this version, to which three more can now be added. Strikingly, in view of the above discussion, only eight contain a complete second variant version. Hammer divided these manuscripts into three groups: group α, a full second variant text; group β, which reverts to the vulgate after the prophecies; and group γ, of an uncertain relationship to the rest but probably closer to α (a further five manuscripts are unclear). The first part of these texts shows some reworking of Books I–IV but nothing out of the ordinary; it is the latter half that differs radically. The kind of reworking done in the first half is so different from what happens in the latter part that one might think they were the product of two different types of rewriting by different people at different times.

However, the distinction between these different versions is rarely clearcut.[18] As is shown in Julia Crick's survey of the manuscripts of *DGB*, now increased to more than 220,[19] and in greater detail by Michael Reeve and

---

[15] Georgia Henley, 'Transnational Book Traffic in the Irish Sea Zone: A New Witness to the First Variant Version of Geoffrey of Monmouth's *De gestis Britonum*', *North American Journal of Celtic Studies* 4, no. 2 (2020): 131–62; Henley, 'Reading Geoffrey of Monmouth in Wales: The Intellectual Roots of *Brut y Brenhinedd* in Latin Commentaries, Glosses, and Variant Texts', *Viator* 49, no. 3 (2018): 103–28, at 113–21.

[16] Michael Reeve dryly described the lack of an edition as 'a gap hard to lament' (*DGB*, x). It does, however, remain one of the few pieces of medieval Arthurian literature not to have encountered its editor.

[17] Hywel Emanuel, 'Geoffrey of Monmouth's *Historia Regum Britanniae*: A Second Variant Version', *Medium Ævum* 35 (1966): 103–10; cf. also Crick, *The Historia Regum Britanniae of Geoffrey of Monmouth, IV*, 15–16, 181. Hammer's papers relating to this are currently held in the Department of Anglo-Saxon, Norse, and Celtic along with a collection of microfilms of Geoffrey manuscripts.

[18] Cf. Henley, 'Reading Geoffrey of Monmouth in Wales'.

[19] Julia C. Crick, *The* Historia Regum Britanniae *of Geoffrey of Monmouth, III: A Summary Catalogue of the Manuscripts* (Cambridge, 1989); Jaakko Tahkokallio, *Monks, Clerks, and King Arthur: Reading Geoffrey of Monmouth in the Twelfth and*

Wright in their edition,[20] even clear vulgate manuscripts show a high degree of contamination (or to be more charitable, influence) from different parts of the tradition. When we also allow for the manuscripts that are part vulgate and part first or second variant, we find a wide range of complexity:[21] for example, [54] §§1–117 second variant + §§118–end vulgate; [106] §§1–149 first variant + §§150–end vulgate; [55] §§6–108 first variant + §§111–17 vulgate + §§118–77 conflation of two branches of the vulgate tradition + §§178–end conflation of vulgate and first variant. Even setting aside contamination within a single version, the upshot is that we have multiple combinations of the sections that go to make up *DGB*: pure vulgate throughout; pure first variant; pure second variant; vulgate + first variant; vulgate + second variant; first variant + vulgate; second variant + vulgate. In such cases, the fault lines, where the text changes version, are in the expected places, and it would be reasonable to suppose that in some cases the change from one version to another was deliberate, as not all manuscripts would sustain accidental damage in the same places.[22] However, in addition we find many manuscripts where the shift is at an unexpected place: for example [66], where the manuscript begins and ends as a second variant text but has a section of the vulgate in the middle.[23] In such cases, one might suppose that the change was forced upon the owner(s) because of accidental loss of text and the need to infill it from whatever version was to hand.

Two main factors seem to have been at play here, and it is important, if possible, to distinguish between them: the deliberate rewriting to create a new version, on the one hand, and inadvertent error or damage, on the other, which required the infilling of text. It is likely that the sheer size of *DGB* may well have given rise to more change than might occur in a smaller work. A single copy would have been a big book, whether we are thinking of a large-format bi-columnar version or a smaller, fatter volume – either of which would have

---

Thirteenth Centuries (Helsinki, 2013), esp. 18–42; Tahkokallio, 'Early Manuscript Dissemination', in *A Companion to Geoffrey of Monmouth*, ed. Henley and Smith, 155–80, at 170–74 (monastic copies), 174–75 (personal copies).

[20] *DGB*, xxxi–li.

[21] For ease of reference (and because the specific manuscripts are not relevant to the discussion), I use the reference numbers that were adopted by Crick, *The Historia Regum Britanniae of Geoffrey of Monmouth, III*, and employed in *DGB*, enclosed in square brackets.

[22] This account does not include the addition of small sections and phrases in certain groups of MSS, e.g. *pudibundus Brito*, the Seaxburh phrase, etc. (Crick, *The Historia Regum Britanniae of Geoffrey of Monmouth, IV*, 90–112).

[23] For the manuscript, see *DGB*, xxxviii, and Crick, *The Historia Regum Britanniae of Geoffrey of Monmouth, III*, 107–10. For another good example of this phenomenon [55], see David Dumville, 'The Origin of the *C*-Text of the Variant Version of the *Historia Regum Britanniae*', *Bulletin of the Board of Celtic Studies* 26 (1974–76): 315–22.

been hard to use and move about – and more prone to damage. In addition to these factors, we have to allow for all the things that scribes do when they copy: the minor changes in wording within a version, whether deliberately or accidentally, whether textually significant or not, or the larger changes caused by, for example, a scribe turning over two or more folia at once. All of these, whether micro or macro, change the text, and much would have been unintended. We are primarily interested here in deliberate change of the kind that distinguishes a vulgate text from a first variant from a second variant. Even so, we very often have to do that as we peer through the fog of minor differences, changes, and variant readings.

We return to Geoffrey's Latin text below, but we can now turn to the Welsh renderings of his texts, known as *Brut y Brenhinedd*.[24] If the Latin texts of Geoffrey offer complexity, the Welsh versions (with the earliest copies dating to the mid-thirteenth century) are even more bewildering, with multiple versions being created in different centres in Wales based on different versions of Geoffrey's work; the text was clearly in high demand, but it seemed not to matter precisely which text was available to be translated or copied. Some twenty-four manuscript copies can be dated to between 1250 and 1500.[25] They are conventionally divided into several redactions (usually labelled after the oldest copy): in the thirteenth century, we have the Llanstephan 1 version,[26] the

---

[24] For a detailed overview, see Brynley F. Roberts, 'Astudiaeth Destunol o'r Tri Chyfieithiad Cymraeg Cynharaf o *Historia Regum Britanniae* Sieffre o Fynwy' (PhD diss., University of Wales, Aberystwyth, 1969); and more recently, Roberts, 'A Web of Welsh *Bruts*'; Patrick Sims-Williams, *Rhai Addasiadau Cymraeg Canol o Sieffre o Fynwy* (Aberystwyth, 2011); Owain Wyn Jones, 'The Most Excellent Princes: Geoffrey of Monmouth and Medieval Welsh Historical Writing', in *A Companion to Geoffrey of Monmouth*, ed. Henley and Smith, 257–90, esp. 273–82; Ben Guy, 'The Reception of Geoffrey of Monmouth in Wales', in *A Companion to Geoffrey of Monmouth*, ed. Henley and Smith, 494–97. For a more general discussion of textual fluidity in medieval Welsh texts, see Thomas M. Charles-Edwards, 'The Textual Tradition of Medieval Welsh Prose Tales and the Problem of Dating', in *150 Jahre 'Mabinogion': Deutsche-Walisiche Kulturbeziehungen*, ed. Bernhard Meier and Stefan Zimmer, Buchreihe der Zeitschrift für celtische Philologie (Tübingen, 2001), 23–39; and for a discussion in line with what is suggested here, see Henley, 'Reading Geoffrey of Monmouth in Wales'.

[25] Roberts, 'A Web of Welsh *Bruts*', 148–49; see also now Patrick Sims-Williams, 'An Unpublished Thirteenth-Century Version of *Brut y Brenhinedd* in Peniarth MSS 24 and 314iii', *Studia Celtica* 57, no. 1 (2023): 15–46.

[26] An edition of selected passages is Brynley F. Roberts, ed., *Brut y Brenhinedd: Llanstephan MS. 1 Version* (Dublin, 1971); for more recent discussion, see Roberts, '*Brut y Brenhinedd* ms. National Library of Wales, Llanstephan 1 Version', in *L'Historia regum Britannie et les 'Bruts' en Europe, Tome I: Traductions,*

Peniarth 44 version,[27] the Dingestow version,[28] and the Peniarth 21/23 version (probably derived from an archetype older than the Llanstephan 1 version);[29] then in the fourteenth century the Cotton Cleopatra version.[30] But in addition there are several composite versions, such as the Red Book version, which is a combination of the Llanstephan 1 and Dingestow versions.[31] What is clear from even these briefest of descriptions is that the tradition was extremely complex and prone to the same criss-crossing influences as we see in the Latin texts of Geoffrey. In many respects, the tradition is even more complex than the Latin one, even though there are fewer surviving manuscripts: for example, it is clear that some of the Welsh translators had access to more than one version of Geoffrey's Latin texts, certainly both the vulgate and the first variant that seems to have circulated widely in Wales.[32] Furthermore, there is clear evidence that different redactions came into contact with one another in terms of shared passages and notably in the similarity in the forms of Welsh names across different redactions.[33] While the variation in Latin texts of Geoffrey began within a few years of the vulgate being released in the twelfth century, the Welsh versions of Geoffrey suggest that a similar mixing and merging of versions was ongoing from the late twelfth and thirteenth centuries onwards.

All of this raises some interesting questions, not all of which have been clearly voiced in the scholarship to date. That may be because they are unanswerable, though that does not mean they are not worth asking. For

---

adaptations, reáppropriations (xiie–xvie siècle), ed. Hélène Tétrel and Geraldine Veyssere (Paris, 2018), 71–78.

[27] A full preliminary edition of Peniarth 44 can be found in Roberts, 'Astudiaeth Destunol'.

[28] Brynley F. Roberts, 'Fersiwn Dingestow o Brut y Brenhinedd', *Bulletin of the Board of Celtic Studies* 27 (1976–78): 331–61; the text is edited in Henry Lewis, ed., *Brut Dingestow* (Cardiff, 1942).

[29] Patrick Sims-Williams, ed., *Liber Coronacionis Britanorum*, 2 vols (Aberystwyth, 2011); cf. also Ceridwen Lloyd-Morgan, 'Un manuscript illustré de *Brut y Brenhinedd*: Aberystwyth, National Library of Wales, Peniarth 23C', in *Historia regum Britannie et les 'Bruts' en Europe, Tome II*, ed. Tétrel and Veysseyre, 429–48.

[30] John Jay Parry, ed. and trans., *Brut y Brenhinedd: Cotton Cleopatra Version*, Medieval Academy of America Publications 26 (Cambridge, MA, 1937); for discussion, see Pierre-Yves Lambert, 'À propos de la traduction galloise du ms. London, British Library, Cotton Cleopatra B.V', in *L'Historia regum Britannie et les 'Bruts' en Europe, Tome I*, ed. Tétrel and Veysseyre, 81–103.

[31] For details, see, for example, Roberts, 'A Web of Welsh *Bruts*', 149; cf. also Sims-Williams, 'An Unpublished Thirteenth-Century Version'.

[32] Sims-Williams, *Rhai addasiadau*, 8–10.

[33] Sims-Williams, *Rhai addasiadau*, 6–9; Roberts, 'A Web of Welsh *Bruts*', 153–54; cf. Brynley Roberts, 'The Treatment of Personal Names in the Early Welsh Versions of *Historia Regum Britanniae*', *Bulletin of the Board of Celtic Studies* 26 (1972–74): 274–90.

example, what would a Welsh translator or scribe do if he encountered a gap in his text, whether by eyeskip or the loss of a quire or more? There seem to be several possibilities depending on the circumstances: if he was in a well-stocked scriptorium or library, another Welsh copy might have been to hand, whether of the same redaction or a different one. Failing a Welsh text, he might have turned to a Latin text (of whatever version), located the relevant passage, and translated that (or had it translated). But all of this raises a question that is rarely asked. The working, often implicit, assumption is that we think of texts of Geoffrey sitting in libraries with scriptoria, such as St Davids, Valle Crucis, or Gloucester. But what about an *uchelwr* (nobleman) in his house in fourteenth-century mid-Wales who has inherited a scruffy copy of a *Brut*, or perhaps a Latin *DGB*?[34] He knows it is battered and worn, but how does he know whether it is complete? By that period, Geoffrey's narrative would have been fairly familiar, at least the famous bits, but, if a quire were missing from the seemingly endless list of kings in Books III or IV, would he notice, or would he even care? If he were of a completist mindset, how would he go about checking? The question becomes more pointed if we move back a century or so when the Galfridian story would have been less familiar. Presumably he would need to collate his copy with another one, perhaps by going to the local monastery or to the Norman castle up the road, and, if gaps were located, he would copy out, or have copied out, the relevant sections from his neighbour's copy into the margins of his own. But what if that neighbour owned a different variant version, and the texts did not really match at all?[35] Probably the relevant sections would have been copied anyway, and the existing text modified to link it to the insertion; hence the rise of copies with mixed texts.

A detailed examination of the make-up of texts of Geoffrey's *DGB*, whether in Latin or Welsh, suggests, then, that some parts of the tradition were awash with variants, ranging from low-level verbal differences to the kinds of major structural differences note above; and that only relates to copies that were broadly intact, and even then readers would probably have had to make do

---

[34] On lay-readers and owners the evidence is poor, but outside the institutional structures that would have offered a protective framework for manuscripts, the survival rate must have been much lower; see Crick, *The* Historia Regum Britanniae *of Geoffrey of Monmouth, IV*, 215–16, 219; Tahkokallio, *Monks, Clerics, and King Arthur*, 29–33.

[35] This issue has not always been recognised in other textually complex fields: for example, in medieval Welsh law, a great deal of work assumes that the owner of a law text would have been aware of where there were gaps and what text had been added to the end of his copy or inserted elsewhere; but, if he did not have the opportunity to compare his text with another copy, how would he know what he was missing? For a recent discussion, see Sara Elin Roberts, *The Growth of Law in Medieval Wales c. 1100–c. 1500* (Woodbridge, 2022), esp. 133–59.

with whatever version was to hand, and, as noted, not all copies were preserved in libraries where other copies were available. On the other hand, broken and damaged copies would have been even more vulnerable to unexpected insertions and additions from other sources, and furthermore those changes might have occurred not at the usual fault-lines of a relatively complete text, as we have seen above, but perhaps where a quire or part of a quire was lost or the last few pages of the copy had fallen away. That said, we also need to remind ourselves not to over-emphasise the variation, as some strands of the tradition preserve a pretty clean vulgate text of *DGB*.

But, in all of this swirl of variants of different shapes and sizes, one thing jumps out, namely a very broad and inclusive notion of what counted as a text of Geoffrey's *DGB* or its Welsh translation, much broader than anything modern readers or editors would countenance. Modern editors are generally preoccupied with deciding to which variant version a particular text belongs or to which redaction of *Brut y Brenhinedd* it is to be assigned. But it is not clear that such concerns troubled our medieval redactors, scribes, and readers, who may well have delighted simply to have laid hands on a relative complete copy, whatever the variant version. In other words, however much difference there was between the variants, they still remained within the frame of something that could be attributed to Geoffrey and be called *DGB*, or whatever other name that particular copy travelled under. Very rarely are the differences between texts noted by the scribes or annotators of manuscripts: the only instance of this seems to be the first-variant copy preserved in Aberystwyth, National Library of Wales, 13210 [4], which has a colophon identifying it as *hystoria Brittonum correcta et abbreviata*;[36] no other first- or second-variant manuscript contains such a comment, but it suggests that this text was better ('correcta') and shorter ('abbreviata'), both virtues that might commend it to readers. Interestingly, this text has been described as containing a conflation of a first- and second-variant version,[37] but the comment in its colophon only makes sense if someone had been comparing the text with other copies and could say that it was better or shorter than some other version. Furthermore, it suggests that one scribe at least saw some point to the variant versions. A comment that also implies purposeful reworking is to be found in the poem that prefaces Madog of Edeirnion's version of the work (Cardiff, South Glamorgan Library, MS 2.611, fols 9v–10r [55]):

> Aures praefata pascent quia sunt breviata.
> Arte refrenata, placide satis examinata.
> Arma, viri, facta sunt sub brevitate redacta, ...

---

[36] Crick, *The* Historia Regum Britanniae *of Geoffrey of Monmouth, III*, 6–7; *The Historia Regum Britanniae of Geoffrey of Monmouth II*, ed. Wright, lxxviii–lxxix.
[37] *DGB*, xxxii.

[Ears will feed on them, since they have been abridged,
restrained by art, and weighed quite pleasantly.
The battles, oh men, have been cut short for the sake of concision.][38]

These comments may serve as a bridge to thinking about variation in other texts of this period. Two groups of texts may prove useful in this regard: first, medieval Welsh hagiography, where at the hands of different redactors we see texts radically changing shape, content, and language, but again without any explicit indication of why they are doing it. Finally, we can return to the works of Gerald of Wales, where in some cases he does tell us what he is doing and why.

Welsh hagiographical texts are preserved in both Latin and Welsh, but it is rare to find multiple lives of a single saint; more often, there is a single surviving life of a saint in either Latin or Welsh. There are two exceptions to this: the multiple lives of St David and those of Gwenfrewy (Winifrede).[39] The lives of the former have received most attention and offer some interesting examples of reworking.[40] I follow Richard Sharpe in seeing the longest life preserved in Vespasian A. xiv as most closely representing the life that Rhygyfarch composed in the late eleventh century.[41] What we can observe here is a gradual process of abbreviation that works in different ways depending on

---

[38] See Joshua Byron Smith, 'Madog of Edeirnion's *Strenua cunctorum*: A Welsh–Latin Poem in Praise of Geoffrey of Monmouth', *North American Journal of Celtic Studies* 6 (2022): 1–14, at 10 (ll. 19–21).

[39] There is insufficient space to discuss the latter here, but there is recent excellent work; the four Latin versions of her life are now available in new online editions and translations: David Callander, ed. and trans., *Vita Sancte Wenefrede (Anonymous; Claudius)* (Aberystwyth, 2023); Callander, *Vita Sancte Wenefrede (Composite; Lansdowne)* (Aberystwyth, 2023); Callander, Vita Sancte Wenefrede *(Robert of Shrewsbury; Laud)* (Aberystwyth, 2023); and Callander, Vita Sancte Wenefrede *(Robert of Shrewsbury; Trinity)* (Aberystwyth, 2023); all available online at https://saints.wales/theedition. For a recent excellent discussion of the Welsh lives, see Jane Cartwright, 'The Welsh versions of the Life of Gwenfrewy', in *Seintiau Cymru, Sancti Cambrenses: Astudiaethau ar Seintiau Cymru/Studies in the Saints of Wales*, ed. David Parsons and Paul Russell (Aberystwyth, 2022), 237–67.

[40] See Russell, 'Translating Saints: The Latin and Welsh Versions of the Life of St David', in *Seintiau Cymru, Sancti Cambrenses*, ed. Parsons and Russell, 101–18; Jenny Day, 'The Later Lives of St David in NLW MSS Peniarth 27ii, Llanstephan 34, and Peniarth 225', in *Seintiau Cymru, Sancti Cambrenses*, ed. Parsons and Russell, 118–53.

[41] Richard Sharpe, 'Which Text Is Rhygyfarch's *Life* of St David?', in *St David of Wales: Cult, Church and Nation*, ed. J. W. Evans and J. M. Wooding (Woodbridge, 2007), 90–106. The standard edition is now Sharpe and John Reuben Davies, ed. and trans., 'Rhygyfarch's Life of St David', in *St David of Wales*, ed. Evans and Wooding, 107–55. For the debate, see Russell, 'Translating Saints', 101–4; cf. also Russell, 'Gerald of Wales and the Rewriting of Saints' Lives: The Hagiographical Fragments

the preferences and aims of the redactors and the use to which they wished to put the text. In addition to being very long and verbose, Rhygyfarch's original life is replete with local Welsh detail, much of which was removed in the 'Nero-Digby' version that was intended for consumption outside Wales;[42] as the life became shorter, another casualty was sometimes the episodes relating to Ireland, which were compressed or removed entirely. Another kind of abbreviation involved the removal of the long section on David's monastic rule; this happened twice in different parts of the tradition: in the Lincoln Cathedral 149 version and then independently in Gerald's Life of David.[43] In the latter, this was almost certainly related to his well-known antipathy to all things monastic, but in the former it may have been an easy way to remove a section that would have been of minimal interest to a church congregation. The Lincoln 149 redaction is part of a legendary, deriving originally from Leominster, and most lives absorbed into such a format tend to be shortened to fit. In that case, we know that the shortening took place in at least two phases, the earlier phase preserved in the Welsh translation of the life that is based on a longer version of the same redaction.[44]

Gerald's Life of David offers us a useful way into Gerald's well-known propensity for rewriting.[45] Unlike most of this works, where he is rewriting and mainly expanding on himself, in some of his hagiography he was reshaping the work of others. In the case of David, he took a Nero-Digby version of the text, already significantly shortened from the original, and reworked it further. None of that is very surprising, but importantly in the preface he tells

---

in London, British Library, Cotton Vitellius E. vii', *Journal of Medieval Latin* 32 (2022): 209–39, at 213–26.

[42] Sharpe, 'Which Text Is Rhygyfarch's *Life* of St David?', 104–5. The Nero–Digby text, labelled after two of its main manuscripts, is edited in J. W. James, ed. and trans., *Rhigyfarch's Life of St David: The Basic Mid-Twelfth-Century Latin Text with Introduction, Critical Apparatus and Translation* (Cardiff, 1967).

[43] On the latter, see immediately below, 38–9.

[44] Russell, 'Translating Saints'.

[45] Robert Bartlett, 'Rewriting Saints' Lives: The Case of Gerald of Wales', *Speculum* 58 (1983): 598–613; Russell, 'Gerald of Wales and the Rewriting of Saints' Lives'. The life was edited as *Vita S Dauid* in Brewer, ed., *Giraldi Cambrensis Opera*, vol. 3 (London, 1863), 377–404; their text, which is not very accurate and also classicised, was essentially taken from Henry Wharton, *Anglia Sacra*, ii, (London, 1691), 628–40 as the single manuscript then known was damaged in the Cotton fire. A new edition is Paul Russell, ed. and trans., *Gerald of Wales: Vita Sancti Dauid* (Aberystwyth, 2023), online at https://saints.wales/theedition/ (based on London, British Library, Royal 13. C. I, a manuscript with a Glastonbury provenance but unknown to the editor of the Rolls Series). For a recent discussion of Gerald's hagiography, see Stephanie Plass, *A Scholar and His Saints: Examining the Art of Hagiographical Writing of Gerald of Wales*, FAU Studien aus der Philosophischen Facultät 17 (Erlangen, 2020), 61–115.

us what he is doing and why.[46] He begins by claiming he is turning it into a text written *scolastico stilo* and then details how he is doing that:[47]

> Lectionis igitur antique et propemodum iam antiquate, sicut nec uerba, sic neque rerum hic series, nec continentia requiratur. Correctionis quippe lege seruata, Domino inspirante, qui interdum que abscondit a sapientibus reuelat paruulis, et superflua rescindi, et defectiua suppleri, et minus exquisite dicta mutari, in hac presenti pagina lector inueniet.
>
> [There should be no need for an old-fashioned nor even antiquated mode of writing neither in words, the arrangement of the narrative, or in content. But maintaining the rule of correction, with the inspiration of the Lord who sometimes reveals to little children what he keeps from the wise (Matt. 11:25), the reader will find in these present pages that which is superfluous cut back, that which is missing supplied, and that which is less artfully composed revised.]

This is also another work that Gerald returned to at a later stage and made some additions. This was unknown to the editor of Rolls Series edition, who was unaware of the copy of the Life of David in London, British Library, Royal 13. C. I, but close comparison shows that the Royal manuscript, though a later manuscript, contains a developmentally earlier version of the text than that in the fragments preserved in BL Cotton Vitellius E. vii, which can be seen to represent his second and perhaps third attempts; the base text of the Vitellius version has been rewritten in places and then marginal notes were also added. These would have been incorporated into a fair copy, but no manuscript copy has survived, though Henry Wharton essentially created the equivalent to a fair copy in his printed text, made before the Cotton fire, thus preserving a complete text.[48]

Elsewhere in Gerald's output, his tendency to rewrite or to take over sections of text from one work to another is well known – for example, the reworking of the famous section on beavers[49] – though not always viewed

---

[46] *Vita Sancti Dauid by Gerald of Wales*, ed. Russell, §1. For a more detailed discussion of the whole passage, see Russell, 'Gerald of Wales and the Rewriting of Saints' Lives', 61–115.

[47] On scholasticism in Gerald generally and his work on other saints' lives, see the discussion in Bartlett, 'Rewriting Saints' Lives', 605–13.

[48] Wharton, *Anglia sacra*, ii, 628–40; not all of the inaccuracies and errors of this edition were ironed out in the Rolls edition, and others were introduced.

[49] *Itinerarium Kambrie*, ii. 3 (James F. Dimock, ed., *Giraldi Cambrensis Opera*, vol. 6, (London, 1868), 115–18); also taken over into *Descriptio Kambrie*, i. 5 (Dimock, ed., *Giraldi Cambrensis Opera*, vol. 6, 173–75); a section of it had already appeared in *Topographica Hibernica*, i. 26 (Dimock, ed., *Giraldi Cambrensis Opera*, vol.

with enthusiasm.[50] However, it is important to pay attention to these additions as they tell us important things about Gerald's concerns with both content and style. Negative comments aside, the Rolls editions did usually print the longest versions including all the additions, though more recent work on *Topographia Hibernica* is based on the shortest redaction, ironically a version that Gerald would have been keen to suppress.[51]

Gerald's rigorous control of his own output seems to have put him in a position to decide when enough additional annotation has been gathered to justify a new recension of one of his works; the new version was always longer, never shorter, even though occasional passages might be excised or replaced. That control was maintained, as far as we can tell, for the whole of his life, to the extent that he could not only offer the chapter at Hereford a new *Topographia* but also offer to revise their copy of *Speculum ecclesiae*.

While very little of Gerald's work seems to have escaped his own oversight, there are some indications that other work had been produced at least in draft. Robert Bartlett's edition of the *History of Llanthony Priory* attributes it convincingly to Gerald, even though it is not claimed by him in his own list of works.[52] I have suggested that he had drawn up notes for a Life of Patrick while he was in Ireland.[53] In both these cases, and certainly in the latter, it might be argued that he regarded these works as incomplete and so not to be mentioned. The *History of Llanthony* seems to have been continued after his death, and so perhaps he regarded it as unfinished. Alternatively, as Bartlett has proposed, it was his last work, and he never updated his bibliography.[54] Such was Gerald's control over his work that he has influenced later editors of his works into following his recensional arrangements, and indeed it is difficult to do otherwise with the works of this kind.[55] However,

---

5, (London, 1867), 58–59); for the first recension version, see John T. O'Meara, ed., 'Giraldus Cambrensis in *Topographia Hibernie*: Text of the First Recension', *Proceedings of the Royal Irish Academy: Archaeology, Culture, History, Literature* 52 (1948–50), 113–78, at 129–30; for discussion, see Michael Faletra, 'Giraldian Beavers: Revision and the Making of Meaning in Gerald's Early Works', in *Gerald of Wales*, ed. Henley and McMullen, 111–25.

[50] Dimock was especially scathing: Dimock, ed., *Giraldi Cambrensis Opera*, vol. 6, lxvii–lvxiii.

[51] For example, O'Meara, ed., 'Giraldus Cambrensis in *Topographia Hibernie*'.

[52] Robert Bartlett, ed. and trans., *The History of Llanthony Priory*, Oxford Medieval Texts (Oxford, 2022); cf. also Bartlett, 'Gerald of Wales and the *History of Llanthony Priory*', in *Gerald of Wales*, ed. Henley and McMullen, 81–96.

[53] Russell, 'Gerald of Wales and the Rewriting of Saints' Lives', 226–36.

[54] *The History of Llanthony Priory*, ed. Bartlett, xxxvi.

[55] For an attempt to break out of this model in relation to *Topographia Hibernica*, see Nóirín Ní Bheaglaoi, '*Libri corrigendi*'; and Bheaglaoi, 'Two Topographies of Gerald of Wales?', *Scriptorium* 67, no. 2 (2013): 377–93.

given Gerald's attempts to recover earlier copies from circulating, he might regard our ability to distinguish recensions as a failure on his part. If he had succeeded in gathering them all in, we would only be working with the latest version and would never have been able to unpick his working methods in the way we can. That said, if he had become bishop of St Davids (or even archbishop), perhaps he might never have continued to annotate his works anyway, being far too busy with church business.

As it is, we can only assume that in the years between recensions of his Irish and Welsh works (and perhaps others), he was gradually making additions and rewriting sections. Some of his working methods are visible in the mass of marginal annotation, with some added on pasted-in slips of vellum, on the pages of the copy of one of his later works (1208–16), *Speculum duorum*, preserved in Vatican, Biblioteca Apostolica Vaticana, Cod. Reg. Lat, 470, fols 50r–77r, in which the text and its burden of annotation give every impression of being about to collapse in on itself.[56] It was clearly a cumulative process but one that he controlled. But, if as a speculative exercise, we imagine that he had not been in control of his own works in such a rigorous way (possibly because he died earlier and others took over the work of revision or no one gathered in all the copies of earlier recensions), what might have been the outcome? One possibility is that his Irish and Welsh works at least might have ended up looking like the different versions of Geoffrey's *DGB* – assuming they became as popular as Geoffrey's work – especially if we set aside the modern notion of three different versions. One conclusion arising from this is that perhaps only Gerald's controlling presence kept the flood of possible variants at bay.

Turning back to Geoffrey, from a modern perspective most of his readers are extremely grateful not to have to wrestle with the churning mass of variants in the different texts and variants. But one cannot help thinking that the kind of improbable stemmata that are produced as part of the narrative of the development of Geoffrey's text(s) and their translations can distort the reality of reading these texts in the twelfth and thirteenth centuries (and indeed beyond). As Brynley Roberts has pertinently observed:

> Laboriously modern editors strive to show these amalgams and borrowings in stemmata. But stemmata are static and we need to use our imagination as we read them, lest we lose sight of the flow and flux implied by so many lines of descent from multiple sources and in the more ambiguous verbal reminiscences that editors annotate. Stemmata are diagrams of cultural communities; texts were adapted, and manuscripts written by real people, for real people, and real patrons.[57]

---

[56] See Yves Lefèvre, R. B. C. Huygens, Brian Dawson, and Michael Richter, eds and trans, *Speculum Duorum or the Mirror of Two Men* (Cardiff, 1974), lvii–lxvi; for digital images of the manuscript, see https://digi.vatlib.it/view/MSS_Reg.lat.470.

[57] Roberts, 'A Web of Welsh *Bruts*', 168.

One way of thinking about Geoffrey's work is to think in Geraldian terms about how they were rewritten; in that light, should we be thinking that the first variant is the product of a single rewrite or a cumulative build-up of annotation of the kind that Gerald did? By contrast, the second half of the second variant of *DGB* looks very much like a systematic rewriting of the Arthurian narrative in which the Arthurian focus is sharpened by downplaying other parts of the narrative. Be that as it may, by using the lens of Gerald's more perspicuous methods of working to view Geoffrey's practices, we might think about the variation and fluidity in different ways. From that perspective, the nameless scribe who described a first variant text of *DGB* as 'correcta et abbreviata', or Madog's claim for his version 'breviata ... arte refrenata ... sub brevitate redacta', may not be very far away from Gerald providing a text that is 'melioratum ... et emendatum'. If nothing else, perhaps we should think more about valuing the complexity of these texts and how they work rather than constantly attempting to smooth them out. They are not always amenable to straight lines, whether in terms of transmission or editorial thinking.

3

Precarious Reimaginings of the British History in the English Brut Tradition

JOHN J. THOMPSON

My contribution to this celebratory volume has been prompted by Siân Echard's sterling published work on an important foundational period for English historical writings. I am thinking, particularly, of her continuing scholarly fascination with Geoffrey of Monmouth and his close contemporaries and the Anglo-Latin literary traditions and scholarly networks surrounding them. Such networks inspired an academic and popular interest in, and occasional scepticism regarding, Geoffrey's version of the story of Arthur and the British history. Echard's pioneering work has highlighted the importance of linking the earliest writing and reception of such works with the Angevin literary culture associated with Henry II's court. In this essay, I now wish to turn to a much more intensively studied later period in English literary history in an attempt to understand how Latin and vernacular renderings of the Galfridian historical narrative fared in relation to the academic and popular historical writings associated with Tudor metropolitan and court culture during the reigns of Henry VII and Henry VIII. By taking this approach, I think it is possible to identify the terms in which the English historical imagination in this later period dealt with the multiple interpretations of Arthur and the beginnings of British history that had been built up over two hundred years and more. That narrative was finally shaped for posterity by what might be described as an almost all-encompassing Tudor culture of compliance to the received wisdom of historical truth transmitted to sixteenth-century readers by the English Brut tradition rather than by any new forensic understanding of the nature of historical evidence.[1]

---

[1] I am here building on the earlier account in John J. Thompson, 'Re-imagining History through the English Prose Brut Tradition', in *L'Historia Regum Britannie et les 'Bruts' en Europe, 2, Production, Circulation et Réception (XIIe–XVIe siècle)*, ed. Hélène Tétrel and Géraldine Veysseyre (Paris, 2018), 345–63. For the purposes of this

William Caxton's prologue for his printed edition of Malory's *Morte Darthur* offers a convenient starting point for this discussion.[2] As is well known to modern scholarship, Caxton's vernacular account again raises the centuries-old anxieties regarding questions of historical veracity surrounding Arthur. He writes: 'dyuers men holde oppynyon / that there was no suche Arthur / and that alle suche bookes as been maad of hym / ben but fayned and fables / by cause that somme cronycles make of hym no mencyon ne remembre hym noo thynge ne of his knyghtes' (sig. [Aijv]).[3] Caxton here takes on the role of neutral observer – or, perhaps, better, sets up a straw man – regarding the diverse opinions that informed this debate. He does so in conversation with certain 'noble and dyuers gentylmen of thys royame of Englond' to whom he expresses the apparent concerns raised because of the opinions of others who simply do not believe in Arthur because of his absence from some chronicle accounts. Caxton then describes how a nobleman in his company countered such negativity by enumerating a range of proofs regarding Arthur's authenticity. He mentions the survival of Arthur's tomb at Glastonbury and the account of his death and later removal to the abbey reported in the *Polychronicon* ('in the v book the syxte chappytre / and in the seuenth book the xxiij chappytre'), the accounts of Arthur's exploits in Boccaccio's *De casu principum*, and also 'galfrydus in his brutysshe book', who offers a life of Arthur. And then there are the relics and artefacts associated with Arthur's court now preserved in Westminster, at Dover castle, and in Winchester, as well as the ruins of Camelot still in Wales. Moreover, Arthur's exploits are celebrated widely across Europe, mainly in French and Welsh vernacular texts but also in Dutch, Italian, Spanish, and Greek versions and also sometimes (but not often enough) in English. All this seems sufficiently evidence-based to assuage many of the lingering doubts Caxton gives voice to in the prologue and strengthens his resolve to print Malory's prose text, which immediately follows.

Caxton refers to two different Brut chronicle items in his prologue as he sets up his case, of course. 'Galfrydus in his brutysshe book' evokes the figure

---

essay, it is important to stress that the late medieval 'English Brut tradition' referred to throughout comprises items written in Latin, insular French and Middle English.

[2] *STC* 801; the abbreviation refers to A. W. Pollard and G. R. Redgrave, *A Short Title Catalogue of Books Printed in England, Scotland, and Ireland ... 1475–1640*, 3 vols (London, 1926); revised edn, W. A. Jackson, F. S. Ferguson, and Katharine F. Pantzer (London, 1976–91).

[3] The Caxton print can probably be dated at earliest to mid-1485, probably within a month of Bosworth and Henry VII's accession. For this tentative dating, see S. Carole Weinberg, 'Caxton, Anthony Woodville, and the Prologue to the *Morte Darthur*', *Studies in Philology* 102 (2005): 45–65. For a modern edition of the prologue, see *Caxton's Own Prose*, ed. N. F. Blake (London, 1973), 107.

of Geoffrey of Monmouth and his twelfth-century account widely known in the later Middle Ages as *Historia Regum Britanniae* (originally called *De gestis Britonum*).[4] Some reference to his role as the progenitor of the entire medieval Brut tradition in a discussion of Arthur at this time is hardly unexpected or surprising. On the other hand, the vagueness of this general reference stands in marked contrast to the scholarly precision with which the anonymous nobleman had initially directed us to the *Polychronicon* and to Book 5, Chapter 6 and Book 7, Chapter 23 of that item even before the name of Geoffrey is brought into the reported conversation.

Since we are dealing here in the prologue with an unusually specific bibliographical recommendation from Caxton's social superior regarding reputable historical sources for Arthur, one might initially wonder which particular Latin or vernacular version of the *Polychronicon* (or, indeed, which particular 'brutysshe book') we are meant to keep in mind as Caxton describes his hesitation regarding whether or not to accept Arthur's historicity.[5] He had printed John Trevisa's English translation of Ranulf Higden's Latin *Polychronicon* text in 1482 (*STC* 13438).[6] In 1480 and again in 1482 under the title *Chronicles of England*, he had also printed a text of the Middle English Prose *Brut* (*STC* 9991, *STC* 9992). That item was ultimately derived from the Galfridian Latin source via an Anglo Norman prose intermediary and therefore would have qualified as another vernacular 'brutysshe book' that could be evoked as part of the English Brut tradition in defence of Arthur.[7] As such, it would seem that the anonymous nobleman in the prologue has

[4] For some introductory sense of the intellectual breadth and geographical scope of the Galfridian reach across late medieval and early modern European writing and reading habits, see *A Companion to Geoffrey of Monmouth*, ed. Georgia Henley and Joshua Byron Smith (Leiden, 2020), especially Siân Echard, 'The Latin Reception of the *De gestis Britonum*', 209–34; for a summary list of the Middle English narratives derived directly or indirectly from Geoffrey, see also Elizabeth Bryan, 'The English Reception of Geoffrey of Monmouth', 449–53, at 451.

[5] For Higden's Latin text and its derivative versions, see the classic study in John Taylor, *The Universal Chronicle of Ranulf Higden* (Oxford, 1966). As far as the situation regarding the English translated version by John Trevisa is concerned, see R. A. Waldron, 'The Manuscripts of Trevisa's Translation of the *Polychronicon*', *Modern Language Quarterly* 51 (1990): 281–317; David C. Fowler, *John Trevisa* (Aldershot, 1993) and the characteristically trenchant account of the state of Trevisa textual studies in A. S. G. Edwards, 'John Trevisa', in *A Companion to Middle English Prose*, ed. A. S. G. Edwards (Cambridge, 2004), 117–26.

[6] The Trevisa text must have gained some traction at this time since it was printed again by Caxton's successor, Wynkyn de Worde, in c. 1495 (*STC* 13439) and again by P. Treveris, 'at þe expences of J. Reynes', in 1527 (*STC* 13440).

[7] For a useful overview, see Lister M. Matheson, *The Prose 'Brut': The Development of a Middle English Chronicle* (Tempe, AZ, 1998), Introduction, 1–56.

been reading and endorsing Caxton's other recent printed texts for future intended sympathetic readers, thereby allowing the Caxton prologue to be read as some kind of publisher's blurb.

Caxton's characterisation of himself as initially doubtful about Arthur is interesting in this context because Higden in his *Polychronicon* had not unequivocally endorsed the account of Arthur he found recorded in Geoffrey of Monmouth.[8] Instead, he followed the Galfridian narrative only insofar as its details were corroborated by historical accounts in other reputed twelfth-century writers such as William of Malmesbury and Henry of Huntingdon. Moreover, it is also in Book 5, Chapter 6 of the *Polychronicon* that Higden had momentarily exposed the precariousness of the Galfridian historical record regarding Arthur's European military exploits and many of the marvels surrounding them that he had not found recorded elsewhere. Trevisa, his English translator, spiritedly argues against the historical scepticism regarding such exploits that had been expressed by William of Malmesbury but that Higden shared and had reported to his Latin readers at precisely this point. Trevisa had an entirely different view of the matter, but he faithfully translated Higden's Latin into English, including its author's reservations about Arthur, which are accounted for as 'þe manere of everiche nacioun to overe preyse som oon of þe same nacioun, as þe Grees preyseþ here Alisaundre, and þe Romayns here Octovianus, and Englisshe men here Richard, and Frensche men here Charles, and Britouns here Arthur' (*Lib.* V, *cap.* sextum, p. 337). Trevisa immediately inserts an indignant comment that clarifies exactly where he stands: 'Here William telleþ a magel tale wiþ oute evidence; and Ranulphus his resouns, þat he meveþ a3enst Gaufridus and Arthur, schulde non clerke moove þat can knowe an argument, for it followeþ it nou3t' (*Lib.* V, *cap.* sextum, p. 337.[9]

Caxton's role as devil's advocate in that longstanding scholarly debate about Arthur is therefore not dissimilar to Higden's questioning search of respected historical sources in the *Polychronicon* for reliable historical evidence to confirm the Galfridian narrative. Such scholarly prevarication forms part of a much larger medieval debate, usually conducted in Latin prose, regarding historical truth and the historicity of national myths of origin that had already been aired by writers such as William of Malmesbury and William of

---

[8] In the absence of a modern edition of the relevant part of the Higden and Trevisa *Polychronicon* texts, see the parallel facing-page edition in *Polychronicon Ranulf Higden Monachi Cestrensis*, ed. C. Babington and J. R. Lumby, 9 vols (London, 1865–86), here vol. 5, ed. J. R. Lumby (1874), 336–37.

[9] References are to Lumby, ed., *Polychronicon*. Trevisa's interpolation is also noted in John E. Housman, 'Higden, Trevisa, Caxton, and the Beginnings of Arthurian Criticism', *Review of English Studies* 22 (1947): 209–17; see also Ronald Waldron, 'Trevisa's "Celtic Complex" Revisited', *Notes and Queries* 36 (1989): 303–7.

Newburgh, among others. As I discuss below, similar such uncertainties and hesitations would be aired again by sixteenth-century and later English writers and translators on the topic. If we follow this line of reasoning, then Trevisa, Higden's English translator, has taken up the opposing side in a spirited defence of Arthur that is continued by the anonymous English nobleman in Caxton's prologue. Both Trevisa, the clerk-translator, and Caxton's anonymous nobleman are reducing this scholarly Latin debate into English, to paraphrase Caxton's famous comment on Malory's achievement in the *Morte Darthur*. In effect, their arguments seem to be offering what amounts to two different sides of the same vernacular coin: the story of Arthur is true because of the survival of a range of artefacts and widely dispersed chronicle versions that tell us it is true.

It is hardly a surprise to any of Caxton's readers that his imaginative endorsement of the carefully rehearsed Galfridian view of Arthur's place in English history in his prologue – one that had already been rehearsed in the *Polychronicon* – falls into line with the unqualified enthusiasm for linking the story of British origins to Brutus and Troy found in other vernacular chronicles. The extant corpus of Middle English Prose *Brut* versions is particularly important in this respect since it has already been convincingly argued that these 'brutysshe books' represent the form in which most fifteenth-century and many sixteenth-century and later English readers knew their national history.[10] Over 180 fifteenth-century manuscripts of the different Middle English prose versions survive, with that number augmented by the two Caxton prints in 1480 and 1482. As many as eleven later prints based on the Caxton version were then produced between 1483 and 1528, about half of these by Caxton's successor Wynkyn de Worde (in 1497, 1502, 1515, 1520, and 1528).[11]

More than two centuries of actively copying, printing, reading, and owning 'brutysshe books' obviously impacted differently on English Tudor writers and readers of various stripes who were living through the political and religious upheavals, uncertainties, and polemics of their age. One of the most remarkable features of the extant corpus of Middle English Prose *Brut* versions, for example, is the unusually large number of sixteenth- and seventeenth-century names and possible marks of ownership and readership some of these predominantly fifteenth-century books contain. Other copies

---

[10] For the corpus presented as a synoptic inventory, see Matheson, *Prose 'Brut'*, 67–348. In Thompson, 'Reimagining History', 353–56, I discuss a number of occasions where Middle English *Polychronicon* versions were imaginatively mined by Caxton and others for additional or confirmatory details with which to bolster the account of English history found in Middle English prose *Brut* versions.

[11] *STC* 9996, 9997, 10000.5, 10001, 10002. For the full list of early printed editions, see Matheson, *The Prose 'Brut'*, xxxiii–xxxvi.

look hardly likely to have been read at all.[12] As I shall discuss further below, many such later readers were concerned with understanding on their own terms the origins of English historical identity and the multiple versions of an English national past that had given rise to an undeniably conflicted present in the Tudor period. It almost goes without saying that that search for certainty regarding an authentic national identity was played out at length in both Latin and English texts closely associated with early modern attempts to establish and make more widely known the legitimacy of the English Tudor dynasty both at home and abroad.

The search itself took on many different forms, some less critical or scholarly in their investigations than others. London British Library, Royal MS 18 A LXXV, for example, is a much-delayed final report of a commission, apparently originally set up to investigate Henry VII's Welsh roots and justify his right to the throne after the Battle of Bosworth and defeat of Richard III in 1485.[13] The title in its opening lines makes clear that the document was finally submitted after Edward VI's accession in 1543: 'This dissent of the moost victorious and Chrysten prynce kyng Edward the sext, sonne and heire of king Henry VIIIth, that goeth lynyally to Brute, is true lynage and agreith with the best cronycles in Wales.' The members of the commission are next identified by name with 'per me David Holand of Rwthyn' inscribed at the end of the document. That person is likely to be the same David Holand of Ruthin who formally signed the copy of the Middle English Prose *Brut* now extant in Aberystwyth, NLW MS 21608A with the phrase 'per me davidem holland' on fol 10r. Another marginal inscription on the next page refers to 'the kyngs highest commissioners in the march of wales' (fol. 10v), so suggesting that MS 21608A was once consulted by Holand as he performed his scribal role for the commission. Regardless of the vernacular language in which it was written, MS 21608A may even have been considered by Holand and his associates as 'a brutysshe book' and one of 'the best cronycles in Wales' simply because of its uncritical agreement with the Galfridian view of English history that Holand's manuscript copy of the lineage unambiguously endorses. By 1543 (the year of Henry VIII's death), this would have seemed a world away from any concerns surrounding the events associated with Henry VII's claim to the throne by right of just title of inheritance. It was also long after the ruling Tudor dynasty had first established itself on the political stage at home and abroad. It seems pointless to try and read the survival of Holand's manuscript copy as anything more than a belated and compliant scholarly gesture or even perhaps a gift of some kind to the new boy king on his accession.

---

[12] Thompson, 'Re-imagining History', 359–60.
[13] Further details on the manuscript and references in Thompson 'Re-imagining History', 358–59.

With so much invested in the story of Brutus and the Trojan origins of Britain by so many writers for so long and in so many Latin and vernacular cultural settings, it remains challenging to understand what could possibly have dislodged this potent English myth of origin in either Tudor court circles or in the popular historical imagination of the period. Nevertheless, through an obvious concern to justify his lineage and the Tudor right to the English crown in European circles, Henry VII is credited with having set in motion in the 1505–6 period another long-term historical search for national origins that co-existed with the Welsh project during his lifetime and, similarly, had made the fruits of its labours available for scrutiny long after the first Tudor king had died. Henry granted that project to Polydore Vergil, an Italian who had come to England in 1502 as a papal delegate and who had already enjoyed some distinction across Europe as a Latin scholar displaying versatility and deftness of touch regarding his selection and deployment of written sources.[14]

Polydore was the latest of a number of visiting Italian humanist writers associated with the courts of Henry VII and Henry VIII, several of whom in the early years of the Tudor monarchy before the break with Rome quickly set the tone for courtly propaganda pieces.[15] These were often presented as royal gifts and offered flattering accounts of significant moments that marked the early Tudor court as an important and noble European power, celebrating events such as the union of the two houses of York and Lancaster through Henry VII's nuptials or the birth of his son Arthur as the first rightful Tudor heir to the English throne. There may well have been some expectation on Henry VII's part that Polydore's researches into the remoter reaches of the English past would have quickly borne similar fruit, but that was ultimately not going to be the case.[16] A first draft of Polydore's *Anglica Historia* that can be dated to 1513 survives in a holograph version that was apparently left as a set of working papers in the hands of Federico Veterani, librarian to the dukes of Urbino, during Polydore's visit to Rome and Urbino in 1514–15.[17] That was possibly in anticipation of a presentation copy of this mammoth account of English origins and history being prepared for Henry VIII in Urbino. If that

---

[14] For Polydore's career and writings, see Denys Hay, *Polydore Vergil, Renaissance Historian and Man of Letters* (Oxford, 1952).

[15] David Carlson, 'Politicizing Tudor Court Literature: Gaguin's Embassy and Henry VII's Humanists' Response', *Studies in Philology* 85 (1988): 279–304.

[16] For Polydore's not entirely flattering account of Henry VII and his reign, written hardly more than a decade after the king's death, see Sydney Anglo, 'Ill of the Dead: The Posthumous Reputation of Henry VII', *Renaissance Studies* 1 (1987): 27–47, at 30–32.

[17] The papers now survive as two bound volumes in the Vatican Library as part of the Urbino collection (Urbinates Latini MSS 497 and 498). See Denys Hay, 'The Manuscript of Polydore Vergil's *Anglica Historia*', *The English Historical Review* 54 (1939): 240–51; also Hay, *Polydore Vergil*, 79–81.

really was Polydore's original intention in taking a preliminary unedited draft of his work to Italy, that specific commission seems to have been abandoned, and a fine presentation copy destined for the English royal court was probably never made.

The decision to leave the first draft of his work in Urbino proved fortuitous since, within a few months of his return to England in February 1515, Polydore had his letters intercepted, all his goods sequestered, and his London house closed when he was arrested and imprisoned in the Tower.[18] That was on the orders of Thomas Wolsey, who was acting on information received from Henry VIII's ambitious Latin secretary, Andreas Ammonius, regarding derogatory comments about Wolsey that Polydore is said to have included in his correspondence at a time when Wolsey was expecting to win a cardinal's hat. A series of diplomatic exchanges with Rome seems to have resolved the issue to Wolsey's satisfaction, and Polydore was released in December 1515. But the incident seems to have left its mark on him since this was clearly not a time to incur the displeasure of the king or his senior advisors. As far as his *Anglica Historia* is concerned, Polydore spent the period up until at least 1526 revising his first draft, with some evidence that his writings and revisions may have been known by others in England prior to its appearance in print. A much-revised text dedicated to Henry VIII was only finally published in 1534, taking the history to 1509, with a second revised edition issued in 1546, and a third in 1555, the year of Polydore's death. The third edition was printed after Mary had come to the throne and added an account of Henry VIII's reign to 1537. All three editions were printed in Basle.[19]

Some delay in formulating definitive statements regarding how the Tudor monarchy fitted into the lineage of English kings from the beginnings of history to the present day might perhaps have been expected due to the political situation in England during the protracted period of the Henrician reformations and the pressure on writers associated, however loosely, with the English court to comply with royal expectations. The *Anglica Historia* was offered to Henry VIII in 1534 as primarily a scholarly endeavour written in classical Latin prose rather than a popular vernacular history, but that did not entirely liberate its writer from the obligation to conform. In writing about the origins of Britain, Polydore had with good reason commented on the unavailability of some sources and the intractability of the problems raised by others, despite his determined efforts to sift fact from fiction in the often contradictory versions of the remote past available to him as sources. In his dedication to Henry, he commends Bede's account of British history since the arrival of the Romans and adds that Gildas is of some help for the even earlier

---

[18] Hay, *Polydore Vergil*, 10–14.
[19] Hay, *Polydore Vergil*, 81–85. Hay notes also (186) that the last known letter written by Polydore was addressed to the new queen, congratulating her on her accession.

period.[20] Without going into further detail at this stage, he next comments obliquely on the obscurity or confusion of later accounts 'quae etiam nunc tenebris circunfusa dilucere nequeunt' (which even now are so surrounded by darkness they are unable to bring light). The targets Polydore specifically has in mind become clearer in Book I:18, where he comments that Gildas in his *De Excidio et Conquestu Britanniae* never mentioned Brutus, yet later accounts masquerading as that honest source have erroneously interpolated an account of Brutus as first founder of Britain and credited it to Gildas. No further details are given, but Polydore adds that he has recently published an authentic Gildas edition: this is a reference to the 1525 publication, probably in Antwerp, of Polydore's text of Gildas.[21] It was dedicated to the bishop of London, Cuthbert Tunstall, an associate of Thomas More and an international Tudor diplomat who had just been appointed Lord Keeper of the Privy Seal.

In I:19, Polydore's attention then turns to the Galfridian version of the British history. He endorses William of Newburgh's similarly supportive view of Gildas before quoting him at length regarding Geoffrey's fabricated account of Arthur. Presumably hoping to insulate himself from censure by such means, Polydore asserts, via William's reported words:

> Gaufredus hic est dictus cognomine Arthurus, pro eo quod multa de Arthuro ex priscis Britonum pigmentis sumpta et ab se aucta per superductum Latini sermonis colorem honesto historiae nomine obtexit.

> [This man is cauled Geffray, surnamed Arthure, bie cause that oute of the olde lesings of Brittons, being somwhat augmented bie him, hee hathe recited manie things of this King Arthure, taking unto him bothe the coloure of Latin speeche and the honest pretext of an Historie.][22]

Polydore scornfully refers to this historical fabrication (I:20–21) as 'nova historia' (the new history) or as a vulgar process of truth enhancement for the sake of novelty, here camouflaged in Latin. To make matters worse, he reports (I:21) how Gildas has already attested that the ancient British accounts of

---

[20] Polydore's printed text of the *Anglica Historia* discussed here is available online with a modern English translation at http://www.philological.bham.ac.uk/polverg/ (accessed 18 December 2022). In the following discussion, I also quote from the anonymous early modern English translation uniquely surviving in London, British Library Royal MS 18.C.VIII/IX, for the text of which see *Polydore Vergil's English History*, ed. Sir Henry Ellis, The Camden Society 36 (London, 1846).

[21] See Dennis E. Rhodes, 'The First Edition of Gildas', *The Library* 6 (1979): 355–60.

[22] Ellis, *Polydore's English History*, 29. For Polydore's source for this quotation in William of Newburgh's prologue to his *Historia Rerum Anglicarum*, see William of Newburgh, *The History of English Affairs, Book I*, ed. P. G. Walsh and M. J. Kennedy (Warminster, 1988), 28.

British origins are all lost, leaving no certain trace of Brutus anywhere in the earliest written record since the Roman histories similarly fail to mention him.

British regnal history has to begin somewhere, however, so, faced with such an impasse, Polydore concedes that, for diplomatic reasons, he will begin with Brutus or 'Brito' (I:21). He carefully indicates that he will do so 'non sine stomacho faciemus tum rationis temporis habendae tum malevolentiae deprecandae causa' (not without distaste, both on account of the times and for the reason of avoiding any suggestion of malice). And there is a sense that Polydore has been somewhat similarly backed into a corner later (III:13) when he grants Arthur some limited historical space. He adds that posterity, in the form of popular common opinion ('vulgus'), has raised Arthur to the same legendary status as Roland now enjoys among the Italians. There then follows a summary of the legendary prowess with which it is claimed that Arthur was victorious over the Saxons, took possession of Scotland, defeated the Romans and Lucius, and also some giants, and was advancing to Rome when he was forced to return to Britain to deal with Modred's tyranny. His Glastonbury tomb offers posterity a final legendary ornament, Polydore claims, although he adds that it could not possibly have been constructed until long after Arthur's day.

The preceding account of the place of Brutus and Arthur in the *Anglica Historia* is based on the revised text published in the Basle prints rather than on Polydore's holograph version.[23] In the latter (MS 1, fol. 15r), Polydore had cynically justified the inclusion of material from Geoffrey of Monmouth in his 1513 version because of its accessibility through the recent work of greedy Paris printers.[24] That information is simply not included in the 1534 and later prints of the *Anglica Historia*. Similarly, his criticism of the credulity engendered by Geoffrey's account of Arthur's martial feats in the holograph (MS 1, fol. 63r) is significantly toned down in the printed versions, where, perhaps following the example Polydore found in Higden, the passage has been rewritten to suggest simply that the figure of Arthur has now reached the legendary status of an English Roland in the popular imagination (III:13).[25] There is no specific reference at this point to Geoffrey's role in fabricating an imperial history for Arthur. Instead, that task is reserved in the printed version for Polydore's earlier general discussion of his sources (1:19), where he

---

[23] Hay, *Polydore Vergil*, Appendix II, 187–98 offers a summary account of the main variations between the manuscript and print versions of the *Anglica Historia*.

[24] This is a reference to the first printing and publication of the *Historia Regum Britannie* by Jodocus Badius Ascensius (Paris, 1508). For his prolific career as printer, see Paul White, *Jodocus Badius Ascensius: Commentary, Commerce and Print in the Renaissance* (Oxford, 2013).

[25] For the text in the holograph manuscript at this point, see Hay, *Polydore Vergil*, 199.

basically allows William of Newburgh to speak for him regarding Geoffrey's flawed modus operandi as a history writer.

By 1534, Polydore had obviously decided to approach the issue of Geoffrey as 'uerior poeta quam historicus' (truer poet than historian) with a marginally greater degree of circumspection than he had shown in the 1513 holograph. His dedication of the print to Henry VIII vaguely alludes to works written after Gildas on British origins that offer more darkness than light but adds that he has consulted all available sources, obviously favouring Gildas and the Roman historians for the earliest period yet resorting to expediency and common sense where these and other European sources failed him. Such a consideration has resulted in Polydore's account of the fifteenth century being built up around one of the unadorned annalistic accounts he refers to in his dedication and that he is most likely to have found in a manuscript or print copy of an unidentified London chronicle version. That material was probably supplemented by information derived from the 1516 printed edition of Robert Fabyan's *New Chronicles of England and France* (*STC* 10659), which Polydore certainly later used to add supplementary details regarding London civic history in the 1546 second revised edition of the *Anglica Historia*.[26]

For his account of military and political events in the period 1259–1352 during the reigns of Henry III, Edward I, Edward II, and Edward III, Polydore is likely to have turned to the details originally derived from two other 'brutysshe books'. The *Anglica Historia* text at this point offers a confection of material that seems to have been ultimately taken from Higden's *Polychronicon* and an English prose *Brut* version. In view of my earlier discussion of the Caxton example, one might be tempted to assume that this means Polydore may have enjoyed access to two different printed versions of both sources, at least one of them or possibly both by Caxton. While this may have been the case, I think there are other possible ways in which Polydore could have accessed this combination of material. Middle English Prose *Brut* copies were often supplied with *Polychronicon* material added in supplementary fashion to enlarge or make good suspected lacunae in some extant manuscript copies, for example.[27] More significantly perhaps, there are also a number of Latin prose translated versions of the English Brut tradition that are far more scholarly in appearance and character than the Middle English prose versions. Such materials are likely to have held some considerable appeal for English history writers such as Polydore.

If Polydore had ever had an opportunity to consult the second version of the Latin Prose *Brut*, it is likely to have held some appeal to him as a useful

---

[26] Hay, *Polydore Vergil*, 147–149 and the additions on civic history in the 1546 edition noted by Hay in his Appendix II. For Fabyan, see Julia Boffey, 'Robert Fabyan: Reading and Compiling in Manuscript and Print', in her *Manuscript and Print in London, c. 1475–1530* (London, 2012), 162–204.

[27] Thompson, 'Re-imagining History', 353–56.

source for the later period of English history. It now survives in thirteen manuscripts (including a sixteenth-century copy in Oxford, Bodleian Library, Rawlinson MS B.195). The extant corpus displays much textual variation, but the second Latin *Brut* version has been characterised as 'a deliberate and sophisticated compilation whose purpose was to improve upon the historical narrative presented in the English Brut to 1437'.[28] Polydore had earlier railed against the attempts by some native writers in a fraudulent text he names as *Gildae Commentarium* to implicate Gildas in a Galfridian version of the earliest period of British history (I:18). The precise texts he had in mind at this point in his writing are unknown, but it is fascinating that it is in the extant copies of the Latin *Brut* text that we see a similar tendency re-enacted. Using the broad framework offered by Galfridian regnal history, the prose *Brut* compiler of the second Latin version supplements the earliest account of British history with references to Gildas and William of Malmesbury by name and by adding material ultimately derived from Higden, perhaps through some other Latin intermediary source. The account of English kingship from Alfred until near the end of Edward III's reign is then largely extracted from an extended *Polychronicon* version offering a continuation to 1377. This has been blended with an account that seems closely related – in content but not language – to the vernacular material found in a version of the Middle English Prose *Brut* extended to 1437.[29]

Polydore may well have felt he was on a relatively secure footing when he used some such version of a 'brutysshe book' for his account of thirteenth- and fourteenth-century British history. He was on much less secure ground in the troubled times in which the *Anglica Historia* was first published when he decided to build upon William of Newburgh's twelfth-century brand of clerical truth-telling in dealing with the earliest period of that history. In effect, the printed text of the *Anglica Historia* offers a carefully sceptical scholarly account taking full advantage of William's much earlier assertions that our Galfridian legacy has distorted the facts and created a popularised view of British history regarding Brutus and Arthur. The problem was that by the 1530s, that popular view, often dismissed as mere fiction by Polydore, held considerable sway in influential Tudor court circles.

John Leland was Polydore's most formidable scholarly critic in this respect.[30] A generation younger than Polydore, Leland had been granted a

---

[28] For a list of the Latin manuscripts and highly tentative summary of their textual affiliation with the Middle English 'peculiar versions' to which they are related and from which they are supposedly derived, see Matheson, *The Prose 'Brut'*, 42–46 (second Latin version) and 271–306 (English texts).

[29] The vexed question of whether the Latin text represents a direct translation of a Middle English Prose *Brut* version requires further detailed study.

[30] See the updated account of Leland's life and career in *John Leland, De Viris Illustribus, On Famous Men*, ed James P. Carley with the assistance of Caroline Brett

commission from Henry VIII in 1533 'to peruse and dylygentlye to searche all the lybraryes of monasteryes and collegies of thys your noble realme'.[31] This was a 'laborious journey' that was to engage his attention in the 1530s and 1540s, just before, during, and after the Dissolution of the monasteries. By 1536, Leland's search to discover and catalogue the ancient titles that offer us what remain of the 'monuments' of the British past had already equipped him with sufficient knowledge and influence to write 'Codrus sive laus et defensio Gallofridi Arturii contra Polydorum Vergilium'. For this early negative response to Polydore's account, Leland has forced Polydore to take on the persona of Codrus, the minor poet ridiculed by his Roman betters as someone who annoys by parroting and reading back to others their own work. His robust scholarly defence of a Galfridian reading of Arthur was then further developed for printing in Leland's *Assertio inclytissimi Arturii regis Britanniae* (London, 1544).[32]

In both these works, we remain on familiar territory in terms of the general groundwork that needs to be covered in order to confirm Arthur's authenticity according to an acceptable Tudor scholarly standard. Leland reviews the extant artefacts and relics associated with Arthur in Wales, Dover, Westminster, and, especially, Glastonbury, as well as the remaining topographical and onomastic evidence, stories, and small finds he has come across on his wider local travels. But perhaps of the highest significance for Leland's antiquarian researches is the evidence for Arthur in the old books that must stand as all that still remains of the ruined monuments or, in legal terms, the muniments, confirming our possession of a glorious national past. Leland keenly conveys to his readers the sense that his knowledge of such artefacts far surpassed that of any of his contemporaries. He seems to have read everything that has been written about Arthur's life and afterlife and has a comprehensive knowledge of relevant writings that support his case by writers such as Geoffrey, William of Malmesbury, Henry of Huntingdon, and Gerald of Wales, together with more recent accounts in Higden, Boccaccio, anonymous lives and legends, and other chronicle accounts at home and abroad and small details supporting his case in many other writers. Even Malory and Caxton are afforded a mention.

(Oxford, 2010). See also James P. Carley, 'Polydore Vergil and John Leland on King Arthur: The Battle of the Books', *Interpretations* 15 (1984): 86–100.

[31] This was noted in Leland's 'new year's gift' to Henry, published as *The Laboryouse Journey* in 1549 (*STC* 15445). I have taken the quotation from James P. Carley's *DNB* entry for Leland at https://www.oxforddnb.com/view/10.1093/ref:odnb/9780198614128.001.0001/odnb-9780198614128-e-16416 (accessed 18 December 2022).

[32] *STC* 15440. Leland's Latin scholarship gained significant additional currency among vernacular English readers when R. Robinson's translation of it was printed as *A Learned and True Assertion of the Life of Prince Arthure* in 1582 (*STC* 15441).

Leland shares Polydore's awareness, borrowed from Higden, that the fables that have embroidered the story of Arthur are not dissimilar to those that have crept into the popular accounts of the marvels performed by other great national figures in history such as Hercules, Alexander, and Charlemagne. But he has a low opinion of William of Newburgh and offers the equivalent of a modern textual scholar's explanation for and distrust of the apparent absence of evidence regarding Arthur in Gildas. He regards this as the result of textual losses and contamination, not helped by Polydore's foreign reprinting of a bad copy of the British text: 'Gildas his historie is published abroade of Polidorus, vndoubtedlie a fragment of þe old Gildas, but it is lame, out of order, and maimed, so farre forthe, as if he were now againe restored to life, the father would scarce knowe his chylde.'[33]

It seems fair to say that Leland's negative scholarly reaction to Polydore's treatment of Arthur in the *Anglica Historia* probably set the terms in which many other English writers viewed the work in the 1540s and later as other polemical, chauvinistic, and sectarian concerns came to the fore among the English reading public interested in the earliest origins of the British history.[34] Much has been written on the adverse reaction to Polydore's work and the manner in which a Galfridian reading of British Trojan origins and an Arthurian imperial presence in English history continued to hold sway among Tudor royal printers, later chronicle writers, and, ultimately, the English popular historical imagination. On the other hand, Polydore had brought a revised sense of reliance on forensic evidence in his retelling of the story of recent British history. Paradoxically, his work continued to figure among the proliferation of popular English histories of the Tudor period that were built around the English Brut tradition – works by writers such as Edward Hall, Richard Grafton, and Raphael Holinshed that effectively also became for many vernacular Elizabethan readers the 'books of their monuments' regarding the Trojan origins of their identity.

A particularly instructive example can be found in John Stow's *Summarie of Englishe Chronicles* (*STC* 23319), first published in 1565 and then reprinted in 1566, 1570, 1573, 1574, 1575, and 1590.[35] Stow has been characterised as the most prolific writer of history in the Tudor age. As such, he has left traces as

---

[33] Quoted from Robinson's translation, 79; see also Carley, 'Polydore Vergil and John Leland', 91.

[34] On this general topic, see Daniel R. Woolf, *Reading History in Early Modern England* (Cambridge, 2000).

[35] For the fraught circumstances in which the printing and revising of the *Summarie* took place as part of Stow's longstanding rivalry with Richard Grafton regarding chronicle writing and religious difference, see Ian W. Archer, 'John Stow, Citizen and Historian', in *John Stow (1525–1605) and the Making of the English Past*, ed. Ian Gadd and Alexandra Gillespie (London, 2004), 13–26.

reader and possible owner of several surviving copies of the Middle English Prose *Brut*.[36] Along with Holinshed, he seems to have had access to Leland's unpublished papers and freely incorporated some of that material in his own writings and revisions. Although he probably had access to other options, Stow also used a copy of the *Anglica Historia* (probably in its 1546 or later edition) as a minor source for some topographical and other historical details in his *Summarie*.[37] His comments on Polydore in the section entitled 'A briefe Description of Englande' are polite but non-committal:

> Thus muche I haue thought good to take out of Polydore, touchynge the diuision of England, with the forme and situation of the same. Much other good matter that author doth alledge, whiche here for breuitie I doo omitte, referring those that desyre to know farther herof, to that boke: where he shall fynde the style and story bothe pleasant and profitable. (Fol. 8v; verso of sig. [Aviii])

His words are immediately followed on the next page of Stow's print by his unambiguous celebration of the English Brut tradition beginning: 'The Race of the kinges of England, since Brute the fyrste of this Realme' (fol. 9r; sig. B[i]).

The reference to Polydore just at the point where English regnal history begins in the *Summarie* is interesting. Stow also includes Polydore's name in a one-page summary entitled 'The names of Authours in this Booke aledged' that immediately precedes 'A briefe Description of Englande' (verso of sig. [aiv]). The list is organised alphabetically by first name and acts as a handy index for the reader of writers named in the *Summarie*. In addition to the reference to Polydore, it includes mention of Arnold's *Chronicles*, Bede, Tacitus, the Domesday Book, Edward Hall, several entries for Gildas (including promisingly an item described as 'de gestis Arthuri'), Geoffrey of Monmouth, Giraldus Cambrensis, Hector Boece, John Hardyng, John Leland, John Lydgate, Jean Froissart, John Rastall, John Bale, John Gower, a 'Merlyn chronicler', Matthew Paris, Robert Fabian, St Columbanus, and, finally, William Caxton. We have here a veritable 'who's who' of many of the English writers who had influenced the shape that the origins of English history then took on for Stow in the *Summarie*.

The situation is quite different and the comments on historical writers much more discriminating when we turn to Stow's prefatory remarks in 'To the Reader', the item that immediately precedes Stow's index in the *Summarie* (sig. aiii–[aiv]). Stow uses this opportunity to acknowledge formally by name

---

[36] The manuscripts are identified in A. S. G. Edwards, 'John Stow and Middle English Literature', in *Stow and the Making of the English Past*, ed. Gadd and Gillespie, 109–118, at 109.

[37] For example, material on the description of England could have been found in *Polychronicon* versions including a short extract that Caxton had earlier printed from his Trevisa version as a separate item in 1480 (*STC* 13440a), followed by reprints by de Worde in 1498 and 1502 (*STC* 13440b).

a network of English writers who have acted as his main sources. He writes: 'For I acknowledge, that many of the hystories, that thou shalte reade here abridged, are taken, partely out of Robert Fabian, sometyme Alderman of London, Edwarde Halle gentylman of Greyes Inne, Iohn Hardynge, a great trauailer bothe in foreyne countreis, and also in all writynges of antiquitie' (sig. aiii v). 'To the Reader' immediately follows Stow's formal dedication of the *Summarie* to the mighty land magnate and royal favourite of the time, Lord Robert Dudley, earl of Leicester, Knight of the Garter, Master of Her Majesty's Horse, and member of Elizabeth I's Privy Council.[38] The name of Polydore Vergil is notable for its absence from Stow's acknowledgements at this point. Indeed, all of those named in 'To the Reader' can be said to have been fully conversant with the English Brut tradition perhaps primarily through their ownership, reading, and utilisation of Middle English Prose Brut copies. All of them followed exactly the same Tudor line on the Trojan origins of English history in their writings to which Stow now also compliantly subscribes.

Robert Fabian, the first named writer in the list, is particularly interesting in this respect. His *New Chronicles of England and of France* (*STC* 10659) was first printed in 1516 with updated versions of the work reissued in 1533, 1542 (twice), 1559 (three times).[39] Fabian's *New Chronicles* is advertised to the English book-buying public as, quintessentially, a Tudor and royal publication. Its title page displays a woodcut of the royal arms and various Tudor emblems that are repeated on both the recto and verso of its opening folio and elsewhere in the volume. And we are told in its 1516 colophon that it was 'emprynted by Richard Pynson prynter vnto the kynges noble grace', thereby possibly offering itself to readers as an officially approved English history. The 1559 prints are worthy of particular note since, in the three Elizabethan editions of that year, Fabian's *Chronicle* continues the story of English kingship through to 'the ende of queene Mary', thereby successfully absorbing into the Tudor narrative after the fact some of the most precarious and divided moments in English regnal history.

The various prints of Fabian's *New Chronicles* graphically illustrate what might be termed the Tudor culture of compliance to the patterns of English history promoted by the English Brut tradition in different ways and at different times.[40] Such a culture was only momentarily challenged by Polydore Vergil's writings, if it can even be said to have been really challenged by them at all.

---

[38] See the DNB entry for Dudley (1532/33–88) by S. Adams at https://www.oxforddnb.com/view/10.1093/ref:odnb/9780198614128.001/odnb-9780198614128-e-8160 (accessed December 2022).

[39] *STC* 10660, 10661, 10662, 10663, 10664, 10664.5.

[40] The idea of Tudor complicity is a complex one that I have borrowed from Kevin Sharpe, *Selling the Tudor Monarchy: Authority and Image in Sixteenth-Century England* (New Haven, 2009). In the context of this essay, I think it also helps explain why traditional Catholic voices like those of Cuthbert Tunstall and Polydore Vergil continued to be heard at some level in England during the Henrician changes of religion.

However, I want to conclude by returning to Stow and the reasonableness and humility with which he describes for his Elizabethan audience what his 'history' has become in the readers' blurb that introduces his *Summarie*:

> To the Reader
>
> Diuers wryters of Hystories write dyuersly. Some penne their hystories plentifully at large. Some contrary wyse, briefly and shortly doo but (as it were) touche by the way, the remembraunce and accidents of those tymes, of which they write. Some do with a large compasse discouer as wel the affaires done in foreyn partes, as those that hapned in that countrey, of whiche especially they wryte. And some content to let alone other matters, put in memory only such thyngs, as they themselues haue had experience of, in their own countreis. Amongs whom, good Reader, I craue to haue place, and desyre roome in the lower part of this table. (Sig. aiii)

In modest and homely fashion, we see Stow trying to organise for himself a modest seat at what must have seemed to him a glorious and antique dining table. He is not at all speaking truth to power but instead seems to be negotiating as best he can the multiple Tudor pasts that gave rise to his complicated metropolitan presence as an Elizabethan antiquarian writer and publisher. Polydore Vergil has a somewhat remote but also not entirely anonymous place alongside other 'divers wryters of Hystories' in this schema. Nevertheless, it was still the texts belonging to the English Brut tradition that continued to offer Stow and his Tudor contemporaries and later readers the foundation stones for the earliest British history. That tradition lay at the heart of his attempts to understand what he and others were living through; it was because of that understanding that Stow was equipped to write, revise, print, and publish anew his many *Summarie* versions of English history.

4

The Weight that English Carries: Vernacularity from *Hali Meiðhad* to Chaucer's *House of Fame*

ANDREW GALLOWAY

The term 'vernacularity', launched in the early nineteenth century as a witty troping on 'Latinity', appeared as a critical concept in medieval studies in a 2003 collection of essays (based on a 1999 conference) edited by Fiona Somerset and Nicholas Watson, *The Vulgar Tongue: Medieval and Postmedieval Vernacularity*. Noting the word's 'derivation from Latin *vernacularis* (of a slave)', the editors ticked off its meanings: its invocation of 'a subaltern or local language or style ... accessible to a particular, generally nonelite group'; its association with the natural, the feminine, the fleshly, or the commonplace; its application to the idea of a 'people's language', 'underprivileged and privileged alike', indicating the idea of a 'common tongue'.[1]

These different, even potentially contradictory elements (a 'common tongue' can name an officially or implicitly officially sponsored language or dialect that, like 'standardization', might well repress the variant, subcultural, or 'fleshly' discourses indicated by the other meanings) add up to a complex and highly mobile concept that seems well suited to medieval literary cultures. This even includes Latin in certain forms and uses and certain contexts, since (as Somerset and Watson insist) vernacularity 'describes, not a language as such, but a relation between one language situation and another, with the vernacular at least notionally in the more embattled, or at least the less clear-cut, position'.[2] Twenty years and more later, the comparisons and juxtapositions of the resulting collection still seem freshly promising. Those

---

[1] Fiona Somerset and Nicholas Watson, 'Preface: on "Vernacular"', in *The Vulgar Tongue: Medieval and Postmedieval Vernacularity*, ed. Fiona Somerset and Nicholas Watson (University Park, 2003), ix. I thank the editors of this volume for their repeated stages of advice and support in completing this essay: true followers of Professor Echard in her clarity, innovation, and intellectual courage.

[2] Somerset and Watson, 'Preface: on "Vernacularity"', x.

investigations include consideration of Orm's notorious spelling reform, presenting English homilies in twelfth-century Anglo-Norman Lincolnshire (a means, Meg Worley argues, to help Norman clerics pronounce English correctly when preaching to indigenous locals); Worley further compares Orm's venture to Édouard Glissant's notion of 'forced poetics', whereby the Caribbean poet and philosopher defined an indigenous writer's efforts to claim discursive and formal control within a conquered landscape. Other essays featured discussion of an early fifteenth-century Oxford academic's surprising support (in Latin) of the aptness of English for translating the Bible during the heresy-hunting world of early Lancastrian kingship; consideration of the political pressures behind the linguistic features of competing 'standard' languages in eighteenth-century Serbia and Romania; an investigation of how the imposition of Shakespeare on British colonial India was used as a model for Hindi impositions of Hindustani to suppress (Islamic) Urdu; a comparison of Chaucer's literary canonization in the fifteenth century to the more difficult rise to fame by Langston Hughes; and many more.[3] The invertability of a 'common tongue' in one sense of 'common' into a hegemonic tongue or the *model* of such a hegemonic tongue flickers through many of the essays. That last essay, for example, framed a key question for English from the medieval to the contemporary world language: Larry Scanlon asks, 'we might well ask how the vernacular tradition that emerged in Britain at the end of the fourteenth century could be inherently subversive in its own time and also provide the historical source of hegemony against which the African-American vernacular tradition later struggled'.[4]

As anyone surveying or inhabiting the field over the last two decades will know, the many studies of 'a' or 'the' vernacular have gone on to establish much deeper, richer, and wider investigations of medieval multilingualism. Explorations of the interwoven and alternately prominent uses and combinations of English, Anglo-Norman, and Continental French in medieval England have been especially productive, helping dislodge earlier fixation on the late medieval 'triumph of English, 1350–1400' (to invoke the title

---

[3] Meg Worley, 'Using the *Ormulum* to Redefine Vernacularity', in *The Vulgar Tongue*, ed. Somerset and Watson, 19–30; Fiona Somerset, 'Professionalizing Translation at the Turn of the Fifteenth Century: Ullerston's *Determinacio*, Arundel's *Constitutions*', in *The Vulgar Tongue*, ed. Somerset and Watson, 145–58; Jack Fairey, 'The Politics of ABCs: "Language Wars" and Literary Vernacularization among the Serbs and Romanians of Austria-Hungary, 1780–1870', in *The Vulgar Tongue*, ed. Somerset and Watson, 177–97; Nandi Bhatia, '"Indian Shakespeare" and the Politics of Language in Colonial India', in *The Vulgar Tongue*, ed. Somerset and Watson, 198–219; Larry Scanlon, 'Poets Laureate and the Language of Slaves: Petrarch, Chaucer, and Langston Hughes', in *The Vulgar Tongue*, ed. Somerset and Watson, 220–56.

[4] Scanlon, 'Poets Laureate and the Language of Slaves', 221.

of a chronologically as well as linguistically narrow 1969 study by Basil Cottle, the Cardiff-born medieval English scholar who happened to be a strong supporter of the recovery of Welsh, although no trace of that appears in his two books on the English language).[5] Yet refoundational as are the increasing studies of medieval multilingualism and broader concerns with 'valuing the vernacular', it might be justifiable to think that something has narrowed in the concept, if not the examples investigated, that Somerset and Watson advanced.[6] For one thing, the transhistorical implications of their keyword brought into new relevance for medieval materials the ideas of later postcolonial writers, whose linguistic theories, forged in often highly practical conditions, often focus on the relations between global languages such as French and English and more locally current or indigenous tongues or dialects. Uses of postcolonial approaches to examine medieval English literature have certainly not ceased – three such collections appeared between 2000 and 2005, and related studies continue to emerge[7] – but few of those engage the puzzling problems of a large concept like vernacularity. For another thing, the nature of historical languages as such in 'vernacularity' has not much advanced from the several essays that made overtures to this issue in Somerset and Watson. Watson's own recent and still-emerging magnum opus on 'vernacular theology' explicitly sets aside the details that might be desired by 'language historians', on the grounds that this would overburden an already

---

[5] Basil Cottle, *The Triumph of English: 1350–1400* (New York, 1969). Cottle's second major study of the English language was *The Plight of English: Ambiguities, Cacophonies and Other Violations of Our Language* (New Rochelle, 1975), whose focuses on the illogicalities and confusions in English might seem to emend the implications of the earlier book's title and premise. Yet Cottle's later anatomy of English's 'plight' is based on the proposition that 'English remains very serviceable, and pruned of its grosser faults it would have the highest claim to be the ideal universal tongue' (14). For some of the many major studies and anthologies on multilingualism and the vernacular in medieval England, see especially Jocelyn Wogan-Browne, Nicholas Watson, Andrew Taylor, and Ruth Evans, eds, *The Idea of the Vernacular: An Anthology of Middle English Literary Theory, 1280–1520* (University Park, 1999); Jocelyn Wogan-Browne, Thelma Fenster, and Delbert Russell, eds and trans, *Vernacular Literary Theory from the French of Medieval England: Texts and Translations, c. 1120–c. 1450* (Cambridge, 2016); Christopher Cannon, *The Making of Chaucer's English: A Study of Words* (Cambridge, 1989); and Ardis Butterfield, *The Familiar Enemy: Chaucer, Language and Nation in the Hundred Years War* (Oxford, 2009).

[6] For the latter concept, see the essays collected in Alastair Minnis, *Translations of Authority in Medieval English Literature: Valuing the Vernacular* (Oxford, 2012).

[7] Jeffrey Jerome Cohen, ed., *The Postcolonial Middle Ages* (New York, 2000); Patricia Clare Ingham and Michelle Warren, eds, *Postcolonial Moves: Medieval through Modern* (New York, 2003); Ananya Jahanara Kabir and Deanne Williams, eds, *Postcolonial Approaches to the European Middle Ages* (Cambridge, 2005).

massive study, given its range of materials in 'the vernacular' (French and English). This is likely wise, but I suspect that a closer sociolinguistic analysis might also risk dissolving the fixed category of 'the vernacular', including blurring the tidy boundaries that we assume fundamentally distinguish even one 'language' from another.[8] On their side, linguists rarely invoke the fluid concept of vernacularity, presumably because it is so flexibly relative. Yet increasing attention in linguistics to the relations between peripheral and central cultural and linguistic authority offers new reasons to explore the utility of notions like 'vernacularity'; a start is visible in Nikolas Coupland's reassessment of the sociolinguistics associated with William Labov's studies of 'the Black English vernacular' in revisiting which Coupland considers how ideas of class differences affect the ideological opposition between idealisations of 'standardness' and those of 'vernacularity', although Labov did not use either term himself.[9]

There are signs as well of a return in medieval literary studies to the more conceptually flexible range of the abstract noun 'vernacularity' invoked by Somerset and Watson. Studies by Ardis Butterfield and Christopher Cannon, as well as important work by Laura Wright and others on the multilinguistic origins of standard English, cohere with a more relativist approach than reified treatments of 'the' vernacular allow. Our honorand's study of Arthurian romances of 'courtly' medieval Latin is another case in point: this project shows how Latin can be both the 'intellectuals' *lingua franca*' and reach far

---

[8] Thus while Nicholas Watson's subsequent, in-progress trilogy on 'vernacular theology in England before the Reformation' brilliantly tracks in the current and forthcoming volumes nothing less than the successive dominance of Old English, early Middle English, Anglo-Norman, then Middle English theological writing, Watson declares that his task is too large to address wishes by 'language historians' that he had shown more 'sensitivity to issues of dialect': Nicholas Watson, *Balaam's Ass: Vernacular Theology before the English Reformation; Volume 1; Frameworks, Arguments, English to 1250* (Philadelphia, 2022), xvii–xviii. To be sure, Watson is explicit in how wide and flexible the range of implications in writing in 'a vernacular', including the issue of language: 'it bears emphasizing' (he states at one point) 'that the structure of linguistic relationships to which the word "vernacular" and its medieval synonyms such as "vulgar" refer was far from static, developing gradually across the centuries and talking different forms according to textual situation and especially language' (125). It is not clear if 'language' there refers to 'a language' such as French or English, or to a more detailed range of linguistic elements in either of those or their combinations, although that kind of focus, as the distinguishing remarks on what 'language historians' might want implies, is nowhere featured in the study. Perhaps equally notably, nowhere in Watson's massive new project on 'the vernacular' does the more complexly implicated abstraction 'vernacularity' appear.

[9] See Nikolas Coupland, 'Labov, Vernacularity and Sociolinguistic Change', *Journal of Sociolinguistics* 20 (2016): 409–30.

into French and English secular literatures and readers, offering another way to consider the properties of a 'common tongue' in a direction that few scholars working on 'the vernacular' have sought to further pursue.[10]

What follows here seeks to offer further possibilities for assessing what might be called the theories and practices of vernacularity at two moments of medieval poetics. By 'theories', I mean to focus not on explicit medieval language theory – a substantial subset of late medieval philosophy – but on the less explicit thought about languages or discourses implied in the writings I consider: the early thirteenth-century prose *Hali Meiðhad*, and two late fourteenth-century poems by Chaucer. Although written in what we think of as one 'language', both English, these present widely different statuses of their main language in relation to other kinds of authoritative or abjected language, which in turn might or might not be thought of as different 'languages' from the works themselves. My title's chronology 'from ... to' risks implying a trajectory, but my concerns are in the first instance synchronic, treating each text as an unpredictable *Gestalt* of social and linguistic elements, and emphasizing not some genealogy of ultimate 'triumph' but the relations to the linguistic and social domains of the undervalued vernaculars that these two moments of English writing present. Each includes its own terms for 'low and fleshly, vernacular'; both present their own distinct relations to the language of power. And invaluable as the sophisticated tools of historical linguistics and sociolinguistics are for extending further the concept of medieval vernacularity, what is gained and lost in the 'valuing of the vernacular' in each case can be articulated more fully, I propose, by invoking some of the theories of modern postcolonial thinkers whose lives and thought developed well outside the modern bastions of intellectual patronage and preservation.

Aureola

Debates about indigenous and colonially imposed languages were woven into medieval English scholarship from its origins. Sixteenth-century antiquaries' overtures in 'Anglo-Saxon' studies focused on recuperating from pre-Conquest English the 'true' English origins of post-Reformation culture in the spheres both of religion (as Anglo-Saxons' supposed views of the Eucharist as commemorative rather than a Real Presence) and politics (as the supposedly ancient rather than recent parliament in the 'Anglo-Saxon' *witan*). The seventeenth- and eighteenth-century century histories of English literature began after the Conquest, by tracing what Thomas Warton called 'the gradual improvements of our poetry', in a 'progression' of 'romantic fiction' that

---

[10] Cannon, *Making of Chaucer's English*; Butterfield, *The Familiar Enemy*; Laura Wright, ed., *The Multilingual Origins of Standard English* (Berlin, 2022); Siân Echard, *Arthurian Narrative in the Latin Tradition* (Cambridge, 1998), 236.

originated 'in the fictions of Arabian imagination', including from 'the farthest coasts of Africa', whence it was transmitted to the colonized Bretons and Welsh before emerging into 'our poetry'.[11]

To be sure, there are plenty of signs that the subsequent continuities emphasized by Warton and his editors and continuators gave English literature an implicitly racialized lineage thenceforth, as if having acknowledged its exotic origins from even the 'farthest coast of Africa', subsequent post-Conquest English literature could claim a rich, indeed colonially enriched, range of imaginative resources.[12] Modern scholarship on what has come to be called 'early Middle English', that is, from the century after the Conquest, began with similar though subtler claims of rooted, racially sustained Anglo-Saxon continuity, brought most clearly into focus by those who can claim some similar bloodline connection. The most famous scholar of early Middle English, J. R. R. Tolkien, identified his true origins as the west midlands, to whose early post-Conquest dialects he made some of his most important scholarly contributions. Yet Tolkien's establishment of those origins was peculiarly self-conscious of his displacement and involved a kind of chosen indigeneity. As he explained in a long letter to W. H. Auden in 1955, he had been born in South Africa in 1892, then at the age of three when his father died he was brought to England where, amid further family deaths and poverty, he became preoccupied by philological and particularly Germanic studies. As Tolkien told Auden, his keen sense of home as found in the west midland region confirmed a kind of innate understanding 'by blood' of the early post-Conquest local dialect:

> I am a West-midlander by blood (and took to early west-midland Middle English as a known tongue as soon as I set eyes on it), but perhaps a fact of my personal history may partly explain why the 'North-western air' appeals to me both as 'home' and as something discovered. I was actually born in Bloemfontein, and so those deeply implanted impressions, underlying memories that are still pictorially available for inspection, of first childhood are for me those of a hot parched country. My first Christmas memory is of blazing sun, drawn curtains and a drooping eucalyptus.[13]

---

[11] Thomas Warton, *The History of English Poetry: From the Close of the Eleventh to the Commencement of the Eighteenth Century* (London, 1774), vol. 1, p. v; signature [a1], [b4v]. For the sixteenth- and seventeenth-century antiquaries, see Graham Parry, *The Trophies of Time: English Antiquarians of the Seventeenth Century* (Oxford, 1995).

[12] On the racializing genealogy of English literature implied by Warton and (still more) his immediate successors, who completed his unfinished project, see Helen Young, Shyama Rajendran, and Sabina Rahman, 'The Changing History of English Poetry 1774–1871: Language, Literature and Anglo-Saxon Whiteness', *Textual Practice* 38 (2024): 337–56.

[13] *The Letters of J. R. R. Tolkien: A Selection*, ed. Humphrey Carpenter with the assistance of Christopher Tolkien (London, 2000), 228.

Like Joseph Bédier, lauded editor of foundational Old French texts such as the *Chanson de Roland* from a generation earlier, Tolkien was peculiarly familiar with 'discovered' or created traditions, evidently based on both dislocations from and colonial hyper-identifications with medieval European traditions.[14] In Tolkien's case, self-conscious nostalgia for his west-midland 'blood' might have been an indirect way of accommodating the period's rapidly shifting and dissolving of colonial control in Africa as elsewhere. Two years after Tolkien's departure from his African birth-land in the South African Orange Free State, which had been built around the 1846 fortress that the British Army major Henry Douglas Warden established after beating the Boers, that political entity was in turn dissolved and by 1948 incorporated into the South African government, whose apartheid policies soon brutally resettled Africans outside Bloemfontein. Yet the same period saw other African nations such as Nigeria and Kenya being nationalized. While Tolkien reflected on the drooping eucalyptus tree in a hot parched Christmas in Bloemfontein and welcomed his discovery of ancestral air in the west midlands, Chinua Achebe was writing *Things Fall Apart* (1958). The contemporaneity of their remakings of English was less coincidence than shared history, and it might be apt to consider their theorizing about ancestral and colonial language in combination, as two sides of vernacularity.

With its global success, *Things Fall Apart* notoriously raised questions on the African side about the authenticity of using English for the African novel, in terms at least as imperative as Tolkien's pursuit of the historical roots of a local dialect that had survived and accommodated colonial Norman culture. A conference at Makerere University in 1962 on 'The Future of the African Novel' erupted into argument about whether to continue using English at all. The activist and writer Obiajunwa Wali argued that writing African literature in English was a 'dead end' and insisted that a true vernacular (in the sense of a democratically chosen common tongue) cannot be based on a colonial language.[15] To write in the latter was simply to enrich further the traditions of the colonizing culture. Instead, Wali argued, one should build up indigenous traditions, in Kiswahili or other African languages, to re-establish African literary traditions. Achebe, perhaps not surprisingly given his education at an African satellite college of the University of London as well as what was by then a global English readership, had a different view. Responding to Wali, Achebe postulated that the languages of all the people in a territory and culture constitute the audience of a 'national literature', and should therefore

---

[14] Michelle Warren, *Creole Medievalism: Colonial France and Joseph Bédier's Middle Ages* (Minneapolis, 2011).

[15] Obiajunwa Wali, 'The Dead End of African Literature?', *Transition* 10 (1963): 13–15. For discussion of this debate in the wider context of the development of the novel in Africa, see Mukoma Wa Ngugi, *The Rise of the African Novel: Politics of Language, Identity, and Ownership* (Ann Arbor, MI, 2018).

all be embraced, including the writings in the colonial tongue. For all such writings extend not the 'tradition' of a particular language's literature but the living literature of the people of a territory, who use whatever languages they use, colonial or indigenous or more local. If that is a language all in that territory understand, it is a 'national' language and literature; if that language is known only to some, it is 'ethnic'. A 'new English' could be imagined that would absorb the African traditions, settings, environment of those using it. Achebe was confident that thus reinvented, his English 'will be able to carry the weight of my African experience'.[16]

The pithiness and clarity of these views reflect the pressures of practical consequences under which this critical debate unfolded, in that sense far from most medieval literary conferences and studies. Gaps in Achebe's and Wali's positions were inevitable, questions unanswered. As Christian Mair remarks, just what Achebe's 'new English' might look like remains unclear; so too, there is no guarantee that simply jettisoning English for African languages as Wali proposed could avoid reconstituting the same 'oppressive discursive practices' in an African language if the underlying social structures remained the same.[17] Yet both proposals suggest ideas that, while acknowledging the incomparable differences in the ongoing costs of African postcolonial struggle for literary and intellectual self-determination, could in some ways be applied to the medieval situation to which Tolkien drew attention.

At the center of his focus was the small, rhetorically elegant early thirteenth-century English prose treatise on holy virginity titled *Hali Meiðhad*, written in the western Marches between England and Wales a century and a half after the Conquest, probably at Hereford, where it was preserved. In 1929, Tolkien drew particular attention to one of the two surviving copies, Oxford, Bodleian Library, MS Bodley 34, which includes three Lives of women virgin martyrs and the allegory of the soul as household, *Sawles Warde*, written in a similar dialect. It was one of Tolkien's most influential scholarly contributions to Middle English studies to anatomize this dialect and demonstrate it was closely related to that used for the earliest copy of *Ancrene Wisse* (Corpus Christi College 402), a more widely copied guide for anchoresses. Although eight copies of the latter survive with evidence of more underlying those, as well as two fifteenth-century adaptations for wider audiences, plus translations into French and Latin, Tolkien's attention was narrowly focused on the continuity of this dialect or 'language', with only indirect acknowledgment even of the content and audience. All these works were initially written for religious women, whom Tolkien's most famous student, S. R. T. O. d'Ardenne,

---

[16] Chinua Achebe, 'English and the African Writer', *Transition* 18 (1965): 27–30.

[17] Christian Mair, 'Linguistics, Literature and the Postcolonial Englishes: An Introduction', in Mair, *The Politics of English as a World Language* (Amsterdam, 2003), ix–xxi, at xvii–xviii.

characterizes through the works' allusions and rhetorical sophistication as 'gentle and lettered ... with a knowledge in various degrees of French, written and spoken, and Latin',[18] and as *Ancrene Wisse* implies, some or all of whom would live out their lives in enclosed dwellings attached to a church but under no traditional religious 'rule', leaving much of the guidance of their lives to these rhetorically and linguistically gorgeous regimental works. Tolkien was not the first to notice the shared dialect but, using the common sigla of the manuscripts of this copy of *Ancrene Wisse* and of *Hali Meiðhad*, he was the first to concentrate on its identity, naming this quasi-ancestral tongue 'the AB language'.[19]

Tolkien's focus on this particular English dialect as the key to the works' significance allowed him to dispense with the varied copies and adaptations of all these materials.[20] Virtually ignoring the contents, Tolkien regarded AB's carefully sustained linguistic rules as a rare witness to a west-midlands domain that, although under the rule of French-speaking Normans for over a century, 'contrived in troublous times to maintain the air of a gentleman, if a country gentleman. ... in close touch with a good living speech'.[21] Nearly personifying the dialect with his use of the verb 'contrived', Tolkien pointed to AB's meticulous traditionalism in its weak verb paradigms: the Old English (OE) weak class II verb paradigm with infinitive in -*ian*, a paradigm that in AB absorbed hundreds of further French and Norse verbs to make new Middle English verbs, while changing that verb paradigm to either -*in* or -*ien*. Despite its remarkable absorptive capacity of verbs from French and Norse, for Tolkien, AB presented 'simply the O.E. paradigm preserved in all its details, except as modified by one or two normal phonetic changes of universal application':[22] namely the 'normal' leveling in both late Old English and post-Conquest Middle English of unstressed 'a' to 'e', and the further separation of -*ien* into either -*in* after a long or polysyllabic stem, or -*ien* after a short stem or a stem that received a strong secondary accent, yielding, on

---

[18] S. R. T. O. d'Ardenne, ed., *þe Liflade ant te Passiun of Seinte Iuliene*, EETS o.s. 248 (Oxford, 1961), 177. This edition and linguistic discussion was available from 1936 as a published dissertation, directed by J. R. R. Tolkien. All of the works in the Bodley manuscript are available with translations (which I have consulted) in Emily Rebekah Huber and Elizabeth Robertson, eds, *The Katherine Group (MS Bodley 34): Religious Writing for Women in Medieval England*, TEAMS Middle English Text Series (Kalamazoo, 2016).

[19] J. R. R. Tolkien, '*Ancrene Wisse* and *Hali Meiðhad*', *Essays and Studies by Members of the English Association* 14, ed. H. W. Garrod (Oxford, 1929), 104–26.

[20] For a valuable overview of this range and the uncertain breadth of influences, locations, and training of the author (as well as the likely idiosyncrasies of what might be just an individual scribe), see Watson, *Balaam's Ass*, 348–50.

[21] Tolkien, '*Ancrene Wisse* and *Hali Meiðhad*', 106.

[22] Tolkien, '*Ancrene Wisse* and *Hali Meiðhad*', 118.

the one hand, for OE *locian* 'look' (long *loc-*), AB *lokin*; but for OE *lufian* 'love' (short *luf-*), AB *luuien*.[23] As Tolkien's student d'Ardenne remarked, 'the regular alternation between *i* in Stem 1 and *e* in Stem 2 is remarkably consistent in AB', although d'Ardenne acknowledged that a more pervasive vowel leveling is also visible in AB:

> Since the 2 and 3 sg. of Class II no longer differed from those of other classes [i.e., OE class II *-ast, -að* but OE class I *-est -eð*], while all other classes had 3 sg. and pl. alike, confusion leading ultimately to leveling of *en, eð* was probably an inevitable further step.[24]

Where Tolkien saw stalwart preservation of fine historical distinctions, his most famous student noted comprehensive leveling well underway.

The 'language' Tolkien triumphantly identified for *Hali Meiðhad* and the other 'AB' works is often now treated as much less 'standardizing' than he or d'Ardenne implied; as Jeremy Smith states, AB was 'particular parochial usage belonging to a particular locality in the South-West Midlands'.[25] It is also now emphasized, following d'Ardenne, that even while sustaining the heritage of the main weak verb class, AB consistently leveled (thus from our view, modernized) the forms of its relative and demonstrative pronouns, from Old English distinctions of grammatical gender and singular third-person accusative and dative forms (*him* vs. *hine*) to a Middle English system of natural gender and a single oblique case (*him* for indirect or direct object). This alone led d'Ardenne to demur from Tolkien's unwavering conviction that the copies of A and B were made soon after their originals, perhaps the result of Tolkien's desire to believe that in the copies we have he was in direct contact with the west-midland soil and air to which he was entitled 'by blood'. In contrast, for d'Ardenne, although 'the grammar of AB was and had been for some time ... fairly stable', the pronouns told another story, of a major shift in pronoun systems between the originals and the surviving copies of the AB texts, which predominantly demonstrate the modernized pronouns. D'Ardenne viewed this as a later scribal shift, a view she supported with just one correction, in the *Life of St. Juliana*, of (accusative) 'him' into 'hine'.[26]

Even this may be too simple. Robert McColl Millar finds the combination of two systems for pronouns in the same general dialect to be a catalyst for wider changes in early Middle English: in general, early Middle English shows that the system of demonstrative pronouns, 'suffering from a traumatic loss of

---

[23] D'Ardenne, *Seinte Iuliene*, 234.

[24] D'Ardenne, *Seinte Iuliene*, 237–38.

[25] Jeremy Smith, 'Standard Language in Early Middle English?', in *Placing Middle English in Context*, ed. Irma Taavitsainen, Terttu Nevalainen, Paivi Pahta, and Matti Rissanen (Berlin, 2000), 125–39, at 131.

[26] D'Ardenne, *Seinte Iuliene*, 222.

specified reference to a given set of functions', was freely combined with more traditional distinctions of grammatically gendered and oblique-case relative and demonstrative pronouns. AB shows the 'modern' pronoun system more often than even later texts of the same general dialectical area (such as *Owl and the Nightingale*).[27] The combination of modernization and tradition that Tolkien minimized, and that d'Ardenne explained away as the gap between the lost originals and the surviving copies of AB, is seen by Millar as a condition of AB. Rather than contriving, with a few 'natural' instances of historical change, a faithful restoration of an Anglo-Saxon linguistic heritage, the users of AB seized on the most modern pronoun scheme at hand, even where more traditional systems of pronouns were available. An unusual *modernity* seems to govern the features of this dialect at a key structural level, even as its verb forms carry traces of more archaic traditions. Given that the syntax of medieval French, both continental and insular, is structured around the verb, even the grammatical category of the verb as the main vehicle for older English elements in AB might be seen as a structural response to an Insular French environment.[28]

All this might lead us to question the assumptions behind Tolkien's philology.[29] Yet the *idea* of a canonical 'language' in AB might not be only the fanciful result of Tolkien's carefully fostered nostalgia. If negotiating selectively with 'alien', 'common', and 'rooted' language is a condition of any postcolonial writer (including Tolkien himself), it is also the condition of the author or authors of the AB texts. Alongside *Hali Meiðhad*'s paradoxical layers of linguistic modernity and traditionalism can, for instance, be considered the many moments in the work where certain disparaged kinds of 'alien' and often cacophonous language are invoked but expunged, projected onto the many oppressive and vile pagan, rapist, domineering husbands and alien and degrading circumstances. Other kinds of language, in contrast, showing the way to salvation, purity, communal peace, tend to absorb Latin rhetorical symmetries as well as display more traditionally English assonance and alliteration. Thus, although *Hali Meiðhad* has often been criticized for its ethical and intellectual simplicity, its hypocrisy (as d'Ardenne puts it) in emphasizing 'merely temporal advantages of virginity' which makes the motives for pursuing virginity no less 'base' than the reasons for seeking marriage

---

[27] Robert McColl Millar, *System Collapse, System Rebirth: The Demonstrative Pronouns of English, 900–1350 and the Birth of the Definite Article* (Oxford, 2000), 195–205, 221–22, 284, 292.

[28] 'The verb is the principal element or "heart" of the sentence [in Old French], and all other elements are secondary to it': William W. Kibler, *An Introduction to Old French*, 3rd edn (New York, 1986), 3.

[29] As does Watson, *Balaam's Ass*, 249–50.

that the work condemns,[30] its subtlest messages about the distinction between purity and contamination emerge from its elaborations of the social as well as aesthetic features of linguistic heavens and hells.

Consider for example this line amid *Hali Meiðhad*'s roundly vehement contrasts between the pure and exalted life of chosen virginity and the bestially slavish life of a wife, who serves a husband like the wild boars the prophet wrote of who rotted in their dung: 'ha in hare wurðinge as eaueres forroteden – þet is, eauereuch wife þet is hire were þre`a'l ant lieuð i wurðinge, he ant heo baðe' (they rotted in their dung as do boars – that is, every wife who is her husband's thrall and lives in dung, he and she both).[31] As usual, this statement includes leveled demonstrative and relative pronouns ('þet'), but in contrast to that leveling is the meticulously inserted 'a' in 'þreal', a miniature superscript addition (here represented with inverted commas).[32] Elsewhere in this manuscript, as initially here, that word is spelled simply 'þrel', revealing what must have happened in pronunciation to this reflex of an Old AB Language 'æ' before 'l' groups. Other words with that phonemic ancestry are often spelled 'ea' in AB texts, perhaps a diphthong, but perhaps also a consistent preservation of something that *looks* like the earlier 'æ', a morphological contrivance since, as the variation shows, it was pronounced simply as slack 'e'. This suggests selective traditionalism in nouns' as well as verbs' phonology or in some cases simply in spelling, which preserved (with some effort) written traditions or quasi-traditions against scribes' actual pronunciation. Since other predictable developments in phonology are fully allowed in AB, such as *lokin* for OE *locian*, the rules for this seem socially gestural, subtle inflections of the kind that identify the members of a selected discursive community, whose signalling of membership and distinction in this instance would require knowledge of how things were supposed to look in writing, though no one could tell the difference in speech. The corrector knew that it was important to mind your 'þreals'.

The unusually careful attention to establishing the proper, semi-archaic spelling of this word in particular is perhaps not an arbitrary choice. Emphasis on thralldom is pervasive in *Hali Meiðhad*, to a degree suggesting an established trope among at least some members of the community, a trope that is elaborated in remarkable rhetorical detail throughout the treatise. Post-Conquest serfdom, we know, or are supposed to think, with its ties to obligations to farm and pay rent, marriage fees, and work-rent, is not chattel slavery, which supposedly quickly faded after the Norman Conquest, for reasons that remain debated (perhaps involving the Normans' general dislike of that institution, or perhaps their displacement of it with other kinds, as when William the Conqueror brought in Jews from cities on the Continent

---

[30] D'Ardenne, *Seinte Iuliene*, xlvii.

[31] Bella Millett, ed., *Hali Meiðhad*, EETS o.s. 284 (London, 1982), 6/29–30 (cited by page and line).

[32] For the manuscript, see N. R. Ker, *Facsimile of Ms. Bodley 34: St Katherine, St. Margaret, St. Juliana, Hali Meiðhad, Sawles Warde*, EETS o.s. 247 (London, 1960), fol. 57.

and later Norman kings defined them as 'the king's serfs': bondage to the king's needs conferring on them a much-resented independence from other lords' demands).[33] The idea of slavery after slavery is, of course, potent and significant in new ways. It is not hard to imagine at least memories of more direct chattel slavery – semantically and perhaps often enough socially blurred into serfdom (*servi* in both case) – in the less Normanized area where the AB texts were preserved and almost certainly created. The Domesday Book (1086) records that over 15 per cent of the numbered population in earlier Herefordshire were slaves, *servi*, distinct from 'villeins' and 'bordars'; the proportion is 18 per cent in Shropshire; and over 26 per cent of the population in Gloucester were slaves. The figures are probably low: bondwomen seem not always counted.[34] Slave-trading, which had reached from the Scandinavian northeast to the western midlands and thence to Wales and Ireland, continued into the twelfth century. The Anglo-Saxon Chronicle at Peterborough, one of the few English historical writing projects that continued after the Conquest, states that in 1081, William the Conqueror led an army into Wales and there 'gefreode fela hund manna' (freed many hundreds of people).[35] Nearby Bristol was a prominent marketplace. A Latin *Life of St. Wulfstan* from the 1120s by William of Malmesbury, who states that he translated it from a (now lost) Old English *Life* by a late eleventh-century monk, presents one of the saint's miracles as his ability to persuade Bristol authorities to outlaw the slave trade. William's twelfth-century Latin narrative lingers over the horrors of this in a way that is not paralleled by earlier English mentions of slave-markets, and since William's eleventh-century English source is lost, we do not know how much the vividness of the description comes from William himself:

> Homines enim ex omni Anglia coemptos maioris spe questus in Hiberniam distrahebant, ancillasque prius ludibrio lecti habitas iamque pregnantes uenum proponebant. Videres et gemeres concatenatos funibus miserorum ordines et utriusque sexus adulescentis, qui liberali forma, aetate integra, barbaris miserationi essent, cotidie prostitui, cotidie uenditari.
>
> [For they would buy up men from all over England and sell them off to Ireland in hope of a profit, and put up for sale maidservants after toying with them in bed and making them pregnant. You would have groaned to see the files of the wretches roped together, young persons of both sexes, whose youth and respectable appearance would have aroused the pity of barbarians.][36]

---

[33] Robin R. Mundill, *England's Jewish Solution: Experiment and Expulsion, 1262–1290* (Cambridge, 1998), 45–71.

[34] H. C. Darby and I. B. Terrett, eds, *The Domesday Geography of Midland England* (Cambridge, 1954), 73, 127, 19.

[35] Susan Irvine, ed., *The Anglo-Saxon Chronicle: A Collaborative Edition: 7: MS E* (Cambridge, 2004), 92.

[36] *Vita Wulfstani*, ed. and trans. M. Winterbottom and R. M. Thomson, *William of Malmesbury: Saints' Lives* (Oxford, 2002), 101–3.

As late as 1170, Irish regions were still trafficking English slaves, as legislation by a synod at Armagh shows.[37]

Whether long-established agrarian laborers or recent transports from elsewhere, slaves would present an at least somewhat alien language as well as legal status, further threatening the linguistic standards of an English-speaking local elite in the Anglo-Norman world. While we can of course never hope to capture their range of languages, consider this climax of *Hali Meiðhad*'s denunciation of marriage, where we as readers and listeners become the object of both visual and auditory abuse:

> His lokunge on ageasteð þe; his ladliche nurð & his untohe bere makeð þe to agrisen. Chit te ant cheoweð þe ant scheomeliche schent te, tukeþ þe to bismere as huler his hore, beateð þe ant busteð þe as his ibohte þrel ant his eðele þeowe. [15/26–30]

> [His gazing on you frightens you. His loathly noise and his wanton uproar make you frightened. He chides you and nags you and shamefully disgraces you, ill-treats you insultingly as a lecher does his whore, beats you and buffers you as his purchased thrall and his born slave.]

The passage is rife with only loosely sourceable words, bespeaking a multilingual understory that opens into new revelations at every statement. 'Nurð', 'noise', is perhaps from Dutch 'norren' (grumble, growl), and has no later attestations in Middle English; it also appears throughout the 'A' copy of *Ancrene Wisse*, suggesting the word served in AB generally as an idiom for abusive and alien and non-Anglo-Norman dissonance. Other linguistic refinements further reveal AB's social imaginary. An 'ibohte þrel' is a chattel slave; but 'his eðele þeowe' is less certain. Is it 'noble slave', as *eðele* would normally mean? 'Natural' or 'native' are better, since those evoke the Latin legal term later used for serfs, *nativi*.[38] Both 'þeowe' and 'þrel' are used throughout the treatise. Is there a distinction?

By carefully nourished memory or real threat, *Hali Meiðhad*'s most prestigious linguistic register and meticulously guarded orthographic consistency are presented as freedom from slave language. By the same token, its language is distinguished not only by its curated traditionalism but also its capacity to access otherwise unattested vernacularities, keyed to the servile worlds of those who have not chosen the virginal, anchoritic life. Thus the word 'cader', a stray borrowing from Welsh *cadair*, 'cradle' (as Tolkien first noted),[39] appears in *Hali Meiðhad* to invoke servility in bearing and nursing children:

---

[37] David A. E. Pelteret, *Slavery in Early Mediaeval England: From the Reign of Alfred until the Twelfth Century* (Woodbridge, 1995), 78–79.

[38] See Millett, *Hali Meiðhad*, 44n. Millett does not associate this with the Latin term.

[39] Tolkien, '*Ancrene Wisse* and *Hali Meiðhad*', 115.

Ant hwet, þe cader fulðen, ant bearmes umbe stunde, to ferkin ant to fostrin hit, so moni earm-hwile, ant his waxunge se let, ant se slaw his þrifte; ant euer habbe sar care ... [18/19–22]

[And, look! – the filth in the cradle and sometimes in your lap, to swaddle it and feed it for so many weary hours, and its growth so sluggish, and so slow its thriving! And ever to have intense worry ...]

Unattested earlier in English, *cader* was familiar enough to be expanded in further elaborations in *Hali Meiðhad* of servility versus freedom, the axis around which the treatise as a whole rotates:

Lutel wat meiden of al þis ilke weane, of wifes wa wið hire were, ne of hare werc se wleateful þe ha wurcheð imeane, ne of þet sar ne of þet sut i þe burþene of bearn ant his iborenesse, of nurrices wecches, ne of hire wa-siðes of þet fode fostrunge, hu muchel ha schule ed eanes in his muð famplin, nowðer to bigan hit ne his cader-clutes; þah þis beon of to speokene vnwurðliche þinges, þes þe mare ha schawið i hwuch þeowdom wifes beoð, þe þullich mote drehen, ant meidnes i hwuch freodom þe freo beoð from ham alle. [18/32–19/8]

[Little does the maiden know of all this same misery: of the wife's woe with her husband, nor of their deed – so disgusting! – that they do together, nor of that pain nor of that grief in the carrying of a child and birth, of the nurse's vigils, nor of her woeful times in the raising of that child, how much food she should stuff into his mouth at one time, neither to bespatter it nor its cradle-clothes. Although these are unworthy things to speak of, they show all the more what slavery wives are in, who must endure them, and in what freedom maidens are in, who are free from them all.]

The presence of such Welsh derivatives as *cader* and *cader-clutes*, especially in connection with the travails of *nurrices*, suggests linguistically and physically intimate settings for these contacts: a true mother-tongue of mixed language, which those with aspirations for more sustained intellectual and stylistic freedom would presumably recognize. As d'Ardenne notes, the AB *Life of Seint Margarete* also has *genow*, 'jaws' (Welsh *geneu*), and *Ancrene Wisse* has *baban*, 'baby', with Welsh *-an*, either directly derived or imitated from Welsh.[40] Such language bespeaks settings where others' clamoring bodily needs displace the women's own aspirations; eating, shouting, and demands for sexual gratification all threaten to drown out prayers in these works in AB. Such clamorous multilingualism of intimate household settings is contrasted with the freedom from servitude extolled in AB's other kinds of discursive and lexical control, balanced on a fine edge of carefully preserved archaism yet adaptability.

---

[40] D'Ardenne, *Seinte Iuliene*, 179; supported by Andrew Breeze, 'Welsh *baban* 'Baby' and *Ancrene Wisse*', *Notes and Queries* 40 (1993): 12–13.

To approach *Hali Meiðhad* in these terms implies a different linguistic and literary range of vernacularity than the teleological perspective in which 'early Middle English' like other medieval Englishes has often been seen from the late nineteenth century on. While revisiting Tolkien's extraordinarily insightful philological knowledge, it is also important to critique these now-visible aspects of it. Tolkien's sense of entitlement 'by blood' to understand the character or attitude ('air') of the personified language of the early Middle English west midlands, its contriving 'in troublous times to maintain the air of a gentleman, if a country gentleman ... in close touch with a good living speech', supports the argument by J. D. Sargan that the entire category of 'early Middle English', which on the one hand has seemed to stand outside the genealogy of medieval English language and literature from 'Anglo-Saxon' poetry on, has, on the other hand, often been recruited all the more fully into a racializing genealogy of English, as either degraded Anglo-Saxon or prospective Chaucerian English.[41] To address this, Sargan proposes a 'reparative codicology' that would focus on the typically fragmentary and marginal presence of English in the early Middle English period, and to use that fragmentariness as such to point away from racialized origins or teleologies and toward communities 'of under-represented readers in the negotiation of institutional Latinity'.[42] Yet we should be cautious before assuming that 'institutional Latinity' is as oppressive to such communities as post-Reformation perspectives have tended to insist. Latinity can be a part of, even a sublime ideal in, the vernacularity of non-Latin writings at any point in the pre-Reformation expanse.[43]

As a final small example from *Hali Meiðhad* of this large topic, consider the treatise's presentation of its supreme ideal, the shining heavenly crown of virginity: 'a gerlondesche schinende schenre þen the sunne, "auriole" ihaten o Latines ledene' (11/18; a diadem shining brighter than the sun, called 'aureola' in the Latin language). Yet orthography for once fails, at least in scribal endeavors. The earlier and most linguistically consistent of the two surviving copies of *Hali Meiðhad* – the crucial basis for AB – transmits the Latin 'aureola' as the incomprehensible 'an urle'; the other, less consistently AB copy spells it not as Latin but French, 'aureole'. The Latin word in the modern text is modern conjecture, confirmed by the word used in the same passage to mean 'language' as such, *ledene*, which is generalized from its etymological meaning of 'Latin' as shown by the otherwise redundant specifier, *Latines*. At

---

[41] J. D. Sargan, 'Filling in the Gaps: Early Middle English, Nationalist Philology, and Reparative Codicology', *Textual Practice* 38 (2024): 211–34.

[42] Sargan, 'Filling in the Gaps', 224.

[43] Watson's survey of post-Reformation disparagement of the supposedly Latin-bound medieval church well demonstrates the distorting power of this bias (*Balaam's Ass*, 46–58). So far, however, *Balaam's Ass* does not consider points where Latinity is an ideal *within* 'the vernacular' that Watson charts.

this rhetorical climax, but in the layers of forgotten etymologies and scribal failures, the treatise's pursuit of rhetorical, orthographic, and discursive purity reaches its limit. Like the spiritual sublimation of bodily virginity itself, the capacity of *Hali Meiðhad* to elevate its *ledene* to a sublime ideal of heavenly vernacularity is premised on a realm beyond itself, leaving even the most meticulous scribes and readers subject to a cacophonous discursive world always on the threshold of thralldom.

Chaucer's Tout-Monde: The Muddy Bottom of the Well of English

In her foundational study of the blending and swapping of what we consider 'language' in England and France, Ardis Butterfield pithily observes that 'Chaucer may have written in English, but English was not a single language for him.'[44] To anchor and deepen this point, Butterfield finds particularly relevant Jacques Derrida's essay, later published as a book, *Monolingualism of the Other: Or, the Prosthesis of Origins*, where the philosopher sinuously unfolds an idea found in many of his writings: that no language (however cognitively all-encompassing as for Derrida language always is) is ever able to supply an 'outside', is capable of any true metacommentary on language, also always involves a state of 'translation'.[45] This nearly Wittgensteinian paradox unfolds playfully around Derrida's central proposition there, that 'I have only one language; it is not mine.'[46] But his focus turns uniquely personal, invoking – with what seems poignant restraint – Derrida's semi-alienated relations to French education, language, and colonial culture as a 'Franco-Maghrebian', an Algerian Jew, a frame that allows Derrida to dwell on both the totalizing and self-constituting claim of a 'mother tongue' and acknowledge how little of it is in his control. Thus, before we take all of this as a blandly general condition, we should note that Derrida seems to grant that this was a distinct feature of growing up 'inhabiting' colonial French, a state of detachment producing what he calls a kind of 'disconcerting' effect:

> The language called maternal is never purely natural, nor proper, nor habitable. *To inhabit:* this is a value that is quite *disconcerting* and equivocal: one never inhabits what one is in the habit of calling inhabiting. There is no possible habitat without the difference of this exile and this nostalgia … That is all too well known. But it does not follow that all exiles are equivalent. From this shore, yes, *from this* shore of this common drift, all expatriations remain singular. [original emphasis][47]

---

[44] Butterfield, *The Familiar Enemy*, 285.

[45] Butterfield, *The Familiar Enemy*, e.g., 97–101, 129–301, etc.

[46] Jacques Derrida, *Le monolinguisme de l'autre ou la prothèse d'origine* (Paris, 1996); I quote from the translation by P. Mensha, *Monolingualism of the Other, or, The Prosthesis of Origin* (Stanford, 1996), 1.

[47] Derrida, *Monolingualism*, 58.

The allusions to postcolonial relations and to a dominant 'common drift' of language and tradition were likely even more pointed in the lecture's English delivery at a conference on the 'mother tongue' in Louisiana hosted by Édouard Glissant, the Caribbean philosopher and poet. This is significant because Glissant's lifelong focus was on the need for all poetics to be open to the discursive 'opacities' produced by including local and oppressed peoples' creoles, a fundamental 'poetics of relation' that ought to generate in more culturally dominant speakers a sense of being 'disconcerted'. Glissant describes 'disconcerted' in this way: a process in which we learn 'that the Other is within us and affects how we evolve ... In spite of ourselves, a sort of "consciousness of consciousness" opens us up and turns each of us into a disconcerted actor in the poetics of Relation.'[48] It seems likely that Derrida's focus on a 'quite *disconcerting* and equivocal' condition of 'monolingual' speakers, however universalized, also nodded to Glissant's theories, which offer a central concept of *métissage* as a 'meeting and synthesis of two [linguistic and cultural] differences', in which he presents creolization as 'an endless *métissage*, its elements refracted and its consequences unforeseeable'.[49]

Glissant's views might be invoked as better guidance for the late rather than early medieval context, since it is in the post-Black Death period where, as Echard indicates, a poet like Gower writing in Latin might negotiate a 'constant relation' to vernacular languages.[50] Glissant's decades-long ruminations on what he calls a 'poétique de la relation' always take their point of departure in the layers of colonial and decolonializing languages of his native Martinique, emphasizing the ideal capability of any language to serve as entry to the plethora of marginal, oppressed, and creolized voices – but especially French (which Glissant proposed arrived in the Caribbean before French had hardened into its standardized metropolitan identity), whose capability for 'relation' in his view opposes the totalitarianism of any monolingual intent.[51] Discourse, he insisted, should be allowed a 'right to opacity' even in a common tongue, respecting the marginal and oppressed speakers who could thereby retain some of their own distinct and even hidden traditions.[52] This offers a poetic as well as ethical and social ideal, namely what Glissant called the *tout-monde*, the 'poetics of the whole world'. This Glissant considered could be invoked even within a single colonial language, but it would need to be established not just by 'créolisme' – i.e., instances of creole – but 'créolisation': a continuous

---

[48] Édouard Glissant, *Poétique de la Relation* (Paris, 1990); trans. Betsy Wing, *Poetics of Relation* (Ann Arbor, 2010), 27.

[49] Glissant, *Poetics of Relation*, 34.

[50] Siân Echard, 'How Gower Found His *Vox*: Latin and John Gower's Poetics', *The Journal of Medieval Latin* 26 (2016): 291–314, at 292.

[51] Glissant, *Poetics of Relation*, 45.

[52] Édouard Glissant, *Le discours antillais* (Paris, 1997); trans. J. Michael Dash, *Caribbean Discourse: Selected Essays* (Charlottesville, 1997), 3.

possibility of marginal tongues and their underrepresented speakers. Only in this way can the 'dead end' ('une situation "bloquée"') of the Caribbean, where 'French-speaking West Indians' have achieved 'the ultimate in subhumanity', be overcome.

With his mention of 'une situation "bloquée"', Glissant might be invoking Wali's famous challenge for African writers of the 'dead end' of writing in English. Indeed, Glissant framed his view of a kind of standard (French) as not only exacerbating the physical torments of the abject in the West Indies ('the salt of death on exhausted men') but also 'the terrible and definitive muteness of those peoples physically undermined and overwhelmed by famine and disease, terror and devastation'. The erasure of these people is possible because of the discursive tyranny of the 'ideal of universal transparency' imposed by 'the West' (a 'project' not a 'place').[53] More upliftingly, in later interviews Glissant advanced his ideal of perpetually open creolization as the epitome of his 'poetics of relation': 'une sorte de variance infinie des sensibilités linguistiques', which would not, he added, require infinite knowledge of languages, for translation would become the 'essential art'. By this means, 'each [person] will be more and more penetrated by that [infinite variation], not by one single poetic and one single economy, structure, and economy of his language, but by all this fragrance, this bursting out of the poetics of the world'.[54]

Placing a writer like Chaucer beside this consideration of recovering profoundly silenced colonized subjects might seem undeserved; Chaucer, after all, figures so prominently in traditions of British literary and linguistic imperialism that the climax of the Caribbean writer Jean Rhys' 1927 story, 'Again the Antilles', is when a racist plantation owner scorns a socially alienated 'colored' intellectual for misattributing to Shakespeare a line by Chaucer, a line reeking of British noble elitism ('he was a very gentle, perfect knight').[55] Nonetheless, Chaucer's attention to converging discourses, despite his enduring post-medieval authority as the 'well of English vndefyled',[56] might be placed beside Glissant's endless and socially signifying linguistic 'relations'. For just as Chaucer was living at a time of increasing variation between English and other languages, so during every working day and reading night he was engaged with Latin, continental French, Anglo-Norman, and, perhaps most of all (as a customs and other civil service officer) the 'mixed' language of inventories and accounting, which variously presents Latin prepositions, French articles, English nouns, and ambiguously Latinate abbreviated forms of linguistically unclassifiable words. Instead of considering Chaucer

---

[53] Glissant, *Caribbean Discourse*, 2.
[54] Édouard Glissant, *L'imaginaire des Langues: Entretiens avec Lise Gauvin* (Paris, 2010), 27, my trans.
[55] Jean Rhys, *The Left Bank and Other Stories* (Freeport, NY, 1927, rept 1970), 93–97.
[56] Edmund Spenser, *The Faerie Queene*, ed. Thomas Roche, Jr. (Harmondsworth, 1978), IV.32.

narrowly in terms of a French, Latin, or Italian 'tradition', we might consider Chaucer and the mixed language.

To do so involves, again, a crossover from 'literary' to 'linguistic' investigations. The range of multiple 'languages' within 'English' points not only to the multilingual poetics in which Butterfield among others has more deeply located Chaucer during the war with France, but also one of the pivotal debates over the last two decades in historical linguistics, the goal of which is to identify the forces behind what appears to us as a movement toward monolingual English and an increasing focus on an idea of standardization. Ideology as well as practice matters. Changes in the strength of the *concept* of English as a distinct language are crucial to how Chaucer allows it to serve as his matrix of relation to other tongues, and for the social interactions that increasingly centered on English and thereby invited a notion of a common English. By the 1370s, as Laura Wright and others have shown – at what happened to be the start of Chaucer's most important literary production – Middle English was becoming a markedly stronger option in the code-switching that had long persisted between the various languages or the 'mixed' language that pervaded England, and the strength of the English option continued even as the wider social range of users of written English interacted, often in conflict. As Wright argues, driving the linguistic changes was accelerating and geographically widening contact between London 'trading professionals' and their increasingly far-flung contacts, all of whose post-plague rising standards of living after the devastating population losses elevated the social and political power of such mercantile agents for whom English was the main tongue. In Wright's view, for which there is much evidence, social and political conflict increased within this more linguistically egalitarian circumstance: 'As living standards for the masses improved, so those masses began to protest and rebel, and to express what they had to say in writing. That voice was English rather than Anglo-Norman or medieval Latin.'[57]

This was not, therefore, a development driven by the profoundly oppressed, despite increasing social and economic opportunities for and increasing protests by the surviving peasants after the demographic collapse from the Black Death, including the 'peasants' revolt' of 1381.[58] Yet this process, as Wright and many others have demonstrated, was also not driven by the royal administration. Against earlier views of a Lancastrian 'language program', these views argue

---

[57] Laura Wright, 'Rising Living Standards, the Demise of Anglo-Norman and Mixed-Language Writing, and Standard English', in Wright, *Multilingual Origins*, 515–32, at 516.

[58] Substantial recent studies of this are Mark Bailey, *After the Black Death: Economy, Society, and the Law in Fourteenth-Century England* (Oxford, 2021); and Christopher Dyer, *Peasants Making History: Living in an English Region, 1200–1540* (Oxford, 2022).

that England's flourishing international trade and its mercantile communities had far more influence on the spread of language standardization than the crown or government.[59] The idea of a centralized standardization of London or Westminster English cannot explain the direction in which these changes occurred (*to* Westminster rather than mainly *from* it), the halting stages in which they occurred, or the forms of English that resulted by the end of the fifteenth century. The process Wright describes eventually produced an English displaying plenty of elements from London dialect but not other key features of London English, such as present plural *-n*, third-person present *-th*, *atte* for 'at the', and so on, all of which vanished while features from economically powerful regions elsewhere were added, such as the northeast with its wool trade: 'them' for London 'hem'; and so forth. The social corollary to this is that in an increasingly common language, direct conflicts would be all the more visible.[60]

Chaucer's *Book of the Duchess*, his first datable poem, from soon after the early death of John of Gaunt's first wife Blanch of Lancaster, on 12 September 1368, enacts a microcosm of this process, delicately elevated to display this issue to (and presumably to seek patronage from) one of the most powerful lords of England. The poem presents the poet's encounter with a Black Knight caught in an endless solipsistic cycle of complaint about 'White's' death. This is clearly courtly lyric, to which the poem bows throughout, but from which it decisively distances itself, even as it makes clear its (hope for or fact of) patronage by John of Gaunt, whose son Henry would later claim the throne. A literary and linguistic French matrix for *Book of the Duchess* is indicated not only by the pastiche of French sources used and recast for the poem but also by the model of French 'complaint' first glimpsed in Chaucer's poem by the narrator's own pre-vision reading of 'a romaunce' (i.e., in French)

---

[59] For demolitions of the earlier views of a centralized 'language program', see Michael Benskin, 'Chancery Standard', in *New Perspectives on English Historical Linguistics: Selected Papers from 12 ICEHL, Glasgow, 21–26 August 2002; 2; Lexis and Transmission* (Glasgow, 2004), 1–39; Gwilym Dodd, 'The Rise of English, the Decline of French: Supplications to the English Crown, *c.* 1420–1450', *Speculum* 86 (2011): 117–50.

[60] In these terms, Wright focuses on the tumultuous London conflicts of the mid-1380s, e.g., Caroline M. Barron and Laura Wright, eds, *The London Jubilee Book, 1376–1387: An Edition of Trinity College Cambridge MS O.3.11, Folios 133–157*, London Record Society 55 (London, 2021). Other domains of culture show similar dangers in using English in the 1380s, well captured by two studies: Steven Justice, *Writing and Rebellion England in 1381* (Berkeley, 1996); and Nicholas Watson, 'Censorship and Cultural Change in Late-Medieval England: Vernacular Theology, the Oxford Translation Debate, and Arundel's Constitutions of 1409', *Speculum* 70 (1995): 822–64.

containing translations of Ovid's Ceyx and Alcyon.[61] Here, Chaucer loads his English with the weight of other tongues, including Classical stories, for the first time inserting that material directly into English. Chaucer's retelling of Ovid's Ceyx and Alcyon ends, however, as abruptly as Blanche's life, with an emphatic incompleteness of Alcyon's final long complaint that drops into untranslatability just before she attempts suicide at the sight and the sound of her husband's talking corpse bidding her farewell: 'With that hir eyen up she casteth / And saw noght. "Alas!" quod she for sorwe, / And deyede within the thridde morwe. / But what she sayede more in that swow / I may not tell yow as now; / Hyt were to longe for to dwelle ...' (209–17).

The Book of the Duchess goes on to show the narrator's visionary encounter with the Knight, who is suspended like Alcyon in courtly 'complaint'; his grief is also untranslatable, to the narrator at least: opaque, in Glissant's terms. Meanwhile, Chaucer's narrator overtly plays the role of an ignorant monolinguist of another kind, in being unable to perceive the world of poetics he encounters. The narrator misunderstands not French as such, but the metaphors and figures of speech that the Black Knight uses, just as the Knight's displacement of language from communication into poetic figurality demonstrates an absence of any adequate contact-language between distinct social realms. Although both speaking in English, the implicit failure of either to grasp the resulting 'créolisation' is presented as the real disorder the poem addresses:

> I stalked even unto hys bak,
> And there I stood as stille as ought,
> That, soth to saye, he saw me nought;
> For-why he heng hys hed adoun,
> And with a dedly sorwful soun
> He made of rym ten vers or twelve
> Of a compleynte to hymselve –
> ...
> He sayd a lay, a maner song,
> Withoute noote, withoute song;
> And was thys, for ful I kan
> Reherse hyt; rytht thus hyt began ...
> 458–74

With brash confidence in being able entirely to capture the Knight's lyric, 'for ful I kan / Reherse hyt', the youthful narrator sneaks up on the knight rather than establishing any basis for communication, then with perverse precision slightly miscounts what the Knight recites – the 'lay' is neither ten nor twelve

---

[61] James Wimsatt, *Chaucer and His French Contemporaries: Natural Music in the Fourteenth Century* (Toronto, 1991), 126–31. Chaucer is quoted from Larry D. Benson, gen. ed., *The Riverside Chaucer, Third Edition* (Boston, 1986).

lines but eleven. Revealing his more profound distance from that kind of poem, the narrator then proceeds to misunderstand for almost the rest of the dream-vision the Knight's address to Death – a use of apostrophe crucial to the Knight's elegantly French figurality. In forcing the Knight to engage in explanation, however, the poet imposes on the Knight a kind of linguistic penance (to invoke the poem's overall structure of quasi-confession). For the problems of communication run both ways, as one exchange especially shows, where the Knight takes up each word the narrator has uttered in order to question and reject it, in irritable corrections of word choice and the burdens those carry, a tragicomic version of lyrical interlace:

> 'By our Lord', quod I, 'y trowe yow **wel**!
> Hardely, your love was **wel** beset;
> I not how ye myghte have do **bet**'.
> '**Bet**? Ne no wyght so **wel**', quod he.
> 'Y **trowe** hyt **wel**, sire', quod I, 'parde!'
> 'Nay, **leve** hyt **wel**!' 'Sire, so do I;
> I **leve** yow **wel**, that trewely
> Yow thoghte that she was the beste
> And to beholde the alderfayreste,
> **Whoso** had loked hir **with your** eyen'.
> '**With myn**? Nay, **alle that hir seyen**
> Seyde and sworen hyt was soo.
> And *thogh they ne hadde, I wolde thoo
> Have loved best my lady free* ...'
> 1042–55 [my emphases]

Initially, the Black Knight insists on making his hyperbole objective fact, resisting all the comparative and relativist words that the narrator offers, since those imply a merely subjective judgment. However, by the end of this interchange, the Knight concedes, in the final statement I have italicized, that he can attest as fact only his own feelings: he cannot extend solipsistic hyperbole into even a claim of shared reality. This is a crucial step in his 'healing', a moment when interacting with the 'monolinguistic' narrator forces the Knight to acknowledge that his language of hyperbole is an idiolect not a universalizing vernacular, that his grammar and diction must be modified into relativist and comparatist forms for communication to occur. As Alcyon's suicidal response to her own earlier lament precisely demonstrates, addressing the dead by apostrophe might be a principle of lyric and complaint, but it is by that same principle no basis for communication. Apostrophe is a path to social death.

By debating the many kinds of figural and hyperbolic language the Knight uses, the poem puts on display the need not for English as such but for any means of making linguistic contact, bridging what is throughout *The Book of the Duchess* alarmingly divided thought-worlds, even when language in our sense is not the barrier. In Glissant's terms, Chaucer obliquely introduces creolization into the world that his half-deaf narrator misprises, only to show that the noble Knight is similarly caught in a dead end of language by being unable to acknowledge and express the physical suffering and losses of others, including his own White. Both the Knight and the narrator learn that their 'shared' language is never fully their own. Both, in this sense, become 'disconcerted', as Glissant followed by Derrida describes that term. The result does not leave the obtusely 'common' narrator in any position of authority; rather, in what many critics have seen as the narrator's healing of the Knight's sorrows by leading him to acknowledge the facts in plain language, the process provides the Knight a lesson in power: he must learn to speak the language of the commoners in order to gain full control, a lesson that Gaunt's son put to practical use when on 30 September 1399, the new king of England, Henry IV, announced and had recorded in parliamentary records his claim, in English, to 'Þis rewme of Yngland, and þe corone with all þe membres and þe appurtenances', an English eruption that the parliamentary clerk emphasized by rendering the rest of the proceedings in Latin rather than the usual (and soon resumed) Anglo-Norman.[62]

Hints of the adoption of an *idea* of a 'standard English' by the king were, of course, momentous, but it is more suited to the evidence to see this as following, rather than instigating, the production of that notion in the 'trading professionals' and yet lower social spheres. The most explicit poetic microcosm of this movement from low to high social embrace of the idea of a common English is Chaucer's *House of Fame*, written perhaps a decade after *The Book of the Duchess*, a few years after he had begun receiving an annuity from John of Gaunt.[63] This was also during a time when Chaucer was employed in the laborious position of controller of the wool custom in the City of London, thus losing his position as mainly a courtier to become a lay civil servant.[64] In this poem, an unnamed but implicit idea of 'common tongue' emerges both as language welded to the highest social and national authority, as identified with specific authors and the 'matter' they purveyed in the frigid House of Fame, as well as a more fecund generation of ungovernable and infantile language in the whirling house of Rumor. An Eagle, straight from Dante, has taken Geoffrey to each of these socially and economically contrasting domains of language-making in order for Geoffrey to gain 'tydynges' as a reward for having served the God of Love in poetry. This basic purpose situates the whole poem in a

---

[62] David R. Carlson, ed., *The Deposition of Richard II: 'The Record and Process of the Renunciation and Deposition of Richard II (1399) and Related Writings* (Toronto, 2007), 58.

[63] Martin M. Crow and Clair C. Olson, eds, *Chaucer Life-Records* (Oxford, 1996), 271–75.

[64] Crow and Olson, *Chaucer Life-Records*, 148–270. On the possible relevance of this change of circumstances, see Robert J. Meyer-Lee, 'Literary Value and the Customs House: The Axiological Logic of the House of Fame', *The Chaucer Review* 48 (2014): 373–94.

belated relation to courtly literature; but the poem's progress itself seems to move backward toward linguistic origins, into the very birth of language itself. Before reaching those depths, we travel through educational discourse, though even this is aimed at the material origins of language as broken air. The Eagle explains to Geoffrey that only natural 'weight' governs all things ('light thing upward, and downward charge' [746]), including language – which is so light it floats up to Fame's Castle; once he has brought Geoffrey there, however, the Eagle neglects to mention, all rules are off except Fame's purely willful choice. But her 'castle' is in the neighborhood of the demotic hubbub from the House of Rumor, where utterance is a cacophonous and clearly even more primeval array of diffused impulses and ungovernable consequences:

> Tho saugh y stonde in a valeye,
> Under the castel, faste by,
> An hous, that Domus Dedaly
> That Laboryntus cleped ys,
> Nas mad so wonderlych, ywis,
> Ne half so queyntelych ywrought.
> And ever mo, as swyft as thought,
> This queynte hous aboute wente,
> That never mo hyt stille stent.
> And therout com so gret a noyse
> That, had hyt sonden opon Oyse,
> Men myghte hyt han herd esely
> To Rome, y trowe sikerly.
> And the noyse which that I herde,
> For al the world ryght so hyt ferde
> As doth the rowtynge of the ston
> That from th'engyn ys leten gon.
> And al thys hous of which y rede
> Was made of twigges, falwe, rede,
> And grene eke, and somme weren white,
> Swiche as men to this cages thwite,
> Or maken of these panyers,
> Or elles hottes or dossers
> That, for the swough and for the twygges,
> This hous was also ful of gygges,
> And also ful eke of chirkynges,
> And of many other werkynges;
> And eke this hous hath of entrees
> As fele as of leves ben in trees
> In somer, whan they grene been;
> And on the roof men may yet seen
> A thousand holes, and wel moo,
> To leten wel the soun out goo ...
>   1918–50

The messiness of birth – the 'noyse' of emergent language – precedes articulation, culminating in the (completely arbitrary) distinctions of good and bad fame that Fame imposes. The passage taking us from the Ovidian and French (*Roman de la rose*) matrix of Fame's House to Rumor engulfs the reader in pragmatic language of the kind otherwise found only in accounting documents. Chaucer's range of options for describing satchels ('Swiche as men to this cages thwite, / Or maken of these panyers, / Or elles hottes or dossers') offers the kind of documentary terms found in 'mixed' language of urban and legal inventories and trade.[65] Forms based on 'hott' (a Germanic word for a basket to carry earth or stones) are attested in Latin (*hottarius, hottator, hottata*) before Anglo-Norman or Middle English.[66] 'Panyer' is widely recorded in Latin records (*panerium*) with some French from the twelfth century, some of which might be considered English (first clearly English attestation is *Havelok*, c. 1300).[67] 'Dosser' (a basket carried on one's back) appears in Latin and French from the twelfth century and remains actively cited in Anglo-Norman through the fourteenth century but is first attested in English here – and never again in Chaucer, although a few later writers use it.

Such words from 'mixed' language escape the category of any particular language; indeed, Chaucer compares Rumor's tidings to non-linguistic noises signifying only physical events, as the sound of a catapult signifies a flying stone ('the rowtynge of the ston / That from th'engyn ys leten gon'). As Wright's studies show, 'mixed' language gradually was shifting from a Latin matrix toward an English-one (e.g., generally from 'De iiij d. pro dimidio dosser zabuli empto' [1433 Bath records]; to 'a dosser off chekyns' [1462]); but in Chaucer's period, language-marking of many such words had not been settled.[68] Rumor's house is not simply multilingualism; it is non- or proto-lingualism, whose potentiality as 'language' is indicated by the path of the infantile shapes of the 'tydynges' that squeeze through the roof holes until

---

[65] Wright, 'Rising Living Standards'; Laura Wright, 'On Variation in Medieval Mixed-Language Business Writing', in *Code-Switching in Early English*, ed. Herbert Schendl and Laura Wright (Berlin, 2011), 191–218.

[66] 'Hottarius' (hod-carrier) from 1198 in Latin: *Dictionary of Medieval Latin from British Sources* (Turnhout, 2015), online by subscription; 'hote' from 1235 in Anglo-Norman: *The Anglo-Norman Dictionary* on Anglo-Norman.net; 'hotte' from 1295 in Middle English: *Middle English Dictionary* in the Middle English Compendium online; but none or all of these might be considered as various languages until later uses in full Anglo-Norman or English matrices.

[67] 'Panerium' from 1194 in Latin matrices: *Dictionary of Medieval Latin from British Sources*; 'panier' in Anglo-Norman from the thirteenth century: *Anglo-Norman Dictionary* (but note at Parliament Rolls of 1382, 'lour panyers quieles ils appellent dorsers', showing the transposition between the terms as well as between the languages). 'Panier(e)' was clearly in Middle English only from 1300: *MED*.

[68] References from the *MED*, s.v. dosser.

arriving at Fame's palace, where 'she gan yeven ech hys name, / After hir disposicioun' (2111–12). The social nexus of such proto-language in trade and travel is disclosed near the end of this (apparently) incomplete poem, as if finally reaching the scandalous origin of a common tongue:

> And, Lord, this hous in alle tymes
> Was ful of shipmen and pilgrimes,
> With scrippes bret-ful of lesinges,
> Entremedled with tydynges,
> And eek allone be hemselve.
> O, many a thousand tymes twelve
> Saugh I eke of these pardoners,
> Currours, and eke messagers,
> With boystes crammed ful of lyes
> As ever vessel was with lyes ...
> 2021–30

'Tydynges' is the only reward the Eagle has offered the narrator, and tidings he gets, with no guarantee of truth-value. But he will return (if only with the abrupt cessation of the poem) with a vision of language's broader material and social truths, including the demonstration not only that documentary language from traders and travelers escapes any linguistic fixity but also that any individual 'ruling' of language, most visibly by Fame herself, is at best the action of an arbitrary despot, whose massive roof the famous authors are compelled to uphold as their special form of servitude. The only escape from that fate that Chaucer presents for a writer (coyly identified as a collector of 'tydynges') who faces both noble and variously mercantile creators and transmuters of the word – both of whom turn out to be scandalously amoral in their verbal promiscuity – is to bear witness to the murky origins of a language that would soon issue from the trumpets, and eventually the armies, of Fame.

* * *

By virtue of both the postcolonial and the historical linguists' views, *Hali Meiðhad* and Chaucer's two early poems stand out as instances not of some inexorable 'progress' or 'rise' of English literature but of extraordinary moments of assessment, measurable not by rises or falls but by other instances. Those assembled here are, of course, the ideas of Achebe, Wali, Glissant, and to some degree Derrida on colonial and decolonizing language: a series of possible frameworks for the broad (and usefully elusive) earlier theory of vernacularity, all of which offer ways of reconceiving the particular elements and histories of premodern English that historical linguists past and present have elaborated and debated, and of appreciating anew the literary works that emerged from those still, and perhaps necessarily, opaque linguistic situations.

I do not mean to reconcile any of the differences between these kinds and aims of understanding, much less between individual cases of each kind, which of course are only sampled here. Against both the postcolonial and the linguistic theory, the ideas of language, discourse, *ledene*, *tydynges*, advanced by the vernacular and *vernacularizing* medieval writers offer partial echoes or anticipation but also partial silence – silence either because they lacked any similar concepts or consciousness, or had such different circumstances and aspirations, and their languages such different affordances, that their focuses led elsewhere. For the two medieval cases considered here, those 'elsewheres' would be very different indeed. Their indication of the worlds that language inhabited and created, however, seem enabled by unusual participation, in ways not always clear to us or even to them, in the lowest as well as highest social, spiritual, and metaphysical uses and registers of language, along with a persistent focus on the circulation between or intrinsic coexistence of these seeming opposites. For all of that, the brilliant assessments from the margins of colonial and decolonizing cultures are apt co-theories, helping views from the midst of western studies better comprehend their own limitations and reawaken their unexploited past literary and critical possibilities.

PART II

GOWER'S BOOKS AND BOOKS OF GOWER

⇥ 5 ⇤

Gower's Ovidian Aesthetic and Its Discontents[1]

R. F. YEAGER

Asserting that John Gower knew his Ovid backwards and forwards requires no fresh evidence to sustain. Some room remains, necessarily, for source-related argument over his reliance on that work or this writer, but a legion of studies extending over the past century and a half has shown beyond doubt that Gower owed his greatest debts to Ovid's corpus. One might go further, to maintain that Gower, no less than Salutati or Montaigne, imbibed at Ovid's fountain an insatiable thirst for poetry; but unlike them, from Ovid Gower inhumed poetic craft as well, learning more about making verse through his reading of Ovid than from any other.[2] Indeed, as Andrew Galloway has remarked, without exaggeration, '[Gower's] approach to antiquity was almost exclusively focused on an author who had long held court in the medieval schoolroom and monastic libraries (with both of which Gower shows many signs of contact): Ovid.'[3]

That said, however, it is no less equally true that over the course of his almost fifty-year career Gower's engagement with Ovid took a variety of forms, leaving significant questions ponderable but unanswered. One such, which I'll not pursue here much beyond raising it, concerns when Gower's initial encounter with Ovid took place. Galloway, like most others, assumes a schoolroom familiarity, and while I have no firm reason to disagree, the sad fact is that we know next to nothing solid about Gower's education. Very likely,

---

[1] It is a privilege and a pleasure to offer this essay in partial recompense to Siân Echard, a friend and colleague of long standing, whose nonpareil studies of Gower's poetry, especially of the Latin, I have found essential for an understanding of his work. As do all Gowerians, I owe her much.

[2] For Salutati, see *Coluccio Salutati de laboribus Herculis*, ed. B. L. Ullman (Padua, 1951), III.11; for Montaigne, see *Essais*, 1.26: 'De l'institution des enfants' ('On Education').

[3] See Galloway, 'Gower's Ovids,' in *The Oxford History of Classical Reception in English Literature, Vol. I: 800–1558*, ed. Rita Copeland (Oxford, 2016), 435–64, at 437.

he learned his letters in Latin – that was the way literacy usually began – but how much of his early study included Ovid (and which Ovid? – more on that later) we can't say. What the extant record of his work does tell us, however, is that initially at least the Ovidian model had competition. Assuming we have understood the chronology of his work correctly, Gower began his poetic career writing Anglo-French – and the *Mirour de l'Omme* exhibits very little directly traceable to Ovid.[4] It has been sometimes suggested that Gower's elected language indicates a decision about audience, French being the parlance of the aristocracy during the reign of Edward III, when we believe the *Mirour* was written. While this is likely true, it is no less worth remarking that many of the sources present in the *Mirour* – e.g., the *Roman de la Rose*, Christian Fathers, biblical prophets, Seneca, Cato's *Distichs*, Gregory, Ambrose – continue to be common throughout Gower's subsequent *oeuvre*; Ovid, however, is named only once in the *Mirour*, to the effect that 'patience is a virtue', and near-quoted once, though in that instance his verse is attributed to 'Ly clerc Orace' – that is, Horace.[5]

What precisely to make of this must be left for another essay, but here it seems pertinent to observe, with Robert R. Edwards, that Gower may be 'the poet who most overtly seeks to become an author in trilingual medieval England'.[6] Taken in that light, the formal choices inherent in the *Mirour* would then suggest that Gower's early poetic ambition was pointing him in an altogether un-Ovidian direction, guided by a conception of 'author' closer, perhaps, to Langland's – that is, vernacular moral assertion, albeit directed

---

[4] Galloway, in the aforementioned essay, holds up possible parallels for Gower's Satan in Ovid's Jupiter, and his Invidia with the latter's Aglauros, but hardly sounds convinced himself, in the end (441).

[5] *MO* 14089–91: 'O Pacience, comme toy prise / Ly sage Ovide en son pprise, / Disantque toute autre vertu …' (O Patience, how the sage Ovid in his writing praises you, saying that any virtue …). *MO* 10948–50: 'Ly clerc Orace auci s'en pleigne, / Si dist bien que la sort humeine / S'est a un tendre fil penduz' (The clerk Orace also complains, saying – rightly – that a slim thread suspends human fate); cf. Ovid, *Ex Ponto*, IV.iii.35, 'omnia sunt hominum tenui pendentia filo' (All things human hang by a slender thread), and also *CA* VI.1513–14: 'The happes over mannes hed / Ben honged with a tendre thred', and the Latin side-note: 'Oracius. Omnia sunt hominum tenui pendencia filo.' All references to Gower's poetry are taken from *The Complete Works of John Gower*, ed. G. C. Macaulay, 4 vols (Oxford, 1899–1902). Unless otherwise specified, translations are my own.

[6] Robert R. Edwards, *Invention and Authorship in Medieval England* (Columbus, 2017), xxix. In this, he was following Echard's lead, who noted in 2004 that 'Gower's eye seems to have been on more than one afterlife'; see 'Last Words: Latin at the End of the *Confessio Amantis*,' in *Interstices: Studies in Middle English and Anglo-Latin Texts in Honour of A.G. Rigg*, ed. Richard Firth Green and Linne R. Mooney (Toronto, 2004), 99–121, at 100.

at a different audience class – than to a form of historical and literary self-awareness that Edwards ultimately intends by 'authorship', and traces to a classical ethos. So when, and perhaps why, did Gower start to think of Ovid in a serious manner as a guide to the craft?

The first extensive evidence we have of a serious shift of Gower's creative direction toward Ovid comes surprisingly late, circa 1381–82, in the so-called *Visio Anglie* that he eventually added to a longer poem he had in progress, the *Vox Clamantis*.[7] That the *Visio* was initially conceived as a stand-alone poem is rendered probable by more factors than can be accounted for here, but for present purposes three in particular stand out. The first is the extraordinary preponderance of quotation in the *Visio* from the broad Ovidian corpus, as has been so often noted.[8] Stylistically, this heavy reliance on Ovid sets the *Visio* apart from Books II through VII of the present *Vox*, where – and this is the second factor – Gower's borrowings from Ovid are significantly outweighed by quotation, sometimes of several lines together, from Christian medieval writers, especially Peter of Riga, Alexander Neckham, and Godfrey of Viterbo.[9] Third, as Alastair Minnis clarified a number of years ago, the formal *accessus* that preface the *Visio* and Books II and III of the present *Vox* evince Gower's focus there on a commentary tradition originally biblical, rather than on the classics per se. These three prologues, moreover, differ in type, bespeaking different origins. Minnis has identified the *forma tractandi* of the opening of the *Visio* as an Apocalypse prologue, modelled on Gilbert of Poitiers; that of Book II, which describes the entire work, albeit noticeably minus the *Visio*, Minnis terms 'Aristotelian', in the manner of Thomas Aquinas, among others; and that of Book III he traces to the *artes praedicandi*, thus connecting all three prologues with commentaries on the prophetic books of the Bible – what was known as the *forma prophetialis*.[10]

About Gower's Ovid all of this should tell us several things, primary among them that what we know today as the *Vox Clamantis* represents the third

---

[7] Maura Nolan has argued that the shock of the Revolt transformed Gower from a 'Boethian' poet to an 'Ovidian' – that is, one who recognised the need to write from the heart as well as the head, a shift coincident with the *Visio*. See Nolan, 'The Poetics of Catastrophe: Ovidian Allusion in Gower's "Vox Clamantis"', in *Medieval Latin and Middle English Literature: Essays in Honour of Jill Mann*, ed. Christopher Cannon and Maura Nolan (Cambridge, 2011).

[8] For an overview, see Macaulay's notes to the Latin works.

[9] For Peter of Riga, the basic study remains Paul E. Beichner, 'Gower's Use of *Aurora* in *Vox Clamantis*', *Speculum* 30, no. 4 (1955); and further his edition of the *Aurora*: *Aurora Petri Rigae Biblia Versificata*, ed. Beichner, 2 vols (Notre Dame, 1965). For Neckham and Godfrey, see Eric W. Stockton, *The Major Latin Works of John Gower* (Seattle, 1962), 342–470, *passim*.

[10] See Alastair Minnis, *Medieval Theory of Authorship: Scholastic Literary Attitudes in the Later Middle Ages*, 2nd edn (Philadelphia, 1988), 168–77.

version of three, which, had one or the other of the directions apparently intended in *Vox* II and III dominated, would have resulted in distinctly different poems. Neither of these *Voxes* would have been so strikingly Ovidian as the *Visio*, but rather much closer in tone and purpose to the *Mirour de l'Omme*. This in turn suggests that Gower's full investment in Ovid was in progress for some time. That argument gains resonance from the relative infrequency of quotations taken from the *Heroides* in the *Vox*, and from the nature of those taken from the *Metamorphoses*, outside of the *Visio*.[11] Generalising broadly, what we find in *Vox* II through VII, most of which was probably written in the mid-1370s, if not somewhat earlier, are brief Ovidian borrowings far outnumbered by those from the *Aurora*, the *Speculum Stultorum*, and Godfrey's *Pantheon*.

For evidence beyond the *Visio* of Gower's significant engagement with Ovid, then, we best look to the *Confessio Amantis*, into which he borrowed multiple stories from both the *Metamorphoses* and for the first time significantly from the *Heroides* – an observation that prompts several others. One, intriguing though of lesser importance, has to do with dates. Since we believe that the *Visio* was likely completed around 1382, a contemporary date for the start of the *Confessio* seems possible – a supposition proffered to little fanfare some years ago.[12] A second observation is of greater implicative significance, however, and begs commensurate attention. It can be introduced by a question: Can we imagine what moved Gower to turn more toward the *Metamorphoses* as a source for his work?

Clearly, we cannot be certain of his full motivation, but several answers seem possible. Most obvious, perhaps, is that the *Metamorphoses*, and the *Heroides* too in that regard, are superb repositories of narratives. Once Gower decided to frame the *Confessio* as the Lover's shrift, the need for exempla with which Genius could illustrate his teachings must have become apparent. For medieval writers traversing this ground, Ovid had few competitors. That

---

[11] By my count, there are thirty-six lines derived from the *Metamorphoses* in *VC* II–VII, twelve from the *Heroides* (compare forty-seven from *Ars Amatoriae*), but the moment of their inclusion may post-date and thus reflect Gower's deeper involvement with both while writing the *Visio*. Because Gower continuously revised his work, precise dating is difficult. Macaulay's copy-text for the *Vox*, Oxford, All Souls College MS 98, is in a single hand and begins with the *Visio*, therefore establishing production of the MS post-1381. David R. Carlson, 'Gower's Early Latin Poetry: Text-Genetic Hypotheses of an *Epistola ad Regem* (ca. 1377–1380) from the Evidence of John Bale', *Mediaeval Studies* 65 (2003): 293–317, convincingly posits a pattern of long-term textual migration from school exercises to 'finished' poem but which, in consequence, underscores the problematics of chronological placement of most lines or portions.

[12] R. F. Yeager, 'Gower's Lancastrian Affinity: The Iberian Connection', *Viator* 35 (2004): 483–516.

notwithstanding, however, there is another reason, both likely and compelling, and with broader implications, that I believe drove Gower's deeper investment in Ovid's work, and in the *Metamorphoses* especially.

It is important, when thinking of Ovid, to recognise that his poetry presents more than one face to the world. The pivot point is of course his exile to Tomis in AD 8, and for good cause. Ovid's work prior to that – *Epistulae Heroidum, Medicamina Faciei, Amores, Ars Amatoriae, Remedia Amores, Metamorphoses*, and the never-completed *Fasti*, on which he was engaged when banished – is fundamentally different from the post-exilic poetry, *Tristia* and *Epistulae ex Ponto*, in more ways than can be well addressed in brief space. I shall, in consequence, focus on two aspects with particular relevance for my larger argument. The first is that, while Ovid's tone and the emotionally lighter subject-matter of his pre-exilic verse would, one can easily imagine, have struck Gower as unsuitable to foreground in the kinds of poetry he was writing before 1381, the special new demands of the *Visio* and the *Confessio Amantis* apparently changed his mind.[13] Both of those poems are about transformation, and this of course comprises the core of Ovid's work, in the *Metamorphoses* especially. That the bulk of Gower's borrowings from Ovid apparently diverges toward opposite ends in the *Visio* and the *Confessio* does not affect this central fact. Gower understood that his new subject was transformation, and he turned more purposefully than he had earlier to the poet most concerned with that.

The second point about Ovid's new appeal for Gower also involves transformation. Although the Ovidian pastiche of the peasants' devolution into monsters is vivid and memorable, the over-arching pattern of transformation projected, first in the *Visio*, then finally by the *Vox* itself, while unrelentingly admonitory, nevertheless through the power of God ultimately must be seen to bend toward the hopeful and positive. Following a clutch of lines dependent upon Peter of Riga's *Aurora*, Gower takes the *Visio*'s last line from the *Remedia Amoris*: 'Sit prior et cura cura repulsa nova' (And let new concerns drive away the old – compare Ovid: 'Et posita est cura cura repulsa nova').[14] As is often remarked, from a modern perspective, what social improvement Gower projects at the end of the *Visio* is starkly qualified, and comes at the expense of the peasantry in chains.[15] However, Gower brings

---

[13] Gower borrows many lines and parts of lines from the *Amores, Ars Amatoriae, Fasti*, and the *Metamorphoses* in Vox II–VII, but most are unrecognisable without careful textual comparison. Matter from those poems, *Metamorphoses* especially, takes on greater importance in the *Visio* and the *Confessio Amantis*.

[14] Text and translation from *The Art of Love and Other Poems*, trans. J. H. Mozley (London, 1969).

[15] 'Sic cum rusticitas fuerat religata cathenis, / Et paciens nostro subiacet illa

the completed *Vox* to a close more inclusively, in lines that some have taken for echoes of *Piers Plowman*:

> Ad bona set pronus audiat ista bonus
> Hec ita scripta sciat malus, ut bonus ammodo fiat,
> Et bonus hec querat, ut meliora great
>
> [Yet the man prone to what is good should listen to this.
> Likewise, the bad man should know these writings so that he may presently become good,
> And the good man should seek them out so that he may do better.][16]

A reasonable assumption, for better or worse, would be that this includes hope for the peasants too, provided they behave.[17]

These are complex issues, but what stands out from all of them, regarding Gower's view of Ovid in the 1380s, is that at that point for him the Roman poet apparently represented continual, but potentially ameliorative, change – the latter largely because, I think, Gower's own project to correct king and kingdom was built of hopeful aspiration. Personal and social improvement is Gower's consistent theme, beginning with the *Mirour*, and with the ascension of Richard II he had a focus more facilitative than society at large, one that, because of Richard's position, could service dual purposes simultaneously. Hence the Aristotle-like admonitions in the *Vox* directed at Richard, several times revised, and the royal encounter on the Thames, actual or not, in the initial version of the *Confessio*. But so optimistic a reading of the *Metamorphoses*, while useful at the outset of a new reign, is of course only one of the many ways to look at Ovid. Gower would have continued to find Ovidian aesthetics personally supportive, and Ovid's unrelenting puncturing of epic aspiration compatible with his own eirenic beliefs. Yet there is a less effectual, even a bleaker, Ovid, too, to be reckoned with. Over time, Gower's outlook changed.

A full discussion of why and how would take me far away from my subject, and so must await another occasion. Obviously Richard's darkening rule played a major part. But the 'Ovidian discontents' of my title are of a more personal nature and cut closer to the bone. Gower, as he aged, grew concerned to establish – and ensure – his legacy as an *auctor*, a relatively

---

pede, / Ad iuga bos rediit, que sub aruis semen aratis / Creuit, et a bello rusticus ipse silet.' *VC* I.2093–96.

[16] 'Qui bonus est audit bona set peruersus obaudit, / Ad bona set pronus audiat ista bonus. / Hes ita scripta sciat malus, ut bonus ammodo fiat, / Et bonus hec querat, ut meliora gerat.' *VC* VII.1471–74.

[17] Nolan, 'Poetics of Catastrophe', 133, projects a kinship Gower felt with the 'demands of the peasants for self-determination', as it was also 'the obsession of clerks and poets'.

new ambition at the beginning of the fifteenth century, but one both he and Chaucer, and Lydgate later, were making possible by sharing it. A number of factors influenced that concern, for which there is more than ample evidence, most concretely his self-designed tomb. Chief among those factors must be his likely encounter with the figure and ideas of Francis Petrarch. Let me be clear: no evidence has surfaced yet of Gower's reading any work of Petrarch's, let alone the slim possibility that he could have crossed paths with the poet himself, as exists with Chaucer.[18] But Chaucer knew at least one of the *rime* (132, 'S'amor non è'), and the *Obedientia ac fide uxoria mythologia* (the story of Giselda);[19] he clearly must have known too what Petrarch represented in Italy: laureation, and the centrality of Virgil to any claim of poetic *auctoritas*.[20] Put another way, and perhaps more to the present point, Petrarch – and through him, Virgil – stood for *posterity*, a concept in connection with a life of letters that Petrarch more or less re-invented, framing poetic immortality solidly around Virgil in the process.

To some degree, by the turn of the century it would seem from the trajectory of Gower's writing that he was prepared to accept much of this. Paradoxically, perhaps, his close reading of Ovid, who continually engaged in measuring himself against Virgil, and failing – or does he? – would have contributed.[21] Consider Ovid's opening lines of the *Amores*, a work that Gower knew well:

> Arma gravi numero violentaque bella parabam
> edere, materia conveniente modis.
> par erat inferior versus – risisse Cupido
> dicitur atque unum surripuisse pedem.

---

[18] See, e.g., Derek Pearsall, *The Life of Geoffrey Chaucer: A Critical Biography* (Oxford, 1992), 104: 'Chaucer could have met Petrarch or Boccaccio on his way down from Genoa to Florence, Petrarch at Arqua or Padua ... but it is extremely unlikely that he did.'

[19] The 'Canticus Troili' (*Troilus and Criseyde*, I.400–20); for text and translation of 'S'amor non è', see Robert M. Durling, ed. and trans., *Petrarch's Lyric Poems: The Rime Sparse and Other Lyrics* (Cambridge, MA, 1976), 270–71; for *Obedientia ac fide uxoria mythologia* (Clerk's Tale), see *Rerum Senilium Libri* XVII.3; English translation in *Francesco Petrarch: Letters of Old Age*, ed. and trans. Aldo S. Bernardo, Saul Levin, and Reta A. Bernardo (New York, 2005), vol. 2, 655–68.

[20] Pearsall, discussing the *House of Fame*, and paraphrasing C. S. Lewis, takes a contrary view of what Chaucer thought of Italy: he '"medievalizes" what he found in the Italians'. Perhaps, but for Chaucer as for Gower, views of the 1370s need not be the same twenty years on. For Pearsall, see *Life*, 110–11; for Lewis, see 'What Chaucer Really Did to *Il Filostrato*,' *Essays & Studies* 17 (1932): 56–75.

[21] See Alessandro Barchiesi and Philip Hardie, 'The Ovidian Career Model: Ovid, Gallus, Apuleius, Boccaccio', in *Classical Literary Careers and Their Reception*, ed. Philip Hardie and Helen Moore (Cambridge, 2010), 59–88, esp. 59–65.

> [Arms, and the violent deeds of war, I was making ready to sound forth – in weighty numbers, with matter suited to the measure. The second verse was equal to the first – but Cupid, they say, with a laugh stole away one foot.][22]

In its first line, Ovid sets his *Amores* next to the *Aeneid*, beginning in grand imitation of Virgilian dactylic hexameter, and then backs off, into his own preferred elegiac pentameter, with clever reference to Cupid stealing 'one foot'. At the end of Book I, the ever-competitive Ovid returns to Virgil, alluding to the latter's three works, and apparently framing his predecessor's *oeuvre* in immortal terms (I.xv.25–28):

> Tityrus et segetes Aeneiaque arma legentur,
> Roma triumphati dum caput orbis erit
> donec erunt ignes arcusque Cupidinis arma,
> discentur numeri, culte Tibulle, tui
>
> [Tityrus and the harvest, and the arms of Aeneas, will be read as long as Rome shall be capital of the world she triumphs o'er.][23]

The 'dum' (as long as) in line 26 is a qualifier, however, hinting against Rome's imperishability, and so perhaps against Virgil's; and in the succeeding two lines (27–28) Ovid replaces Rome with Cupid, re-introducing him as another coordinate of time, one perhaps more favouring Ovid himself: 'donec erunt ignes arcusque Cupidinis arma, / discentur numeri, culte Tibulle, tui' (as long as flames and bow are the arms of Cupid, thy numbers shall be conned, O elegant Tibullus). Although the lines eventually resolve themselves into a compliment to Tibullus, the trick of the verse, by delaying his naming, tempts the reader to apply the description, at first, and incongruously, to Virgil, then to Tibullus – and eventually to Ovid himself, who later identifies with Tibullus

---

[22] Text and translation from *Heroides and Amores*, trans. Grant Showerman, 2nd edn, revised G. P. Goold (London, 1977), vol. I, I.i.1–4.

[23] The lines play upon Virgil's self-composed epitaph, 'Mantua me genuit, Calabri rapuere, tenet nunc / Parthenope; cecini pascua rures duces' (Mantua bore me, Calabria snatched me away, now Parthenope holds me; I have sung pastures, countryside, leaders) and possibly, as Edwards has pointed out, also provisional lines removed from the beginning of the *Aeneid*: 'Ille ego qui quondam gracili avena / carmen et egressus silvis vicina coegi / ut quamvis avido parerent arva colono, / gratum opus agricolis, at nunc horrentia Martis / arma viurmque cano' (I am he who once tuned my song on a slender reed, then, leaving the woodland, constrained the neighbouring fields to serve the husbandman, however grasping – a work welcome to farmers: but now of Mars' bristling arms and the man I sing); see Edwards, *Invention and Authorship*, 96–97.

while mourning him (*Amores* III.ix.1–68).[24] Read closely, however, like so many of Ovid's expositions, the elegy for Tibullus cuts in several directions, before bringing Ovid himself out on top (7–8, 13):

> ecce, puer Veneris fert eversamque pharetram
> et fractos arcus et sine luce facem ...
> fratris in Aeneae sic illum funere dicunt
>
> [See, the child of Venus comes, with quiver reversed, with bows broken, and lightless torch ... In such plight, they say, he was at Aeneas his brother's laying away.]

The trick here is that, with Aeneas dead, and Cupid bow- and torchless, it's Ovid himself who is left, singing alone, 'the glory of the Paeglignians'.[25] The epithet is shrewdly chosen.[26]

Gower thus might well have retained Ovid as a model, seeking in his ambitious footsteps the literary immortality that the latter so often wrote about: the way forward is there to be followed. Chaucer, after all, includes Ovid with Virgil (albeit while ahead of Homer, nonetheless following Virgil in the list), Lucan, and Statius as one of the *auctores primi* to whom he sends his 'litel bok', *Troilus and Criseyde*.[27] And 'moral Gower' had obviously read a poem

---

[24] i.e., 'pascitur in vivis Livor; post fata quiescit, / cum suus ex merito quemque tuetur honos. / ergo etiam cum me supremus adederit ignis, / vivam, parsque mei multa superstes erit' (It is the living that Envy feeds upon; after doom it stirs no more, when each man's fame guards him as he deserves. I, too, when the final fires have eaten up my frame, shall still live on, and the great part of me survive my death). Text and trans. Showerman, *Heroides and Amores* I.378–79. Joseph D. Reed, 'Ovid's Elegy on Tibullus and Its Models', *Classical Philology* 92, no. 3 (1997): 260–69, makes the similar point, that 'Ovid's revisionary treatment is part of his parodistic absorption of Tibullus into Ovidian poetics' (261).

[25] 'Paeglignae dicar gloria gentis.'

[26] The fuller passage is instructive here, not least for its competitive geography: 'Mantua Vergilio, gaudet Verona Cattullo / Paeglignae dicar gloria gentis ego / quam sua libertas ad honesta coegerat armas / cum timult socias anxia Roma manus. / atque aliquis spectans hospes Sulmonis aquosi / moenia, quae campi iugera pauca tenent / "Quae tantum", dicat, "potuistis ferre poetam / quantulacumque estis, vos ego magna voco."' (Mantua joys in Virgil, Verona in Catullus; 'tis I shall be called the glory of the Paeglignians, race whom their love of freedom compelled to honourable arms when anxious Rome was in fear of the allied bands; and some stranger, looking on watery Sulmo's walls, that guard the scant acres of her plain, may say, 'O thou who couldst beget so great a poet, however small thou art, I name thee mighty!'). In present context, the comparison of 'anxious Rome' with 'Paeglignians, race whom their love of freedom compelled to honourable arms' would seem suggestive.

[27] *T&C* V.1786, 1792.

commended to him, 'to vouchen sauf, ther nede is, to correcte'.[28] But in his new verse – after he finished the *Confessio* for the first time, at an unknown date, but certainly by the early 1390s – Gower again moves away from Ovid.

It is important, however, to stress *new* verse. Of the major, and secondary, pieces clustered immediately around the turn of the new century – the *Cronica Tripertita* and *In Praise of Peace, O recolende, Rex celi Deus* – only the last shows any Ovidian influence.[29] Thirty-four of the fifty-six lines of *Rex celi Deus*, presumably assembled in celebration of Henry IV's 'election' on 30 September 1399, are wholly or in part borrowed from Ovid, most from *Ars Amatoriae* and *Tristia*. Gower's immediate source was not Ovid, however, or not Ovid directly: rather, it was his own *Vox Clamantis*. The bulk of the *Rex celi Deus* appears there, first written with Richard II in mind. Gower, perhaps working under pressure of time, merely recycled and re-arranged his existing material, conforming it the better to fit Henry.[30] More indicative, clearly, of Gower's new Ovid-less direction is that his last major Latin poem, the *Cronica Tripertita*, where one might expect to find Ovidian fingerprints, contains not a trace of Ovid at all.[31]

How to explain this late shift away from Ovid? Short of resurrecting Gower himself, we have no sure way to know, obviously. And indeed there may have been a confluence of reasons. Galloway has plausibly suggested that Gower's developing blindness cut off 'his ability to browse big books', and that the politics of his final years called for 'simpler, sententious verse'.[32] Siân Echard, in a typically acute essay on Gower's poetics that includes close study of *O*

---

[28] *T&C* V.1856, 1858.

[29] *O Deus immense*, although sometimes dated 1399–1400 (e.g., George R. Coffman, 'John Gower, Mentor for Royalty: Richard II', *PMLA* 69, no. 4 (1954): 953–64), was probably written earlier, around 1397–98, as general advice to kings, and does not reflect the charges brought against Richard at his deposition.

[30] The borrowed lines come from *VC* VI. xviii* 1159–98*, originally composed for Richard II. The evidence is that the original lines appear alone in MSS Oxford, Bodleian Library MS Digby 138, Dublin, Trinity College MS D.4.6, and Hertfordshire, Hatfield House; in Oxford, Bodleian Library MS Laud 719, and Lincoln, Cathedral Library MS 235 (A. 7. 2) they appear together with a version revised after the ascension of Henry IV. The five other extant MSS of *VC*, including Oxford, All Souls College MS 98 (Macaulay's copytext), contain this revised, post-usurpation version, inscribed over erasure. What seems clear is that in *Rex celi Deus* Gower recycled his own work, from the pre-usurpation *VC*; the substitution of the revised portion occurred after Henry's election.

[31] The sources are predominantly the articles of Richard II's deposition in the so-called 'Record and Process' of the 'Parliament' of September 1399, and the Old Testament; see David R. Carlson's commentary in *John Gower: Poems on Contemporary Events*, ed. Carlson, trans. A. G. Rigg (Toronto, 2011), 330–81.

[32] Galloway, 'Gower's Ovids', 456.

recolende and *Rex celi Deus*, has argued persuasively that in these late poems, and in *In Praise of Peace*, 'Gower found his *vox*... in the polyphony of his double – or rather triple – tongue.'[33] Yet a third reason, in no way incompatible with these, may be a narrowing preoccupation with posterity – a 'Petrarchan gaze', one might call it – uncoverable in the verse of Gower's closing years, and in the concerns of the literary circle around him.

Populating that circle with any exactness is more difficult in Gower's case than in Chaucer's. As far as we know, Gower wrote no occasional verse addressed to contemporaries, nothing comparable to Chaucer's 'Truth' (to Vache), 'Lenvoy a Scogan', or 'Lenvoy a Bukton', that could suggest a relationship based around letters. The closest he came to that mode of writing are his addresses to royalty, variously to Richard and to Henry, and to Chaucer himself, in the early version of the *Confessio Amantis*.[34] But after Chaucer – and the kings, for it is important to hold them in mind – the list of literary conversants is essentially blank.[35] The existence of such a Gowerian circle can be inferred, notwithstanding. The evidence is two short poems present in many manuscripts of Gower's work, one probably by Gower himself, one possibly not.[36] The latter, *Quam cinxere freta*, is a mere two unisonant hexameter couplets (possible translations are provided in the following pages): 'Quam cinxere freta Gower tua carmina leta / Per loca discreta canit Anglia laude repleta. / Carminis Athleta satirus tibi sive Poeta / Sit laus completa quo gloria stat sine meta.' In Oxford, Bodleian Library MS Fairfax 3 (Macaulay's copytext for his edition), the verses are prefaced by the heading 'Epistola super huius opusculi sui complementum Iohanni Gower a quodam philosopho transmissa' (A letter about the completion of this, his little work, sent to John Gower by a certain philosopher).[37] The 'quodam philosopho' has been tentatively identified as Ralph Strode, a Fellow of Merton College, Oxford, and possibly the Strode to whom, alongside Gower,

---

[33] Siân Echard, 'How Gower Found His Vox: Latin and John Gower's Poetics', *Journal of Medieval Latin* 26 (2016): 291–314, at 314.

[34] *CA* VIII.2941*–56*.

[35] Gower calls attention to Richard's interest in the *Confessio*, not only in English at the beginning of the Ricardian version (*CA* Prol.24*–92*) but also in the Latin *Explicit* in that version. See esp. Echard's discussion, 'Last Words', 101–5; and further David R. Carlson's of the Henrician replacement, in Carlson, *Gower and Anglo-Latin Verse* (Toronto, 2021), 148–49.

[36] Echard, for example, counts twenty-nine of the forty-nine known manuscripts of the *Confessio* containing *Quam cinxere*, cautioning that a significant number have lost final leaves: see Echard, 'Last Words', 100.

[37] For text and translation, see *John Gower: The Minor Latin Works*, ed. and trans. R. F. Yeager (Kalamazoo, 2005), 86; Macaulay prints the poem at the end of the *Confessio*, *Works*, III.479.

Chaucer commended his *Troilus*.[38] There is some evidence – very slight – that Strode wrote verses, and it is possible *Quam cinxere* should be attributed to him.[39] Certainly the straining after ornate affect evident in the metrical handling of the verses smacks of the schools; 'Athleta' in line 3 is rare in contemporary Latin, and appearing – if it is Gower's – only here, in any form in his trilingual corpus.[40]

Strode's authorship, if actual, is interesting in several ways. If the 'opusculi' referred to in the prose heading is the *Confessio*, following which all known copies of *Quam cinxere* appear, then it may provide some proof of when Gower finished at least one version of his major English poem – for Ralph Strode died in 1387.[41] More implicative for present purposes, however, is what *Quam cinxere* can tell us about the existence and interests of Gower's literary circle. There are several ways to understand *Quam cinxere*. Some years ago, I translated it this way: 'O Gower, enclosed by the sea and filled with praise / England, throughout many regions, recites your joyous poetry. / Master of verse, satirist – or Poet – for you / May praise be full where glory stands without end.'[42]

Although the above is the more likely, a second possibility is this: 'How decorated for wreathing, Gower, your felicitous poetry! / Throughout diverse places England sings, full of praise. / Master of verse, satirist, or rather Poet, to you / May praise be full, where glory stands without end.'

The most immediately suggestive words in either version – the powerful words, one might say – occur in the third line: 'satirus ... sive Poeta', and the fourth: 'laus completa quo gloria stat sine meta'. Gower was certainly a satirist, in the manner understood in the Middle Ages. 'Poeta' however invokes something new: *authorship* of a classical sort. It is high praise and vaults Gower into company with 'Virgile, Ovide, Omer, Lucan, and Stace.' That unavoidable reading urges others similar: 'quam cinxere' as 'how decorated

---

[38] The idea that Strode was the author of *Quam cinxere* and *Eneidos, bucolis* originated with Macaulay: see his note, *Works*, III.549–50.

[39] 'A marginal note in the *Catalogus vetus* of Merton College describes Strode (with the Christian name added later as "Rad.") in these words: "nobilis poeta fuit et versificavit librum elegiacum vocata *Fantasma Radulphi*" [He was a noble poet and versified a book of elegies called *Fantasma Radulphi*].' J. D. North, 'Strode, Ralph (d. 1387), Scholastic Philosopher and Lawyer', Oxford Dictionary of National Biography, 25 May 2006, https://doi.org/10.1093/ref:odnb/26673.

[40] The *Dictionary of Medieval Latin from British Sources* lists it as the 5,535th most frequent word. For discussion of Gower's own use of schools-based 'mannerism', see Carlson, *Anglo-Latin Verse*, 155–61, at 161.

[41] North, 'Strode, Ralph': 'Strode died in London in 1387, judging by a record of his will, now lost.'

[42] *Gower: Minor Latin Poems*, 86.

for wreathing' (one would assume with laurel), 'quo gloria stat sine meta' as unending literary fame, with 'glory' being a potentially freighted choice.[43]

Many of these elements recur in a second poem, *Eneidos, bucolis*, also sometimes attributed to Strode – though here, the greater sophistication of the verses almost certainly implicates Gower's authorship. The comparison in *Eneidos, bucolis* is directly with Virgil, whose *Aeneid*, *Bucolics*, and *Georgics* are contrasted with the *Mirour de l'Omme*, *Vox Clamantis*, and *Confessio Amantis*:

> Eneidos, bucolis, que georgica metra perhennis
> Virgilio laudis serta dedere scolis;
> Hiis tribus ille libris prefertur honore poetis,
> Romaque precipius laudibus instat eis.
> Gower, sicque tuis tribus est dotata libellis
> Anglia, morigeris quo tua scripta series.[44]

> [The meters of the *Aeneid*, *Bucolics*, and *Georgics*, woven together by Virgil, have given matter of perennial praise to the schools. On account of these three books, he is preferred in honour over all poets, and Rome bestows upon them its chief praises. Thus too, Gower, with your three little books is England endowed, where you accommodate your writings to serious things.]

Ultimately, the poem prefers Gower over Virgil, on grounds that while Virgil wrote only in Latin, Gower composed in three languages ('trinis tria scribere carmina linguis', line 9), and on Christian topics rather than pagan ('Ludus et in studiis musa pagana suis / Set tua Cristiicolis fulget scriptura renatis', lines 14–15).

It is instructive to set these two short poems briefly beside *Quia unusquisque*, a colophon unquestionably Gower's work.[45] This appears in most manuscripts of the *Confessio Amantis* and would seem to contribute to a discussion about literary value ongoing in *Eneidos, bucolis* and *Quam cinxere*. 'Because each one is obliged to impart to others what he has received from God', Gower writes in *Quia*, he will describe 'three books especially composed by him ... for the purpose of bringing instruction to the attention of others' (*Quia unusquisque*

---

[43] Interestingly, an alternative headnote to *Quam cinxere* in seven manuscripts reads 'operis' rather than the diminutive 'opusculi', appearing in ten; seven more have both ('operis vel opusculi'). As Echard observes, '*operis* has its appeal ... with its connotations of Latinate *gravitas* and *auctoritas*' (Echard, 'Last Words', 107).

[44] Macaulay, *Complete Works*, IV.361.

[45] As, apparently, many scribes did: of the forty-nine extant MSS of the *CA*, fifteen place *Quam cinxere* directly ahead of *Quia unusquisque*. See *A Descriptive Catalogue of the English Manuscripts of John Gower's Confessio Amantis*, ed. Derek Pearsall and Linne Mooney (Cambridge, 2021), and Echard, 'Last Words', Appendix, 113–15.

prout a Deo accepit aliis impartiri tenetur... tres libros per ipsum ... doctrina causa compositos ad aliorum noticiam).[46] Taken together, the two poems – *Quam cinxere* and *Eneidos, bucolis* – register a similar recognition: the laurel wreath of lasting poetic fame is the goal, Virgil and his three works the model to be emulated (or surpassed) to secure it. And as *Quia unusquisque* suggests, if properly effected, the endeavour can be godly. We can, I think, consider *Quam cinxere, Eneidos, bucolis,* and *Quia unusquisque* fruits of conversation within Gower's literary circle, one that perhaps included Strode for a time, but certainly Chaucer – who would have brought to that discourse Petrarch, if not *in propria persona* then certainly as an influential voice.[47]

It is worthwhile, in this regard, to think further, briefly, about what Chaucer ventriloquising a Petrarchan 'voice' would have contributed. For one thing, perhaps, the idea itself of a circle devoted to discussion of literary matters: Petrarch outlines the shape of an ideal gathering of that kind in his *Familiares* XVIII.10; such a group existed in Florence, focused around his work.[48] Chaucer calls Petrarch 'the lauriat poete',[49] suggesting his possible knowledge of Petrarch's self-orchestrated laureation ceremony in Rome in 1341, and – more importantly – of the content, if not the actual text, of the accompanying 'coronation oration' Petrarch delivered there on 8 April. If so, Chaucer might have shared such of Petrarch's thoughts as these: 'The poet's reward is beyond question multiple, for it consists, firstly, in the charm of

---

[46] For full text, see Macaulay, *Works*, IV.360.

[47] Sebastian Sobecki has suggested that a 'Chaucerian' circle met in Southwark and included 'Gower and the Kentish magnates of the Tooley Street enclave, such as Lord Cobham and Sir Arnold Savage, civil servants and scriveners based in Southwark and perhaps even the household of [Bishop] Wykeham's Winchester residence.' He also opines Thomas Usk might have made one, and names two Southwark scriveners, John Brynchele and Thomas Spencer, as well. See Sobecki, 'A Southwark Tale: Gower, the 1381 Poll Tax, and Chaucer's *The Canterbury Tales*', *Speculum* 92, no. 3 (2017): 650. Brynchele and Spencer, while owners of copies of, respectively, the *Canterbury Tales* and *Troilus*, were scribes, but also brothel-keepers, among other unsavoury enterprises, and so seem unlikely members of a Gowerian circle. On both, see Martha Carlin, 'Thomas Spencer, Southwark Scrivener (d. 1428): Owner of a Copy of Chaucer's *Troilus* in 1394?', *Chaucer Review* 49, no. 4 (2015): 387–401. A likelier possibility, for a Gowerian circle, would be Richard Maidstone, who did adopt Gower's plain-style hexameters in his *Concordia facta inter regem et cives Londonie*; see A. G. Rigg, *A History of Anglo-Latin Literature 1066–1422* (Cambridge, 1992), 285. His participation, however, would have been short-lived: Maidstone died in 1392.

[48] Letter to Francesco Nelli; see *Letters on Familiar Matters*, vol. 3, ed. and trans. Aldo S. Bernardo (New York, 2005), 61; on the 'Petrarchan Academy', see David Wallace, *Chaucerian Polity: Absolutist Lineages and Associational Forms in England and Italy* (Stanford, CA, 1997), 264–65.

[49] Quotation from the 'Clerk's Tale', IV (E). 31.

personal glory ... and secondly, in the immortality of one's name.'[50] The outward manifestation of that glory was clear: 'Great poets, having attained to the highest and most illustrious mastery of their art, have received the laurel crown they had deserved.' And for Petrarch, the supreme example of poetic mastery, who gave his own laureation meaning, was 'Virgil, the very father of poets.'[51]

But Gower had problems with Virgil. As in Ovid's work, a clear distrust, even a detestation, of the worldly pretensions of *imperium* runs through Gower's writing. When Ovid speaks of it, and of Augustus, it is difficult to accept the triumphalism of those passages ingenuously.[52] Gower, who understood government as a compact between ruler and ruled, would not have missed Ovid's scepticism submerged in such passages.[53] For Gower also equated empires with tyrants.[54] *Vox Clamantis* VI.623–26, intended to advise the young Richard II, captures his views succinctly:[55]

> Non te pretereat populi fortuna potentis
> Publica, set sapiens talia fata cave.
> Vita Pharaonis et gesta maligna Neronis,
> Que iusto regi sunt fugienda docent.
>
> [Let not the people's common weal escape your eye,
> By being wise avoid calamities.
> Pharaoh's life and Nero's wicked deeds teach us
> Those things from which a just king should flee far.][56]

---

[50] The sentence following would have interested both Richard II and Henry IV: 'This immortality is itself two-fold, for it includes both the immortality of the poet's own name and the immortality of the names of those whom he celebrates.'

[51] Quotes from 'Petrarch's Coronation Oration', trans. Ernest Hatch Wilkins, *Studies in the Life and Works of Petrarch* (Cambridge, MA, 1955), at 305, 304, 302, respectively.

[52] See, e.g., *Metamorphoses* XV.807–70; *Tristia* I.ii.95–110; and also Gower, *Rex celi Deus*, 39, 47; and further Leo C. Curran, 'Transformation and Anti-Augustanism in Ovid's *Metamorphoses*', *Arethusa* 5 (1972): 71–91, esp. 82–90.

[53] See Matthew Giancarlo, 'Gower's Governmentality: Revisiting John Gower as a Constitutional Thinker and Regiminal Writer', in *John Gower: Others and the Self*, ed. Russell A. Peck and R. F. Yeager (Cambridge, 2017).

[54] The exemplary case is Gower's assessment of Alexander's insatiable will to conquer as 'a failure of both self-governance and adherence to moral education', the opposite of a model to emulate. See Charles Russell Stone, *From Tyrant to Philosopher King: A Literary History of Alexander the Great in Medieval and Early Modern England* (Turnhout, 2013), 142.

[55] John H. Fisher identified this section of *VC* as an 'Epistle to the King'; see Fisher, *John Gower: Moral Philosopher and Friend of Chaucer* (New York, 1964), 107, 183–85, 302, n. 28.

[56] See also *CA* VII.2905–17, 3073–83, 3103–41 for succinct statements of Gower's

This position never wavers: Gower's harshest charge in the *Cronica Tripertita* against the deposed Richard is tyrannical imperialism.[57]

For Gower the Ovidian, these beliefs apparently meant most of a creative lifetime skirting the *Aeneid* (and minimising Aeneas himself, as a betrayer, of Troy, of Dido) – a point that will be rejoined below.[58] No quotation from Virgil's epic occurs until the *Visio Anglie*, and there only on two occasions, in undistinguished lines.[59] More tellingly, despite the suspicion of various scholars that Virgil's poem lies behind some of Gower's descriptions, in the *Visio* especially, these two lines are also the only certain evidence that he read the actual *Aeneid*, or indeed any of Virgil at all.[60] Gower never quotes, or alludes to, either the *Eclogues* or the *Georgics*.[61] They are not his kind of poetry, of course, but clearly he knew of them, or had some idea, and from early on: at the very least, both works are often mentioned in instructional commentaries such as Servius's, which one can reasonably suppose was part of Gower's schooling. And Gower had other opportunities, as well.

So it is important to be clear about what is intended by 'read'. If, for example, Gower derived his centonic style in the *Visio* from Proba, then he encountered there a great deal of Virgil, though perhaps not in an appreciable way.[62] On the other hand, if by 'read' is meant the complete *Aeneid*, cover-to-cover, or the *Eclogues* or the *Georgics*, poring over them the way he

---

view of royal responsibility vis-à-vis the people and the law; *CA* VII.3102–3386 and VIII.3064–79 on tyranny specifically.

[57] See, e.g., *Cronica* III.27-32.

[58] See *CA* I.1091–1106,1124 (Troy); IV.78–137; VIII.2552–53; (Dido). Siân Echard has interrogated, and dismissed, the notion that Gower's use of 'canam' in line 2 of the initial Latin poem of the *CA* is an intentional nod to 'Arma virumque cano ...' that opens the *Aeneid*. See 'With Carmen's Help: Latin Authorities in the *Confessio Amantis*', *Studies in Philology* 95 (1998): 1–40, esp. 27.

[59] I.e., *Aeneid* IV.173 at *Visio* 1231; *Aeneid* VI.727 at *Visio* 1403.

[60] See, among others, Maria Wickert, *Studien zu John Gower* (Cologne, 1953), esp. 51–52.

[61] Stockton has claimed, *Major Latin Works*, 451, 479, that *Eclogues* X.69 ('Omnia vincit amor') influenced *Vox* VI.999, and III.93 ('latet anguis in herba') *Cronica* II.345; both, however, were commonplaces. Gower also uses the former in the prologue to the *Visio*, 7, in *Ecce patet tensus*, 3, and an altered version at *Vox* V.147 ('Sic amor omnia domat'); cf. also, famously, Chaucer, *Canterbury Tales* I(A).162. Gotthard Walz, *Das Sprichwort bei Gower mit besonderem Hinweis auf Quellen und Parallelen* (Nördlingen, 1907), 56, finds it in multiple *loci* in French, as well as in Sophocles' *Antigone* 781ff. (56, n. 1). Stockton himself recognises the latter as 'proverbial' (479); its use was too widespread by the fourteenth century to base an originary claim on it. Cf. Chaucer, *Canterbury Tales*, III (D).1994–95, V(F).512, and citations in Walz, 20.

[62] See R. F. Yeager, 'Did Gower Write Cento?', in *Recent Readings: Papers Presented at the Meetings of the John Gower Society at the International Congress on*

obviously had over Ovid, then one needs first to ask after their accessibility. Christopher Baswell lists thirty-seven extant manuscripts of Virgil's three works 'copied in England during the Middle Ages, or produced elsewhere but owned in England up to the dissolution of the monasteries in 1542'.[63] Of these, ten contain the *Eclogues*, *Georgics*, and the *Aeneid* together; and, while twenty-five (including binding fragments) were produced prior to Gower's death, only two were copied in England in the fourteenth century. In contrast, six derive from the thirteenth century, twelve from the twelfth – and ten from the fifteenth. Of the twelfth-century manuscripts, however, eight have annotations in fourteenth-century hands.[64] These are interesting numbers, for several reasons. They imply that, first, as the many later annotations in earlier manuscripts indicate, what initially seems a fourteenth-century dip in production of *Aeneid* copies results from plenitude, not a contemporary lack of interest. So Gower undoubtedly could have come by a Virgil, had he wanted.[65] Second, if Gower indeed found an *Aeneid*, he would likely have discovered the *Eclogues* and *Georgics* alongside it – which makes his apparent lack of interest in either (not even the Fourth *Eclogue*) quite striking. More striking still, however – and this is the third point – is how little use Gower seems to have made of Virgil's works, if copies were readily available. It implies that the two previously mentioned borrowings identifiable in the *Visio* resulted not from *in propria forma* reading of the *Aeneid*, but possibly came from an excerpt, perhaps a school commentary or florilegium, instead.

This conclusion, moreover, is suggestive in turn. Notably, first, it helps to explain in part Gower's puzzling treatment of Virgil in poems written prior to *Eneidos, bucolis* and (if his) *Quam cinxere*. 'Virgil' – a character, not the poet – appears just three times in Gower's *oeuvre*, at first glance somewhat strangely cast as a magician, and as a befuddled lover. These narratives draw exclusively, however, not on any life of the poet Gower would have encountered in, say, the grammars of Servius or Donatus, or derived from any of Virgil's works, but rather on what Domenico Comparetti has called the 'Virgil of popular legend.'[66] Thus, in his sole entrance in the *Mirour de l'Omme*

Medieval Studies, Western Michigan University, 1983–88, ed. R. F. Yeager (Kalamazoo, 1989), 113–32.

[63] See Christopher Baswell, *Virgil in Medieval England: Figuring the Aeneid from the Twelfth Century to Chaucer* (Cambridge, 1995), Appendix I, 285–308, at 285.

[64] Listed by Baswell, *Virgil*, 389, n.1.

[65] Indeed, as early as 1379–80, Gower might have got a look at an *Aeneid* through Chaucer, who seems to have been working directly from the text while writing the *House of Fame*. See, among others, Baswell, *Virgil*, 220–48.

[66] See Domenico Comparetti, *Vergil in the Middle Ages*, 2nd edn, trans. E. F. M. Benecke (London, 1908; rpt Hamden, 1966), 239–357; but also the corrective of Fabio Stok, 'Virgil between the Middle Ages and the Renaissance', *International Journal of*

(14725–48), 'Virgil' becomes the creator of a magic mirror that alerts the Romans to approaching enemies – a role Gower re-creates for him, albeit to different purpose and in more elaborate detail, in the *Confessio Amantis* V.2031–2208. The unsuccessfully amorous Virgil surfaces, briefly, at *CA* VI.98 and VIII.2714–17.

That Gower should turn to such stories rather than the work of the poet himself casts light, I think, not only on that distaste for Virgilian epical triumphalism noted earlier, but highlights as well two ancillary points of attendant relevance. The first of these underscores Gower's aversion to Aeneas. The kind of alternative material that yielded him the magician and amorous Virgil would also have presented Gower with conflicting views of Virgil's hero, not all of them flattering. The suspicion, traceable to at least the fifth century BC,[67] that Aeneas together with Antenor betrayed Troy is maintained by Servius,[68] and followed in the versions of the Troy story that were Gower's better sources: Dictys Cretensis's *Ephemeris belli Troiani*, Dares Phrygius's *De Excidio Troiae Historia*, Guido delle Colonne's *Historia destructionis Troiae*, and – in different form – Benoît de Sainte-Maure's *Roman de Troie*. Gower engages with this negative Aeneas in *Confessio* I.1077–1128, using Antenor and Aeneas as examples of 'ipocrisie'. Betrayal, although classified as a form of Sloth, also underlies Aeneas's treatment of Dido, as detailed in *Confessio* IV.77–137.

The second ancillary point concerns Gower's general rejection of military adventurism (a sentiment he shared with Ovid), which in literary terms manifests itself as a nearly career-long concomitant avoidance of epic, particularly in its medieval incarnation as chivalric romance.[69] Not that he wasn't aware of such works: in the *Mirour*, he cites 'Lancellot et Boors' (1473), Lancelot in *Cinkante Balades* (43.3:17), 'Lancelot et Tristrams' in *Traitié pour les amantz marietz* (15.1:2), Lancelot and 'Gunnore', Tristram and Ysolde, Galahot 'with his ladi' in *Confessio* VIII.2500–4. But it is telling how no trace of the *Roman d'Eneas*, with its 'themes of patriarchy: militant aristocracy, the foundation of empire, and the establishment of royal power through battle', surfaces in Gower's work.[70] The poem was popular with the landholding class, of which Gower was a better-read member.[71] He had a high chance of knowing it.

---

the *Classical Tradition* 1 (1994): 15–22; and further Michael P. Kuczynski, 'Gower's Virgil', in *John Gower: Essays at the Millennium*, ed. R. F. Yeager (Kalamazoo, 2007), 163–87, esp. 174–80.

[67] For a compact version of the history, see Reinhold Meyer, 'The Unhero Aeneas', *Classica et Mediaevalia* 27 (1966): 195–207.

[68] E.g., his comment on *Aeneid* I. 242 – although Servius is not consistent on this point. See Robert A. Kaster, *Guardians of Language: The Grammarian and Society in Late Antiquity* (Berkeley, 1988), 169–97, esp. 190.

[69] On Gower's eirenic philosophy, see R. F. Yeager, 'Pax Poetica: On the Pacifism of Chaucer and Gower', *Studies in the Age of Chaucer* 9 (1987): 97–121.

[70] Quotation from Baswell, *Virgil*, 200.

[71] Another such was Henry Despenser, bishop of Norwich 1360–1406, whose

Along with those of Ovid, as noted above, of far greater influence, doubtless, on Gower's thinking about Virgil, Aeneas, and epic were the views of Augustine. The latter's critique of Virgil in the *Confessions* Gower could only take to heart (not registering, probably, how much the *Confessions* were shaped by the *Aeneid*);[72] Augustine's related remarks on empire in *De civitate Dei contra paganos*, few but withering, would have driven the lesson home.[73] Indeed, what mildly surprises, given Gower's singular familiarity with the works of Augustine – and possibly the allegorised Virgil of Fulgentius as well[74] – is that he never turned his hand to an alternative epical form that J. Christopher Warner has identified as 'Augustinian': poems that 'induce a vision of Augustine's spiritual journey in the experience of their readers and ... claim by that motive a justification for the poet's vocation'.[75] On further reflection, however, that Gower *wasn't* drawn in such a direction (coming closest, perhaps, only in the *Visio Anglie* and there, one thinks, incidentally) would seem further proof of how staunchly Ovidian he was, little valuing Virgil, for most of his life.

And yet, the disquieting problem I believe Gower discovered in his last years with Ovid as an aesthetic model was posterity – and hence Gower's discontent. Certainly he could feel, with Petrarch, that 'the desire for glory is innate not merely in the generality of men, but in greatest measure in those who are of some wisdom and some excellence',[76] or say, with Ovid, 'the thought of the listener excites the toiling writer; excellence grows when it is praised, and the thought of glory is a powerful spur'.[77] But as a poet of continuing transformation, and earth-bound love, Ovid fell short of that Petrarchan high seriousness that promised permanence. Virgil, alone, possessed that.

---

copy is now London, British Library MS Add. 34114 (*olim* Spalding). See further Holly James-Maddocks and R. F. Yeager, 'Bishop Henry Despenser and Manuscript Production in Late Medieval Norwich', *New Medieval Literatures* 25 (forthcoming); and Baswell, 'Aeneas in 1381', *New Medieval Literatures* 5 (2002): 8–58.

[72] On the relationship between the *Confessions* and the *Aeneid*, see in particular John O'Meara, 'Augustine the Artist and the *Aeneid*', in *Mélanges offerts à Mademoiselle Christine Mohrmann*, edited by L. J. Engels, H. W. F. M. Hoppenbrouwers, and A. J. Vermeulen (Utrecht, 1963), 253–61.

[73] *Confessions* I.xiii; *City of God* III, xiv.IV.iii, xv, xvii.

[74] Gower definitely knew Fulgentius's *Mitologiarum*, referring to it variously in the *Confessio*. His knowledge of the *Expositio Virgilianae continentiae secundum philosophos moralis* is difficult to determine, for lack of clear evidence.

[75] Warner, *The Augustinian Epic: Petrarch to Milton* (Ann Arbor, MI, 2005), 2. Warner's major examples post-date Gower, but his insight in anchoring the type in Petrarch's *Secretum* and *Africa* merits attention.

[76] 'Coronation Oration', trans. Wilkins, *Studies in the Life and Works*, 305.

[77] 'Excitat auditor stadium, laudataque virtus / crescit, et immensum gloria calcar habet.' *Ex Ponto* IV.2, ll. 35–36.

⊰ 6 ⊱

Gower's Allusive Forms: Anaphora and Political Desire in the *Visio Anglie*

STEPHANIE L. BATKIE

Medieval history writing is no stranger to embellishment or flourish. A description in *Knighton's Chronicle* of Robert Knollys' attack on Auxerre in February of 1358 tells of how the overwhelming effect of the English charge caused the townspeople to jump from the city walls to escape, if not death, then a death more painful and horrifying than that promised by the river below them. Knighton comments wryly that 'thus it was that many more were killed by terror than by the sword', and attributes this success to 'fama diuine gracie Anglorum' (the reputation of the English, by divine grace).[1] The chronicler here rather exceeds his charge of reporting historical events by '[copying] the most authentic texts he could find',[2] instead garnishing his record with details that give urgency and motion to the scene. The account orients Knighton's audience by blending the factual and descriptive with postulations of both the people's terror and the role of divine providence. In a similar manner, the Chandos Herald, narrating the aftermath of the failed negotiations at Poitiers in 1356, comments that 'if you had no part in the battle, it would have been a fine thing to watch'.[3] At these climactic moments, authorial intervention removes us momentarily from the action in order to describe both its horrific effects and to signify our critical distance from them: we are aware of both what took place on the battlefield and our absence from it. But the effect in both texts is nevertheless emphatic regarding the level of violence we are

---

[1] 'Sique factum est, quod multos plures occiderunt terrore quam gladio.' *Knighton's Chronicle 1337–1396*, ed. G. H. Martin (Oxford, 1995), 165.

[2] John Taylor, *English Historical Literature in the Fourteenth Century* (Oxford, 1987), 47.

[3] Richard Barber, ed., *The Life and Campaigns of the Black Prince: From Contemporary Letters, Diaries, and Chronicles, Including Chandos Herald's 'Life of the Black Prince'* (London, 1979), 100.

asked to imagine taking place, and each text works hard to create a sense of drama, experienced as part of reading the historical past.

Far from being extraneous, these moments of authorial commentary or interpretation within medieval chronicle fundamentally shape the writing of history in the later Middle Ages. Medieval narrative histories, especially when dealing with moments of crisis, function through a bifurcated sense of form: a tension between chronological organisation, in which temporal progression provides the primary chronicle-structure, and the use of affective and emotional engagement to create political and historical meaning.[4] The former is governed largely by the *ordinatio* required by a linear narrative – chronicles are constructed around events unfolding in time that show the desire or need of a particular group in a particular political space, made visible by their actions. The latter, affect and emotion, often offer a form of resistance or opposition to the overarching chronicle-logical *ordinatio*. They encourage readerly attention to surplus poetic details and, in doing so, open paths for obverse modes of hermeneutic engagement. As we shall see, affective *ductus*, or 'the way by which a work leads someone through itself' in order to '[set] a viewer or auditor or performer in motion within its structure', can work in concert or in counterpoint to other organisational structures, like those provided by the chronicle-form.[5] This resistance to chronicle-logical *ordinatio*, these moments where the poetic or affective causes us to pause, to visualise, to extrapolate, or to orient ourselves become, I argue, an important part of how these texts engage the past and how historical texts make visible the political structures they imagine.[6]

The union or tension between these two textual categories, *ordinatio* and *ductus*, give us the textual 'shape' of a piece of historical narrative. In her

---

[4] For *ordinatio* as part of *inventio* in medieval rhetoric, see Geoffrey of Vinsauf, *Poetria Nova*, in *Les artes poétiques du XII et du XIII siècle: Recherches et documents sur la technique littéraire du moyan age*, ed. Edmond Faral (Paris, 1924), lines 43–125; Geoffrey of Vinsauf, *Poetria Nova*, trans. Margaret F. Nims (Toronto, 2010), 20–22.

[5] '*Ductus* ... [gives] an experience more like traveling through stages along a route than like perceiving a whole object. The art of the Middle Ages does not hold up a perfect "globed fruit" but leads one in a walk along converging and diverging paths.' Mary Carruthers, 'The Concept of Ductus, or Journeying through a Work of Art', in *Rhetoric beyond Words: Delight and Persuasion in the Arts of the Middle Ages*, ed. Mary Carruthers (Cambridge, 2010), 190.

[6] I use this idea here in the way Jacques Rancière uses it to discuss the role of literary language in political *aesthesis*: 'The literary qualities of these texts, or their "literarity", refers at once to the excess of words available in relation to the thing named; to that excess relating to the requirements of the production of life, and finally, to the excess of words vis-à-vis the modes of communication that function to legitimate "the proper" itself.' Rancière and Davide Panagia, 'Dissenting Words: A Conversation with Jacques Rancière', *Diacritics* 30, no. 2 (2000): 115. See also Panagia, *Rancière's Sentiments* (Durham, 2018), 51–54.

work on medieval romance, Siân Echard has proposed a textual technology in which the material things populating narrative romance become a site of tension between the mundane and the magical. She finds these objects straddle the line between familiar, useful items and supernatural talismans: the ring that allows one to become invisible, for example, or the purse that is never empty. These material objects, particularly weapons, become 'a kind of two-way mirror. From one side, we see the fantastical technology of romance; from the other, the contemporary reality of combat. And that two-way view crystallises for us that romance is itself a thing.'[7] I propose that medieval narrative reportage functions in much the same way. Rather than a collocation between the practical and the fantastic as in romance, however, these texts work by juxtaposing affective poetic forms and narrated historical events to produce the 'thing' or, perhaps more appropriately, the 'material form' of the political past. Following Echard's argument about the materiality of romance, I would like to argue that a turn to ductile, material poetics gives us history writing as a machine of affective forms. That is, authors use rhetorical and poetic techniques, techniques materially present in the language on the page, to initiate aesthetic responses in readers that generate affects and desires around the 'experienced' historical events. As we read, we can be moved down the page by the progression of time, but more commonly by a poetics that generates forms of readerly desire in its audience: desires such as an interest in moving forward in the narrative, the desire to celebrate or condemn events being described, or desires that follow along with hegemonic, state-sanctioned modes of political subjectivity. The initiation of such desires might work to confirm previously held assumptions regarding political power readers bring with them into the text, but not necessarily. Similarly, the text itself may share the political desires of the individual figures or groups they describe in their pages (that of rulers or, conversely, of those rebelling against them), but they often do not. If these sets of *desiderata* (reader and text, text and *materia*) do not align, the familiar *ordinatio* of chronicle (the lives of kings, the progression of dates, the delimiting of noteworthy events, etc.) comes up against an oppositional, affective *ductus* – the path by which we are drawn through the text. Reading with this in mind, we quickly find that each chronicler approaches how much or how little *ductus* aligns with *ordinatio* to create their account's particular poetic landscape. As such, we can begin to categorise different types of historical narratives based on how they conflate or delineate these two structures and these two forms of political desire. Finally, we can use

---

[7] Siân Echard, '*De Ortu Walwanii* and *Historia Meriadoci*: Technologies of/in Romance', in *Handbook of Arthurian Romance: King Arthur's Court in Medieval European Literature*, ed. Leah Tether, Johnny McFadyen, Keith Busby, and Ad Putter (Berlin, 2017), 498.

this to uncover a wider range of historical approaches to seemingly familiar events, like those taking place in the London of June 1381.

In the dream-vision of the *Visio anglie*, Book 1 of Gower's *Vox clamantis*, Gower charts the 1381 attack on the city and the assault on the Tower of London in anything but a straight line. Rather than relying on measured chronology, the *ordinatio* he enlists is one of fluid and recursive emotional response generated through poetic forms and literary allusion. As David Carlson and Maria Wickert note, the taking of the city happens in three different forms and from three different perspectives.[8] We first see the peasants, transformed into beasts, precipitating the fall of New Troy; we then see Gower made into an exile in his own home by the ravaging crowd; and we see him finally on a Boethian-inspired ship, tossed amid the waves of political turmoil. The third of these reflects figuratively on the unrest the poet is supposedly witnessing and, much like the ship itself, is unmoored from solid or dependable points of chronological reference. In part, we might say that this is Gower taking full advantage of the affordances of the dream-vision form.[9] But more critically, the accumulative narrative effect is to transform a recorded sequence of historical events experienced by many into a personal, affective text whose *ductus* doubles the ruin of the city by dislocating readers' sense of historical space and time.[10] And nowhere is this more apparent than in the portions of the text where Gower uses poetic forms, forms so evident they seem almost

---

[8] Carlson finds that Gower used 'three differing approaches to telling the same thing' when it comes to the events in the *Visio*: a 'historical-legendary version', an 'uncannily disorienting type of exile', and finally, an allegorical version in 'the figure of a ship at sea beset by a storm'. David R. Carlson, 'Gower *Agonistes* and Chaucer on Ovid (and Virgil)', *The Modern Language Review* 109, no. 4 (2014): 936–37. Wickert uses a slightly different scheme, which divides the poem into the 'Beast Vision', the 'Troy Vision', and the 'Ship Vision'. She is careful to note that 'the three visions do not represent independent stages of an historical occurrence ... instead there appear to be [between visions two and three] chronological overlappings, or at least obscurities'. *Studies in John Gower*, trans. Robert J. Meindl (Washington, DC, 1981), 31.

[9] For an incredibly useful analysis of how the oft-overlooked dream vision form of the poem shapes its meaning, moving it from political critique to internal, moral critic that interrogates and recognises the poet's own complicity, see Andrew Galloway, 'Reassessing Gower's Dream Visions', in *John Gower, Trilingual Poet: Language, Translation, and Tradition*, ed. Elizabeth Dutton, with John Hines and R. F. Yeager (Cambridge, 2010).

[10] Matthew Irvin also discusses this phenomenon, arguing that the ship and the use of Ovid's exilic poetry in this section of the *Visio* shows us how Gower 'takes the *political* position of exile onto his textual persona' and in so doing creates an affective political sphere. Irvin, *The Poetic Voices of John Gower: Politics and Personae in the Confessio Amantis* (Cambridge, 2014), 38–39. For more on Gower's struggle as a shipwrecked exile in the *Vox*, see Kobayashi Yoshiko, 'The Voice of an Exile: From

material, physical objects themselves, to align the chaotic terror he wants to convey with what it *feels* like to read about it.

Throughout the poem, Gower's lines often work to dramatically and concretely disrupt the flow of events being described, much as the larger *ordinatio* of the text folds in and over itself. He accomplishes this in a variety of ways, using what Ian Cornelius has called his 'unbridled imagination' to sculpt internal rhyming patterns, polyptoton, classical allusion, and so on that alter the rhythm of events from measured linear chronology to a kind of syncopated, poetic time.[11] These forms circle back, echo, counter, and distort. Despite (or perhaps because of) his claims to *reportage*, Gower is not counting the hours or beating out the timely progression of events; he is sounding out and lyrically embodying the disorienting response he is (supposedly) experiencing. There is much yet to be said regarding his interest in such techniques, particularly in how he uses them to draw together his position towards the classical past and the political perspective he holds in the rest of the *Vox*. Here, however, I would like to focus on only one example: his dramatic use of anaphora as a formal counterpoint to the more overt use of quotations from authoritative sources, mainly Ovid. Carlson, in his commentary on the *Visio*, locates four places in the poem where Gower uses extended anaphora: the first, a dazzling series of anaphoric sequences in one of his early descriptions of the allegorised beast-peasants' monstrous and bloodthirsty condition (623–70); the second and third, in which he dips into a kind of *occupatio* in glossing over the various horrors of his flight (1415–20) and laments what he has seen during his 'wakeful sleeps' (2141–46); and the fourth, detailing the assault and taking of the Tower of London by the surging, insurgent crowd (1743–64). In some sense, we can tie this affection for anaphoric form to Gower's larger propensity to turn to Ovidian allusion at moments of political and poetic crisis. Carlson notes that anaphora was a useful form for Ovid across much of his writing and that 'Gower appears to have been attracted to the Ovidian anaphoras with unusual frequency.'[12] Of course, Ovid is not alone in his use of the figure. There are other sources Gower draws from for anaphora, most directly the *Speculum stultorum*, but whereas Nigel Wireker uses anaphora as part of the comedic fabric of his writing, for Gower (as often for Ovid) it is anything but.

My interest is in how Gower's anaphora affords a stuttering kind of horror that, in each of the examples listed above, is curiously bound up with expressions of political desire either on the part of the poet or on the part of the

---

Ovidian Lament to Prophecy in Book I of John Gower's Vox Clamantis', in *Through a Classical Eye*, ed. Andrew Galloway and R. F. Yeager (Toronto, 2016), 339–62.

[11] Ian Cornelius, 'Gower and the Peasants' Revolt', *Representations* 131 (2015): 23.

[12] John Gower, *Poems on Contemporary Events: The* Visio Anglie *(1381) and* Cronica Tripertita *(1400)*, ed. David R. Carlson, trans. A. G. Rigg (Toronto, 2011), 190, n. to lines 623–34.

antagonists he describes. Moreover, this connection between narrated desire and formal response, I would argue, operates differently in this poem than in the political writing of Gower's contemporaries. In Gower, the *ductus* and *ordinatio* of the poetic line become entangled with resistance to political desire, and they generate a field in which an obverse aesthetic takes over from chronological distance or propagandistic control – the two other modes we often find structuring narrative histories. Gower clearly (and quite famously) does not share in the desires of the peasants in 1381, but his mode of countering them works along lines more affective and formal than authoritative and critical because he sees shifts in *affect* as the primary *effect* of their actions. And affect turns out to be quite important for Gower.

The June events of 1381 reveal for Gower the stark fragility of political and social sense inasmuch as they demonstrate in dramatic fashion how easily markers of meaning can be captured and made to re-signify and restructure. A flexibility of signification is something that, elsewhere in the *Visio* and the *Vox*, we might most closely associate with Gower's willingness to reframe and rephrase quotations and references in his Latin work. Maura Nolan, in discussing how quotation works in the larger *Vox*, notes that 'Gower determinedly sustains a tension between deference to Latin authority ... and the display of poetic skill embodied in the fearless abandon with which he redeploys classical words and images while ruthlessly exploiting both their past and present meanings.'[13] Throughout the *Visio*, and indeed in all of Gower's Latin writing, we can see this willingness to make others' words do other things. But 1381 is different. Despite the freedom (and pleasure) he takes in reworking the literary architecture of the classical past, Gower nevertheless strenuously objects to the rebels' desire to do the same with the physical symbols and bodies that structure political authority. And so, in the midst of a poem famous for the dizzying array of quotations and modified references, Gower does something unexpected. He counters the peasants' ability to redeploy the sense of the physical symbols of monarchic power with a shift into allusive forms rather than allusive quotations.

In his formal choices, I find, Gower makes a case for feeling politically. Consider the description of the Tower's fall, rendered in a sequence of cascading images poetically hooked together through anaphoric repetition:

> O quam tunc similis huic naui Londoniarum
>   Turris erat, quod eam seua procella quatit.
> Turris egens muris, vbi sumpsit petra papiri
>   Formam, quam penetrans sordida musca terit.
> Turris, vbi porta sibi seras ferre recusat,
>   Quo patitur thalamus ingredientis onus.

---

[13] Nolan, 'Historicism after Historicism', in *The Post-Historical Middle Ages*, ed. Elizabeth Scala and Sylvia Federico (New York, 2009), 81–82.

Turris, vbi patula furiis via restat, et omnis
>   Rusticus ingrediens res rapit atque loca.
Turris, vbi vires succumbunt debilitati;
>   Turris, vbi virtus non iuuat vlla viros;
Turris in auxilium spirans, custode remoto,
>   Et sine consilio sola relicta sibi.
Turris in obprobrium patricidaque sanguine feda,
>   Cuius ineternum fama remorsa volat.
Turris, vbi rupta spelunca fuit leopardi,
>   Ipseque compulsus vt pius agnus abit.
Turris, vbi pressit vi tegula feda coronam,
>   Quo cecidit fragili sub pede forte caput.
Turris, non thuris olefacta salute sed egra,
>   Lugens non ludens, tedia queque ferens.
Turris diuisa linguis Babilonis ad instar;
>   Turris, vt est nauis Tharsis in ore maris.
Sic patitur pressa vicii sub gurgite turris,
>   Nescio qua morum parte parare viam.
Quisque dolet, sed non vt ego, dum talis amarum
>   Spectat ad interitum naufraga Cilla meum.
Hec ita sompnifero vigilans quasi lumine signa
>   Vidi, quo timui dampna futura rei.

[O now, how similar was the Tower of London to
>   That ship, as savage storms rattled it.
The Tower – missing its walls, whereby its rock took the form
>   Of paper, gnawed to pieces by the burrowing, filthy flea.
The Tower – where the gate refuses to accept its bar,
>   Where the bedchamber endures the burden of penetration.
The Tower – where the wide road spread open for the wrathful, and every
>   Penetrating peasant plundered things and places.
The Tower – where strength gives way to weakness,
>   The Tower – where virtue helps no man,
The Tower – sighing for aid, its warden removed,
>   And left alone, without counsel.
The Tower – teeming with blood amid disgrace and patricide,
>   Whose chewed-up fame flees for eternity.
The Tower – where the leopard's cave was broken,
>   And, driven out, he departed like a tender lamb.
The Tower – where, with its strength, the filthy paving stone strikes down the crown,
>   Where the mighty head topples under the brittle foot.
The Tower – not smelling of frankincense, but of ill health,
>   Lamenting not singing, it bore its suffering.
The Tower – in the image of Babylon, was divided into tongues.
>   The Tower – like the ship of Tharsis in the mouth of the sea.

> Thus, the Tower, overwhelmed, suffers under the flood of vice
> And does not know, for its part, where to find the familiar
> path.
> Thus all might grieve (but not as I do, as long as shipwrecking
> Scylla sees such a bitter ruin for me).
> Watchful, I saw these signs as if by a sleepy light,
> Whereby I feared the disasters of things yet to come; lines
> 1743–70.][14]

The language marches us down the page in disorienting but no uncertain terms. There are references here: biblical allusions to Babylon and the ship of Tharsis, both of which signify sinful excess, and the mention of Scylla, reminding us of the Boethian-ship Gower finds himself on. We also get momentary heraldic imagery here in the leopard, an image taken from the royal arms[15] – but no direct quotation. Most of Gower's description comes through his persistent use of personification as the peasants sweep through the building. The act of penetration by the crowd – the disruption of the 'normal' flow of movement through the Tower by opening up passageways to alien bodies and forces – is something that we feel more than we see. We *feel* the Tower brought low both physically and symbolically though the prosopopoeia framing the rebels' violations: it '[sighs] for aid' (1753), it 'bore its suffering' (1762), and it was 'overwhelmed' by the 'flood of vice' (1765) that overtopped its walls and rushed through its open(ed) doors. We see the space not through its own characteristics or its intended purpose, but through the movement of the rebellious forces rushing through it. In the absence of the king, it is open and available for realignment – which is precisely what happens upon the arrival of the rebel crowd.[16] In penetrating the Tower's defences, the peasants redefine the physical components of the building. Walls are no longer a sign

---

[14] Latin passages from the *Visio* are taken from Rigg's and Carlson's edition. Translations are my own.

[15] The *lion passant guardant*. Gower, *Poems on Contemporary Events*, 211, n. to line 1302. Interestingly enough, Richard himself is never named in the *Visio* and only referred to in oblique terms or by his title, *rex*. See Gower, *Poems on Contemporary Events*, 211, n. to line 1302.

[16] N.B. Gower allegorises the king's departure as transformative to the royal person as well, rendering him here as both a leopard and a lamb. Curiously, the peasants themselves, much like the space of the Tower, are also relatively undefined in this passage. We hear no descriptions of who they are or what they do. Indeed, we get almost no direct syntactical reference to them at all. The verbs here are almost entirely governed by the Tower herself, and if the actions of the rebels are mentioned, they are in the passive voice. The lack of clear description of individual leaders or details about the participants is also noted in Mark Bailey, 'The Peasants and the Great Revolt', in *Historians on John Gower*, ed. Stephen Rigby and Siân Echard (Cambridge, 2019), 184.

of royal authority. They are now indicative of the anger and power of the mob, and they become a measure of movement, making visible the scale of the crowd's anger and achievements.[17]

The apparent counter to this is the dominant poetic feature of the passage: the anaphora on 'The Tower' (*Turris* ... *Turris* ... *Turris* ..., etc.), which takes over the allusive quality by turning to Ovidian form rather than Ovidian quotation. It is tempting to take the anaphora as an attempt to stabilise the space of the royal fortress inasmuch as these lines inscribe the name of the building again and again, seemingly in an attempt to re-solidify it through language. This feels doubly true when we consider the connection between the figure and Ovidian *auctoritas*. Sylvia Federico has argued this point elsewhere; finding in Gower's language the desire to re-establish clear lines of sense and sensibility. 'Gower attempts', Federico writes, 'to smooth over London's internal conflicts in a mirage of completion, construct cohesive boundaries, and explain and blame away violations of those boundaries.'[18] However, she points out that the more Gower attempts this, the more his project slips away from him, often producing quite the opposite effect. Her reading, which addresses this passage in particular, works by deconstructing the text to reveal the implications of images, metaphors, and references that undermine the poet's attempts to stabilise the scene (and the world) around him, with particular reference to the use of sexual desire and gendered personification. I would go further. Gower, as much as he would like to render the world legible and dependable once more, is not trying to do this at all in the *Visio*, and this is not how the *ductus* of the formal allusion functions. The effect of figures like anaphora here (and even his quotations elsewhere in Book I) does not secure the Tower through poetic *compositum* or generate a kind of 'poetics of security' but rather renders the Tower as a site of affective response.[19] Or, perhaps more accurately, as a site of affective participation as

---

[17] The ability of the rebels, however well organised, to gain access to the Tower, a fortified complex of buildings designed to withstand significant armed assault, is a matter of some speculation, even in modern scholarship. It was not, presumably, accomplished by military action, and it seems likely that the rebels either benefitted from sympathisers within the Tower or entered through a show of force, even if not by force itself. See Juliet Barker, *1381: The Year of the Peasants' Revolt* (Cambridge, MA, 2014), 259–61. For the idea that the increasingly fortified Tower also historically indicates increasing royal anxiety and instability when it comes to the king's relationship with the commons (which we see coming violently to a head here), see Kristen Deiter, *The Tower of London in English Renaissance Drama: Icon of Opposition* (New York, 2008), 28–44.

[18] Sylvia Federico, 'A Fourteenth-Century Erotics of Politics: London as a Feminine New Troy', *Studies in the Age of Chaucer* 19 (1997): 129.

[19] I am thinking here of Frédéric Gros's arguments about form of security as Stoic self-composition, which in turn develops into the policing of the modern 'sovereign

the reader comes to feel the sense of not only the events Gower describes but also the nature of the political power they disrupt.

To put this in other terms, I am arguing here that the anaphoric form of this passage reveals that the Tower inhabits the political or social effect not of an *appareil* (a successful apparatus of state power) but rather of a *dispositif* (an open assemblage of significations open for capture and redistribution).[20] The peasant assault opens the Tower up to new signification, and what Gower's text generates is the disorienting horror as we shift from assumptions about the Tower as disciplinary and the Tower as dispositional. When he describes the rebels' movement through the physical space of the building, we see the Tower undergo an architectural *de casibus*, transforming from an image of royal authority into one marked primarily by violation and debasement. Before the uprising, as a symbol of power, it performed a disciplinary function: it consolidated vertical, political authority over the public imagination inasmuch as the sense of the Tower brought individuals into its structure of meaning both by organising bodies within it and in projecting signifying power over the urban landscape. It penetrated the cultural consciousness to establish political *consensus*, that feeling-together that manifests, stabilises, and augments hierarchical identities.[21] But when the building in Gower's account is penetrated in turn, the represented movement of the rebels through space gives way to a revealing process of capture.

While we might be spectators to the represented routes the peasants take as they forcibly enter and possess the building, we participate in the shame and violation that emerges primarily from the figurative language around the Tower's personification. A sharp divide occurs between Gower's narrative representation of what the peasants want (claiming the spaces of the building

---

state'. Gros, *The Security Principle: From Serenity to Regulation* (London, 2019). On *compositum* as a *desideratum* for political poetry, see Stephanie Batkie, '"Compositum in Compedibus": Scribal Panegyric in Ms Rawlinson B214', in *'Of Latine and of Othire Lare': Essays in Honour of David Carlson*, ed. Richard Firth Green and R. F. Yeager (Toronto, 2022).

[20] Gower's sense of the building creates a 'distributive arrangement of peoples, spaces, and times that may be available in the operational logics of technical objects but that do not determine how and why they function as they do at any given point of time'. The critical difference here is that the *dispositif* (rather than the *appareil*) 'moves us away from the idea of media objects as tools of domination and towards a consideration of them as sentimental instruments that arrange dispositions, attentions, and perceptabilities'. Davide Panagia, 'On the Political Ontology of the Dispositif', *Critical Inquiry* 45, no. 3 (2019): 715–16. This shift into objects as tools for perceiving structures of power and meaning should put us in mind of Echard's argument about the material and textual technologies of romance (above).

[21] Jacques Rancière, *Dissensus: On Politics and Aesthetics*, trans. Steve Cocoran (London, 2010), 38.

for their own symbolic purposes) and how readers are asked to feel about it. This is violation; this is desecration. And thus, Gower turns to metaphors of rape, which are themselves intensified by the extended anaphoric *prosopopeia* in the passage. The description of the assault on the building clearly carries with it overtones of not just violation but sexual violation as walls are breeched, gates are forcibly held open, and the building is 'defiled with blood amidst disgrace' (1755).[22] The city of London, by extension, becomes a vulnerable widow – desired and ripe for plunder:

> A dextrisque nouam me tunc vidisse putabam
>   Troiam, que vidue languida more fuit.
> Que solet ex muris cingi patuit sine muro,
>   Nec potuit seras claudere porta suas.
>
> [Just then, I believed I saw to my right New
>   Troy who, listless as a grieving widow, was tormented.
> She who was once engirded with walls is now wall-less, spread open,
>   Nor was the gate able to close fast its bolts; lines 879–82.]

The effect is not subtle. We follow the eye of the dreamer along the same path taken by the angry crowd, from the outer walls into the inner, private spaces of the building, travelling in their wake as they molest the integrity of both city and structure. The conflation of sexual attack and the political desires of the peasants should also not be underestimated. In Federico's reading, the attack on the personified Tower draws from the earlier allegorisation of the bestial nature of the peasant-rebels:

> The previous description of the rebels as generally brutish is extended here into a realm of ferociously masculine sexuality as the physical bounty of the feminine city is plundered by the animals; the madness 'plunged into any – and everything forbidden' [*in vetitum quodlibet ipse ruit*; line 900]. The initial shape-change of the rebels into animals is revised again as the invaders take on a human, criminal form to correspond with the city's transformation into a vulnerable woman.[23]

---

[22] There is the possibility of a pun here, if we are willing to read for it. The word used for 'defiled' here is *feda*, which we would commonly read as *foeda* (filthy, repulsive, abhorrent). However, there is also the potential for an aural pun with *feta*, meaning 'pregnant', 'filled', or 'bearing'. In this latter option, we get unsettling overtones of how sexualised the penetration of the Tower's space might be, and how the incursion makes the space 'pregnant with blood and shame'. The aural similarity of the *foeda* and *feta* is disturbing on a linguistic level, and it is tempting to read in this moment a meaningful conflation on Gower's part.

[23] Federico, 'A Fourteenth-Century Erotics of Politics', 132. N.B. This is in keeping

Gower uses the references to rape (callous and freighted as they are here) to chart our path through this moment, and in so doing, to convey the magnitude of the shift into dispositional. Or, more accurately, into the always-already dispositional. We are drawn, through the language of imagined sexual assault, into an understanding of just how unstable the signifying power of the Tower is, and always has been, and the metaphors govern our response to this revelation.[24] His understanding of the structure as a location not for authoritative power but rather as an assemblage of its own, vulnerable in its sense and signification, is what is both revealed and unavoidable, and his strategy here is to capture his sense of horror at the recognition rather than to attempt to erase or remedy it, to make it fundamental to how his text functions.[25]

But it is important to note that this is not always the case. Other versions of these same events will organise the relationship between *ordinatio* and

---

with (although not likely a direct reference to) the *città-donna* motif in Italian lyrics of the period, in which the city is imagined as a desirable yet vulnerable woman, enticing in the political power she promises but withholds from the exiled, would-be lover. Alternatively, the *città* represents a source of desire the masculine spectator can neither claim nor protect from conquest and penetration from her enemies – something much closer to what we see here. In the Italian tradition, as Catherine Keen writes, 'The sexual and physical violence of so much of the visual rhetoric associated with the *città-donna* and with her hapless exile-lover offers an exploration of the tensions and fragilities of societies whose dynamics of development involved painful and frequently violent ruptures with the conventions traditionally governing both politics and culture, and reveals uncertainty about where to turn in the quest for a new stability.' Keen, 'Sex and the Medieval City: Viewing the Body Politic from Exile in Early Italian Verse', in *Troubled Vision: Gender, Sexuality, and Sight in Medieval Text and Image*, ed. Emma Campbell and Robert Mills (New York, 2004), 168.

[24] What is at stake here is how and what the Tower signifies. Rather than reflecting the sense and meaning shining out from royal authority, the Tower is not illuminated but itself illuminates – it generates its own meaning, which is necessarily unstable and open to re-signification. The 'curves of visibility' the Tower *qua dispositif* makes possible reveal not 'a general source of light which would be said to fall upon pre-existing objects: it is made of lines of light which form variable shapes inseparable from the apparatus in question ... Each apparatus has its way of structuring light, the way in which it falls, blurs and disperses, distributing the visible and the invisible, giving birth to objects which are dependent on it for their existence, and causing them to disappear.' Giles Deleuze, 'What Is a Dispositif?,' in *Michel Foucault: Philosopher*, trans. Timothy J. Armstrong (New York, 1992), 160.

[25] Of course, there is also a noteworthy tension here between the always-already of the dispositional Tower and the singular act of rape the *prosopopeia* imagines. Bringing its own sense of horror, we must ask ourselves if Gower's image imagines a rape not as a temporally bounded event but as a permanent and atemporal state. This, obviously, creates a very different set of horrors for readers who are asked to consider the feminised body of the Tower in this way.

ductus to more directly counter the peasants' desires/complaints by drawing back from a lyric mode in favour of a critical, authoritative distance. In his version of the storming of the Tower, for example, Thomas Walsingham also lingers with unusual detail over what happens inside the king's bedchamber, but he does so in a more traditional chronicler's vein. Like Knighton or the Chandos Herald, he deploys a great deal of literary flourish, depicting the scene in the 'colourful' language characterising his general approach to the events of the day: these are not just peasants who enter into the king's private quarters but 'the most vile of the peasants' (*non solum rusticos, sed rusticorum abjectissimos*), and they enter not as a group but individually (*non plures, sed singulos*).[26] Their fearlessness in moving through the spaces of the building without thought of royal opposition is what seems to dismay Walsingham the most, and he brings all his rhetorical power to bear as he describes their actions within:

> Et cum haec omnia facerent, et, ut diximus, plerique soli in cameras concessissent, et sedendo, jacendo, jocando, super lectum Regis insolescerent; et insuper, matrem Regis ad oscula invitarent quidam; non tamen, – quod mirum dictus est, – audebant plures milites et armigeri unum de tam inconvenientibus actibus convenire, non ad impediendum manus injicere, nec verbis secretissimis mussitare.

> [And when they had done all this, as we say, [the rebels] withdrew (both as a group and individually) into the chamber. There they grew even more insolent, sitting, lazing, and jesting on the king's bed; on top of this, some jeered at the king's mother for kisses. Moreover, which is amazing to say, the many soldiers and armed men did not dare to meet a single one with opposing action, nor to throw up their hands to impede them, nor even to mutter words in secret.][27]

Rather than inserting himself into the scene by claiming direct experience as Gower does, Walsingham opts for the guise of a kind of sermonising distance, which transforms the scene into something closer to the exemplary. As readers, we get enough affective language-forms to produce obverse desires that counter what we see enacted by the intruders; moreover, these moments of poetic or rhetorical flourish are meant to draw careful attention to the specific

---

[26] In his description of a text that is quite rhetorically savvy, Saul's choice of 'colourful' as a descriptor may comment both on the evident emotion with which Walsingham writes as well as the attention to his use of rhetorical 'colour'. Nigel Saul, *Richard II* (New Haven, 1997), 69, n. 52.

[27] Thomas Walsingham, *Chronica Monasterii S. Albani*, ed. Henry Thomas Riley, Rerum Britannicarum Medii Ævi Scriptores 28, part 1 (London, 1965), 459. Translation my own.

political objections the peasants hold. The incredulity of the 'jacendo, jocando' towards the opening of this passage, for example, is almost tangible as the intruders not only lie down on the king's bed but joke and jest upon it, bringing the full weight of their contempt to bear on a location that was seen as the site of one of their complaints: the charge that the king conduced business with a favoured few in inaccessible spaces, like his bedchamber (*thalamus*), rather than in open, public audiences.[28] Quite apart from the physical damage enacted upon the furniture, the symbolic weight of this gesture rests on the destruction of the status of the chamber as a private, protected, or secret location from which the king might direct the business of the realm. As the rebels penetrate the room, they transform it into a newly accessible space and use their (momentary) access to erase the ability of the *thalamus* to divide royal governance into visible and invisible elements.

Walsingham's focus on the *thalamus* is noteworthy inasmuch as it aligns the action specifically with the body of the monarch, much as we see in the *Visio*. For both Walsingham and Gower, this is critical to how they see the dispositional status of the Tower. But elsewhere, we see chroniclers taking other valences of the *thalamus*-space. In Froissart, for example, we see the rebels penetrate the bedchamber not of the king, but of his mother. The intruders in the *Chroniques* direct their attention to Joan's bed with such ire that she faints, whereupon her attendants spirit her from the increasingly chaotic building via the Water Gate.[29] Walsingham's (and Gower's) insistence on the royal rather than maternal *thalamus* shifts the tenor of the episode from one of potential sexual violence against a feminine body to that which metonymically challenges the affairs of state. While this threat still certainly carries

---

[28] Juliet Barker notes that, while Walsingham's account is confused about some historical details, 'the attack on the royal bed was true enough: Thomas atte Sole of Gravesend, Kent, confessed that he was in the king's bedchamber on 14 June and that he "ran through the bed of the lord king with his sword saying 'that was for the traitors found there such as [Nicholas] Heryng and others'"'. Heryng was a landholder and public official in Dartford whose properties were attacked earlier in the uprising and who was eventually executed. Barker clarifies the import of the sword-thrust into the royal bed as a revolutionary gesture: 'Atte Sole was not implying any sexual liaison: medieval kings frequently held private audiences with petitioners and courtiers while sitting at state in the royal bed, hence the symbolism of its destruction by the rebels. This was a blow aimed at those who did not do their business openly with the king, when he held public courts but secretly, in his private chambers, to which only a favored few were admitted.' Barker, *1381: The Year of the Peasants' Revolt*, 261. See also R. B. Dobson, ed., *The Peasants' Revolt of 1381* (London, 1970), 172, 191; and Edgar Powell and G. M. Trevelyan, eds, *The Peasants' Rising and the Lollards: A Collection of Unpublished Documents Forming an Appendix to 'England in the Age of Wycliffe'* (London, 1899), 10.

[29] Dobson, *The Peasants' Revolt of 1381*, 191.

the possibility of violence against Richard's flesh, and possibly sexual threat as well, the event enacts humiliation on both bodies of the king – public and private. Such an invasion of *privité* is noteworthy for its *insolentia* as much as for physical damage, and the *St Albans Chronicle* and the *Visio* both use the space to define the limits of political subjecthood: there are those who should have access to the chamber, and there are those who should not.

The difference between Walsingham and Gower lies in the how each author manages the relationship between *ductus* and *ordinatio*. Whereas Gower privileges the former, giving us the Tower personified, Walsingham opts for the latter, casting the Tower as figurative, a building that creates rather than accepts signification. Both authors use the *thalamus* as part of their narrative, but in Walsingham it is a sign of monarchic power and (for the peasants) royal corruption – a powerful symbol upon which to record their complaint. They acknowledge its signifying power and desire to subvert its effects by taking control of what it means. For readers, on the other hand, the *thalamus* focuses Walsingham's critique on questions of access and the definition of different categories of the political subject. Both come to bear on the room itself and are read through the interaction between bodies and material objects (walls, doors, mattresses) and in the relationship of threat and stasis between the guards and the invaders: the latter move with ease, the former remain inert in word, deed, and even thought.[30] There is certainly feeling and even emotion here, but the textual *ductus* nevertheless remains embedded in the chronicle-logical – Walsingham is treating events as they happen, lingering over some and passing lightly over others as his perspective dictates. *Ordinatio* comes from the temporal progression of actions as they unfold in the chamber, and Walsingham works to draw readers' sensibilities along 'appropriate' channels by positioning them within the critical perspective that looks back and over. We see the political desire of the peasants, but that desire is accessed in the gap between us as readers *registering* the desire and the *peasants* feeling it.

In this, Walsingham's purpose is to organise affective response in the wake of public trauma, making use of the chronicler's distance in order to draw the lines of history where they 'ought' to go. His chronicle-form depends on that combination of critical distance and affect to produce the 'thing' of narrative history; it is a careful balance that works here because the political desire of the peasants is recorded but not shared. He is therefore able to use rhetorical affect as resistance to directly counter what he reports while nevertheless adhering to the *ordinatio* governed by

---

[30] 'Audebant plures milites et armigeri unum de tam inconvenientibus actibus convenire, non ad impediendum manus injicere, nec verbis secretissimis mussitare' (Walsingham, *Chronica Monasterii S. Albani*, 459, discussed and translated above 000).

the 'official' chronology. *Ductus* is present, but not dominant as it is in Gower. It supports *ordinatio* by resisting the narrated desires the author finds distasteful, embodying the distant position of the state and generating political and cultural stability. Gower is not so fortunate: there is no earthly stability to be found in the *Visio*. For that, we must turn to God, as he does in the final chapters. When *ordinatio* and *ductus* ostensibly align with hegemonic political desires, however, different measures are required, and this is where we can see the use of form and poetics as a possible mechanism for opposition. For texts produced under dominant or even totalitarian systems of political rule, it is in the affective and poetic forms that we find resistance, even if it is resistance that is not entirely deliberate. We find, essentially, the ways in which poetic language evades capture by revealing contrary affective forms.

To take a slightly unexpected example (and one also discussed by Federico),[31] Richard Maidstone's *Concordia* describes at length Richard's triumphal procession into London as part of the 'reconciliation' of the king and the city's citizens in 1392. This poem is most often discussed as an example of propaganda, or at the very least, state-approved panegyric.[32] The corporation of the city had been at odds with the crown over money, and in 1392 Richard forced the governing body to submit a lavish display of pomp and submission that emphasised royal control over the coffers and *corpus* of the urban space.[33] Writing under very different circumstances than Walsingham and Gower, Maidstone nevertheless structures political desire along lines that echo what we see in the 1381 accounts, namely in the use of the bedchamber as metonymic for political subjectification. Rather than focusing on a physical location, however, Maidstone locates a purely figurative *thalamus* as a prominent part of the political and civic landscape, imagining it not as a place but as an abstracted location of political desire and subjection. And affect is governed not by chronicle-distance but by the royal gaze.

In his entry into the city, Richard is described as moving through the streets as a bridegroom approaching his beloved: his beauty is emphasised, his affections are engaged, and he is entreated (obliquely) to mercy by a speaking voice that calls on his on marital duty and position:

---

[31] Federico, 'A Fourteenth-Century Erotics of Politics'.

[32] For the most complete argument on this, see David R. Carlson, *John Gower, Poetry and Propaganda in Fourteenth-Century England* (Cambridge, 2012), 93–109.

[33] For details on the metropolitan conflict, see the introduction to Maidstone, *Concordia: The Reconciliation of Richard II with London*, ed. David R. Carlson, trans. A. G. Rigg, (Kalamazoo, 2003), and Caroline M. Barron, 'The Quarrel of Richard II with London 1392–7', in *The Reign of Richard II: Essays in Honour of May Mckisack*, ed. F. R. H. Du Boulay and Caroline M. Barron (London, 1971).

Lux, tibi, Londonie, rumor amenus adest;
Namque tuum regem, sponsum dominumque tuumque,
    Quem tibi sustulerat Perfida Lingua, capis.
Invidiosa cohors regem tibi vertit in iram,
    Desereret thalamum sponsus ut ipse suum;
Sed quia totus amor tuus est – et amantis ymago
    Formosior Paride – nescit odisse diu.
Adde quod in miseros semper solet hic misereri,
    Nec habet ultrices rex pius iste manus.

[A pleasant rumour has arrived! A light to you, O London!
For your king, your spouse, and your lord,
    (Whom Wicked Tongue had stolen away) you embrace
        once more.
Its hostile troops turned the king to anger towards you,
    So that the bridegroom himself forsook his marriage-bed.
But because your love is complete, and the face of the lover
    Is lovelier than that of Paris, he is unable to hate for long.
In addition, inasmuch as he brings comfort to the miserable in
    his mercy,
        Such a tender king does not have vengeful hands; lines
            20–28.][34]

Additionally,

Hic licet accensus foret in te, Troia, parumper,
    Grata modo facies se docet esse piam.
Non poterat mordax detractans lingua tenere
    Quin cuperet thalamum sponsus adire suum.
Qui libertates solitas tibi dempserat omnes
    Nunc redit, et plures reddere promptus eas.

[It is right, O Troy, that he was inflamed against you for a while,
    But his beloved face [now] shows itself to be affectionate.
A biting, disparaging tongue could not detain
    The bridegroom who longs to approach the bedchamber!
He who withdrew all accustomed liberties from you
    Now he returns, ready to restore more of the same; lines
        39–44.]

In the above passages, the 'marriage-bed' and 'bedchamber' are both the *thalamus*: the king 'desereret thalamum' (24) when ill rumour abounded, and 'cuperet thalamum sponsus adire suum' (42) upon his return to the city. The description of Richard's disposition (and his physical beauty) is decidedly

---

[34] All text from the *Concordia* is taken from Maidstone, *Concordia*. Translations are my own.

panegyric – Maidstone seeds these lines with justification for Richard's anger and praise for his (supposed) mercy and forgiveness. But the eroticising of the panegyric form, accomplished by the dual layering of the *thalamus/sponsus* language and the allusions to Troy (and to Paris in particular), positions the *concordia* Richard is looking for within a potent conflation of royal desire and royal authority.[35] This time, unlike in the *Visio*, we as readers are on the desiring-side, complicit in (if not necessarily approving of) what is about to happen.

In both Gower and Maidstone, the referential and penetrative powers of the figurative (or personified) *thalamus* are powerful and dangerous, but in the *Concordia* the promise of the bedchamber initiates royal rather than rebel desire and the threat of royal, not rebel, violence. The lines of force are inverted. Maidstone makes it clear that Richard desires the city, but (at this moment) the city does not appear to desire him back. Elsewhere, the poet will make much of the citizens' apparent gratitude and pleasure in their monarch's return, but in the *thalamus*-sections the action as well as the desire is one-sided. The only expression of civic response is in the verb 'capere' (22) and in the assurance that the city's 'love is complete' (*Sed quia totus amor tuus est ...*) (25). From a translator's perspective, we might read *capere* here as 'seize' or 'grasp', but it can also simply be the more benign (and more ambiguous) 'get' or 'receive' – an important but unresolved distinction. The linguistic flexibility between 'seize' and 'get' opens the door (as it were) to the king's presence and authority as being inevitable but also perhaps un-asked for. After all, it is the poet who proffers the invitation to penetrate the metaphorical space, not the people of the city. And while Richard is (like Paris) a bridegroom who is looking to do some seizing of his own, we hear nothing in this passage of the city's willingness to be 'taken'. What we do see is the royal person using his prerogative to enter, to possess, and to enjoy, and his desire exists beyond and outside of any reciprocation or consensual acceptance. The *thalamus* thus becomes the staging-ground for the threat of marital rape, a violence that might be slightly 'muted' by the shadow-image of Paris hovering over Richard's face – or amplified by it. The poem works to bifurcate the resonances of the erotic by affording readers a view of and a view from within Richard's political desire, and we are pulled along in the erotic realignment of civic space as a result, willingly or no.

In some sense, what we see here is what is often assumed to be Gower's conventional desire in the *Visio* – the political ability to make public space

---

[35] The Trojan connection here is particularly interesting in that it conjures up, through Paris, a narrative of erotic desire but also of erotic abduction – both of which lead to well-known civic disaster. It is a curious choice on Maidstone's part, and Federico offers much insight into how slippery (and telling) this alignment is, noting how complex the English political associations were around the classical abduction-narrative of Paris and Helen. Federico, 'A Fourteenth-Century Erotics of Politics', 123–26.

and structure legible and stable. Richard's progress through the city re-establishes lines of motion and aligns the physical geography of the city with his reassertion of royal power. The use of the bridegroom/*thalamus* metaphor here is integral to the effort: Richard is entreated, invited, and encouraged to penetrate the chamber/city, to lay claim to its space and affordances. He walks down streets, he passes by spectators, he pauses before decorations and performances and then moves on. In the end, he will invite the now-subjected citizens to enter into his own, royal space once the lines of power have been re-inscribed.[36] It is Richard's motion that arranges consensual space in his royal wake by enforcing representation of and for the bodies he passes. Moreover, the position of the textual spectator is bound to Richard's spatial perspective – unlike the civic spectators, we track his movement, looking *at* him, perhaps, but also following along *with* him. In this, the readerly eye moves through the city by floating laterally alongside the king, regarding him but also seeing the city and its inhabitants through his progress. Maidstone uses his language not just to track Richard's movement but to bring the space and people we are moving through into alignment with the royal gaze as well. The king's physical presence becomes an embodying and solidifying *appareil* for political power.

But how complicit is Maidstone in this effort? We are comfortable in seeing Gower's *ductus* and affective language as a counter to what he is describing in the *Visio*, but Maidstone is usually categorised as willingly championing the affective landscape Richard seeks to create. I would argue, however, that there are in fact elements of unexpected poetic resistance to be found in Maidstone's poetics. Richard's presence brings everyone around him into line and flattens them out into props for making visible his own magnificence. We see this most clearly in an anaphoric passage of Maidstone's own, in which Richard makes his gradual way through the catalogue of guildsmen during his approach to the city. In the text, we see the variety of trades, arrayed along the procession-route, waiting patiently (it seems) for Richard and Anne to pass them by. The pattern amounts to something of an 'Old Macdonald' list, in which 'Here a …' 'There a …' (*Hic … Ibi … Hic … Ibi*) march down the page:

---

[36] N.B. It is at the moment of royal invitation into the royal space of Westminster that Anne delivers her plea on the people's behalf, positioning herself as the mediatrix asking for mercy for the city and its inhabitants on account of their contrition and reverence for the king. Upon his acceptance of her request and the restoration of the city's liberties, the crowd has a particularly chilling response: they fall prostrate before Richard (*prostrata ruit*) and cry out (*acclamat*) 'Vivat rex! Vivat semper! Vivat bene! Vivat!' (May the king live! May he live always! May he live well! May he live!; lines 539–41). The benediction (in the subjunctive mood) carries biopolitical overtones in that it places the desire for the king's continued life in the mouths of the newly re-subjugated populace.

Secta docet sortem quemque tenere suam:
Hic argentarius, **hic** piscarius, secus illum
    Mercibus **hic** deditus, venditor atque meri;
Hic apothecarius, pistor, pictor, lathomusque;
    Hic cultellarius, tonsor, et armifaber;
Hic carpentarius, scissor, sartor, **ibi** sutor;
    Hic pelliparius fulloque, mango, faber;
Hic sunt archifices, **ibi** carnifices, **ibi** tector;
    Hic lorimarium pannariusque simul;
[**Hic**] vaginator, **hic** zonarius, **ibi** tector;
    Hic candelarius, cerarius pariter;
Hic pandoxator, **ibi** streparius, **ibi** iunctor;
    Est **ibi** pomilio, sic avigerulus **hic**.
'A' super 'R' gratis stat in artibus hic numeratis
...
Hic cirotecarius bursistaque, caupo coqusque:
    Ars patet ex secta singula queque sua.

[Their livery shows that each one keeps to his own group:
Here a goldsmith, **here** a fishmonger, following him
    Here a devoted mercer, and a wine-seller,
Here an apothecary, a baker, a painter, and a mason,
    Here a cutler, a barber, and an armorer,
Here a carpenter, a cutter, a tailor, **there** a cobbler,
    Here a skinner and a fuller, a shop-monger, a smith,
Here are the archers, **there** the butchers, **there** a thatcher,
    Here a spurrier and a draper also,
Here a scabbard-maker, **here** a girdler, **there** a weaver,
    Here a chandler, together with a wax-maker,
Here a brewer, **there** a stirruper, **there** a joiner,
    There as well was an apple-seller, **there** so a poulterer.
'A' above 'R' stands freely in the guilds here numbered,
...
Here a glover and a purse-maker, an innkeeper and a cook.
    Each individual craft lies open by their own livery ...;
    lines 80–95.]

The repetition makes the gathered crowds an immediately recognisable catalogue both for Richard and for readers. Each group is present and accounted for, and as we follow the king, the display and reception of each guild has two effects: (1) it recognises and performs the distinctions of each guild's various occupations, and (2) it transforms the bodies standing along the road into units of measure. In the first instance, we are told that 'Ars patet ex secta singula queque sua' (Each individual guild is clear through its own livery) (95) and 'Secta docet sortem quemque tenere suam' (Their livery shows that each one keeps to his own group) (80). The guilds here are representative in that groups of individual bodies are arranged by their membership in a given guild-company, and the guilds themselves are arranged by order of precedence; those associated with the city's merchant-oligarchs take pride of place. Even though each group is easily identified by the poet by virtue of their distinctive clothing, as readers we see neither the identifying garments nor the assembled numbers. A single stand-in figure, devoid of any markings apart from the craft-assignment given by the text, assumes a metonymic function and represents the entirety of his 'phalerata cohors' (decorated troop) (79). The display as a whole is impressive: the poet likens the scene of assembled and organised Londoners as 'formas ordinis angelici' (forms of angelic order) (97) and claims that the grandeur and beauty of the scene is clear to anyone who might see it.

The anaphora creates this effect. It seems initially to stabilise the scene, reflecting the way Richard's person stabilises urban space. On the other hand, however, with Gower's anaphora lingering in the background, we might also find it conveys an unwitting sense of political horror. The order and beauty Maidstone celebrates in the guildsmen is possible because the actions and the agency of the crowd have been converted into a curiously static and motionless tableau. The list of guild-companies is recognisable but inert, devoid of the motion that their association with a given craft comes from. We are told of scabbard-makers, joiners, brewers, carpenters, smiths, glovers, barbers, and more, but they have been rendered as bloodless abstractions, notable for their difference from one another but not for the work and workings that might otherwise animate them.[37] The only ones moving here, in fact, are Richard and (more obliquely) Anne. It is their progress that gives life to the scene and that offers the organised perfection Maidstone is describing. As they pass through the streets, lined for four miles with the waiting people, individual bodies become decoration and a form of measurement – a spatial list that marks not only the breadth of trades represented but also how Richard's progress through them makes their assembly legible. Bodies transition from gathered crowds, to metonymic representatives, to spatial markers through which Richard's process can be measured and marked.[38] His movement, in a distinct contrast

---

[37] For the distinction between the labour catalogue and the signifying power of the assembly, see Andrew W. Cole, 'Scribal Hermeneutics and the Genres of Social Organization in Piers Plowman', in *The Middle Ages at Work: Practicing Labor in Late Medieval England*, ed. Kellie Robertson and Michael Uebel (New York, 2004).

[38] There is a strong sense here of how Simone Weil beautifully and horrifically describes the effect of force: it is that which turns bodies into things: 'From [force's] first property (the ability to turn a human being into a thing by the simple method of killing him) flows another, quite prodigious too in its own way, the ability to turn a human being into a thing while he is still alive. He is alive; he has a soul; and yet – he is a thing. An extraordinary entity this – a thing that has a soul. And as for the soul, what an extraordinary house it finds itself in! Who can say what it costs it, moment by moment, to accommodate itself to this residence, how much writhing and bending,

to that of the peasants in Gower and Walsingham, realigns spaces according to *status*, thereby establishing *concordia*. Richard's movement subordinates ranks of bodies from which individuality and action have been erased, and political signification is fixed by the way he (and the poem) transforms his subjects into a striated, signifying system.

The readerly and royal gazes align, and we are drawn into the *ordinatio* of Richard's measured (and measuring) pace, but not without some difficulty on the part of the poet. Throughout the early parts of the procession, Maidstone's descriptive voice quickly begins to falter due to his inability to account for or detail the overabundance of bodies, trimmings, and expenditure:

> Quis numerare queat numerum turbe numerose,
>   Que velud astra poli densius inde fluit?
> Milia viginti iuvenes numerantur equestres;
>   Qui pedibus pergunt non capit hos numerus.
>
> [Who would be able to number the number of the numerous crowd
>   Which flows thence, more thickly than the stars of heaven?
> Twenty thousand young, mounted men are numbered –
>   No accounting can number those who proceed on foot;
>   lines 67–70.][39]

Along with the (in)visible guildsmen and spectators, the celebratory decorations adorning civic buildings and spaces are also notable in their excess, but rarely fully described:

> Ornat et interea se pulcre queque platea:
>   Vestibus auratis urbs micat innumeris.
> Floris odoriferi specie fragrante platea,
>   Pendula perque domos purpura nulla deest,
> Aurea, coccinea, bissinaque tinctaque vestis
>   Pinxerat hic celum arte iuvante novum.
> Quos tulit ante dies istos plebs ista labores,
>   Quas tulit expensas, os reserare nequit.
> Quid moror? Ecce, dies transit …

---

folding and pleating are required of it?' The reification of the assembled crowd, the transformation of individual people into inert markers of measurement, locates the horror of this scene for the reader firmly within Richard's imposition of royal will through force. Weil, 'The Iliad, or the Poem of Force', in *War and the Iliad* (New York, 2005), 5.

[39] This passage also shows a particularly notable use of polyptoton on *numerare*, another of Gower's favourite tropes and that I have tried to capture in the translation: 'Quis numerare queat numerum turbe numerose, / Que velud astra poli densius inde fluit? / Milia viginti iuvenes numerantur equestres; / Qui pedibus pergunt non capit hos numerus.'

[Meanwhile, each street ornaments itself beautifully:
>   The city shines with countless golden draperies,
> The streets are fragrant with the splendid perfume of flowers,
>   Purple hangings are not lacking in any home.
> Cloths infused with golden, cochineal, and white dyes
>   Have embellished here a fresh canopy with pleasing skill.
> Before this day, the people speak of such labours,
>   They speak of such expenses – one mouth cannot disclose them all.
> But why do I delay? Behold, the day passes ...; lines 57–65.]

Here too we find anaphora, as lines 63–72 open with '**Quos** / **Quas** / **Quid** / **Regis** / **Quis** / **Que** / **Milia** / **Qui** / **Custos** / **Quos**.' But we also find something approaching *occupatio*, in which the inability or choice not to describe something is used to draw attention to it. *Occupatio* is about the idea of opening spaces through which readers are invited to look, but not guided through – a very different *ductus* from the organised, visual, and visible progression Richard models. This is a technique Gower will use as well, and usually to gesture toward something beyond his ability, poetically or emotionally, to render into verse, and in so doing he causes them to become affective, participatory *ductus* rather than part of narrative chronicle. In the *Concordia*'s description of the physical spectacle of the crowded city, we see something similar. Maidstone continually emphasises the 'unaccountable' excesses the citizens of London provide, apparently at their own incentive. The extreme measures and wealth that we see in the decorations of the progress-route are paradoxically multiplied in their lack of description. We are invited to imaginatively colour in fantastical details, which, interestingly enough, have no cost (labour or monetary) attached to them. In this, we participate in the erasure the text initiates.[40] The text deliberately elides the way in which activity here is royally determined – as with the gathering of the guildsmen, nothing about this is voluntary. Thus, we also become complicit in and, by extension, absorbed into Richard's consensual perspective, and repetition (anaphora) is married to erasure (*occupatio*) to produce a particularly powerful sense of state power.

Moreover, the same is true for the poet. In the *Concordia*, readers' imaginations can supply unlimited extravagance in the decorations and expenditures

---

[40] Susan Phillips describes the use of *occupatio* in the *House of Fame* along similar lines: she sees Chaucer's use of gossip as something that '[produces] the *promise* of surplus rather than surplus itself ... This promise of multiplicity is the source of the poem's narrative tension, as readers are everywhere led to read the fulfilment of that promise. Surplus is continually invoked but never realised because the rhetoric of multiplication operates in tandem with the trope of *occupatio*, withholding multiplicity even as it pretends to reveal it.' Phillips, *Transforming Talk: The Problem with Gossip in Late Medieval England* (University Park, PA, 2007), 75.

that are not described, that are labour-less, and that have been denied their circulatory power because Richard has restructured the products of labour into products of praise, even as he restricts civic identity to position within a representative catalogue. But the poet cannot speak of it. The goal of Richard's punishment is a kind of political and economic *contrapasso*, and what we see in Maidstone's *occupatio* follows this desire: labour and purchasing power made impotent, powerless, labour shaken loose from systems of exchange. The banners and flags and flowers come from nowhere, mean nothing, and cost a great deal. For his part, Maidstone's poetics pick up on this effect and echo (or even amplify) it by swallowing even these emptied material objects into the text's poetic gaps. Many hands have done this work, many mouths would likely be required to speak of it. But he has only one. He cannot report what he sees, and we hear in his *occupatio* an eerie echo of the way Richard's presence silences those around him: 'Aurea rex dum frena trahit et sistere cogit / Dextrarium, proceres mox populusque silent' (The king then draws back on the golden reins and collects his halted / steed; the people and the nobles now fall silent; lines 130–31). This places the poetic voice not as a floating eye, moving alongside Richard in a position of privilege, but amid the subjugated populace, who also fall quiet before the royal presence.

I do not necessarily want to read in Maidstone the kind of counter to political desires we see in Walsingham's description of the peasants rummaging around in Richard's bedclothes; his poetics include the possibility of formal resistance but are not in themselves particularly affective. We can be moved by what we read, but this affect occurs along very different lines than that invited by Walsingham's discontent. Furthermore, this kind of formal analysis I am suggesting for the *Concordia* depends on a deeply diagnostic reading: we uncover the symptoms of one living under a totalitarian regime rather than recognise an active attempt to oppose it. However, the two ends of the spectrum, Walsingham's affective realignment *of* and Maidstone's formal participation *in* political desire structure how each of these texts imagine the 'thing' of history by negotiating the lines between affective *ductus* and structural *ordinatio*. Gower, I would argue, splits the difference. Whereas Walsingham's aesthetic displays a counterrevolutionary spirit that tries to reclaim signification about what the Tower means, and whereas Maidstone uses extended poetic figures to produce the effect and extent of Richard's royal power (approvingly or no), Gower embeds his resistance to the Tower's fall in allusive forms that reconfigure history as an affective machine.

His elegy for the Tower, 'quo patitur thalamus ingredientis onus' (where the bedchamber endures the burden of penetration; line 1748), balances the way in which *raptus* becomes rape, embedding both within a poetics that convey not stability but stupefied horror. This response is one we are supposed to share with the poetic voice, and it forms a version of history for which the *techne* of Gower's writing becomes both visible and critical. The anaphora is not easily missed, and its Ovidian origins are likewise legible for any reader who would also be likely to recognise the range of Ovidian quotation Gower employs in the poem. As others have described, Gower's turn to the exilic Ovid carries strong political and lyric tones, and he uses the *Tristia* and the *Ex ponto* to carry readers into that exile with him. By adding into this the formal allusion to Ovid in his anaphoric Tower, however, Gower shifts readers into a different, more diffuse affective orientation. Anaphora is about repetition, and it generates a circular field that looks backward to lines past and forward to anticipated lines to come; its motion does not adhere to the kind of temporal progression that marks chronicle-*ordinatio*. Anaphora resists the teleology of cause and effect, the teleology of epic, thereby making it something uniquely Ovidian. Like Ovid, Gower here does not engage with a grand narrative, legible in its stabilising and national purpose. Like Ovid, he turns to lyric expression, materialised in language that is 'stuck' in an experienced (or dreamed) present. Like Ovid, he laments rather than critiques.

This has strong political as well as literary implications. By allowing formal allusion rather than borrowed fragments of text to anchor his description, Gower attempts a resignification that escapes the limits of the chronicle and the coercion of the propagandistic. The *Visio* is neither obverse desire nor performative panegyric. The conflation of the violated *thalamus*, the gendered *prosopopeia*, and the Ovidian anaphora capture how Gower's sense/sensation of the scene creates the sense/meaning of the political events for his readers. In so doing, he stakes a claim for historical narrative's ability to control not just aesthetics but *aesthesis*.[41] In the *Visio*, Gower's vision is intentionally fragmented, illuminating not a stable political landscape but one that is – and always has been – unreliable. Echard has argued convincingly for this very perspective across her readings of Gower's Latin works, clearly showing how poetry, and specifically Latin poetry, is, for Gower, 'a means by which he effects a mimesis of the political uncertainties of his age'.[42] It is this sense of uncertainty that flavours the entirety of the *Visio*, separating it out from both the other chronicles of the period and also from the rest of the *Vox*. It should also be a quality we associate more strongly with Gower, particularly as we consider the ways in which he imagines his historical narrative of the past contributing to and shaping the political present.

---

[41] My use of *aesthesis* here comes from Rancière's discussion of the relationship between the distribution of the sensible and the functions of political enunciation. Jacques Rancière, *The Politics of Aesthetics: A Distribution of the Sensible*, trans. Gabriel Rockhill (London, 2004), 39.

[42] Siân Echard, 'Gower's "Bokes of Latin": Language, Politics, and Poetry', *Studies in the Age of Chaucer* 25 (2003): 129. This is as true in the extended work of the *Vox* as well as in the marginal Latin verses to the *Confessio amantis*. See Echard, 'With Carmen's Help: Latin Authorities in the Confessio Amantis', *Studies in Philology* 95, no. 1 (1998).

7

Gower and the Heavens: The 'Dull' and the Divine in *Confessio Amantis*

WILLIAM GREEN

Ruling stars

Book VII of *Confessio Amantis* presents the reader with a constellation of interruptions to Gower's poem; it is a singularity that seems to disrupt the poem's narrative and seems to be in danger of destroying its form. The dialogic frame falls away: Amans does not speak until the very end of the book, when he interjects with the plea 'Do wey, mi fader, I you preie.'[1] This is a sentiment the reader is likely ready to join in voicing, as one has found not the expected moral exempla pertaining to a category of mortal sin (lust is the expected topic) but is instead presented with discourses on the liberal arts and examples of kingly policy, totalling well over five thousand lines, and that, we are told, consist of the instruction that Aristotle provided to Alexander.

This seeming structural misalignment of Book VII has always presented difficulty for critics of the poem. As Elizabeth Porter noted, it 'has been variously described as a "general digression on education", "a minor theme", or conversely, as "the heart of the matter"'. For Porter, the 'critical disagreement over the place of Book VII in the structure of the poem neatly epitomises the larger disagreement concerning the nature of Gower's poetic achievement in this his major English work': is it primarily a 'graceful and skillful' love poem, or is it instead 'the culminating expression of Gower's social and political philosophy'?[2] Others of the relatively small number of

---

[1] *Confessio Amantis* (hereinafter *CA*), Book VII.5408. I refer to the edition of G. C. Macaulay, ed., *John Gower's English Works*, 2 vols, EETS e.s., 81–82 (London: 1900–1).

[2] Elizabeth Porter, 'Gower's Ethical Microcosm and Political Macrocosm', in *Gower's* Confessio Amantis, ed. A. J. Minnis (Cambridge, 1983), 135. Porter identified these two positions as dominant in criticism from, respectively, 'British commentators', on the one hand, and 'their American counterparts', on the other, while arguing that 'these views are not necessarily opposed and that *Confessio Amantis* has a unity of conception'.

critics who have turned their attention to this section of the poem approach the sense of bafflement it inspires by seeking to answer what purpose is served by the multitude of disquisitions on varied and obscure topics: as Tamara O'Callaghan once asked, voicing a perhaps common critical sentiment, if 'the book is, in fact, a "mirror for princes" ... why, then, does Gower include a seemingly obscure and uninspiring passage on the fifteen stars, fifteen stones, and fifteen herbs? How does such a passage fit into the poem's primary theme of kingship and secondary theme of love?'[3] Other writers have, of course, in keeping with the critical exasperation surrounding this section of the poem, reversed the priority of those elements of the work; Book VII does the critic no favours in resolving what the poem as a whole is, or what it is about.

In addition to a sense of (critically productive) uncertainty about the contents and structure of Book VII and its relation to the rest of the work, another curious rhetorical topos is often in evidence in criticism of this section of the poem. It is, unfortunately, the critic tells us, dull, very dull, and an apology is in order to the reader as, despite the critic's best intentions and good sense, it nevertheless has been taken up as a topic.[4] Writing on Book VII in a Festschrift for his doctoral supervisor J. A. W. Bennett, M. A. Manzalaoui in 1981 began his contribution by presenting the usual attitude of the critic to this, the second longest book in the poem:

> To choose Book VII of the *Confessio Amantis* as one's topic is to load oneself with the handicap of a subject most critics have found dull. True, we have become less prone today to dismiss as otiose the frequent departures in medieval narrative or expository structure from the straight and narrow path of post-Renaissance linearity; both medievalist scholars and our contemporary imaginative writers have accustomed us to non-sequential leaps from one realm of vision to another, to unfamiliar parallelisms, analogies, and ectypes, to unexpected and unauthorized bedfellows, long since revealed to be as common in the conceptual field of the Middle Ages as in the bed-sitters of modern fiction. But it is this particular excursus which has been found hard to accept, this summary of learning, ethics, and statecraft, interrupting the Lover's confession, and diminishing the impact of the main emotional exposition, the string of narrative *exempla*, and the texture of imagery and poetic language.[5]

---

[3] Tamara O'Callaghan, 'The Fifteen Stars, Stones and Herbs: Book VII of the *Confessio Amantis* and its Afterlife', in *John Gower, Trilingual Poet: Language, Translation, and Tradition*, ed. Elizabeth Dutton, with John Hines and R. F. Yeager (Cambridge, 2010), 139.

[4] A notable exception to this view was, as Porter also points out, that of John Fisher, who argued that 'the whole framework of the *Confessio*, the whole manipulation of expectation, was intended to focus attention upon this "digression" ... Book VII of the *Confessio Amantis* appears not as a digression but as the heart of the discussion.' See John H. Fisher, *John Gower: Moral Philosopher and Friend of Chaucer* (New York, 1964), 197–98.

[5] M. A. Manzalaoui, '"Noght in the Registre of Venus": Gower's English Mirror

Manzalaoui admits that these 'complaints' are not without 'some justice', noting in Gower's defence that '[he] has warned the reader early on that his *Confessio* is at least partly a work of advice for a ruler'; yet Manzalaoui feels the need to insist that 'nor is this section without its true poetic touches'.[6] Aesthetic value is invoked as a defence for the reading that is about to be performed.

The presence within the material of 'true poetic touches', in other words, provides a defence against the reader's initial apprehension of dullness. Yet surely in a poem as vast as *Confessio Amantis* there are many other passages that provide all of the poetry without as large a measure of the apparently dull. Why turn to Book VII, with all its seeming tedious didacticism and narrative torpor, at all? For Manzalaoui, Book VII seems mainly to have been of interest because of what it has to tell us about Gower's access to the pseudo-Aristotelean *Secretum Secretorum*, brought to medieval English attention in large part by Roger Bacon and his redaction of the Latin translation of the Arabic text (supposedly translated in turn from a lost Greek original).[7] For Manzalaoui, Gower's use of the *Secretum Secretorum* and his other sources in Book VII, notably Brunetto Latini's *Livres dou Trésor*,[8] is worth reading because it allows us to place Gower in relation to other medieval men of learning and their 'scientific' understanding, as opposed to unlearned superstition. Manzalaoui finds interest in the 'self-consistent synthesis' the poem attempts in its 'reconciling of faith and proto-scientific determinism', which he sees in evidence in, among other places, the rubric that heads the astronomical section of Book VII and addresses the question of planetary influence. For Manzalaoui, 'the contrast' that Gower as compiler and composer of Book VII presents

> with Roger Bacon is informative. Bacon, making use of the *Secretum*, contends that the welfare of the world lies in the virtuous use by the scientist of the determined affinities and forces of the physical world. Gower, presumably expanding upon the two brief passages in the *Secretum* which make the same point, calls for a man both wise and good to restore the rule of will into the cosmic system, a thing made possible through the action of Grace:

---

for Princes', in *Medieval Studies for J. A. W. Bennett aetatis suae LXX*, ed. P. L. Heyworth (Oxford, 1981), 159.

[6] Manzalaoui, '"Noght in the Registre of Venus"', 159.

[7] Manzalaoui had produced an edition of Middle English versions of the text for the Early English Text Society (M. A. Manzalaoui, ed., *Secretum Secretorum: Nine English Versions*, vol. 1, EETS o.s. 276 (Oxford, 1977)). The second volume, to contain a commentary, was never published.

[8] As identified by Macaulay, who provides correspondences between passages of Book VII and Latini's work in the notes to his edition of *CA*. On Gower's knowledge of Latini, see additionally Julia Bolton Holloway, 'Brunetto Latini and England', *Manuscripta* 31, no. 1 (1987).

> Lege planetarum magis inferiora reguntur,
> Ista set interdum regula fallit opus.
> Vir mediante deo sapiens dominabitur astris,
> Fata nec immerito quid nouitatis agunt.

The cerebral side of Gower enjoys the clarity and system of scientific teachings, the turning from the inchoate beliefs of 'the lewed people' to the explanations of the 'Philosophre' (ll. 319–67). But his poetic side does not miss the opportunity to mention the 'fyrdarke' and gliding star into which fiery exhalations are shaped by the imagination of those who do not know of 'Assub' and 'Eges'.[9]

Gower's poetic sensibility, therefore, excuses some of his didactic excess, even if it does not obviate the resulting dullness. For O'Callaghan, too, a reading of Book VII and its obscure passages helps us to view Gower in a different light; in a discussion of the rather obscure astrological, geomantic, and herbal passages therein, she concludes:

> Gower's inclusion of the material in book VII, and its reception, calls into question traditional views of the poem which regard the love-vision as central and book VII as a digression, or which see the poem as appealing to some presumed interest of Richard II, and perhaps Henry IV, in 'courtly love'. Under the influence of the passage of the fifteen stars, fifteen stones and fifteen herbs, 'moral' Gower is transformed into 'scientific' Gower.[10]

More recently, Seb Falk has read Book VII and argued, *contra* O'Callaghan, that 'Gower's science is part of an education in morality' and that it is imperative to 'be careful not to mistake the depth or purpose of Gower's technical writing', as the 'scientific content' has been 'taken out of its original context'.[11] For Falk, the reason for an examination of Book VII is in order to examine 'Gower's use' of 'some of his lesser known sources', which 'reveals subtle but significant features of his scientific interest ... and offers new insights into the debated issue of his scientific expertise'. In Falk's

---

[9] Manzalaoui, 'Gower's English Mirror for Princes', 178–79; I discuss the Latin poem quoted here below in part III; Echard and Fanger, whose translations of the Latin poems of *CA* I rely on herein, translate it as follows: 'By starry law the lower things are ruled, / But now and then that rule may prove deceptive. / With God's help wise men dominate the stars; / And fate quite rightly brings on new surprises' (Siân Echard and Claire Fanger, *The Latin Verses in the* Confessio Amantis*: An Annotated Translation* (East Lansing, 1991), 77).

[10] O'Callaghan, 'Fifteen Stars, Stones and Herbs', 156.

[11] Seb Falk, 'Natural Sciences', in *Historians on John Gower*, ed. S. H. Rigby with Siân Echard (Cambridge, 2019), 524.

reading, 'Gower's worldview is decisively shaped by the astral sciences';[12] and careful attention to Book VII shows that 'the poet incorporated some ideas [e.g., in modern terms, geomancy, alchemy, astronomy] further from the mainstream of modern science and that although scholars have previously thought them ... "not quite respectable", they were in fact widely accepted and copied'. But Falk concludes that

> whether the poet fully understood the mathematical implications of the science he described is moot; his aim was to educate and entertain more than to inform ... Whilst narrow focus on a selection of scientific details has revealed something of Gower's sources and place among contemporary learning, this is perhaps not how Gower's readers experienced his poetry; he bathed his readers in sciences, and they surely let the learning wash over them.[13]

Medieval encounters with Gower's text, then, are presented as a passive experience. For Falk here, the riddle of Book VII is answered thus: Gower's learning, with its secondary considerations of accuracy and with its careful treading of the line between licit and illicit knowledge, was for entertainment, and, perhaps, while diverting, also providing moral instruction, with Gower himself, through his deployment of astrological learning, 'lifting his readers' eyes to the divinely-ordered universe'.[14]

I think that all of these critics are correct insofar as they argue that Book VII has something to teach us despite the sense of tedium it tends to (or, at least, is imagined to) elicit in its readers, that it contains something of importance, which, due to this apparent dullness, has escaped critical notice.[15] It is this

---

[12] Falk, 'Natural Sciences', 494.
[13] Falk, 'Natural Sciences', 24–25.
[14] Falk, 'Natural Sciences', 24–25.
[15] David Lawton, in 'Dullness and the Fifteenth Century', *ELH* 54, no. 4 (1987), has argued that the poets of the later fifteenth century, including Lydgate, presented themselves in their poems in a 'guise' of dullness, a 'humility topos of an intensely specific kind', with the result that much of importance in their works has often been overlooked. Lawton recognises that this self-presentation 'owes much to Chaucer', though he does not discuss Gower's similar self-presentation in *CA*. Lawton is not 'primarily' concerned with 'the received reputation of the fifteenth century' (762) but demonstrates how these authors' appeals to dullness are part of a careful political self-fashioning and positioning. I am interested, on the other hand, in the way that our perception of certain texts as dull, and our willingness to take professions of dullness at face value, may point to moments of epistemological discontinuities, both in terms of subsequent critical evaluations and as reflected in the texts themselves, and I find Lawton's discussion of George Ashby's debt to Gower and specifically to Book VII of *CA* (771–72) to be suggestive in these terms.

critical commonplace of dullness itself in the scholarship considering Book VII of *Confessio Amantis* in which I am interested, however, and I argue below, through a reading of Siân Echard's recent contributions to critical practice as applied to premodern textual artefacts, that it is precisely this critical reaction that should be of interest to us as researchers writing about the literatures of medieval Europe. As scholars and critics, we often tend to set the mundane, the ordinary, the boring, aside in our studies, favouring instead the exceptional or the exciting upon which we, quite understandably, prefer to turn our critical faculties. When we do turn to items more representative of the undifferentiated mass of medieval textual production, it is often seen as a tedious exercise in service of proving some larger point about the canonical, exceptional texts upon which literary scholarship remains focused. I suggest that critical engagement with the categories of the dull, the tedious, or the boring might aid us in multiple ways: first, in recognising that our bias toward (reading, teaching, and writing about) exceptional literary works often serves to obscure the fact, even as we know better, that much of medieval textual production was dedicated to creating or copying materials that even we as specialists often find dull or unrewarding to read; second, and I think far more importantly, it allows for a realisation that a response that imputes dullness to a text is often, or should be, a warning that we have reached the edge of our understanding of the products of a culture that had in many ways radically different epistemologies than our own. Trained as we are to read difficult texts, the moments in a work where we apprehend dullness – the kind of response *Confessio Amantis* has been subject to in the centuries since its appearance, one that the poem at times seems to anticipate eliciting – are those in which we might fruitfully look more closely for the traces of a relation with the world that as modern rather than medieval subjects we are no longer able to access, where we might see more clearly the textual remains of medieval European cultures as objects embedded within a system of relations to the world that have long since been submerged within our own modern methods of signification. It is precisely the alienness of the material that we perceive of as dull in which we might attempt instead to see medieval textual productions as the once-live objects that informed medieval subjectivities; it is in the boring that we might gain insight into the fundamental differences between our own modes of being and theirs.

Criticism and the Inaccessible

In her recent work, Siân Echard has encouraged those of us who engage with medieval manuscript materials to consider how the institutional environments in which the manuscripts we consult are contained, and the ways access to them is controlled and structured by these environments, determine our encounters with them and how we engage with them.[16] Within the confines of modern manuscript reading rooms, she says, we engage with medieval books more as observers than as readers as a medieval user of the same book might have conceptualised the latter term: we take notes silently, rather than reading aloud communally; we look to marginal notations for traces of past readers' interactions with the materials, unable to 'add to that conversation, which has now become fixed'[17] both because of the archival mission and associated surveillance apparatus of the institutional context, and, perhaps *a fortiori* because of our own sensibilities about the book-as-object's fragility and importance as an historical artefact; as an object that exists, in some way, in a different cultural and temporal dimension than our own. Medieval codices are no longer books in the sense that a medieval writer, reader, or listener would have understood the term, because the contextual relation of these artefacts to those who are able to access them today has changed: they are now (rightly) preserved, and, as their keepers allow, viewed, observed, investigated, but not used for the purposes for which they were produced in the manner that those who made them and their contemporaries would have done.[18]

Echard's meditation on the shelfmarks of London, British Library, Cotton MS Otho A.xii, and its companion Cotton MS Otho A.xii* (note the asterisk), a sixteenth-century transcription made before the Cotton Library fire, is characteristic of her scholarship: insightful, erudite, and original; and most of all, attentive to what others might find unremarkable or easy to overlook. She interrogates the asterisk as a bibliographic sign: what, exactly does this particular asterisk represent?

---

[16] See particularly Siân Echard, 'Containing the Book: the Institutional Afterlives of Medieval Manuscripts', in *The Medieval Manuscript Book: Cultural Approaches*, ed. Michael Johnston and Michael van Dussen (Cambridge, 2015) and Echard and Andrew Prescott, 'Charming the Snake: Accessing and Disciplining the Medieval Manuscript', in *The Cambridge Companion to Medieval British Manuscripts*, ed. Orietta Da Rold and Elaine Treharne (Cambridge, 2020) as well as her earlier 'House Arrest: Modern Archives, Medieval Manuscripts', *Journal of Medieval and Early Modern Studies* 30, no. 2 (2000).

[17] Echard and Prescott, 'Charming the Snake', 263.

[18] Elsewhere in this volume, Elaine Treharne astutely discusses the concept of what she terms 'plenitextuality' or 'textual wholeness', which allows a consideration of 'how medieval manuscripts are conceived and perceived *as whole books* from the moment of intentionality of the compiler or scribe to the books' present lives in libraries, archives, and private collections as wholes or whole fragments or fragments with holes' (below, 171), and my argument here is, I think, along similar lines: our relationship with the physical artifacts containing the remnants of medieval textual production is always produced in relation to the totality of the artefactual history of that object, and this operates in such a way as to make inaccessible, above and beyond temporal and cultural distance, the idea of the *book* that a medieval user would have had in relation to the object as well as to the text contained therein.

Was Otho A.xii* being offered as a kind of prosthesis, a replacement for the missing medieval manuscript? Did 'see also' in Otho A.xii and the asterisk on the transcription imply a kind of hierarchy? ... This seemed, in short, a contradictory object, an artifact that both required institutional recognition ... and yet could also be put in a separate, asterisked category, one where it might be overlooked.[19]

For Echard, although the asterisk 'is in part simply a routine institutional gesture', it is also moreover an invitation to consider the object from outside the ordinary perspective of the ontology of the book imposed by the institutional structures of the archive. As she says, it is 'useful' to consider something as mundane and easy to overlook as the naming conventions of these manuscripts, themselves layered with institutional history, 'because to do so allows [one] to consider the implications of the institutional markers ... that frame the transcript. By paying attention to mundane or unremarked practices, we can open up a conversation about the ways that books are constructed, and reconstructed, in the archives that hold them.'[20]

Echard also deploys an 'attention to the mundane or unremarked' to great effect in another domain within her readings of Gower and his modern reception. As she has pointed out, looking to typographical features of the print tradition of Gower's works, printers' '[design] decisions have had lasting effects on how we read, and teach, Gower'; that while something like the use of italics can 'assur[e] us, for example, that it is acceptable to skim or skip the Latin',[21] the Latin apparatus, as she has ably shown, is in fact an essential component of the work. Our readings of medieval texts, her work tells us, are structured by the choices the editors of the books we encounter, as well as those of the other editors of the text throughout its editorial history, because of their editorial attention; for instance, comparing the sixteenth-century edition of Gower by Thomas Berthelette, she notes that while 'Berthelette used Caxton's edition',

> he added some missing passages, and expanded considerably on the prefatory matter, writing an extensive introduction which praised Gower's language and the moral value of the stories contained in the *Confessio*. He also made some additions and changes to Caxton's table of contents, changes which subtly reorient a reader's perception of the text. He tends, for example, to include entries for the parts of the *Confessio* that are focused more on information than on narrative – the signs of the zodiac in Book VII are one instance. A reader of Berthelette's edition might see the *Confessio* as a kind of encyclopedia, as well as the story compendium Caxton suggests it to be.[22]

---

[19] Echard, 'Containing the Book', 96–97.

[20] Echard, 'Containing the Book', 97.

[21] Siân Echard, 'Gower in Print', in *A Companion to Gower*, ed. Siân Echard (Cambridge, 2004), 125–26.

[22] Echard, 'Gower in Print', 116–17.

The extent to which *Confessio Amantis* is encyclopaedic, is a compendium of stories, is a mirror for princes, is a love poem, is, as we have seen above, still a matter of critical debate. As Echard points to here, if editorial interventions are able to promote, rather than fabricate, one or another reading, surely the work is, to some extent, all of them. Why do we so often, not heeding this advice, insist on applying our modern categories in this way, attempting to determine whether the text is this or is that, when a more useful answer might be that it contains within it a multiplicity of features in which we can discern, or with which we can impose, this or that category, from moment to moment?

Echard has herself written of the reception of Gower's work as dull, of 'the inherited notion of schoolmasterly dullness'[23] that the figure of Gower carried with it in the twentieth century and 'the legacy of the Chaucer–Gower pairing'.[24] In doing so, Echard never quite, so far as I am aware, presents an explicit argument that Gower is *not* dull: certainly, she says, there is something in the text, as well as in the historical context, that has meant the charges levelled at him by (particularly nineteenth-century) critics of a dullness, a schoolmarmish didacticism, resonated in the way that they did, and have. Certainly, too, for Echard there is much we find in Gower's poetic corpus that is *not* boring, that is poetically captivating – but for her to take the contrary, to work to convince us that Gower's work is unfairly held in lower esteem than that of his contemporaries, is beside the point; we gain, rather, from reading Gower's work *despite* its supposed, or apparent, dullness, by noticing and paying attention to what has been overlooked by other readers and often previous critics *precisely because of* their qualities that (at least post-medieval) readers have found dull. Gower's work is self-evidently interesting, or at least should be, given due attention.[25]

The approach in evidence in these interventions – the insistence that examining the overlooked is not merely productive of new readings but is

---

[23] Siân Echard, 'Introduction', in *A Companion to Gower*, ed. Siân Echard (Cambridge, 2001), 19.

[24] Echard, 'Introduction', 22.

[25] Echard and Claire Fanger, in the introduction to their translation of the Latin verses of *Confessio Amantis*, make more-or-less this argument directly: 'We had also, however, a reason [i.e. in translating the Latin verses] that might be described as ideological rather than practical. Gower's Latin poetry – indeed, most medieval Latin poetry – has not in general been highly thought of or much praised for its literary merits. The poor reputation of medieval Latin writing is almost certainly aggravated by the fact that, even where translations exist, they are usually in prose, and seldom make a strong attempt to evoke such literary or poetic qualities as the work might in fact have. Since Gower's writing is often thought, by many people not well acquainted with it, to be without humor, awkward, or dull – since, in other words, Gower's reputation has already suffered enough – it seemed advisable for his admirers not to exacerbate the situation by enclosing his delicate feet in the cement shoes of prose. Our attempt to capture Gower's poetry with our own is not just a vote of confidence; it is an effort, though a modest one, to aid in the rendering of a fair judgment on his work' (xxix).

in fact able to reveal that which constitutes our readings – is representative of the value of Echard's critical approach and of the originality of her scholarship. It is also a habit to which, as her doctoral student, I am very grateful to have been taught, and in which to have been encouraged. In my own writing, I have elsewhere argued that medieval textual records that seem to a modern reader unremarkable and repetitive can unexpectedly allow us to approach difficult-to-access questions of medieval people's temporal subjectivities.[26] Applying Echard's approach of 'paying attention to [the] mundane or unremarked' to our readings of texts opens new possibilities of seeing that are otherwise impossible, of attending to readings that make an approach to differences in epistemologies and qualia that would be otherwise unrecoverable. Of course, remarking on the unremarked is, one may rightly point out, perhaps the foundation of literary criticism. But I am talking here not about *method*, but rather about *objects*. As scholars and critics, we tend, naturally, to focus our attention on the exceptional rather than the commonplace – but in so doing we elevate the unique, unusual, the singular, the abnormal, at the expense of the kinds of texts that would most often have been encountered by users of medieval manuscript books. What wasn't, and hasn't been, I wonder, celebrated as novel and remarkable, but instead was so familiar as to be wholly *un*remarkable? Why do we, as scholars, not more often turn to these materials – the copious, the *boring* – in order to stage our encounters with the medieval, and with those who wrote and read these books?

Dulled Sense

While Gower's modern critics have sought to defend his work against its reception as staid and dull, or at least to present a case for reading it despite its supposed dullness, *Confessio Amantis* is a poem that at times seems to presuppose the label. The Latin verses that begin the work are puzzling in ways apart from the riddle of the final couplet:

> Torpor, ebes sensus, scola parua labor minimusque
> Causant quo minimus ipse minora canam:
> Qua tamen Engisti lingua canit Insula Bruti
> Anglica Carmente metra iuuante loquar.
> Ossibus ergo carens que conterit ossa loquelis
> Absit, et interpres stet procul oro malus.[27]

---

[26] William Green, 'Time and Commemoration in English Monastic Hagiography', *Journal of English and Germanic Philology* 120, no. 1 (2021).

[27] *CA* Prol.i.

[Dull wit, slight schooling, torpor, labour less,
Make slight the themes I, least of poets, sing.
Let me, in Hengist's tongue, in Brut's isle sung,
With Carmen's help, tell forth my English verse.
Far hence the boneless one whose speech grinds bones,
Far hence be he who reads my verses ill.][28]

Criticism of these lines has understandably focused on the riddle, the humility topos expressed by the poet (*minimus ipse minora canam*), and the role of Carmentis, the prophetic nymph of Ovid's *Fasti* who is looked to for aid as the speaker attempts, famously, to shape his verses into 'Hengists's tongue'. But what muse is invoked here? Carmentis is not called upon in the vocative, but is rather instrumentalised in the ablative (*Carmente ... iuuvante loquar*).[29] The first couplet, on the other hand, ending on *canam*, presents us perhaps with a wry echo of the *Aeneid*;[30] this is a use of irony appropriate to the *Confessio*, I think, because of both its length and its speaker's profession (or affectation) of age and impotence, in evidence here at the very beginning of the poem as it is at the very end. The cause of the poet's singing of these insignificant, inferior (*minora*, again with a wry nod to the poem's length) verses is identified as the four abstract ideas presented in the strong first line of this couplet: *torpor* (sluggishness, listlessness, sloth); *ebes sensus* (a dull or insensitive faculty of perception); *scola parua* (little schooling) and *labor minimus* (very little work). I say 'ideas', but I think here, as throughout the poem, there is rather a degree of personification occuring: the syntax of the first line, beginning with 'torpor' standing alone, before the resolution provided by the verb in the second line, at first sounds as if it is these qualities that are being addressed.

---

[28] For the Latin verses of *CA*, I quote the translations of Echard and Fanger, *Latin Verses*, here at 3.

[29] On the relationship between the multiple voices and languages of the poem and their personifications here, see Siân Echard, 'With Carmen's Help: Latin Authorities in the *Confessio Amantis*', *Studies in Philology* 95, no. 1 (1998).

[30] Echard has also remarked upon the parallel of Gower's use of *canam* in the first Latin poem in *CA* with *cano* in the first line of the *Aeneid* in Echard, 'With Carmen's Help', 27, where she notes that 'the opening line of the *Aeneid* ... is a standard weapon in the arsenal of the medieval writer of epic and may be echoed in the verb chosen here' but concludes that 'if there is a hint of Vergil in the Latin verse, it is submerged in the medieval encyclopedist-compiler of the prose and the English. This is an academic exercise.' I agree. The first two lines of the opening Latin poem of *CA* are meant to echo this 'standard weapon', and to be recognised by a reader as so doing, but to immediately subvert the expectations of this recognition: our poet is singing under the influence of torpor, dullness, ignorance, and laziness, rather than about arms and the man.

Are not torpor, dulled perception, lack of schooling, and an aversion to work not only the *cause* of the poem but also, in some way, its subject?

The poem's much-discussed prologue that follows these Latin verses continues its meditation upon the idea of dullness. 'We also', the narrator tells us,

> In oure tyme among ous hiere
> Do wryte of newe some matiere,
> Ensampled of these olde wyse ...
> Bot for men sein, and soth it is,
> That who that al of wisdom writ
> It dulleth ofte a mannes wit
> To him that shcal it aldai rede,
> For thilke cause, if that ye rede,
> I wolde go the middel weie
> And wryte a bok betwen the tweie,
> Somwhat of lust, somwhat of lore,
> That of the lasse or of the more
> Som man mai lyke of that I wryte:[31]

Of course, Gower's 'middle weie', and the degree to which it succeeds, has long been debated. Certainly, on the whole the 'lore' greatly outweighs the 'lust' throughout Gower's (ostensible) attempt to smuggle learning into his readers' minds by making it more palatable, wrapping it in what is said to be a lover's confession. But the speaker here remains preoccupied with both potential accusations of dullness and the reputation of learning generally: proverbially, to those who read 'wisdom'[32] all day, the result is a 'dulled wit', something the speaker of the Latin verses professes to have in abundance.

Gower does not merely anticipate a readerly complaint of dullness but also works through the poem's framing devices to provide the reader with a way to respond to this anticipated (and often, in the centuries since, actual) reaction. One question the poem's prologue leaves basically unanswered is what the subject of the work is supposed to be: 'somwhat of lust, somewhat of lore', yes, but what are we to take this to mean, especially when the subject introduced in Book I is love, rather than lust? The Prologue provides us with clues, many of which have attracted critical attention: the narrator's (at least, if not Gower's own) world-weariness, for example; the request from Richard in the middle of the Thames for the poem's composition; the complaints regarding the church, and the retelling of Nebuchadnezzar's dream and the

---

[31] *CA* Prol.4b–21.

[32] 'Transmitted wisdom, wise teaching regarding temporal matters; sound advice; also, a piece of good advice, a wise saying; a sage observation'; *Middle English Dictionary* s.v. 'wisdom', n., 4(a).

decline of the world; the hope for a new Arion able to sing warring factions to peace and accord. But none of these alone gives us much of a sense of the matter of the work as a whole, nor do they explain the relationships among 'lust', 'lore', and the figure of the lover. The poem, of course, comes to be about those things that Genius relates in his instruction of Amans, but the way these elements of 'lore' interact remains unclear, despite scholarship's attempts to discern a plan or pattern.

R. F. Yeager reports that he 'ha[s] begun to think it probable that a growing thoughtfulness about the nature and urgencies of time contributed mightily' to the composition of the poem and its language(s), and asserts that 'time in all its various manifestations' was 'central to Gower's plan for the *Confessio Amantis*'.[33] I agree: time is a recurring preoccupation of the poem, albeit one among many such, and one that has received less critical attention than others. For Yeager, Gower's attention to time stems from his understanding of England as a nation, existing within time, having a past, present, and future and, crucially, as Yeager points out, for 'a knowledgeable Christian like Gower' the proper observation of time-calculation 'demanded reference to multiple systems' (i.e., the *temporale* and the *sanctorale*), each of which imbued time itself with 'moral and logistical meaning'; the calculation and tracking of time, then, 'has a fundamentally moral rationale'.[34]

Concern with time is abundant in the surviving literature from the turn of the fifteenth century in a peculiar way. It has often been discussed in terms of the development of a medieval sense of so-called 'science' in a way that is thought to have at least laid the foundations for our own: the reception of Chaucer's treatise on the astrolabe is a chief example here. But I think Yeager's understanding, that for Gower, 'mundane time has intense urgency', which orders 'a progression of opportunities for moral intervention, personal and political',[35] aids us in beginning to see the deep cultural currents that led to a preoccupation with time that underlies the extensive production in the late English Middle Ages of texts described as astronomical or astrological, and also including subjects often deemed even more esoteric such as alchemy. The literary works produced within this moment of epistemological instability often, in navigating such cultural change, may in reaction present us with a copiousness, an overabundance, of material that in some way speaks to these changes but that elicits in readers for whom this change is no longer immanent a sense of dullness that risks critical foreclosure.

---

[33] R. F. Yeager, 'Amans the Memorious', in *Later Middle English Literature, Materiality, and Culture: Essays in Honor of James M. Dean*, ed. Brian Gastle and Erick Kelemen (Newark, DE, 2018), 95.

[34] *Yeager*, 'Amans the Memorious', 98.

[35] *Yeager*, 'Amans the Memorious', 99–100.

Perhaps the most basic question *Confessio Amantis* seems to want to resolve is that of why things occur, why events have certain results, a question that for Gower is bound up with the epistemological status of the stars and planets and their role in ordering time and history. It is a question that the poem equivocates about, even as it offers answers that sound, in isolation, in one tongue but not the other, definitive. Provoked by Gower's horror of the unruled, unrestrained mob, the poem discusses what it is that determines the outcome of events. Evil must come from man, not God; nevertheless 'yet som men wryte / And sein that fortune is to wyte, / And som men holde oppinion / That it is constellacion, / Which causeth al that a man doth: / God wot of bothe which is soth.'[36] Is it fortune or fate, on the one hand, or 'constellacioun', the alignment of the planets, on the other, that causes men to be good or evil? Is behaviour predestined by chance, or is there a deterministic planetary influence at work? God knows.

The voice of the Latin annotator also knows, or, rather, at first glance appears to know. In the margins, the speaker repeats the question but proceeds to offer a corrective that is lacking in the English verse:

> Some propose, as is said, that it is by the means of the chance of fortune, and some by the influence of the planets, that the results of events necessarily have happened. But it is preferable for it to be said that those things which we call in this world success and misfortune come to pass according to the deserts of men as befitting the judgement of God.[37]

Eventually, the narrator of the English poem tells us that 'man is overal / His ogne cause of wel and wo',[38] but rather than following the Latin in finding it preferable to ascribe these results to God's judgement of the merits or demerits of human beings, the English text turns to the figure of Fortune's wheel.

We find a similar ambiguity in Book VII. The book purports to relate the knowledge of various subjects as taught to Alexander by Aristotle, and is organised into two overarching divisions – 'philosophy' and 'policy'. Astronomy, alongside arithmetic, music, and geometry, is a branch of mathematics, itself a portion of 'Theorique', the first part of philosophy. But by far the largest part of the discussion of all of 'philosophy' in Book VII deals with the twin subjects of astronomy and astrology. This topic receives 880 lines, compared to the 830 dedicated to all the other elements of 'philosophy'

---

[36] *CA* Prol.528–33.

[37] 'Nota contra hoc, quod aliqui sortem fortune, aliqui influenciam planetarum ponunt, per quod, vt dicitur, rerum euentus necessario contingit. Set pocius dicendum est, quod ea que nos prospera et aduersa in hoc mundo vocamus, secundum merita et demerita hominum digno dei iudicio proveniunt' (*CA* p. 19, marginal note at line 530).

[38] *CA* Prol.546b–47.

combined. Prior to the beginning of the astronomical section, Genius tells us that knowledge of astronomy takes primacy for an understanding of terrestrial matters: without it, all other science is in vain; it flies above the other sciences as an eagle flies above the earth.[39] While some of the astronomical material that Genius relates in the book is a compilation of lore found in Gower's sources, especially in Latini's *Livres dou Trésor*, Gower's use of these in this astronomical section is sporadic, and, once again, the voice of the Latin apparatus works against that of the English verse.

Two of the Latin verses of Book VII bear noting in particular in relation to the long discussion of astronomy. In the English verse, Genius has this to say about the importance of the discipline of astronomy:

> Benethe upon this Erthe hiere,
> Of alle thinges the matiere,
> As tellen ous thei that ben lerned,
> Of thing above it stant governed,
> That is to sein of the Planetes.
> The cheles bothe and ek the hetes,
> The chances of the world also,
> That we fortune clepen so,
> Among the mennes nacion
> Al is thurgh constellacion,
> Wherof that som man hath the wele,
> And som man hath deseses fele
> In love as wel as othre thinges;
> The stat of realmes and of kinges
> In time of pes, in time of werre
> It is conceived of the Sterre:
> And thus seith the naturien
> Which is an Astronomien.
> Bot the divin seith otherwise,
> That if men weren goode and wise
> And plesant unto the godhede,
> Thei scholden noght the sterres drede;
> For o man, if him wel befalle,
> Is more worth than ben thei alle
> Towardes him that weldeth al.[40]

Here, as in the Prologue, we see two opposing camps of thinking regarding celestial influence, now identified as the 'Astronomien' and the 'divin'. For the astronomer, all earthly events are the result of planetary influences, 'conceived of the Sterre' and effected through the workings of 'constellacioun', the

[39] *CA* Book VII, lines 625–32.
[40] *CA* Book VII, lines 633–57.

particular conjunctions of heavenly bodies; the theologian, on the other hand, says that men need not dread the stars if they are godly. A brief attempt is then made to reconcile these seemingly contradictory positions: 'Bot yit the lawe original, / Which he hath set in the natures, / Mot worchen in the creatures, / That therof mai be non obstacle, / Bot it stonde upon miracle / Thrugh priere of som holy man.'[41] The operations of the celestial bodies, governed by laws ordained by God, thus work upon earthly creatures according to their natures; this, however, can be overcome by a 'miracle' through the intercession of the 'priere of som holy man'. Unfortunately for Amans, the astronomical lore that follows, including discussions of the natures of the planets, the signs of the zodiac, the fifteen stars, and so forth, does very little to explain how the information it provides might relate to questions of causality or physical determinism.

The fourth Latin poem of Book VII, heading this section, does not help clarify the situation and echoes the ambiguity and confusion of the discussion of causal priority found in the Prologue. Lower things (*inferiora*), the Latin verses tell us, 'by starry law ... are ruled': 'But now and then that rule may prove deceptive. / With God's help wise men dominate the stars; / And fate quite rightly brings on new surprises.'[42] The point of Genius's discussion of astronomy, then, would seem to be for the hearer to become one of these *vir sapiens* who dominate the stars with God's help (*deo mediante*), but even so, it seems, causal priority remains unsettled: the 'starry law' (*lex plantearum*) can *sometimes* deceive (*interdum ... fallit*), and fate still brings new and unexpected occurrences.

What, then, is the point of the inclusion of this mass of astronomical material? The straightforward answer is that it was thought, at this historical juncture, to be in some way important for an educated subject to know, and that similar material had been circulating in compendia for some time (like the *Livres dou Trésor* and the *Secretum Secretorum*). But why does it continue to reappear, interjecting itself into the middle of Gower's poem? I think we may begin to see an approach to an answer through the conjunction of the end of Book VII's astronomical discussion and the second set of Latin verses we encounter in Book VII, heading the section beginning the discussion of 'Theorique', which contains the subdisciplines of theology, physics, and mathematics, of which astronomy forms a major part (and to which the greatest proportion of verses in the philosophical section of the book are dedicated). At the end of the astronomical section, which concludes the discussions of both mathematics and indeed of 'Theorique', there is a passage that traces the development of the knowledge of astronomy from its ancient origins and

---

[41] *CA* Book VII, lines 658–63.

[42] Echard and Fanger, *Latin Verses*, 77, translating the lines: 'Lege planetarum magis inferiora reguntur, / Ista set interdum regula fallit opus. / Vir mediante deo sapiens dominabitur astris, / Fata nec immerito quid nouitatis agunt' (*CA* Book VII iv).

reiterates its primacy: 'The science of Astronomie, / Which principal is of clergie / To dieme between wo and wel / In thinges that be naturel, / Thei hadde a gret travail on honde / That made it ferst ben understonde.'[43]

The period was one in which medieval understandings of astronomy, cosmology, and temporality were in flux: whereas in prior centuries, scholastic conceptualisations of the heavens in Western Europe revolved around the calendar-reckoning practice of *computus*, astronomical lore as a feature of the description of astrological practices had gradually become more widespread, and more accepted, coinciding with the spread in the Latin West of Arabic mathematical and astronomical texts (including classical astronomical and astrological sources preserved in Arabic translations), as well as the emergence of the almanac (itself, of course, bearing an Arabic name) as the primary calendrical tradition rather than the earlier computstical model.[44] Following the discussion in the *Speculum Astronomiae* of Albertus Magnus, Gower traces the genealogy of astronomical knowledge: from Noah, who was the first 'that this science write' (line 1450), to Nimrod, then (through some obscure intermediaries) to Ptolemy, whose astronomical work known as 'Almagest' was known to Western Europe in the later Middle Ages through a Latin translation of an Arabic translation, to Alfraganus, to a planisphere made by 'Gebuz and Alpetragus'; other biblical figures (Abraham and Moses) are then imputed as possible astronomers, and finally 'Hermes':

> Above alle othre in this science
> He hadde a gret experience;
> Thrugh him was many a sterre assised,
> Whos bokes yit ben auctorized.
> I may noght knowen alle tho
> That writen in the time tho
> Of this science; bot I finde,
> Of jugement be weie of kinde
> That in o point thei alle accorden:
> Of sterres which thei recorden
> That men mai sen upon the hevene,
> Ther ben a thousend sterres evene
> And tuo and twenty, to the syhte
> Which aren of humself so bryhte,
> That men mai dieme what thei be,
> The nature and the properte.[45]

---

[43] *CA* Book VII, lines 1439–45.

[44] On the esoteric and potentially illicit material of Book VII, see Falk, 'Natural Sciences', cited above; on the late history and influence of the computistical tradition as it intersected with new astronomical thought and observational practices, see Laurel Means, '"Ffor as moche as yche man may not haue þe astrolabe": Popular Middle English Variations on the Computus', *Speculum* 67 no. 3 (July 1992): 595–623.

[45] *CA* Book VII, lines 1477–92.

This passage, tracing the development of astronomical lore or learning, ends the long astronomical section of Book VII, seeking to ground (as did its source) the potentially esoteric discipline in a biblical origin. But I would read this, as the closing gesture in the astronomical section, and indeed of the whole discussion dedicated to 'Theorique', against the Latin poem that opens the section on theorique and its constituents:

> Prima creatorem dat scire sciencia summum:
> Qui caput agnoscit, sufficit illud ei.
> Plura viros quandoque iuuat nescire, set illud
> Quod videt expediens, sobrius ille sapit.[46]

> [This first science [i.e., theology] leads us to our Maker;
> Who learns the principle can leave the rest.
> Sometimes it serves men not to know too much;
> The sober man can see what knowledge serves him.][47]

This admonition toward judiciousness in learning appears to undercut (especially) the inclusion of the glut of astronomical lore that forms the largest proportion of the discussion of theorique; it also seems to express the same weariness with overmuch reading seen before in the Latin verses of the Prologue. The better part of wisdom, for the speaker of the Latin verses, is an understanding of when to stop reading.

We see, at least in relation to the astronomical material included in *Confessio Amantis*, a tension between the plenitude, indeed the excess, of the English poem, and the correctives the Latin verses offer us toward judiciousness, toward an acknowledgement of the dullness produced by an excess of reading and study. I think that it is precisely this tension, and especially the reaction that subsequent generations of readers and critics have had, and that the speaker of the Latin verses anticipates – that this stuff is *dull* – that should in fact alert us that this is precisely where something interesting is happening. Why, after all, *would* we elaborate upon material that the text itself acknowledges is difficult, is contradictory, is boring, meant to be skimmed or ignored, why *not* favour instead something more captivating, about which we might have something to say, against which we might produce a commentary that is more arresting? Tedium as a critical reaction may often indicate a locus in the text where our epistemological framework is unable to account for that which we have encountered. If the surviving texts of the late English Middle Ages show us a time in which modern epistemological structures, such as science, can be said to begin to emerge, it then also provides us with the opportunity to engage with

---

[46] *CA* Book VII, ii.
[47] Echard and Fanger, *Latin Verses*, 74–75.

the world that pre-existed, and was submerged by, this emergence, through the artifacts produced in such a moment, and specifically through engagement with the material contained within them that is so copious and seemingly unremarkable that our critical sense at first directs us away from it, trained as we are to seek out the unusual. How do we begin not only to *critique* but to transcend our epistemological boundaries, to unthink the modern idea that that which isn't 'science' is categorically different from knowledge, is instead perforce religious, superstitious? Perhaps less judiciousness in our selection of readings, a re-evaluation of the incisive tendencies our critical training provides us, is in order, one that would allow us to centre the quotidian and enter into a different relation with the material we have received from the past that is marked with categories like 'difficult' and 'dull'.

8

A Knight at the Roxburghe (Club): George Granville Sutherland-Leveson-Gower and the Textual Transmission of *Balades and Other Poems by John Gower*

DAVID WATT

When I learned this volume was being compiled in honour of Siân Echard, I immediately thought of four books. This seemed fitting since I immediately thought of her when I encountered these books in the summer of 2008. The books are catalogued consecutively in the British Library catalogue because they are intimately related to each other. The first is London, British Library MS Add. 59495, a trilingual Gower manuscript completed in 1400 that is also known as the Trentham Manuscript (and referred to hereafter as the Trentham Manuscript).[1] The second book, MS Add. 59496, is a transcription of the Trentham Manuscript completed by Henry Strachey in 1764 (hereafter Strachey's Transcription). The third and fourth books are even more closely connected: MS Add. 59497 is the page proofs for the edition of *Balades and Other Poems by John Gower* that George Granville Sutherland-Leveson-Gower presented to the Roxburghe Club in 1818 (hereafter Earl Gower's Proofs) and MS Add. 59498 is one of the one hundred copies of this edition that were printed from the corrected proofs (hereafter Earl Gower's Edition).[2]

---

[1] On the dating of this manuscript and its significance, see Sebastian Sobecki, '*Ecce patet tensus*: The Trentham Manuscript, *In Praise of Peace*, and John Gower's Autograph Hand', *Speculum* 90, no. 1 (2015): 925–59. For a different argument about dating, see David Watt, '"Mescreauntz", Schism, and the Plight of Constantinople: Evidence for Dating and Reading London, British Library, Additional MS 59495', in *John Gower in Manuscripts and Early Printed Books*, ed. Martha Driver, Derek Pearsall, and R. F. Yeager (Cambridge, 2020), 131–51. See also Craig E. Bertolet, 'Gower's French Manuscripts', in *The Routledge Research Companion to John Gower*, ed. Ana Sáez-Hidalgo, Brian Gastle, and R. F. Yeager (New York, 2016), 97–101.

[2] On the Roxburghe Club and its editions, see David Matthews, *The Making of*

I thought of Siân when I encountered these four books that summer because they seemed to be curated with her expertise in mind and because I knew at that point that I would get to learn more about them when her *Printing the Middle Ages* appeared later that year.[3]

In her chapter 'Aristocratic Antiquaries: Gower on Gower', Echard demonstrates that the eighteenth- and nineteenth-century reproductions of verse in the Trentham Manuscript reveal that it was considered 'an artifact to be reproduced and passed along from one century to the next, with each generation having its own ideas about what parts of that artifact should be reproduced, and how'.[4] I agree with Echard's view, and it has led me to reassess the edition of *Balades and Other Poems by John Gower* that George Granville Sutherland-Leveson-Gower (hereafter Earl Gower because he held that title from 1803 to 1833) made for the Roxburghe Club. By reconstructing the process by which Earl Gower edited the *Balades and Other Poems*, I aim to show that his editorial approach was both innovative and reflective of ideas that were circulating among members of the Roxburghe Club in its early years. Earl Gower used Strachey's Transcription to establish his text while employing other print technologies to convey aspects of the Trentham Manuscript's physical characteristics. When seen in the context of other early Roxburghe Club editions, Earl Gower's edition of John Gower's *Balades* invites us to reconsider the Roxburghe Club members' activities as editors and audience, for it reflects their sophisticated understanding of textual transmission as an interaction between what Jerome McGann calls its linguistic and bibliographic codes.[5] When considered from this perspective, the editions made by early members of the Roxburghe Club provide insight into developments in the editing of Middle English texts while reminding us that editorial decisions are often influenced by technological and financial considerations as much as scholarly principles.

The title page of *Balades and Other Poems by John Gower* proclaims that it was 'Printed from the Original Manuscript in the Library of the Marquis

---

Middle English (Minneapolis, 1999), 87. For more on the texts in these manuscripts, see R. F. Yeager, ed. and trans., *John Gower: The French Balades*, TEAMS Middle English Texts Series (Kalamazoo, 2011); Siân Echard, 'Gower: French Poetry', in *The Encyclopedia of Medieval Literature in Britain*, ed. Siân Echard and Robert Rouse (Chichester, 2017); and Peter Nicholson, 'The French Works: The Ballades', in *The Routledge Research Companion to John Gower*, ed. Sáez-Hidalgo, Gastle, and Yeager (New York, 2017), 312–20.

[3] Siân Echard, *Printing the Middle Ages* (Philadelphia, 2008). I draw mainly on the chapter 'Aristocratic Antiquaries: Gower on Gower', 97–125.

[4] Echard, *Printing*, 118.

[5] Jerome McGann, *The Textual Condition* (Princeton, 1991), esp. 'The Socialization of Texts', 69–83.

of Stafford at Trentham.'[6] In his preface to the edition, Earl Gower explains that he will not provide a lengthy description of the Trentham Manuscript because one already exists:

> An account of the Manuscript in the Marquis of Stafford's Library, containing Gower's French Balades and other Poems, will be found in the appendix to the second volume of Warton's History of English Poetry, and in the Illustrations of Gower and Chaucer, by the Revd. H. J. Todd, whose judicious remarks render unnecessary any further observations on the subject.[7]

Echard has shown that the Trentham Manuscript held a special place in the library of the first marquess of Stafford, who was also son of the first Earl Gower and father of the Earl Gower who presented John Gower's *Balades* to the Roxburghe Club in 1818. According to Echard, the manuscript's 'twin connections to the Lancastrians and to the noble house of Gower' were used by several generations of Yorkshire Gowers to suggest a genealogical link between their family, who owned the manuscript, and the medieval author.[8] It seems likely that Earl Gower decided to base his Roxburghe Club edition on the Trentham Manuscript because of its importance to his family, yet it is curious that he did not include 'In Praise of Peace', which is addressed to Henry IV, if he wanted to emphasise a Lancastrian connection. Earl Gower explains that he did not include this text, the only English poem in the Trentham Manuscript, because it had already been printed 'in Urry's Edition of Chaucer's works'.[9] The availability of a printed text did not preclude other club members from selecting texts for their editions: almost all of the books presented to the society in its early years were editions of texts available in early printed books, not manuscripts. Nonetheless, it seems as though Earl Gower took the Roxburghe Club directive to reprint scarce works very seriously: he justifies his decision to edit the 'French Balades' by reminding readers that they 'are supposed not to exist in any other MS'.[10] Thus Earl Gower emphasises the originality of

---

[6] London, British Library, MS Additional 59498, fol. 1r.

[7] MS Add. 59498, fol. 4r. Rev. Henry J. Todd, *Illustrations of the Lives and Writings of Gower and Chaucer: Collected from Authentick Documents* (London, 1810), 95–108 effectively covers the same ground as Thomas Warton, *History of English Poetry, from the Close of the Eleventh to the Commencement of the Eighteenth Century*, 3 vols (London, 1775–81).

[8] Echard, *Printing*, 118. Cf. Shayne Husbands, *The Early Roxburghe Club, 1812–1835: Book Club Pioneers and the Advancement of English Literature* (London, 2017), chapter 8, esp. 141–42.

[9] MS Add. 59498, fol. 4r.

[10] MS Add. 59498, fol. 4r.

the Trentham Manuscript and of his Roxburghe Club Edition by insisting that both are the earliest examples of their kind.

Although Earl Gower's Edition does not include every text in the Trentham Manuscript, it does use the technology at his disposal to represent many of its textual and physical features. Paradoxically, Earl Gower's reliance on Strachey's Transcription of the Trentham Manuscript to make his edition provides the clearest evidence that he wanted his edition to represent the medieval book's physical and textual characteristics as faithfully as possible. It is unlikely that a modern editor with access to the Trentham Manuscript would make much use of an eighteenth-century copy of the Latin and French poems to create a critical edition, yet the notes on this manuscript and Earl Gower's Proofs reveal that Strachey's Transcription was used to set the text of his edition. Contemporary readers are likely to question the sincerity of Earl Gower's claim to have printed his edition from 'the original manuscript' since it is clear, according to Echard, that Strachey's Transcription 'became the copy text for the edition of Gower's *Balades* produced in 1818 for the Roxburghe Club'.[11] While Earl Gower would not have used the term 'copy text', I believe it is likely that he considered the Trentham Manuscript to be the basis for his edition insofar as it determined the way he represented its linguistic and bibliographic codes. Although Earl Gower used Strachey's Transcription in the way many editors would use a copy-text, there are nevertheless practical and theoretical reasons for thinking that Earl Gower was in earnest when he described his edition as being printed from 'the original manuscript'.

From a practical perspective, Earl Gower had several good reasons for using Strachey's Transcription to make his edition. First, the printer seems to have found the script that Henry Strachey (1736–1810) used to be very legible. Earl Gower's Proofs contain a few errors introduced by the printer, but there are very few instances where this seems to have arisen because of a misreading of the script. The exception that proves the rule is the introduction of 'Meras' for 'Merci' (fol. 18 of MS Add. 59497), but most of the other errors of this kind involve the substitution of individual letters, which could have had several different causes. Second, Earl Gower had every reason to think it was an accurate and complete transcription of the Trentham Manuscript. A note on the eighteenth-century manuscript reassures its readers, 'This is a true copy of the Original and is Examined By me Hen: Rooke 1764' (fol. 38r). The transcription is not entirely error-free, but a new transcription would likely have introduced some errors as well. A new transcription would also have come at a cost. Another Roxburghe Club member, Samuel Egerton Brydges, describes how 'the books in which I was engaged for the press occupied much of my time; and the long transcripts necessary were laborious and fatiguing. They

---

[11] Echard, *Printing*, 117.

were enough to suppress my imagination and deaden my powers of original thought.'[12] We cannot know whether Earl Gower would have made an edition of Gower's *Balades* if he did not have access to Strachey's Transcription, but it is certain that a new transcription would not have reduced the steps between the Trentham Manuscript and the edition. Moreover, we would be unlikely to regard a new transcription of the Trentham Manuscript as a copy-text: it would simply provide a way of making the text of 'the original manuscript' available to the printer, which is what Earl Gower used Strachey's Transcription to do. Ultimately, then, Earl Gower had practical reasons for providing Strachey's Transcription to the printer even if he considered the Trentham Manuscript to be what contemporary editors would call his copy-text.

From a more theoretical perspective, the corrections Earl Gower made to his Proofs reveal that while he provided the printer with Strachey's Transcription to set the text, he clearly considered the Trentham Manuscript to be his copy-text in the sense that W. W. Greg defines it.[13] Earl Gower's Proofs make it clear that while the printer used Strachey's Transcription to set the text, Earl Gower deferred to the Trentham Manuscript when dealing with substantives (diction) and accidentals (spelling, punctuation, and capitalisation).[14] There are only two instances where the final edition follows Strachey's Transcription over the Trentham Manuscript on either grounds. The first appears on fol. 32r of the page proofs and edition, where the correction changes 'Seine' in the proofs to read 'Sein', as it does in the transcript rather than 'Lein' as it appears in the Trentham Manuscript. Later, in a note that appears on fol. 52r, Earl Gower adopts the transcript's expansion of 'Alexandrum' in a marginal note rather than strictly adhering to the Trentham Manuscript's reading of 'alexdru*m*'. Elsewhere, Earl Gower defers to the Trentham Manuscript on matters of substantials and spelling other than when he makes emendations of his own – that is, when he chooses a reading that is not witnessed in either manuscript. Earl Gower admits in the preface that he does not follow the Trentham Manuscript for punctuation because, he writes, 'the pointing has been so little attended to in the MS, that it has been judged better to omit it altogether'. This would not disqualify the manuscript from being a copy-text according to Greg's definition because punctuation falls under the rubric of accidental. Earl Gower writes that he followed the Trentham Manuscript when it came to another accidental: 'The spelling of the original has been faithfully adhered to.' If we accept Greg's definition, then, Earl Gower seems to have considered the Trentham Manuscript to be his copy-text even if he provided the printer with Strachey's Transcription to set the text.

[12] Husbands, *Early Roxburghe Club*, 110.

[13] W. W. Greg, 'The Rationale of Copy-Text', *Studies in Bibliography* 3 (1950).

[14] Erik Kelemen provides an excellent summary of these considerations in *Textual Editing and Criticism: An Introduction* (New York, 2009), 102.

Even if most of the available evidence shows that Earl Gower was keen to follow the text of the Trentham Manuscript as closely as possible, he did make several interventions as an editor. Most of these appear in the notes, and they often supply missing or lost text. Many of these emendations consist in the expansion of names to match the text or the provision of grammatical endings to Latin words. Emendations occur more rarely in the text of the poems, and they are mostly to be found in a cluster in which he adopts '-sse' endings rather than '-sce' as it appears on fol. 15r of the Trentham Manuscript (e.g., 'Gentilesse', 'lesse', 'noblesse', 'destresse'), possibly in reaction to the use of the '-ste' endings on fol. 13r of the transcription and fol. 15r of the page proofs ('Gentileste', 'leeste', 'nobleste', 'destreste'). There are a few other emendations: whereas 'damont' appears in all copies, Earl Gower amended it to 'damour' on fol. 14v of the final edition; he emends a phrase that appears as 'vn lieus' on fol. 35r of the Trentham Manuscript and 'lieus' in the transcription and page proofs to 'liens' on fol. 51r of the final edition. It is tempting to speculate that Earl Gower's limited interventions may have been informed by his understanding of what Beresford describes as the Herculean task of the editor. In *The Twelve Labours of Hercules, Exhibited in a Running Parallel with Those of an Editor*, Beresford quotes (with reasonable accuracy) Johnson's Preface to Shakespeare:

> An editor must have before him all possibilities of meaning, with all possibilities of expression: – such must be his comprehension of thought, and such his copiousness of language. Out of many readings possible, he must be able to select that, which best suits with the state, opinions, and mode of language, prevailing in every age, and with his Author's particular cast of thought, and turn of expression: – such must be his knowledge, and such his taste. Conjectural criticism demands more than humanity possesses; and he that exercises it with most praise, has frequent need of indulgence.[15]

Johnson's words, and their currency in early nineteenth-century bibliographic discourse, suggest that we might interpret Earl Gower's approach to emendations as an indication of the way he understood his role as an editor.

A passage in a book written by another member of the Roxburghe Club, Thomas Frognall Dibdin's *Bibliomania*, strengthens this argument and helps to explain why Earl Gower's identification of 'the original manuscript' in his family's library was an important legitimising claim from both an editorial

---

[15] James Beresford, *Bibliosophia; Or, Book-Wisdom; Containing Some Account of the Pride, Pleasure, and Privileges, of That Glorious Vocation, Book-Collecting; II. The Twelve Labours of An Editor, Separately Pitted against Those of Hercules* (London, 1810), 76. The passage he cites is taken from Samuel Johnson's Preface to *Shakespeare's Plays* published in 1765.

and genealogical perspective. 'In regard to the Greek and Latin Classics', Dibdin writes, 'the possession of these original editions is of the first consequence to editors who are anxious to republish the legitimate text of an author. Wakefield, I believe, always regretted that the first edition of Lucretius had not been earlier inspected by him.'[16] Earl Gower could have no such regrets, for he not only inspected the manuscript that he considered to be authoritative – correctly, given what Sebastian Sobecki has shown about Gower's involvement in it – but used it as the basis for his edition.[17] The notes and alterations Earl Gower made to Strachey's Transcription suggest that he treated it very much in the same way that a modern editor would treat a contemporary transcription. Some of these notes include instances where he makes up for textual loss on Strachey's Transcription rather than on the page proofs: on fol. 10v, for example, he adds the letters 'des gr' and 'nent'. If Earl Gower had used the Trentham Manuscript to correct Strachey's Transcription in its entirety before he provided it to the printer, the latter manuscript would not be considered a copy-text, but his decision not to do that also has a practical explanation. Corrections made to the Strachey Transcription had the potential to cause more confusion than they resolved. Ultimately, then, Earl Gower used Strachey's Transcription in a way that was consistent with his editorial principles for producing an authoritative version of texts as they appear in the Trentham Manuscript.

Other notes that Earl Gower made in Strachey's Transcription demonstrate his commitment to ensuring that his edition would show as much fidelity to the Trentham Manuscript's bibliographic features as its text. For example, Earl Gower makes several notes in the transcription to instruct the printer to print the rubrics in red, which is how they appear in the Trentham Manuscript. The number '1' appears in the top compartment of a large X on fol. 8v of MS Add. 59496, beside 'Rex celi Deus', and the direction 'in red type' appears in the margin. A note on fol. 10v indicates that the partial rubric to the *Cinkante Balades* is 'to begin a page & these broken lines to be printed in red ink'. Other notes provide instructions about how the printer was to make use of the numbers pencilled into MS Add. 59496: 'Where side memorandem occur, they are to be printed as below in small roman type' (fol. 13r). Because these numbers agree with those in the Trentham Manuscript, Earl Gower does not correct them even when the numbers are clearly incorrect: the numeral 'IIII' is used for both the fourth and fifth items in the *Cinquante Balades*. Most of the other instructions provide directions about the edition's layout, including instructions to include a 'blank line' in several instances (fols 31v and 32v).

---

[16] Thomas Frognall Dibdin, *The Bibliomania; Or, Book-Madness; Containing Some account of the History, Symptoms, and Cure of This Fatal Disease* (London, 1809), 69.

[17] See Sebastian Sobecki, '*Ecce patet tensus*', who argues that John Gower's hand appears in the Trentham Manuscript, further strengthening its connection with him.

Detailed directions appear on fol. 32r, where there is textual loss at the end of a Latin poem and the beginning of the *Traitié*: 'An explanatory Note to be inserted here as the end of this poem + the beginning of the French poem [are imperfect from] a leaf taken out of the original copy.' In his note at the beginning of the Roxburghe Club edition, Earl Gower explains that even the blank spaces are meant to signify something about the Trentham Manuscript: 'A leaf containing part of a French poem addressed to Henry the Fourth, and also the title of the Balades and a part of the first of them, having been unfortunately mutilated, blank spaces having been left in those places in the volume.' As Echard shows, Earl Gower's Edition also follows Strachey's Transcription by using blank space to indicate textual loss due to damage or excisions that were made to the manuscript.[18]

One of the most important ways in which Earl Gower's Edition diverges from Strachey's Transcription is that the former uses black-letter typeface to represent the gothic book hand used in the Trentham Manuscript while the latter employs an eighteenth-century script. As I noted earlier, the printer seems to have found Strachey's script to be very legible, and it seems likely that some nineteenth-century readers would have found it more legible than the typeface that appears in Earl Gower's Edition. However, Earl Gower's use of black-letter was a design decision that aligns with the approach other Roxburghe Club members consistently took to their early editions. Critics of the club, then and now, have seen this as a sign that they often deliberately chose to make texts less accessible than they might have done, not only by limiting their print run but by employing typefaces that were deemed unreadable by contemporaries. In his satirical *Bibliosophia*, James Beresford suggests that members of the Roxburghe Club might have chosen to print using black-letter both because it was associated with the origins of print and because it might have the additional benefit of being a deterrent to reading: 'The *Black-Letter Copy* is nearly coeval with the very birth, and being, of the Printer's craft; and if the uncouthly angular configuration – the obsoletely stiff, grim, and bloated appearance, of its characters, "Give pause" to the *modern* reader, – so much the happier for the *Collector*', who will be left 'in that undisturbed possession of his beloved rarities, which gives them all their value'.[19]

Beresford's distinction between collectors and readers is designed to make those who prefer black-letter seem like the foremost of the fools whom Sebastian Brant identifies in his *Ship of Fools* – the one who possesses books but does not value what he can learn from them – yet it also suggests that we might understand Earl Gower's approach to layout from another perspective.[20]

[18] Echard, *Printing*, 118.
[19] Beresford, *Bibliosophia*, 63.
[20] An image and four lines from Alexander Barclay's translation of the *Ship of Fools*, printed by Pynson in 1509, are featured on Dibdin's title page.

Beresford suggests that collectors and readers approach books in very different ways. Whereas collectors take 'but a bird's-eye view of a whole field of page', readers 'may be so inquisitive as to pore through every furrow' that they find it difficult to pass 'through a type so impassable as that which we have described'.[21] Whatever one thinks of the readability of Earl Gower's Edition, its use of typeface and layout does indeed create the impression that he took a bird's-eye view of the whole field of a manuscript leaf. This approach also seems to apply to the work of those Roxburghe Club members who were reproducing the look of early printed books. As Shayne Husbands argues:

> This was a conscious act, designed to reproduce the works as closely as possible to the originals, and in so doing ensuring the continued existence and reading of rare works, increasing the number of readers who could in effect access the original as an artefact in all ways that mattered and also giving back to the book its identity as a valued artefact in its own right, rather than just the carrier of the text, interchangeable with any other bundle of paper that could hold the ink.[22]

Earl Gower's edition of the *Balades* differs from many other early Roxburghe editions because it reproduces the features of a manuscript rather than an early printed book. Nonetheless, black-letter was chosen deliberately to represent the script used in the Trentham Manuscript rather than the script used in Strachey's Transcription or the Roman type used in the paratextual material of Earl Gower's Edition. The combination of black-letter typeface for the text, red ink for rubrics, and a layout that imitated the one employed in the Trentham Manuscript all contributed to the impression that readers were encountering a medieval page when they read Gower's *Balades*.

Earl Gower might well have served more nineteenth-century readers by selecting a different typeface, but his decision to employ black-letter was not just an anti-democratic reflex: it was aligned with the approach taken by other members of the Roxburghe Club and seems to reflect his commitment to reproducing bibliographic aspects of the Trentham Manuscript in addition to the text. In addition to using black-letter typeface to represent the Trentham Manuscript's script, Earl Gower had signatures in the manuscript reproduced lithographically, as Echard explains. John Dent used the same new technology in a book he presented to the society that same year: a reprint of Richard Pynson's *Solempnities and Triumphes Doon and Made at the Spousells and Marriage of the King's Daughter the Ladye Marye to the Prynce of Castile, Archduke of Austrige*. According to Husbands, 'the real significance of this reprint in the context of the club publications is that of the cutting-edge

---

[21] Beresford, *Bibliosophia*, 64–65.
[22] Husbands, *Early Roxburghe Club*, 91.

methods that Dent utilised in 1818 by having it printed by way of the recent invention of lithographic reproduction'.[23] This leads Husbands to conclude: 'When the Roxburghe Club reproduced their rare volumes they also attempted to reproduce as much information from the original item as they could, given the restrictions imposed by the available technology.'[24] Given the limitations any technology presents, decisions needed to be made about what features could and could not be reproduced in any given book. I agree with Echard that Earl Gower may have been motivated to represent the bibliographic features of the Trentham Manuscript in his edition because he hoped its authorship or provenance would establish or strengthen his credentials with fellow book collectors, and his employment of several technologies that could convey the Trentham Manuscript's medieval features to a nineteenth-century audience might have helped him to achieve this goal.

Ultimately, Earl Gower's Edition was designed to please a very specific audience – 'the president and members of the Roxburghe Club'.[25] As Husbands notes, the Roxburghe Club's approach to books has often been belittled as 'merely the hobby and extravagance of Regency aristocratic playboys'.[26] This perception was widespread at the time of the club's formation and has endured to some extent. However, Husbands also notes that only two of the eighteen men present at the club's inaugural dinner 'were peers and a further two baronets'.[27] The other fourteen founding members were not aristocrats, but they did share an extravagant passion for books. Their desire to collect and acquire books brought them together on 17 June 1812, when Lord Blandford purchased the Valdarfer Boccaccio (1471), a book considered to be the rarest available in the sale of the duke of Roxburghe's library.[28] According to Thomas Frognall Dibdin, who attended the sale and the inaugural Roxburghe Club dinner with Earl Spenser, the man who had been outbid, Lord Blandford won the auction by paying £2,260 – a sum equal to the amount paid for the rest of the library. This was clearly an extravagant price, and it is unsurprising that it came to be associated with the height of 'bibliomania', a term that Dibdin used as the title for a book published in 1809 (and later republished in expanded forms in 1811 and 1842).[29] *Bibliomania; Or Book-Madness* has a subtitle

---

[23] Husbands, *Early Roxburghe Club*, 90.
[24] Husbands, *Early Roxburghe Club*, 89.
[25] London, BL, MS Add. 59498, fol. 1r.
[26] Husbands, *Early Roxburghe Club*, 3.
[27] Husbands, *Early Roxburghe Club*, 40.
[28] For a cultural history of the importance of private collections, see Mark Purcell, *The Country House Library* (New Haven, 2017).
[29] The Roxburghe Club Pamphlet uses this term in its account of the club's origins. The pamphlet, which was hand printed by the Ounce Press in 1986, took its text from Robert Chambers, *The Book of Days: A Miscellany of Popular Antiquities in*

that promises the book will provide an account of the *History, Symptoms, and Cure of This Fatal Disease*. Citing Gabriel Peignot's *Dictionnaire de Bibliologie*, Dibdin defines bibliomania as 'a passion for possess[ing] books; not so much to be instructed by them, as to gratify the eye by looking on them. He who is affected by this mania knows books only by their titles and dates, and is rather seduced by the exterior than interior.'[30] Given that the early members of the Roxburghe Club agreed to meet annually to commemorate the sale of the Valdarfer Boccaccio, it is perhaps unsurprising that they have often been associated with the bibliomania that Dibdin critiques. Yet Dibdin's participation in the club and his dedication of *Bibliomania* to Richard Heber, Esq., another of the men who attended the inaugural Roxburghe Club dinner, suggests that the club's commitment to printing books to be presented to other members was an attempt to resist the dangers associated with bibliomania.

At the first anniversary dinner, Dibdin recalls in his *Bibliographical Decameron*, 'it was proposed for each member, in turn, according to the order of his name in the alphabet, to furnish the Society with a reprint of some rare old tract, or composition – chiefly of poetry'.[31] This agreement must have gratified Dibdin, who insisted that 'the reprinting of scarce and intrinsically valuable works' and 'the editing of our best ancient authors, whether in prose or poetry' were two means 'of effectually counteracting the progress of the Bibliomania' as he described it.[32] The first members of the Roxburghe Club followed Dibdin's prescription, for William Bolland had *Certaine Books of Virgiles Aenaeis, Turned into English Meter* printed for presentation in 1814 (the year after the agreement had been made), and Richard Heber had *Caltha Poetarum; Or, The Bumble Bee* printed for presentation in 1815. Five members printed books for presentation in 1816, and another eight were printed for 1817. Earl Gower's Edition, *Balades and Other Poems by John Gower*, was one of nine books printed by club members in 1818.[33] The form and format of the early Roxburghe volumes demonstrate not only the club's devotion to early printing and typographical practices but also their willingness 'to embrace the newest, most cutting-edge technologies of the day such as lithography, which now allowed them to reproduce more exactly

---

Connection with the Calendar, Including Anecdote, Biography, & History, Curiosities of Literature and Oddities of Human Life and Character (1862). The pamphlet also acknowledges material from Thomas Dibdin, *Reminiscences of a Literary Life*, 2 vols (London, 1836), I.374.

[30] Dibdin, *Bibliomania*, 58.

[31] Thomas Frognall Dibdin, *The Bibliographic Decameron; Or, Ten Days Pleasant Discourse upon Illuminated Manuscripts, and Subjects Connected with Early Engraving, Typography, and Bibliography* (London, 1817), 72.

[32] Dibdin, *Bibliomania*, 77, 78.

[33] The prefatory note indicates it was complete on 17 June 1818.

the workmanship that they loved'.[34] Other members were engaged in editing practices both within and outside the club. For example, Joseph Haslewood 'was of sufficient standing as an editor and expert on early literature to have been approached by other editors working in similar areas looking for advice and soliciting collaboration'.[35] In short, the Roxburghe Club was not only precisely the audience that could be expected to read a text printed in black letter but they were also the people most likely to notice and appreciate the way Earl Gower drew on a variety of technologies to represent the textual and physical features of the original manuscripts (or rare early printed books) in their possession. After all, this was something many of the other members of the Roxburghe Club were attempting to do at the same time as Earl Gower.

As I hope to have shown, Earl Gower's Edition represents both the bibliographic and linguistic codes of his source, and this approach is consistent with ideas about textual reproduction that seem to have been circulating among members of the Roxburghe Club. The club's early activities provide an additional reason for thinking that Earl Gower's Edition might have been especially welcome to club members. The fact that this edition was printed for the Shakspeare Press by William Bulmer and Co. in Cleveland-row, St James's, London, is probably fortuitous, but Shakespeare was an important figure for members of the Roxburghe Club and those involved more broadly in bibliographic discourse at this time. As noted earlier, Beresford cited Jonson's Preface to Shakespeare's plays in his tract comparing editors to Hercules. Dibdin, whose *Bibliographic Decameron* was printed by the Shakspeare Press in 1817, also suggests that the desire for a collection of books associated with Shakespeare or his time (or the time in which his sources appeared in print) might have contributed to the disease he was keen to anatomise: 'Such a "Bibliotheca Shakspeariana" might, however, have been only a fresh stimulus to the increase of the black-letter symptom of the *Bibliomania*.'[36] Husbands suggests that one 'literary thread that runs through' editions by early Roxburghe Club members is 'their exploration of texts that provide literary context and relevant background to the works of Shakespeare'.[37] Although Gower's *Balades* do not provide the kind of direct connection to Shakespeare that his account of Pericles in the *Confessio Amantis* might have done, Roxburghe Club members might nonetheless have enjoyed making the more subtle connection between the Trentham Manuscript's ostensible dedication to Henry IV and Gower's cameo appearance in *Henry IV, Part 2* (though it is not entirely clear what they might have thought of Gower's refusal

---

[34] Husbands, *Early Roxburghe Club*, 90.
[35] Husbands, *Early Roxburghe Club*, 24.
[36] Dibdin, *Bibliomania*, 74.
[37] Husbands, *Early Roxburghe Club*, 131.

to dine with Falstaff in Act 2, Scene 1). One of the inscriptions Earl Gower had lithographically reproduced identified this book's contents as follows:

> S[i]r John Gower's learned Poems
> the same booke by himself presented
> to kinge ~~Edward~~ <Henry. T[he] fourth ~~att~~ <or before> his Coronation.[38]

While it is not necessary to know this inscription to understand what is happening in Henry IV, Part 2, it transforms that scene into what we might call today 'an Easter Egg', the kind of material designed to reward insiders for their ability to recognise connections between material only available to them.[39]

Critics from the early nineteenth century until recently have often claimed that early Roxburghe Club members were primarily interested in rewarding insiders for their ability to recognise connections between material only available to them. That criticism seems fair when we consider the nature of private book collections, and it may also apply to the club members' desire to restrict the number of people who had access to their editions: one hundred copies is, after all, a very limited print run. Defenders of the club have argued that one hundred copies are more accessible than one (or in some cases a handful), and the Roxburghe Club should therefore be praised for doing what they did to preserve and circulate rare texts. I would like to suggest that both positions can be true. While I have praised Earl Gower's Edition for representing his source's bibliographic and linguistic code, his use of emerging technologies to imitate features of the Trentham Manuscript would have been costly and difficult to replicate widely. Nonetheless, I hope to have shown that the incorporation of these elements was the result of decisions made by members of the Roxburghe Club based on ideas they seem to have shared about editing, even if they did not articulate them explicitly in writing. 'While often criticized for their lack of scholarly editing', Husbands writes, 'the Roxburghe Club were commonly using editing methods and scholarly frameworks that had not yet become common practice.'[40] The story of their contribution to key developments in the editing of Middle English, especially those undertaken by Frederic Madden and Frederick Furnivall, both of whom edited texts for the Roxburghe Club before editing texts for the Early English

---

[38] London, British Library, MS Add. 59498, fol. 3v.

[39] The *Oxford English Dictionary* explains that this sense of the term originated in computing and describes 'an unexpected or undocumented message or feature hidden in a piece of software, intended as a joke or bonus. Also: a feature of this kind in film, music, and other forms of information or entertainment.' *Oxford English Dictionary*, s.v. 'Easter egg, n. 2', last modified July 2023, https://dx.doi.org/10.1093/OED/5712755404.

[40] Husbands, *Early Roxburghe Club*, 162.

Text Society, is becoming better known.[41] What I hope to have done here is to suggest that the club's commitment to representing the bibliographic code of their source material should be considered just as innovative, for they anticipate the kinds of approaches that more recent critics have called for as the opportunities and challenges presented to us by digital technologies have emerged. While I may not have added anything to Echard's argument that Earl Gower's Edition draws special attention to the Trentham Manuscript as an artefact, I hope to have shown what we might learn about early editorial practices if we accept that the Roxburghe Club edition achieves some of the ends she says it does. Ultimately, the time I have spent with the four books in the British Library catalogued as MSS Add. 59495–98 has allowed me to re-evaluate my understanding of the way that early Roxburghe Club editors used the technology at their disposal to represent their source materials – in this case Earl Gower's 'original manuscript'– in an even more immersive way than I recognised before reading Echard's work.

[41] See Matthews, *Making of Middle English*; esp. chapter 4, 'Turtle Soup and Texts: From the Roxburghe Club to the Camden Society', 85–110; chapter 5, '"The Deadly Poison of Democracy": Frederic Madden, Scholar-Knight', 113–37; and chapter 6, '"Go-a-head-itiveness": Frederick Furnivall and Early English', 138–61.

PART III

HEROES AND THEIR AFTERLIVES

⊰ 9 ⊱

The Idea of *Beowulf* and 'The Book Beautiful'

ELAINE TREHARNE

Throughout Siân Echard's prolific and distinguished career, she has emphasised the fluidity of medieval textualities and technologies of text. Whether her focus is Arthurian literature and its transformation through time, or the shift from manuscript to print, or her newest work on the history of the facsimile, Echard has demonstrated depth, deftness of engagement, and breadth of intellectual imagination.[1] She is a book historian *par excellence*, able to turn her hand to detailed analysis of any technology of text and to the ways in which books have been collected, catalogued, curated, displayed, and interpreted. In a recent outstanding essay, co-authored with Andrew Prescott, Echard zooms in on the experience of a reader in the British Library's Manuscripts Reading Room in London, providing a detailed account of searching that library's many catalogues, handling the physical manuscript, and reconciling all the information to form a scholarly analysis of the whole.[2] Highlighting the 'range of conditions' under which we encounter manuscripts and their representations, Echard and Prescott demonstrate the liveliness of manuscript history and its persistent dynamic. This essay, which considers the life of a manuscript through time, place, and successive meetings with scholars, hopes to honour Siân Echard's contribution to bibliographical studies and to medieval and text technological scholarship. I am grateful for Siân's inspiring scholarship, for her collegiality, and for her generosity, and I am focusing here on some

---

[1] See, among other publications, Siân Echard, *Arthurian Narrative in the Latin Tradition* (Cambridge, 1998); Echard and Stephen Partridge, eds, *The Book Unbound: Editing and Reading Medieval Manuscripts and Texts* (Toronto, 2004); Echard, *Printing the Middle Ages* (Philadelphia, 2008); and Echard, 'House Arrest: Modern Archives, Medieval Manuscripts', *Journal of Medieval and Early Modern Studies* 30 (2000): 185–210.

[2] Siân Echard and Andrew Prescott, 'Charming the Snake: Accessing and Disciplining the Medieval Manuscript', in *The Cambridge Companion to Medieval British Manuscripts*, ed. Orietta Da Rold and Elaine Treharne (Cambridge, 2021), 237–66.

of her great academic loves, medieval literature and manuscript history, by discussing the cross-temporal existences of the Old English heroic poem, *Beowulf*, and the manuscript as a whole that houses it.

Perceiving Textual Objects

All editions of *Beowulf*, all translations, adaptations, and multimedia renditions, are principally concerned with the retrievable and imaginary words and worlds of the poem.[3] Until recently, the print editorial history of *Beowulf* has been almost entirely male-dominated – a narrative of personal and professional combat, a veneration of a poem that is opaque at best; an intellectual wrestling contest that mirrors the world of the poem itself. It is heartening to see new work – like Maria Dahvana Headley's feminist translation of *Beowulf* or the community translation, *Beowulf By All* – bring the poem to fresh audiences, encouraging new approaches to Old English.[4]

In this scholarly and creative work on the text, its origins, and its meanings, what can be so easily lost in print is a sense of *Beowulf* within the context of the whole manuscript book with its systems of production and reproduction: what I would term the plenitextuality (simply the full textual history and potential) of *Beowulf*. Plenitextuality might be thought of as a development from materialist philological concerns, led by Bernard Cerquiglini, Stephen G. Nichols, and Paul Zumthor three decades ago.[5] The plenitext emerges from a comprehensive interpretative analysis of any textual object's core or first order attributes – Intentionality + Materiality + Functionality +/- Cultural Value.[6] *Intentionality* is why, or from whose creativity, something was produced; *materiality* is what it is made of and how it was produced; *functionality* is how the object is received and used; and cultural value is how society (from museums to individuals) give a fiscal, social, intellectual, or emotive value to the object.

---

[3] As shown by the hundreds of published items in Britt Mize's project, Beowulf's Afterlives: Bibliographic Database, at http://beowulf.dh.tamu.edu/. Thanks to Professor Mize and others for their comments on a much earlier version of this essay, delivered as a paper at Texas A&M in 2019.

[4] Maria Dahvana Headley, trans., *Beowulf: A New Translation* (New York, 2020); Jean Abbott, Mateusz Fafinski, and Elaine Treharne, eds, *Beowulf by All: A Community Translation* (York, 2020).

[5] I reframe 'plenitextuality' as 'dynamic architextuality' in Elaine Treharne, *Perceptions of Medieval Manuscripts: The Phenomenal Book* (Oxford, 2021); Bernard Cerquiglini, *Eloge de la variante: Histoire critique de la philologie* (Paris, 1989; trans. *In Praise of the Variant: A Critical History of Philology* (Baltimore, 1999)); Stephen G. Nichols, 'Introduction: Philology in a Manuscript Culture', *Speculum* 65 (1990): 1–10; Paul Zumthor, *Towards a Medieval Poetics* (Minneapolis, 1992).

[6] See further Elaine Treharne and Claude Willan, *Text Technologies: A History* (Stanford, 2019).

My model builds, too, on the traditional book historical research triad of Production, Transmission, and Reception.[7] 'Text' in this sequence is an important thing or information-set transmitted from an author via some or other vehicle, and as something that changes only extrinsically. This model is less capacious than Intentionality plus Materiality plus Functionality plus or minus Cultural Value, where all four attributes are always present, but to varying degrees, in every textual object without exception. My model accounts more effectively for what D. F. McKenzie pointed out decades ago about the sociology of texts: that texts are forms of intentional communication as social, multiple, and transformable through time. Texts are 'recorded forms': 'all forms of texts ... verbal, visual, oral, and numeric data ... everything in fact from epigraphy to the latest forms of discography'.[8] To these, we can now add digital texts and digitised reproductions of texts.

What the book history triad, and perhaps even the 'sociology of text', cannot explain, though, is why one quickly penned note is venerated rather more than others,[9] or how authorial and editorial intentionality precedes production or the physical existence of the text. The model delineating a textual object's full biography – Intentionality + Materiality + Functionality +/- Cultural Value – accounts for the entirety of interpretative potential, then. With a plenitextual approach, one could theoretically construe a full narrative of the technology of textual objects in their global entirety through time.

Before I turn to *Beowulf*, I want to build on this model to consider the textual wholeness that it creates. In *Perceptions of Medieval Manuscripts: The Phenomenal Book*, my argument focuses on investigating how medieval manuscripts are conceived and perceived *as whole books* from the moment of intentionality of the compiler or scribe to the books' present lives in libraries, archives, and private collections as wholes or whole fragments or fragments with holes. This is not to claim that books remain static or the same; on the contrary, a book's state varies through time, but for a medieval producer-user, it seems a book was conceived of, and perceived as, whole. This theory is inspired by the twentieth-century French philosopher Maurice Merleau-Ponty and his concept of the world experienced as immanent (in its wholeness) and transcendent (that is, perspectivally, but still whole in reality). When bits and pieces of a whole textual object are separated out for evaluation, description, or editorial criticism, scholars necessarily narrow or even preclude the full

---

[7] This is the sequence required to accommodate the linear life of a text, and the title of a study by Carlo Caruso, ed., *The Life of Texts: Evidence in Textual Production, Transmission and Reception* (London, 2019).

[8] D. F. McKenzie, *Bibliography and the Sociology of Texts* (Cambridge, 1999; first published as *The Panizzi Lectures*, British Library, 1985), 12–13.

[9] Such as Einstein's note given to a bellboy and sold for $1.6million in 2017 (https://www.bbc.com/news/world-middle-east-41742785). To account for how text can function in this way, cultural value must be understood as integral to textuality.

interpretative potential of the complete object. Meaning is lost. Significances are elided. Not only might one fail to apprehend the text at all but also lose the percipient qualities of that artefact. This is fundamentally applicable to all textual objects, but the focus here will be *books*. The wholeness of books was clear to their medieval illustrators who drew whole miniature books to represent the object in the real world; to compilers, who conceived of objects as voluminous and whole; to poets, scribes, and browsers, who wrote themselves into books, conversed with texts in the margins, and adapted books to suit their own needs.[10]

This wholeness – the need to use all the faculties to interpret the material object in its entirety – was also clear to medieval intellectuals. The *Old English Soliloquies*, preserved only in a manuscript dated to the second half of the twelfth century – London, British Library, Cotton Vitellius A. xv Part I, is a translated adaptation of St Augustine's *Soliloquies*. In it, Reason asks Alfred/ Augustine how he learned about the geometry of the sphere upon which a line was drawn to show the revolution of the heavens:

> Þa cwæð heo: Hweðer geleornodest þu þe myd þam eagum, þe mid þam ingeþance?
> Þa cwæð ic: Mid ægðrum ic hyt geleornode: ærest myd ðam eagum, and syðþan myd þam ingeþance. Ða eagan me gebrodton on þam angytte. Ac siðþan ic hyt þa ongyten hæfde, þa forlæt ic þa sceawunga mid þam eagum and þohte, forði me þuhte þæt ic his mæate micle mare geþencan ðonne ic his mahte geseon, siððan þa eagan hyt ætfæstnodon minum ingeþance.[11]

> [Then Reason said: 'Do you learn with your eyes or with your perception?' Then I said: 'I learned it with both: first with the eyes and after with perception. The eyes brought me understanding. But after I had perceived those things, I abandoned looking with my eyes and thought; because it seemed to me that I could understand much more of it than I could see once the eyes had fastened it in my perception.]

---

[10] All of this is fully explained in Elaine Treharne, *Perceptions of Medieval Manuscripts: The Phenomenal Book* (Oxford, 2021), *passim*. Maurice Merleau-Ponty, *Phenomenology of Perception*, trans. Colin Smith (London, 1958; repr. 2009); published first as *Phénomènologie de la perception* (Paris, 1945).

[11] Old English translation is mine. On 'ingeþance' and its range of meanings, particularly 'inner thought' or 'abstract thought' built upon the information gathered by the senses (as opposed to *intellectus* – the faculty of the incorporeal anima, then, it is *cogitatio*), see Leslie Lockett, *Anglo-Saxon Psychologies in the Vernacular and Latin Traditions* (Toronto, 2011), 340–41. Note in the *DOE* that 'ingeþance' occurs in *Andreas* and in Gregory's *Dialogues, Cura Pastoralis*, and *Soliloquies*: a restricted use. Thomas Carnicelli, ed., *King Alfred's Version of Augustine's Soliloquies* (Cambridge, MA, 1969), 61.

For Alfred in this sequence, which differs from Latin versions of the *Soliloquia* (as least as far as scholarship has revealed to date[12]), the eyes – sight – are the means by which learning is acquired, but he is advised here fuller apprehension of an object is facilitated by the perception, 'ingeþance'. That is, an ocular-centric perspective that only considers what one can see (partial, perspectival, transcendental) results in insufficient understanding; perception – all the senses as embodied consciousness, perhaps – permits a much fuller understanding than just the physical eyes can achieve. Embodied consciousness is how Merleau-Ponty describes the human experience in the world.[13]

Reason goes on to ask Alfred/Augustine further about what it takes to believe in what one is seeing, and the answer takes the reader beyond the conceptual or intellectual and into the realm of the material, and, especially, perception of the object as a whole, in its *wholeness*. Reason asks him:

> Geþenc nu gyf ðines hlafordes ærendgewrit and hys insegel to ðe cymð, hwæðer þu mæge cweðan þæt ðu hine be ðam ongytan ne mægæ, ne hys willan þær-on gecnawan ne mæge …[14]

> [Consider, now: if your lord sent to you a letter of authority and a seal, whether or not you might say that you were able to understand him through those things, and would you be unable to know his will thereby?]

As Leslie Lockett comments about this unique addition to the Latin *Soliloquia*, 'Gesceadwisnes' (Reason or Wisdom) 'illustrates that objects perceptible to the senses – in this case, written words and a seal – can provide a firm basis for *belief* in something that is not currently present to the senses'.[15] In Augustine's *Soliloquies*, as least as far as Alfred or his circle understood the text and transmitted it, the understanding of an object, the materiality of the object, the melding of perception, and then belief in interpretation, is predicated not just on sight of the thing but on the store of knowledge that one can bring to bear for comprehension and interpretation – a *wholeness* that exists in the experience, the previous know-how of the perceiver.

This reading of Alfred's sense of inner thought or perception and his understanding of an object, even though only part of that understanding has been formed through sense data, anticipates some principal concerns of Merleau-Ponty. For Merleau-Ponty, his phenomenological research moves beyond

---

[12] See, for example, Ruth Waterhouse, 'Tone in Alfred's Version of Augustine's *Soliloquies*', in *Studies in Earlier Old English Prose*, ed. Paul Szarmach (Binghamton, 1986), 63–64.

[13] Merleau-Ponty, *Phenomenology of Perception*, 79.

[14] Old English translation is mine. For 'letter of authority', see the *DOE*, s.v., 'ærendgewrit'.

[15] Lockett, *Anglo-Saxon Psychologies*, 341–42.

Cartesian dualism and Husserlian transcendentalism[16] to explain the way in which we, as *embodied consciousnesses*, make our way in the world, persistently understanding and realising objects we encounter as whole and three-dimensionalised, even when we never *see* an object in its entirety (we only ever encounter objects perspectivally). This emphasis on *wholeness* and on what the *Soliloquies* terms 'ingeþance' has important implications, particularly for book and textual historians and critics.

Lives and Books, Bookish Lives

Merleau-Ponty's phenomenological account explains how humans perceive the world around them: perception is dependent on an 'embodied consciousness', and the 'body is the agent of the world'. Perception or embodied consciousness is neither intellectualist nor empiricist. Merleau-Ponty discusses the perception of objects in the world around us as wholes, even when perceivers see transcendentally; that is, perspectivally. An object is always revealed gradually to the perceiver and is to be considered 'inhabited' – both by the embodied consciousness as it apprehends the object, and in the way in which the object is seen by all other objects around it. From my understanding, this is a relational perception, relational in the way the world functions as a complete kind of interwoven scene synchronically and in the sequence in which we know or perceive things through time or diachronically. These synchronic and diachronic axes of comprehension are precisely emulated by the full textual model made up of a textual object's intentionality + materiality + functionality +/- cultural value. An object exists through time biographically, and at any point the system of objects could allow for multiplicities of choices in any one element of these key components. Thus, for example, materialities of a textual object can be one of a number of things (paper, vellum, metal, stone) and its cultural value could be anything from valueless (a piece of junk mail) to nationally valued (the Lincoln Memorial in America) to priceless (the Gutenberg Bible).

In terms of the way that objects, like books, function for the human perceiver in Merleau-Ponty's explanation of the world and one's experience of it:

---

[16] For Husserl, phenomenology is the philosophical task of expounding the world's existence. Transcendental Ego for Husserl is 'consciousness which lies outside the causal order of the natural world and is wholly different from it' according to Komarine Romdenh-Romluc, *The Routledge Philosophy Guidebook to Merleau-Ponty and Phenomenology of Perception* (London, 2010), 9–10: in the Cartesian model, 'the body is an object that belongs in the external world. It is not essentially related to consciousness.'

To see is to enter a universe of beings which *display themselves* ... Thus, every object is the mirror of all others. When I look at the lamp on my table, I attribute to it not only the qualities visible from where I am, but also those which the chimney, the walls, the table can 'see'; the back of my lamp is nothing other than the face which it 'shows' to the chimney. I can therefore see an object insofar as objects form a system or a world and insofar as each of them treats the others around it like spectators of its hidden aspects and a guarantee of their permanence.[17]

In this way, although the view from everywhere is not a view I myself can have, it is a view I can now see as *being* had, a view from which my own perspective is felt to deviate.

There are two particularly critical elements of this phenomenology for book historians: the first is the clear demonstration that the knowledge of textual history and object-in-existence brought to this work by an object's physical and digital dimensions profoundly affects and effects all that is perceptible; the second is the importance of how 'each [cultural object] spreads around it an atmosphere of humanity', which is to say that inherent to a manufactured object is the already-existing possibility for both perception and action: a ball is for throwing or kicking or picking up; a book is for opening, and moving through, and reading. Moreover, the perceiver experiences other human presences in that object. As Komarine Romdenh-Romluc puts it: 'One feels the presence of other selves', even those who 'have long since gone'.[18]

Merleau-Ponty further comments on the biographical essence of an object: 'Whether it be a question of vestiges or the body of another person, we need to *know* how an object in space can become the eloquent relic of an existence.'[19] An object then can be, or perhaps always is, an 'eloquent relic of an existence'. This applies beautifully to books – all books, but particularly historical books that are handmade and therefore imbued with their makers' craft and effort; or books that exist with long and complex biographies through which many users have passed. *Beowulf* forms an excellent example of this phenomenon. Each publication or presentation of the Old English poem known as *Beowulf* contained in London, British Library, Cotton MS Vitellius A. xv Part II is a new relic, a new existence, a new textual object. Each can be the subject of investigation through the analysis structured as Intentionality + Materiality + Functionality +/- Cultural Value, whether the object is Julius Zupitza's 1882 autotype Early English Text Society volume entitled *Beowulf* or Roy Liuzza's

---

[17] Merleau-Ponty, *Phenomenology of Perception*, 82–83. Quoted, with modified translation, in Sean Dorrance Kelly, 'Seeing Things in Merleau-Ponty', in *The Cambridge Companion to Merleau-Ponty*, ed. Taylor Carman (Cambridge, 2004), 74–110, at 76.

[18] Merleau-Ponty, *Phenomenology of Perception*, 202. See Romdenh-Romluc, *Guidebook to Merleau-Ponty*, 172.

[19] Merleau-Ponty, *Phenomenology of Perception*, 406.

2000 translation of that poem; or Robert Zemeckis's 2007 CGI extravaganza of that name.[20] This point has been made in different ways many times before and with multiple referents. Perhaps most famously and startlingly is the question posed by F. W. Bateson to ask: 'If the Mona Lisa is in the Louvre, where then is *Hamlet*?'[21] We can adapt this to consider any literary text, perhaps most critically so when that text has been published or produced in multiple instantiations, like *Beowulf*.

Asking what *Beowulf* is (like the Mona Lisa) creates many ontological issues. Here, two questions focused on wholeness and *Beowulf* in a handful of its various textual manifestations will be posed. These questions can be *asked* in chronological order, though my discussion will break out of chronology: (i) What can one say about *Beowulf* in the context of its eleventh-, twelfth-, and sixteenth-century manuscript, London, British Library, Cotton MS Vitellius A. xv? (ii) How did nineteenth- and twentieth-century scholars, editors, and writers try to make a new 'book beautiful' of *Beowulf*?[22]

'Book Beautiful ... one composite whole'

'Book Beautiful' is a term borrowed from the Arts and Crafts binder and press owner Thomas Cobden-Sanderson, a friend of William Morris, Emery Walker, Edward Johnston, and other craftspeople and social activists in late nineteenth- and early twentieth-century London. In 1901, Cobden-Sanderson wrote *The Ideal Book or Book Beautiful: A Tract on Calligraphy Printing and Illustration and on the Book Beautiful as a Whole*, an essay about what makes a perfect book-artefact.[23] In the *Ideal Book or Book Beautiful*, Cobden-Sanderson writes:

---

[20] Julius Zupitza, ed., *Beowulf: Autotypes of the Unique Cotton MS. Vitellius A. xv in the British Museum with a Transliteration and Notes*, EETS o.s. 77 (London, 1882); Roy M. Liuzza, ed. and trans., *Beowulf* (Toronto, 2012); *Beowulf*, dir. Robert Zemeckis (2007).

[21] F. W. Bateson, 'Modern Bibliography and the Modern Artifact', in *English Studies Today*, ed. Georges A. Bonnard (Bern, 1961), 67–77, at 70. See also Martin Foys's work broadly, but especially 'Medieval Manuscripts: Media Archaeology and the Digital Incunable', in *The Medieval Manuscript Book: Cultural Approaches*, ed. Michael Johnston and Michael van Dussen (Cambridge, 2015), 119–39.

[22] For the movement of a single textual object through time, see now Michelle R. Warren, *Holy Digital Grail: A Medieval Book on the Internet*, Stanford Text Technologies (Stanford, 2022).

[23] Thomas J. Cobden-Sanderson, *The Ideal Book or Book Beautiful: A Tract on Calligraphy Printing and Illustration and on the Book Beautiful as a Whole* (Hammersmith, 1900).

> The Ideal Book or Book Beautiful is a composite thing made up of many parts & may be made beautiful by the beauty of each of its parts – its literary content, its material or materials, its writing or printing, its illumination or illustration, its binding and decoration – of each of its parts in subordination to the whole which collectively they constitute.[24]

Cobden-Sanderson distinguishes between the beautiful written book ('which admits of great nicety and perfection') and the printed book, in which type is 'rigid and implacable', and takes the reader through the individual components of book production, dwelling finally on the 'Book Beautiful as a Whole.'[25] 'Finally', he says, 'if the Book Beautiful may be beautiful by virtue of its writing or printing or illustration, it may also be beautiful, be even more beautiful, by the union of all to the production of one composite whole, the consummate Book Beautiful.'[26] Then he closes with capitals, perhaps angry, and prophetic of the shouting mode in contemporary social media:

> The wholeness, symmetry, harmony, beauty without stress or strain, of the Book Beautiful, would then be one in principle with the wholeness, symmetry, harmony and beauty without stress or strain, of that WHOLE OF LIFE WHICH IS CONSTITUTED OF OURSELVES AND THE WORLD, THAT COMPLEX AND MARVELLOUS WHOLE ... THE TRUE ARCHETYPE OF ALL BOOKS BEAUTIFUL OR SUBLIME.

Cobden-Sanderson sees wholeness as a harmonic and strainless aesthetic, that seems, for him, to be part of a universal system of being. The parts of the single volume unite to form a perfect union, which extends to the book's textual and visual components. What Cobden-Sanderson would make of volumes that are themselves composite is interesting to consider: books that are joined together for thematic or pragmatic or unascertainable rationales; that is, individual books that emerge from the medieval period rebound into a single physical object by later owners, such as Archbishop Matthew Parker or Sir Robert Cotton and their circles of scholars and librarians.[27]

In Cobden-Sanderson's typology, a 'true archetype' for *Beowulf* might be considered to be the poem as it is written by two scribes in the manuscript codex, London, British Library, Cotton MS Vitellius A. xv Part II. This large

---

[24] Cobden-Sanderson, *The Ideal Book or Book Beautiful*, 1.
[25] Cobden-Sanderson, *The Ideal Book or Book Beautiful*, 2.
[26] Cobden-Sanderson, *The Ideal Book or Book Beautiful*, 8.
[27] For the ways in which medieval books have been received and transformed, see, among others, Siân Echard, 'Containing the Book: The Institutional Afterlives of Medieval Manuscripts', in *The Medieval Manuscript Book: Cultural Approaches*, ed. Michael Johnston and Michael van Dussen (Cambridge, 2015), 96–118; and Colin Tite, *The Manuscript Library of Sir Robert Cotton*, Panizzi Lectures (London, 1994).

volume, generally divided into Parts I and II, is often reductively labelled as the *Beowulf*-manuscript, when *Beowulf* is, of course, but a singular textual object surrounded by multiple other texts copied in the eleventh and twelfth centuries. Since we know from scribal error that at least one exemplar preceded the copying of *Beowulf*, perhaps that might be the 'archetype'; or perhaps it is the earliest, now non-determinable instantiation of the core of the poem, spoken aloud or murmured in practice or creatively conceived by the *ur*-poet. The one surviving attestation to the early medieval poem, though, exists in a now-composite manuscript not famed for anything in particular until the later eighteenth century. In Thomas Smith's *Catalogue of the Manuscripts in the Cotton Library*, published in 1696, *Beowulf* is omitted.[28] Indeed, the poem was not itself labelled as part of this codex until the title 'Item 7 Beowulf' was added later in pencil to the blank space left in the earliest Table of Contents.[29]

When faced with a single textual object like this, a large volume made into a whole from two apparently unrelated pre-existing parts, what, in essence, constitutes the primary object of study and what frameworks of interpretation should scholar-librarians provide? For Thomas Smith, and Richard James who wrote the seventeenth-century Table of Contents while the manuscript was in the Cottonian Library, *Beowulf* was not identifiable and not included in the list, so their catalogue description is effectively incomplete, the wholeness of the volume unrecognised. Eileen Joy is prescient in her understanding of the complexities and exigencies of cataloguing from the early modern period onwards and its knock-on effects. In her exemplary 2005 article, 'Thomas Smith, Humfrey Wanley, and the "Little Known Country" of the Cotton Library', Joy reveals the difficulties faced by early cataloguers, the competitiveness among them, and the precarious position they occupied – often on the fringes of scholarly society, and in sporadically paid semi-formal positions.[30] Their cataloguing efforts were, in many respects, heroic. Dorothy K. Coveney, palaeographer and cataloguer in London, is similarly prescient. In her 1950 article, 'The Cataloguing of Literary Manuscripts', Coveney trenchantly surveys the work of the cataloguer:

---

[28] Thomas Smith, *Catalogus librorum manuscriptorum bibliothecae Cottonianae* (Oxford, 1696).

[29] See the digital version of London, British Library, Cotton Vitellius MS A. xv, either online at the British Library website (https://www.bl.uk/manuscripts/FullDisplay.aspx?ref=Cotton_MS_vitellius_a_xv) (at the time of publication, this link was not functional due to the 2023 cyber-attack on the British library; we are hopeful it will be restored), or in Kevin Kiernan et al., eds, *Electronic Beowulf*, 4th edn (https://ebeowulf.uky.edu/#). This folio is two recto.

[30] Eileen Joy, 'Thomas Smith, Humfrey Wanley, and the "Little Known Country" of the Cotton Library', *Electronic British Library Journal* (2005): 1–34, DOI https://hcommons.org/deposits/item/hc:21187/.

He ploughs a lone furrow, frequently self-taught.

None the less, a perusal of the most important catalogues of even the last forty years will, if viewed without sentiment, force one to the conclusion that all too frequently the ploughman is so absorbed in his furrow that he is not always mindful of the objects of the ploughing. The result is a collection of non-uniform, inadequate catalogues which, unlike furrows, may have to serve for a century or more, and may finally even prove to be a disservice to the users, in that their very existence prevented the making of better ones. For the expense factor bars frequent editions, in fact usually renders unlikely any second edition. And it is this inexorable longevity of manuscript catalogues which has prompted the present critical analysis and the suggestion that the time has come to consider what the minimum requirements should be.[31]

Written almost seventy years ago, this critical overview, which places the *user* of the catalogue at the centre of things, is still pertinent in contemporary cataloguing and, perhaps, *especially* now given the tools at our disposal for the creation of online catalogues that present clear metadata allied to, and augmentative of, digital display capabilities. Coveney called then for 'full catalogues' (across the world – railing against American and British scholars' insularity) that serve the 'complete purpose' of all scholars – 'literary researchers, historians, librarians, palaeographers, and others'. She sees in catalogues up to that point the dominance of the interests of 'text-seekers', 'art historians', and 'those interested in heuristic, heraldry, sphragistic, and the like'. She ponders: 'What of the palaeographers'? – those interested in the 'formats, types of parchment and paper, watermarks, methods of ruling and prickmarks, arrangement of text', and so forth. In other words, Coveney is alert to those components that, if fully described, allow the user of the catalogue or the viewer of the book-entry to apprehend the object in its entirety, its wholeness – the *singularity* of the manuscript, then: the surviving volume as a unit, a single thing, an entity, in its singleness and oneness; its 'special excellence', to quote the *Oxford English Dictionary*; its distinctiveness.

Singularity or uniqueness is certainly one value used in the appreciation of a medieval manuscript. The fact that no manuscript is like any other is often remarked upon, and it is because of uniqueness that cultural value is often ascribed to such objects.[32] But singularity need not imply or describe

---

[31] Dorothy K. Coveney, 'The Cataloguing of Literary Manuscripts', *The Journal of Documentation* 6, no. 3 (1950): 125–39.

[32] In literary and historical studies, of course, texts like *Beowulf* are generally extracted from their larger physical contexts for editing and study and treated as if individual objects. Only rarely are whole codices (or whole composite codices) treated in their entirety. Kevin Kiernan's pioneering Open Access *E-Beowulf* is an exception to this, though the title of the book itself would suggest that *Beowulf* is the only focus.

wholeness. Indeed, what essential criteria exist to show how the wholeness of a medieval manuscript is constituted? Often these criteria seem to be codicological ones: the same scribe over a number of folios and texts; quires that appear to have been written with the intention of being one production; a volume of multiple stints bound between boards or kept together as if one object in the medieval period. Yet these, or other, potential criteria are not always systematically applied to medieval textual objects either by cataloguers or by scholars, so that, from catalogues, it can be difficult to ascertain the extent of an extant medieval book. As such, scholars need to ask what it is that is being described to them: a part or the whole of a volume? An extractive record, or the full details. Only with the latter is the book's-existence-in-the-world (its phenomenological reality) discernible.

This is a truly vexed question, then, that depends on choices made by the foundational cataloguers in the field. In Neil Ker's *Catalogue of Manuscripts Containing Anglo-Saxon* – the most influential catalogue in the field of Early English Studies, his idea of an object's wholeness appears to be indicated by individual itemisation.[33] Thus, for example, London, British Library, Cotton MS Tiberius A. iii (a mid-eleventh-century Christ Church compilation, perhaps made for Archbishop Stigand) or Cambridge, Corpus Christi College, MS 303 (a mid-twelfth-century homiliary and hagiography from Rochester) are constituted by Ker as single items, as whole manuscripts, produced presumably in one place as a concerted effort and containing multiple texts. Cambridge University Library, MS Ii. 1. 33 is also treated as one manuscript, one item, though it was almost certainly produced in two different centres (though one of the scribes is evidenced in both centres) over a period of time in the second half of the twelfth century. Reflecting their disparate places and times of origin, Cambridge, Corpus Christi College, MS 367 (an eleventh- to fifteenth-century religious and historical compendium with a south-eastern English origin and a Worcester provenance) is divided by Ker into three separate parts but given the same overall item number, because it is assumed it was bound into this shape of volume in the medieval period. Cambridge, Corpus Christi College, MS 201 (an eleventh-century religious, legal, and romance anthology) is divided into two catalogue items – Item 49, Corpus 201 pp. 1–178, Parts A and B; and Item 50, Corpus 201, pp. 179–272. London, British Library, Cotton MS Julius A. ii is two distinct items in Ker's *Catalogue* – 158 and 159; and Cotton MS Vitellius A. xv is two separate items – 215 and 216 – under a single shelf-mark, because the separate parts (well, they are parts for Corpus 201, but here they are catalogue items) were written in different centuries, one might assume at different places.[34] Some of these codices, then, are divided into 'parts'

---

[33] Neil R. Ker, *Catalogue of Manuscripts Containing Anglo-Saxon* (Oxford, 1957; repr. with Supplement 1990).

[34] Corpus 367, items 62–64, 108–10; Corpus 201, items 49–50, 82–91; Cotton

meriting separate entries under a single catalogue item number and with the same shelf-mark; others are separated into distinct catalogue items but still with the same shelf-mark, because they are, in fact, one whole volume. These decisions surely affect how scholars work with these manuscript materials; *Beowulf* comes to metonymically represent its whole manuscript (the *Beowulf*-manuscript), and far less notice is paid to the *Southwick*-Codex, a separate item in Ker but that was bound by Cotton and his circle with the *Beowulf*-manuscript, for example.[35]

When he considered the way that the evidence needed to be presented, Ker was clearly thinking about Sir Robert Cotton's and Archbishop Matthew Parker's activities as he compiled his *Catalogue* and considered how information should be presented. Idris Bell, keeper of the manuscripts at the British Museum at the time of the bicentenary of the Cotton Fire in 1931, commented on the significance of Cotton's efforts as a collector and conservator. As Colin Tite recalls in his Panizzi lectures, Bell said of Cotton:

> In one respect ... Cotton deserves censure rather than praise as an antiquary. There is not in the whole Cottonian collection a single manuscript which retains its original binding; and there is abundant evidence that Cotton made it his practice not only to rebind such manuscripts as he acquired but to bring together under a single cover volumes of the most diverse nature and provenance.

But 'it would be unfair to condemn Cotton too sharply for failing to rise above the standards of a day when ... the primary interest of a book lay in its contents and authorship rather than in its format and the story of its transmission'.[36] Just, then, as it is unfair to condemn Cotton for his disbanding, reorganisation, and rebinding of medieval textual objects – as a man of his time to whom we should be infinitely grateful – so, too, is it unreasonable to criticise Ker. Ker's reach and influence are great, though, and have effectively shaped the field of Old English literary and historical studies in ways that have not been acknowledged or – where required – modified in the light of the development of fields of scholarly study.

Ker's work is exceptional, brilliant, and will never be superseded in its entirety, but it has created profound structural problems for scholars of early

---

Julius A. ii, items 158–59, 201–2; and Cotton Vitellius A. xv, items 215–16, 280–83. Methods of divisions in parts or items or wholes are not entirely consistent, as has been discovered in the preparatory work for a revised edition of Ker's *Catalogue of Manuscripts Containing Anglo-Saxon*, edited by Elaine Treharne as *Digital Ker: Early English At Stanford* <DigitalKer.stanford.edu>.

[35] See Kiernan, *The Electronic-Beowulf*.

[36] Sir Idris Bell, *Guide to a Select Exhibition of Cottonian Manuscripts*, 8, cited in Tite, *Manuscript Library of Sir Robert Cotton*, 104–5.

English impacting upon how English literary and historical, legal, religious, and scientific texts are approached, researched, and understood. This is not just because of Ker's connoisseurly approach to a manuscript's aesthetic and its cultural value but also through the separation of volumes and parts of volumes in his *Catalogue*. For these distinctions were not based solely on scribal efforts, or codicological scrutiny, or the dates of textual items that correlate, but on the putative dates of their being bound together. Now, and especially in this age of digital display, scholars understand better how tentative such a criterion necessarily is.

Ker's choice in the layout of the *Catalogue* (and its consequences for *Beowulf* research) may have been inspired by Kenneth Sisam. Sisam was Ker's main advisor at the undergraduate level, and his method could have influenced Ker's descriptive and analytical process. In a three-page article in *Modern Language Review* in 1916, Sisam wrote:

> A few years ago, when turning over the *Beowulf* MS., I was surprised to observe that certain facts had escaped notice or attention. And they are worth setting out, if only as an indication of the dangers that beset a historical study in which insufficient attention is paid to manuscript indications, often the clearest indications of time and place.
>
> The MS. volume Vitellius A. xv consists of two separate codices fortuitously brought together by the binder in the sixteenth century.[37]

Sisam gives one subsequent paragraph over to the Southwick Codex (folios 3–94), the first folios in the manuscript, before focusing on the Nowell-*Beowulf* folios. This uncoupling of the first part of the extant codex from the *Beowulf*-manuscript sets a significant precedent for our modern era of textual scholarship, particularly if it was Sisam's influence that encouraged Ker to develop his idea of cataloguing medieval manuscripts using this approach.

Making Parts from Wholes and Wholes from Parts

A scholarly focus on text and on unity of origin or method of production or a specific emphasis on books as principally *parts* – folios, bifolia, quires, booklets, textual units – results perhaps inevitably in the academic dismantling of the manuscript book and its contents.[38] The division of whole manuscripts in Ker's *Catalogue* into separate items contributes to the emphasised

---

[37] Kenneth Sisam, 'The "Beowulf" Manuscript', *Modern Language Review* 11, no. 3 (1916): 335–37, at 335.

[38] Of course, codicological studies necessarily do this, but without forgetting, one would hope, to highlight the physical wholeness of the codex. On the origins of the contemporary codicology, see François Masai, 'Paleographie et codicologie',

fragmentation of the record in the *Handlist* of Helmut Gneuss and Michael Lapidge, which, while reparative in terms of bringing back the predominant Anglo-Latin contribution to early English written culture, reinforces Ker's faux book-wide *distinctiones*, including only books or parts of books that can be dated up to 1100 – their chronological endpoint.[39] Thus, for example, in Gneuss and Lapidge, Cotton MS Vitellius A. xv appears only as half the book it actually is: Part II, the *Beowulf*-manuscript is included, while Part I, the Southwick Codex is not, since it post-dates 1100. In the *Handlist*, Cotton MS Julius A. ii is included as half the object that physically exists and Cambridge, Corpus Christi College, MS 367 appears as one-fifth of the physical extant manuscript book. Such descriptions prepare scholars only partially for what they can expect to find in the archive or library, though one must assume that now researchers will consult online images wherever they can. Fragmentation in the catalogue therefore results in an obfuscation of the voluminous object as it exists and of its reception history as a whole book travelling through time and space at the most basic biographical level.

It was not always thus, as Humfrey Wanley's catalogue demonstrates.[40] Here, codices/volumes of medieval materials, created at different times and in different places, are described as they physically exist. Wanley's catalogue lists objects that contain multiple, potentially unrelated texts – as in the case of Cotton MS Vitellius A. xv, or Corpus MS 367, or Corpus MS 201; he shows them as existing together to form one singular volume. Is it possible that these temporally and spatially heterogenous components should be considered as synergistic and productive, rather than merely separate parts of a coincidental object? Is there a benefit to considering the wholeness of the manuscript book as it physically exists? In the most direct sense, benefit or not, the manuscript *is* now one thing – as with so many premodern books composed of units of varying origins received by modern students. Acknowledging that physical unity in the plenitextual sense would mean simply accepting that all the parts create the whole and can be studied as reflecting or commenting upon each other within a full description and analysis.

Scriptorium 4 (1950): 279–93; and François Masai, 'La paléographie gréco-latine, ses taches, ses methodes', *Scriptorium* 10 (1956): 281–302.

[39] Helmut Gneuss and Michael Lapidge, *Anglo-Saxon Manuscripts: A Bibliographical Handlist of Manuscripts and Manuscript Fragments Written or Owned in England up to 1100* (Toronto, 2014).

[40] Humphrey Wanley, *Antiquae literaturae septentrionalis liber alter seu ... librorum veterum septentrionalium ... catalogus historico-criticus*, volume 2 of George Hickes, *Linguarum veterum septentrionalium thesaurus grammitco-criticus et archaeologicus* (Oxford, 1705; repr. in *English Linguistics 1500–1800* (A Collection of Facsimile Reprints), ed. R. C. Alston (Menston, 1970)), 248.

I will examine London, British Library, MS Cotton Vitellius A. xv as it exists now and investigate its biography to consider how the physical object has been fragmented in scholarship over time and with what consequences. The Table of Contents of the whole codex was first written by Richard James – Sir Robert Cotton's first librarian:[41]

> (ff. 2–3 preliminary) 17th-century Cottonian endleaf; medieval endleaf, containing historical memoranda
> (i) ff. 4r–59v: Augustine of Hippo, *Soliloquia* (acephalous and acaudata)
> (ii) ff. 60r–86v: *Gospel of Nicodemus*
> (iii) ff. 86v–93v: *Debate of Saturn and Solomon*
> (iv) f. 93v: *Homily on St Quintin* (fragment of opening)
> (v) ff. 94r–98r: *Homily on St Christopher* (acephalous)
> (vi) ff. 98v–106v *Marvels of the East*
> (vii) ff. 107r–131v *Letter of Alexander to Aristotle*
> (viii) ff. 132r–201v *Beowulf* [added in pencil having been omitted from original Table of Contents]
> (ix) ff. 202r–209v *Judith* (acephalous)

This is the complete, albeit damaged, Cotton MS Vitellius A. xv, yet scholars never read across its compositeness: folios 4r–93v are called the Southwick Codex; and folios 94r–209v, the Nowell or *Beowulf*-manuscript. The contiguity of Part I – the so-called Southwick Codex – may one day prove to be pertinent to discussions of the place of origin of the whole manuscript, as well as the perceived thematic unification and functionality of the book as seen through the eyes of Sir Robert Cotton and his librarian. Is it possible, then, to say something new, something about the medieval and early modern conceptualisations of manuscript and content by recognising this manuscript as one single textual object? The script of the Southwick Codex, for example, is written in a distinctive twelfth-century hand that deliberately emulates earlier script – but not just any earlier script. It is an earlier script that is specifically localisable to tenth-century Winchester, from a period when a famous group of manuscripts associated with the Alfredian circle was produced.[42] This very deliberate script in the Southwick Codex, with its strong Winchester connection, might be used as a prompt to encourage research on a possible Winchester connection for the eleventh-century part of the codex. One might ask, for instance, could these eleventh- and twelfth-century codices have travelled together, making their way to Sir Robert Cotton's library from Winchester via Southwick? While it would take a significant amount of research (and perhaps a good deal of speculation) to make something of this hypothetical movement, it might provide a starting point.

---

[41] For ease of access, I use the British Library's foliation.

[42] See Elaine Treharne, 'Invisible Things in London, British Library, Cotton Vitellius A. xv', in *Texts, Textiles, Intertext: Essays in Honour of Gale Owen-Crocker*, ed, Maren Clegg Hyer and Jill Frederick (Woodbridge, 2016), 225–37.

Conceptually, too, the deliberately archaic script of the twelfth-century texts in Part I of the manuscript could inspire reflection on the archaism of the Old English classical verse-form at the moment of the copying of *Beowulf* and perhaps *Judith* in the early eleventh-century Part II of the manuscript. The imitative script of Cotton MS Vitellius A. xv Part I presents us with an act of explicit cultural veneration – the recognition in the post-Conquest period of the importance of the pre-Conquest vernacular intellectual and spiritual aesthetic. This, in turn, throws into sharp relief the copying of *Beowulf* and *Judith* around 1010, as their committal to record similarly pays testimony to the earlier Old English poetic form and cultural aesthetic.

Furthermore, the *Life of St Thomas* (now lost), the *Life of St Quintin*, and the prose *Solomon and Saturn* written into the manuscript in the twelfth century present us with spiritual and intellectual parallels for the *Life of St Christopher*, *The Wonders of the East*, and the *Letter of Alexander to Aristotle* in the eleventh-century Southwick Codex. In *Thomas*, if it had survived, we should have seen the travels of the apostle to India – the site of Alexander's conquests. Similarly, in the prose dialogue, *Solomon and Saturn*, we are presented with answers about the mysteries of the world that would delight any participant who momentarily inhabits the world of the *Wonders of the East* or the *Letter of Alexander to Aristotle*. Indeed, answering questions about the size of Noah's ark, or the age of Adam, unites the worlds of all of these sapiential and travel narratives – the distant biblical and the distant exotic, the improbable past and the equally improbable present. The hagiographic texts examine, respectively, conversion and transformation narratives, uniting the New Testament and the antique world with the contemporary Anglo-Saxon and Anglo-Norman. Similarly, the apocryphal work of the Southwick Codex's *Gospel of Nicodemus* is confirmed or augmented by the addition of the deuterocanonical *Judith* to the Nowell Codex. Wisdom literature, theological, exemplary, and global literatures are present in both parts of this single, singular, manuscript and change how the complete physical codex might be read across its temporally distinct parts. Augustine's *Soliloquies* provide fundamentally important spiritual, philosophical, and personal guidance, in a way that Alexander sought from his mentor Aristotle, or that is offered pastorally by the more reflective and homiletic moments in the poem *Beowulf*.

Despite the single book that Cotton MS Vitellius A. xv represents, its metaphorical dismemberment is a feature of the codex's scholarship since the beginning of the nineteenth century.[43] At this point in its history, the poem *Beowulf* became the focus of sustained (and almost entirely male and masculinist) scholarship. In this landscape of textual extraction from manuscripts, nineteenth- and then twentieth-century editors and bookmakers made *Beowulf*

---

[43] The book is more than metaphorically dismembered, of course. The damage to the codex in the Ashburnham House fire in 1731 was so significant that each leaf is now housed in an individual paper frame, the frames being bound into the whole. This makes for a particularly interesting case study of 'wholeness'.

the centre of their Book Beautiful. For William Morris, book-producer, type-creator, translator, and scholar, *Beowulf* was one of the chosen titles for his Kelmscott Press in the 1890s. These fifty-three titles are emulative, venerative acts: a nod to the artistry of preceding craftspeople – like the script of the Cotton MS Vitellius A. xv Part I, or the admiring recounting of history, myth, and ancestral figures in *Beowulf* itself. In his lecture 'The Ideal Book', published in 1893, Morris declared that the commerciality of books undermines their potential as works of art.[44] Utilitarianism undermines a book's potential to be aesthetically pleasing – Morris commented: 'You cannot have a book either handsome or clear to read which is printed in small characters'; 'I would, therefore, put in a word for some form of gothic letter'; and he understood the functionality of the book when he stated, 'the two pages making an opening are really the unit of the book'.[45] The ideal book should be 'printed on hand-made paper', but 'a small book should not be printed on thick paper, however good it may be',[46] and 'a big folio lies quiet and majestic on the table, waiting kindly till you please to come to it, with its leaves flat and peaceful, giving you no trouble of body, so that your mind is free to enjoy the literature which its beauty enshrines'.[47]

Morris's *Beowulf* follows some but not all of his own stipulations about the ideal book (it certainly does not lie 'quiet and majestic on the table'), and even in its paper and print existence, it is clearly part of the system of a handmade book, deriving its overall aesthetic from an imaginary medieval manuscript, with the Troy Type-face at 18 point emulating a refashioning of the Gothic.[48]

But it does not seem designed or intended for easy legibility, and interestingly, the archaic nature of the design and the translation of *Beowulf* by Morris and A. J. Wyatt link directly back to Cotton MS Vitellius A. xv aesthetically and functionally. Just as very few readers interact with Morris's translation of *Beowulf*, so very few read (or, indeed, seemed a thousand years ago to read) all of Cotton MS Vitellius A. xv – and this despite the fact that Cotton MS Vitellius A. xv Part II 'is one of the most viewed items (if not the most viewed) on [the] Digitised Manuscripts site'.[49] Both renderings of the codices

[44] William Morris, 'The Ideal Book', The Bibliographical Society Lecture, 19 June 1893, 1–11; repr. in *The Library* 1, nos 1–2 (1893): 179–86.

[45] Morris, 'Ideal Book', 7–9.

[46] Morris's handmade linen-rag paper was made by Joseph Batchelor and Son in Kent, based on fifteenth-century Italian paper. See the rich digital resource at http://morrisedition.lib.uiowa.edu/images/loveisenough/pageflip.html.

[47] Morris, 'Ideal Book', 11.

[48] Designed by William Morris and cut at eighteen points by Edward Prince.

[49] Personal communication from Dr Julian Harrison, curator at the British Library, 23 September 2020. He adds: 'There are probably several factors behind that (it has been online for longer, it is featured in many university and school syllabuses, there is greater cultural awareness of it).'

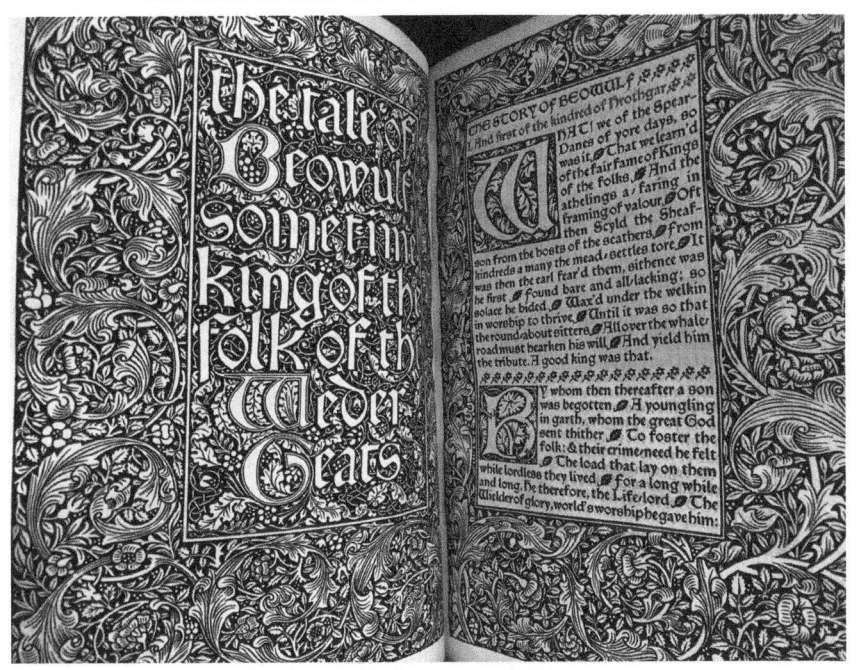

Figure 9.1: William Morris's *Beowulf*.

become, in effect, an *aspect* of bookness, akin to an exhibited artwork, rather than one with which a reader might kinaesthetically and intellectually engage.

Readers throughout the nineteenth and twentieth centuries became engaged in the telling of *Beowulf*, often by subscription, via other cheaper editions than the Kelmscott's. The invention of the economically viable photographic facsimile through the process of Autotyping made a significant difference in the reader's experience of the extracted poem. Two well-known nineteenth- and twentieth-century facsimiles of *Beowulf* permit further consideration of the extracted text within this system of related textual objects. Key to the consideration here is how these editions seek to materially reproduce the text in its manuscript context (as opposed to the Kelmscott 'ideal book', printed but emulative). These are Julius Zupitza's Early English Text Society autotype of the manuscript with his transcription and notes from 1882[50] and Norman Davis's second edition of Zupitza's work, with new collotype photographs (which are the same as used in the Early English Manuscripts in facsimile volume in 1962), and an added preface by Davis.[51]

[50] *Beowulf*, ed. Zupitza.
[51] Julius Zupitza, ed., *Beowulf Reproduced in Facsimile from the Unique Manuscript British Museum MS. Cotton Vitellius A. xv*; introduced by Norman Davis, *Second Edition Containing a New Reproduction of the Manuscript with an Introductory Note*,

The Zupitza edition was designed to be important and special; Furnivall's comment on the EETS edition assures the reader of this in his explanation of the particular size and quality of paper used in the edition and the critique of readers who 'spoil' their copies by normalising the pages' size:

> This book was meant to be of the uzual *demy* 8vo size of the Society's Texts, and the Autotypes were orderd of that size. But as they were printed with a wide margin, it seemed too cruel to cut them down. So the 8vo pages of type have been printed on larger Paper, to suit the Autotypes; and the cutting down of the book to range with the Society's other Texts is left for those Members to order, who like thus to spoil the look of their copies.
>
> F.J.F.
>
> 24 Nov. 1888[52]

It is interesting in this note to read about the fundamental concern with the size of the edition – a highlight that fails to mention Zupitza's facsimile is only millimetres away from dimensional proximity to Cotton MS Vitellius A. xv; that is, the actual membrane of the burnt manuscript is very close in size to the reproduced framed membrane folios of the facsimile. Zupitza does not comment upon this either, presumably because this edition, like so many others, is focused entirely upon establishing the *text* in its narrowest and its *truest* sense. It should be noted however that the size emulation matters in terms of familiarity and haptic engagement; one could argue that interaction with this 1882 facsimile edition is the closest one gets in terms of perspective to the eleventh-century's reader's sensory experience, though, of course, only one text is provided of many in the manuscript book.

In his 'Preliminary Notice' to the EETS facsimile of *Beowulf*, published in 1882 but reprinted with additional commentary and new collotype images in 1959, Zupitza said of his work with the damaged, paper-framed manuscript in the British Library that

> I grudged no pains in trying to decipher as much of what is covered [at the edges] as possible. When, in my notes, I simply state that something is covered, I always mean to say that, by holding the leaf to the light, I was able to read it nonetheless. In case I could not make out what is covered distinctly, I always add a remark to that effect.[53]

EETS o.s. 245 (London, 1959 for 1958), xix. (As an aside, it might be asked how one should cite this volume: as Norman Davis editing Zupitza? Or Zupitza transliterating and annotating and subsequently introduced by Davis?)

[52] *Beowulf*, ed. Zupitza, ii.

[53] *Beowulf Reproduced* introduced by Norman Davis, *Second Edition*, ed. Zupitza, xix.

This description of the reading process represents how the user-reader experiences the *wholeness* of the book – its materiality and content. Zupitza says that he embarked on a physically and intellectually strenuous project, one that, he suggests, involved picking up the bound manuscript book and extending one leaf of the book out separately to the light source, scrutinising the margin at the point of coverage of the paper frame to determine the letter forms underneath that frame. This bodily encounter with the textual object is critically important for accessing the heft and wholeness of the book. Such a physical act would have involved lifting, manoeuvring, turning, peering, in a way that would not be permitted in repositories now for any medieval manuscript, never mind Cotton MS Vitellius A. xv, but it does underscore the importance of taking in all of the textual object in close research through the kinaesthetic and proprioceptive. Phenomenologically, this is the lived experience of encountering the whole book and part of the book's biography. Zupitza's edition and the reedition of Davis in 1959, however, do not allow any such understanding of the retrievability of the manuscript *text*, as Fig. 9.2 illustrates.

In most of the facsimile images in the 1959 reprint – which are very slightly larger than the autotype images from the 1882 edition – there is an elision of the paper frame, showing only the darker manuscript page against a paler regular rectangular background, itself framed by the EETS paper stock and trimming. The images of the burnt membrane of the manuscript in each of these two volumes is relatively close to the size of the actual leaves of Cotton MS Vitellius A. xv, as I say, but otherwise the voluminousness of the bound volumes is not at all like that of the codex in its entirety.

The first edition of Zupitza's EETS facsimile was printed in 1882 to outrage in some quarters, as J. R. Hall revealed in a *Notes and Queries* article:

> When [Professor G.] Stephens, possessed of strong anti-German sentiments, read the reviewer's remarks, he endorsed them in a letter published in *The Athenaeum*, No. 2921 (20 October 1883), 499. Among other things, Stephens asserted that:
>
> the University of Cambridge contemplated the publication of this facsimile edition under the experienced guidance of our great English expert Prof. Skeat. It was in consequence of a London intrigue that the work was eventually put into the hands of Prof. Zupitza, to the great disgust of all right-minded Englishmen. No-one denies the competence of Prof. Zupitza, but none of us can understand why this studied slight should have been put on English scholarship of the highest class.[54]

---

[54] Quoted in J. R. Hall, 'F. J. Furnivall's Letter to the Royal Library, Copenhagen, Asking that the Thorkelin Transcripts of *Beowulf* Be Sent to London for the Use of Julius Zupitza', *Notes and Queries* (1978): 267–72.

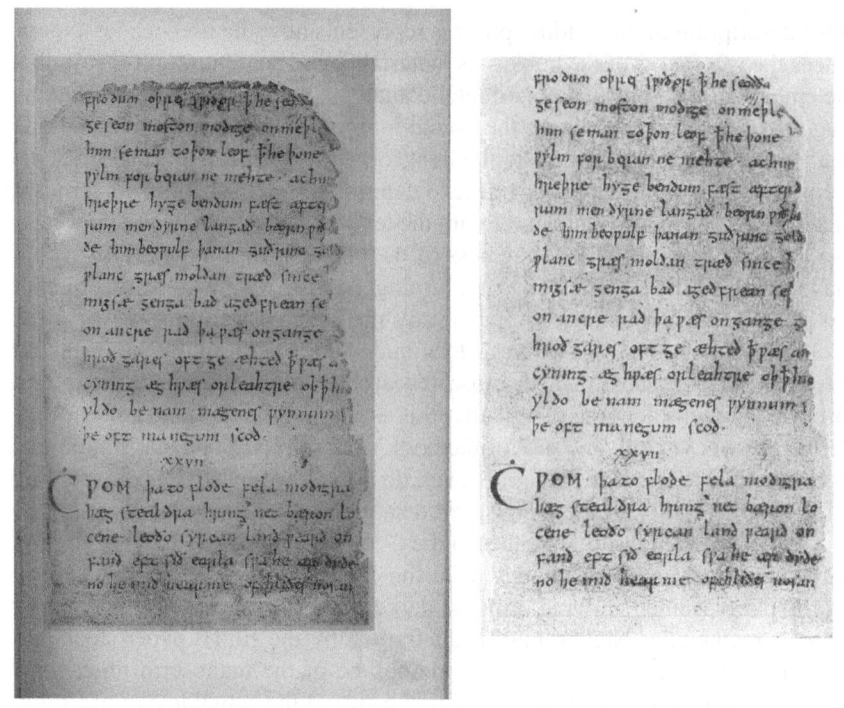

Figure 9.2: Two *Beowulf* facsimiles, Zupitza's edition and Davis' re-edition.

Zupitza's autotype reproduction of the manuscript folios, a process that many hailed as better than other existing methods of photography, 'true' and, in fact, 'for the purposes of original research, [making the "splendid collotype facsimile"] of equal value with the parchment itself'.[55] Autotype was felt to be a permanent photographic record, though, as the Stanford ownership punched into the title-page of one of the Google Books' versions of the EETS edition suggests, the fragility of the book renders it far from 'permanent', and pages are indeed dislodging along the inner margin.[56]

The 1959 volume, on the other hand, is a new edition, made using collotype images, with a whole set of new photographs that were taken for what the revision editor, Norman Davis, called 'this most important volume in the EETS series'. These same photographs were used for the Early English Manuscript

---

[55] Frank Beaumont, 'On *Beowulf*', *Proceedings of the Royal Philosophical Society of Glasgow* 38–39 (1906–7): 201–33. He calls it a 'collotype' at 218.

[56] *OED*, s.v. 'autotype': 1878 Prospectus of 'Autotype Company': 'The public need no longer be content with fading photographs; ask for "Autotypes" or "Chromotypes".' There are two different Google digitised Zupitza editions, quite different from one another in colour, framing, and paratextual information.

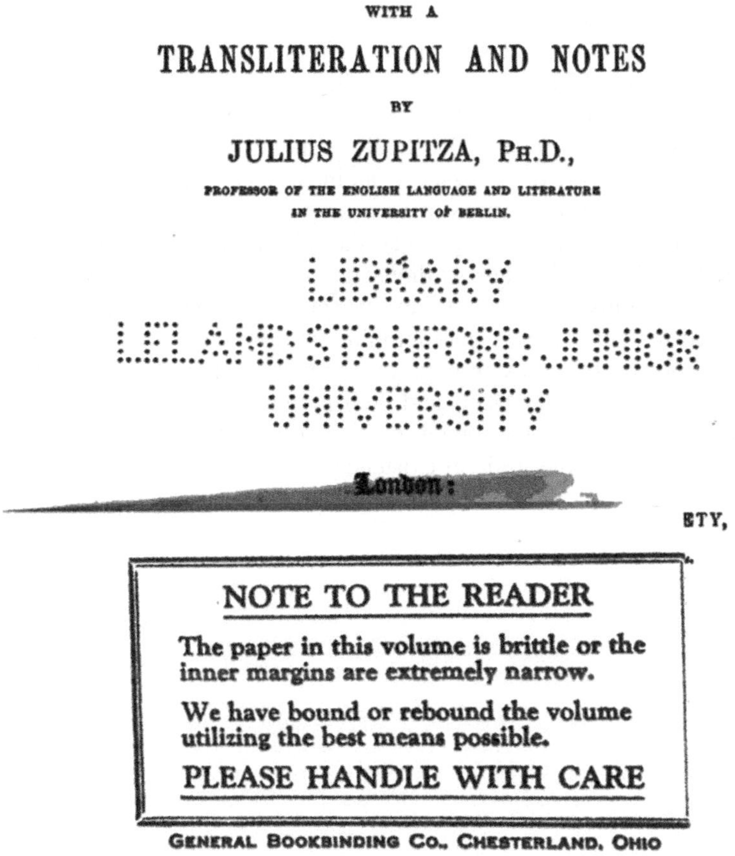

WITH A

TRANSLITERATION AND NOTES

BY

JULIUS ZUPITZA, PH.D.,

PROFESSOR OF THE ENGLISH LANGUAGE AND LITERATURE
IN THE UNIVERSITY OF BERLIN.

LIBRARY
LELAND STANFORD JUNIOR
UNIVERSITY

London:

ETY,

NOTE TO THE READER

The paper in this volume is brittle or the inner margins are extremely narrow.

We have bound or rebound the volume utilizing the best means possible.

PLEASE HANDLE WITH CARE

GENERAL BOOKBINDING CO., CHESTERLAND, OHIO

Figure 9.3: Stanford's copy of the EETS edition of *Beowulf* edited by Julius Zupitza.

in facsimile volume of the Cotton MS Vitellius A. xv Part I that appeared some four years later continuing the tradition of publishing only part of the complex codex.[57] This becomes a mosaic of parts, of images, editions, and facsimiles of parts of the physical book.[58]

57 Kemp Malone, ed., *The Nowell Codex*, Early English Manuscripts in Facsimile 12 (Copenhagen, 1963). Note that Michael Lapidge, for example, in his article, 'The Archetype of *Beowulf*', *Anglo-Saxon England* 29 (2000): 5–41, states at footnote 15 that this EEMF volume presents 'the entire manuscript', when 'manuscript' refers only to part of the whole codex.

58 Though this multiplication of printed images is nothing in comparison with present-day digital plethora, the superabundance of visual, digital, and digitised data.

Finally, the manuscript's meaning does not reside with the poem or renditions, adaptations, translations, and editions of that single text; that should be clear enough. It does not reside in these texts *narrowly* conceived: *texts* as word-symbols on a substrate. One might argue that extractive editions and reproduced aspects – taken individually – can never be considered more than an illusion: that which is, in essence, an incorrect experience. A more correct experience of *Beowulf* resides in an acknowledgement of the wholeness or voluminousness of the textual object; the full interpretative potential resides in tracing *Beowulf* through its thousands of edifices, while understanding the whole manuscript context from which it is drawn. It resides in these inhabited textual things – photographic and digital aspect, metadata, and physical object. It is only through examining, or at least being alert to, the wholeness of physical objects and their systemic relationships that we can move from illusion to the 'being-in-the-world' of *Beowulf*, Cotton Vitellius MS A. xv, or any other relic of existence.

10

Trojan Ghosts in Arthurian Romance[1]

ELIZABETH ARCHIBALD

When Geoffrey of Monmouth describes Arthur's coronation, he notes that the men and women of the court feasted separately because 'the Britons liked to observe the old Trojan custom'.[2] It is surprising that this aside is the only explicit link Geoffrey makes between Arthur and Troy, since in his hugely successful, if historically dubious, *Historia Regum Britanniae*, the two are closely linked by ancestry: Brutus, the Trojan refugee, founds Britain, and Arthur is its most glorious king.[3] Descent from the Trojans is first ascribed to the Britons by Nennius in the ninth-century *Historia Brittonum* and further developed by Geoffrey; Trojan ancestry was claimed for kingdoms and dynasties across Western Europe throughout the Middle Ages and beyond because of the prestige of a connection to the Roman empire, which was founded by Aeneas the Trojan refugee.[4] In coats of arms made for Henry VII and Elizabeth I, Brutus and Arthur appear with Geoffrey's legendary King Belinus, creating a claim 'to an ancient British lineage', and Henry had statues

---

[1] It is a pleasure to offer this essay in appreciation of Siân Echard's many valuable contributions to the study of the Arthurian legend and the classical tradition in the Middle Ages, and also of her good fellowship.

[2] I begin with a work that has been a major focus of Siân's scholarship. Geoffrey of Monmouth, *History of the Kings of Britain*, ix.13, lines 371–77, ed. Michael D. Reeve, trans. Neil Wright (Woodbridge, 2007), 212–13: 'antiquam namque consuetudinem Troiae servantes Britones consueuerant'. This detail is repeated by later chroniclers including Wace, Layamon, and Manning.

[3] See Helen Fulton, 'Historiography and the Invention of British Identity: Troy as an Origin Legend in Medieval Britain and Ireland', in *The Origin Legends of Early Medieval Western Europe*, ed. Lindy Brady and Patrick Wadden (Leiden, 2022), 338–62.

[4] There is an extensive literature on this subject. See for instance Richard Waswo, 'Our Ancestors, the Trojans: Inventing Cultural Identity in the Middle Ages', *Exemplaria* 7, no. 2 (1995): 269–90, and Wolfram Keller, *Selves and Nations: The Troy Story from Sicily to England in the Middle Ages* (Heidelberg, 2008).

of Brutus, Hengist, and Arthur at his palace at Richmond.[5] In the late fifteenth century, the Italian poet Boiardo invented for the ruling house of Ferrara an ancestor with Trojan connections, Ruggiero, a descendant of Hector's son Astyanax (who in this account survived the fall of Troy): 'Fortunately, the household of Priam was large enough to provide ancestry for everybody in Europe.'[6] Ruggiero cannot claim Arthurian family links, but Boiardo 'concocts a grand dynastic scheme, founded on the characteristic interaction of the legend of Troy, the eminence of ancient Arthurian chivalry, and its return through the introduction of a new hero'.[7]

Modern critics frequently link the two legends, in relation to medieval interest in and exploitation of the classical past; Christopher Baswell notes that 'romances of antiquity are generally read as "glorious prehistories"'.[8] Lee Patterson sees Arthur's Roman campaign as 'part of the inevitable process of *translatio imperii*, the westering of empire from Troy to Rome, where it will eventually serve as, in Father Chenu's words, "a providential preparation for the age of Christ"'.[9] According to Baswell, 'Arthurian tradition in England, from Geoffrey onward, nevertheless persistently arranges itself – translates itself – into some analogy of Mediterranean imperial antiquity, especially that of Troy and Rome, by means of narrative parallels, narrative inversions, and such evocative names as "Troynovaunt" [for London].'[10] Baswell suggests a new category of *translatio fabulae* 'by which events are variously retold, reparsed, or challenged as carrying a weight of fact or spurious fantasy'.[11]

Chrétien de Troyes famously refers to the *translatio imperii* in relation to tales of chivalry in the opening of his Arthurian romance *Cligés* as he

---

[5] Christopher Dean, *Arthur of England: English Attitudes to King Arthur and the Knights of the Round Table in the Middle Ages and the Renaissance* (Toronto, 1987), 27; Muriel Whitaker, *The Legends of King Arthur in Art* (Cambridge, 1990), 147.

[6] Riccardo Bruscagli, 'Ruggiero's Story: The Making of a Dynastic Hero', in *Romance and History: Imagining Time from the Medieval to the Early Modern Period*, ed. Jon Whitman (Cambridge, 2015), 167.

[7] Bruscagli, 'Ruggiero's Story', 160.

[8] Baswell, 'Fearful Histories: The Past Contained in the Romances of Antiquity', in *Romance and History*, ed. Whitman, 24–25.

[9] Lee Patterson, *Negotiating the Past: The Historical Understanding of Medieval Literature* (Madison, 1987), 214. He also notes that 'both in their first form and in their later versions, the Arthurian legends, like the Trojan, are persistently marked by the paradox of their origin. Fabrications used to affirm a historical past, their historical authenticity is from the beginning at issue' (206).

[10] Christopher Baswell, 'Troy, Arthur, and the Languages of "Brutis Albyoun"', in *Reading Medieval Culture: Essays in Honor of Robert W. Hanning*, ed. Robert M. Stein and Sandra Pierson Prior (Notre Dame, 2005), 173. He quotes Kellie Robertson's comment that 'the Trojan vernacular was the most influential language never spoken in the British Isles during the Middle Ages' (172).

[11] Baswell, 'Troy, Arthur', 173.

describes his purported source; he claims that chivalry and *clergie* (learning) have moved from Greece and Rome to France.[12] But he does not name Troy or Arthur here – after all, he is praising France, and Arthur ruled in England. Moreover, the Arthur of Chrétien's romances is not the all-conquering action hero of the chronicles but a less impressive *roi fainéant*, a weak king who mostly stays at court passively while his knights go out and have adventures; there is no hint of the early glory days of subjugating Britain, or the continental wars, or the final betrayals and disasters, though they would surely have been known to Chrétien's readers. Sylvia Federico argues that 'the continuum of Trojan, Roman and Arthurian precedent offered a range of possible martial, political and cultural subject positions for the English'.[13] But that continuum is surprisingly infrequently articulated in Arthurian romance, in English or any other language. Baswell's claim that Arthurian tradition 'persistently' rearranges itself to parallel the stories of Troy and Rome seems to me somewhat overstated: Troynovaunt does not appear in many Arthurian romances, though some narrative parallels and evocative names will be discussed in this essay.

One famous example of Trojan heritage is the frame of the late fourteenth-century Middle English poem *Sir Gawain and the Green Knight*, whose opening lines trace the movement from the fall of Troy through the colonisation of Britain by 'Felix Brutus' to the early years of Arthur's reign:

> Sithen the sege and the assaut   was sesed at Troye,
> The burgh brittened and brent   to bronde and askes
> The tulk that the trammes   of tresoun there wroghte
> Was tried for his trecherye,   the truest on erthe ...
> And far over the French flod   Felix Brutus
> On many bonkes ful brode   Bretayn he settes
>   Wyth wynne ...
>
> [After the battle and the attack were over at Troy,
> The town beaten down to smoking brands and ashes,
> That man enmeshed in the nets of treachery – the truest
> Of men – was tried for treason; I mean
> Aeneas, the high-born ...
> And, joyfully, far over the French sea,
> Felix Brutus founds Britain by ample down
>   And bay ...][14]

---

[12] *Cligés*, lines 28–33, ed. A. Micha, CFMA (Paris, 1978), 1; trans. W. Kibler in *Arthurian Romances* (London, 1991), 123.

[13] Sylvia Federico, *New Troy: Fantasies of Empire in the Late Middle Ages* (Minneapolis, 2003), 69.

[14] *Sir Gawain and the Green Knight*, lines 1–4, 13–15, in *The Works of the Gawain Poet*, ed. Ad Putter and Myra Stokes (London, 2014), 239–406; all references are to this edition, cited as *SGGK*. Translations are taken from Keith Harrison, *Sir Gawain*

Thorlac Turville-Petre notes the emphasis in this description of the Trojan diaspora on founding and building; Arthur is introduced in this context, which might be considered positive:[15]

> Bot of all that here bult*,   of Bretaygne kynges   [built]
> Aye was Arthur the hendest*,   as I have herde telle.   [most courteous]
>   (25–26)

In the final stanza of the poem, the sequence Troy–Brutus–Arthur is reversed, rather more briefly and rapidly, and the first line repeated almost exactly:

> Thus in Arthurs day   this aunter bitidde*   [these marvellous things took place]
> The Brutus bokes* thereof   beres wittnesse.   [i.e. *Brut* chronicle]
> Sithen Brutus the bolde burn*   bowed* hider firste,   [man; landed here]
> After the sege and the assaut   was sesed at Troye …   (2522–25)

As Silverstein notes, there are in fact no such Gawain stories in the *Brut*.[16] Much critical ink has been spilled over the implications of this unusual frame in *SGGK*, to which I will return at the end of this essay; but surprisingly few other romances make such explicit connections between the two legends. The links that do appear can take various forms: lineage, names, juxtaposition in manuscripts, material objects. Like ghosts, they are only faintly visible, and their impact can be positive or negative, emphasising the prestige or superiority of the Arthurian world, or its inevitable destruction.[17] Of course my examples are not intended to be comprehensive; I focus on French and English romances, with some reference to German ones.

Allusions to Troy and to the founding of Britain by Brutus occur frequently in the chronicle tradition, but much less often in Arthurian romance.[18] The

---

and the Green Knight: A New Translation (Oxford, 1983), with occasional substitutions; the meanings of some words are ambiguous or disputed.

[15] Thorlac Turville-Petre, 'Afterword: The Brutus Prologue and *Sir Gawain and the Green Knight*', in *Imagining an English Nation*, ed. Kathy Lavezzo (Minneapolis, 2004), 343.

[16] Theodore Silverstein, '"Sir Gawain", Dear Brutus, and Britain's Fortunate Founding: A Study in Comedy and Convention', *Modern Philology* 62, no. 3 (1965): 192.

[17] Echard suggests another useful metaphor in her 'Palimpsests of Place and Time in Geoffrey of Monmouth's *Historia regum Britannie*', in *Teaching and Learning in Medieval Europe: Essays in Honour of Gernot Wieland*, ed. Greti Dinkova-Bruun and Tristan Major (Turnhout, 2017), 43–59.

[18] See Lister Matheson, 'The Chronicle Tradition', in *A Companion to Arthurian Literature*, ed. Helen Fulton (Oxford, 2009), 58–69, and in the same volume Julia Marvin, 'The English Brut Tradition', 221–34. Arthur's descent from Brutus was valuable to English kings asserting their claims to sovereignty over the whole of

English alliterative poets of the fourteenth century seem to have had a particular interest in Britain's Trojan past. In the Alliterative *Morte Arthure*, for instance, Sir Cleges boasts that his family arms date back to the siege of Troy:[19]

> Myn armez are of ancestrye enueryde with lord* [attested by lords]
> And has in banere bene borne sen* Sir Brut tyme, [since]
> At the cité of Troye, þat tyme was ensegede*, [besieged]
> Ofte seen in asawtte* with certayne knyghttez, [assault]
> Fro þe* Brute broughte vs and all oure bolde elders [since]
> To Bretayne þe braddere* within chippe-burdez*. [greater; aboard ships]

Note the use of the first-person 'vs' (1698) to describe the Trojan refugees who colonised Britain. Malory includes a version of Cleges' speech in the second tale in his *Morte Darthur*, 'King Arthur and the Emperor Lucius', which is very closely based on the Alliterative *Morte*:[20] 'Myne armys ar knowyn thorowoute all Inglonde and Bretayne, and I am com of olde barounes of auncetry noble, and Sir Clegis is my name, a Knyght of the Table Rounde. And frome Troy, Brute brought myne elders.'

That is the only reference to Brutus in Malory. When Arthur is dying at the end of the Alliterative *Morte*, the Trojan relationship is invoked, with some repetition of Cleges' earlier speech:

> Thus endis Kyng Arthure, as auctors* alleges, [authors/authorities]
> That was of Ectores blude, the kynges sone of Troye,
> And of sir Pryamous the prynce*, praysede in erthe: [i.e. King Priam]
> Fro thythen* broughte the Bretons all his bolde eldyrs [thence]
> Into Bretayne the brode, as þe Bruytte* tellys. [the *Brut* chronicle]
> (4342–46)

There is no equivalent to this in Malory; indeed, Thomas Crofts argues that Malory deliberately resisted the parallel between Brutus and Arthur. For instance, the Stanzaic *Morte Arthur*, on which he drew heavily in his final tales, alludes to Britain's Trojan origins in describing the final battle between Arthur and Mordred:[21]

Britain; see for instance Christopher Michael Berard, *Arthurianism in Early Plantagenet England: From Henry II to Edward I* (Woodbridge, 2019).

[19] *Morte Arthure: A Critical Edition*, lines 1694–99, ed. Mary Hamel (London, 1984), 162. All references are to this edition.

[20] Sir Thomas Malory, *The Morte Darthur*, ed. P. J. C. Field, 2 vols (Cambridge, 2013), I.165 (V.7); the text is in vol. 1, cited by page number, followed by the book and chapter numbers in Caxton's edition.

[21] Thomas Crofts, *Malory's Contemporary Audience: The Social Reading of Romance in Late Medieval England* (Cambridge, 2006), 146–47; Stanzaic, *Morte*

Sithe Britain* out of Troy was sought*   [Brutus; came]
And made in Britain his owne wonne*,   [dwelling]
Such wonders never ere was wrought,
Never yet under the sun.

But Malory makes no reference to Brutus or Troy at this point.

Brutus is of less interest to continental writers, unsurprisingly. He is absent from the Vulgate and Post-Vulgate cycles, apart from a brief mention in the Post-Vulgate *Queste* of a King Brutus, named for the Trojan because he lives in a castle built by Brutus and his men after Troy had fallen.[22] Elisabeth Lienert, surveying the German tradition, notes that genealogical links with Troy occur only in Albrecht's *Jungerer Titurel* (c. 1270), where the Grail family is said to be descended from the Trojans, and in the opening of Fuetrer's *Buch der Abenteuer* (c. 1480–90), which begins with the Trojan War and moves on to the Grail story, drawing on the *Jungerer Titurel*.[23]

As well as ancestral links, another form of relationship is manuscript context. It is quite common to have Trojan and Arthurian narratives in the same manuscript, and sometimes they are interlinked in complex and interesting ways, reflecting the simultaneous and rapid rise of vernacular chronicles and chivalric romance in the later twelfth century. The *romans antiques*, medievalising French verse accounts of the classical stories of Thebes, Troy, and Aeneas, were produced around 1150 to 1165. The earliest French Arthurian romances are the five poems about the adventures of individual knights by Chrétien de Troyes (c. 1170–90). In the famous Guiot manuscript, Paris, BN, fr. 794 (1230–40), four of the five are followed by the *Roman de Troie* and Wace's *Brut* (the first French version of Geoffrey's *Historia*), and then come Chrétien's *Conte du Graal* and the first two anonymous Continuations, so that history is framed by romance.[24] In a contemporary manuscript, Paris, BN, fr. 1450, the order is more complicated: the *Roman de Troie* and the *Eneas* are followed by Wace's *Brut*, which is interrupted to include the *Conte du Graal*, *Cligés*, part of *Yvain*, and part of the *Chevalier de la Charrete*, after which the

---

Arthur, lines 3376–79, in *King Arthur's Death*, ed. Larry D. Benson, rev. Edward E. Foster, TEAMS (1974; Kalamazoo, 1994).

[22] *La Version Post-Vulgate de la Queste del Saint Graal et de la Mort Artu: troisième partie du roman du Graal*, ch. IX.109, ed. Fanni Bogdanow, 5 vols, SATF (Paris, 1991–2001), II.143–44; trans. Martha Asher in *Lancelot-Grail: The Old French Arthurian Vulgate and Post-Vulgate in Translation*, gen. ed. Norris J. Lacy, 5 vols (London, 1993–96), V.142. King Brutus's unnamed daughter falls in love with Galahad and tries to seduce him, killing herself with his sword when he rejects her; this suggests a number of telescoped Trojan allusions, to Lavinia and Dido.

[23] Elisabeth Lienert, 'Ritterschaft und Minne, Ursprungmythos und Bildungzitat –Troia-Anspielungen in nicht-troianisch Dichtungen des 12. bis 14. Jahrhunderts', in *Die deutsche Troialiteratur des Mittelalters und der frühen Neuzeit, Materialen und Untersuchungen*, ed. Horst Brunner (Wiesbaden, 1990), 200.

[24] Marc-René Jung, *La Légende de Troie en France au moyen âge: Analyse des versions françaises et bibliographie raisonée des manuscrits* (Basel, 1996), 185–86.

Brut continues; Nixon notes that none of Chrétien's prologues are included, so that the romances seem part of the historical continuum.[25] All Chrétien's romances focus on the twelve years of peace described by Wace in which Arthur's knights can go on individual quests; after this, history reasserts itself with the inexorable movement to the final tragedy.[26] Another such compilation manuscript, Paris, BN, fr. 375 (late thirteenth to early fourteenth century), begins with the *Roman de Thèbes* and the *Roman de Troie*, and includes the *Roman d'Alexandre* and Chrétien's *Cligés* and *Erec et Enide*, as well as a number of other texts.[27] Sylvia Huot has pointed out that there is a progression here 'from ancient to contemporary times … from paganism to Christianity', and also an emphasis on 'the story of love and chivalry as ongoing human activities'.[28] She also draws attention to a material connection here between the Arthurian world and Troy: in *Erec*, the story of Aeneas is depicted on Enide's saddle (5289–98).

In one manuscript of the Vulgate Cycle, Bodmer 147 (late thirteenth century), the usual sequence of the Vulgate *Estoire del Graal* is interrupted in a most unusual way after Arthur's coronation, when Merlin instructs Blaise to write down the story of Troy (this echoes the link between the coronation and Troy in my opening quotation from Geoffrey of Monmouth):[29]

> Mes atant se test ores li contes de lui [Arthur] et parlerons de Mellin qui s'en ala a Blaise son mestre et li conta mot a mot si comme le roys Artus avoit esté coronez (et par lui le savons nos encore). Et puis li dist: 'Ge vueil que tu mestes en escrit comment et por quele achoison Troie la grant fu destruite et essilliee.' Et Blaises dist: 'Ce ferai ge moult volontiers, car aussi avoie ge grant desirrier de savoir en la verité.' 'Or prenez donc .i. autre livre et ge t'en diré mot a mot la certaineté, comment et porquoi la guerre commença et les grant batailles et les granz mortalitez qui en furent.' Et Blaises dist: 'Et ge l'escriré volontiers.'

> [But now the story stops talking about him [Arthur] and we will speak of Merlin who went to Blaise his master and told him word for word how King Arthur had been crowned (and through him we know it still). And then he said to him: 'I want you to write down how and for what reason Troy the Great was destroyed and exiled.' And Blaise said: 'I will do it very

---

[25] Jung, *La Légende*, 204–5; Terry Nixon, 'Romance Collections and the Manuscripts of Chrétien de Troyes', in *The Manuscripts of Chrétien de Troyes*, ed. Keith Busby et al., 2 vols (Amsterdam, 1993), I.23.

[26] Wace's *Roman de Brut*, lines 9731–98, ed. and trans. Judith Weiss (Exeter, 1999), 244–47. See Ad Putter, 'Finding Time for Romance: Medieval Arthurian Literary History', *Medium Ævum* 63 (1994): 1–6.

[27] Jung, *La Légende*, 164–66.

[28] Sylvia Huot, *From Song to Book: The Poetics of Writing in Old French Lyric and Narrative Poetry* (Ithaca, 1987), 23.

[29] Quoted in Françoise Vielliard, 'Un Texte interpolé du cycle du Graal', *Revue des histoires des textes* 4 (1974): 317–18 (my translation).

willingly, for I too have a great desire to know the truth about it.' 'Now then, take another book and I will tell you word for word the truth, how and why the war began and the great battles and the great mortality which occurred.' And Blaise said: 'And I will write it willingly.']

The placing of this unique interpolation at the very beginning of Arthur's reign is presumably intended to suggest parallels between the two stories, with the implication of a tragic ending for Camelot, the destruction of a great civilisation. At the end of the Post-Vulgate *Mort Artu*, when Arthur and Lancelot are both dead, King Mark sacks Camelot and destroys most of Logres, including churches, monasteries and Joyous Gard, the Round Table and Lancelot's tomb, to avenge the dishonour he had received there.[30] There is no reference to Troy, but the parallel seems clear enough: the disrespect to Mark is connected to Isolde's affair, and the destruction of Lancelot's tomb might echo the treatment of Hector's body in the Troy story. Juxtaposition is one form of link, then, where the reader must make the connections, and not always between whole narratives. Jung points out that in Paris, BN, fr. 1420 (mid-thirteenth century), Chrétien's *Erec* and *Cligés* are followed by twenty-one verses about Hector from the *Roman de Troie*, presumably implying some sort of implicit comparison or contrast.[31]

Another form of literary kinship is suggested by the appearance in the Arthurian legend of a number of names famous from the Troy story but now applied to minor characters, ghosts haunting the Arthurian narrative. Sir Priamus appears in the Middle English Alliterative *Morte Arthur* and in Malory.[32] In the Alliterative *Morte*, he is a pagan prince whose father has rebelled against Rome; when Gawain defeats him in battle during the Roman War, he agrees to be christened. He describes his father as of Alexander's blood, and his grandfather's uncle as 'Sir Hector of Troy' (2595ff.), and also claims descent from Judas Maccabeus and Joshua, two of the biblical Worthies. Impressed by Gawain's first reply to him, he says that the king who has such a knight (i.e. Arthur) will be Alexander's heir and 'abler than ever was Sire Ector of Troy' (2634–35). Malory includes the reference to Hector in his version of Priamus's speech but omits both Alexander and Hector from Gawain's reply (178–79; V.10). Any reader or listener who knew the Troy story would surely also have recognised the name of Priam as Hector's father; it seems rather a demotion to reintroduce him as a mere knight. A more significant borrowing is the name of Hector himself, given both to Arthur's fosterfather in some texts (he is Antor in the Vulgate and in the Middle English Prose *Merlin*,

---

[30] Ch. 64.701ff., ed. Bogdanow, III.506ff; trans. Asher in *Lancelot-Grail*, V.311.

[31] Jung, *La Légende*, 423–24.

[32] 'Sir' can be applied anachronistically to classical figures, but this Priamus is clearly a medieval knight, not the Trojan king.

but Ector in Malory), and to Lancelot's brother Ector de Mares, who in the Vulgate Cycle is the illegitimate son of King Ban. Does the use of Hector's name for minor characters imply that Camelot outstrips Troy, or is it a way of exploiting Trojan prestige, and a reminder of Britain's link to the legendary city and its heroes? Trojan characters can also change gender in Arthurian romances: in the Post-Vulgate *Queste*, the roll-call of Round Table knights ends with Ecubas (presumably from Hecuba, Priam's queen).[33]

There are many women named Helen in the Arthurian legend, two of whom fall in love with Lancelot and cause him particular trouble; these must be deliberate choices by the romancers to recall the Spartan queen's impact on Troy. Elaine of Corbenic tricks him into making her pregnant with Galahad, whose birth (predestined and a Good Thing) and subsequent arrival at court arouse the wrath of Guinevere. Elaine of Astolat (Tennyson's Lady of Shalott) dies of unrequited passion for Lancelot, but the rumour that he loves her makes Guinevere jealous. The queen's reaction replaces the aggrieved husband's revenge in the Troy story; the result is not a major war, but lovers' quarrels, and in the case of Elaine of Corbenic, Lancelot's exile and temporary madness. Before these Helens, there is the young duchess of Brittany abducted and raped by the giant of St Michel and avenged by Arthur, whose story is told by Geoffrey of Monmouth and later chroniclers, and also by the Alliterative *Morte* poet and Malory; she is named Helena in Geoffrey and Wace. Unlike Helen of Troy, she is a reluctant sexual partner, killed by her abductor's lust. In the account in the Alliterative *Morte*, the duchess is not named, but Troy is explicitly mentioned in relation to the giant's hoard: the messenger tells Arthur that the giant has more treasure than Troy when it fell (886–87). Baumgartner has argued that Wace's account of this episode and of Arthur's battle with the giant recalls not only Brutus's conquest of the giant inhabitants of Britain but also the abduction of the Trojan Helen; Arthur's defeat of the giant is a sort of reparation and return to order and civilisation, in contrast with Paris's crime and the subsequent war.[34] Beautiful women are often compared with Helen; the name seems to be associated with sexual temptation, deliberate or not. In the *Didot Perceval*, Gawain

---

[33] *Post-Vulgate Queste*, ch. II.39, ed. Bogdanow, II.54–55; trans. Asher in *Lancelot-Grail*, V.123.

[34] Emmanuèle Baumgartner, 'Passages d'Arthur en Normandie', in *Le Roman de Brut entre mythe et histoire*, ed. Claude Letellier and Denis Huë (Orléans, 2003), 33. Baumgartner argues elsewhere that the name Helen also recalls the saintly mother of Constantine: see 'Sainte(s) Hélène(s)', in her *De l'histoire de Troie au livre du Graal: le temps, le récit (XIIe-XIIIe siècles)* (Orléans, 1994), 352, 355. She notes that in the Grail lineage, Lancelot's mother Elaine, who ends her life in a convent, is descended from King David (354).

has a sister called Helen; she and Perceval fall in love when they meet at a tournament early on, though she plays no further part in the story.[35]

In German literature too, Trojan characters and scenes are sometimes used as a yardstick to show the superiority of Arthurian characters.[36] In Heinrich von dem Türlin's *Diu Crône* (c. 1220–30), the narrator describes the general grief at Queen Ginover's abduction as greater than that caused by Helen's abduction, which led to the fall of Troy, and continues with an interesting mélange of classical and medieval allusions.[37] Of course it was almost a literary cliché to invoke such mythological scenes; the popularity of the Troy allusion is underlined by the comic reference in Chaucer's *Nun's Priest's Tale* when Chauntecleer is carried off by the fox and the general lamentation is greater than when Troy fell and Priam died.[38] In a beast fable, this is ironic, but references to Troy seem particularly appropriate for Arthurian characters since they are descended from the Trojans.

Comparisons of Arthurian knights with Trojan or Greek warriors do occur, but more might have been expected, especially after Arthur became one of the Nine Worthies along with Hector (in the *Voeux du Paon*, an Alexander text composed about 1312). In Lydgate's *Fall of Princes* (1431–38), Arthur is 'As Ector hardi [brave], lik Ulixes tretable'; the comparison with Ulysses, here characterised as intelligent or reasonable rather than wily, is unusual and surprising.[39] When Malory was writing, Crofts notes, Thomas Talbot, Viscount Lisle, was known posthumously as 'the English Achilles' because of his 'fieriness' after he died in a battle with William Lord Berkeley over manors.[40] The *Gesta regum Britannie* attributed to William of Rennes (c. 1236) says that Arthur surpasses Achilles as Achilles surpasses Thersites.[41] At the beginning of the early thirteenth-century French romance *Fergus* by

---

[35] *The Didot Perceval according to the Manuscripts of Modena and Paris*, ed. William Roach (Philadelphia, 1941; repr. 2016), 103ff. (MS E); trans. D. Skeels as *The Romance of Perceval in Prose: A Translation of the E Manuscript of the Didot Perceval* (Seattle, 1961), 10–11.

[36] See Lienert, 'Ritterschaft und Minne', 203.

[37] *Diu Krône*, lines 11549–49, ed. Gudrun Felder (Berlin, 2012), 191; trans. J. W. Thomas, *The Crown: A Tale of Sir Gawein and King Arthur's Court* (Lincoln, 1989), 129.

[38] Chaucer, *Canterbury Tales*, VII.3355–61, ed. Jill Mann (London, 2005), 617.

[39] Lydgate's *Fall of Princes*, VIII. 2799, ed. Henry Bergen, 4 vols, EETS e.s. 121–24 (London, 1924–27), III.901. Neither comparison is in his sources.

[40] Crofts, *Malory's Contemporary Audience*, 3.

[41] Quoted in Siân Echard, '"Hic est Artur": Reading Latin and Reading Arthur', in *New Directions in Arthurian Studies*, ed. Alan Lupack (Cambridge, 2002), 61.

Guillaume le Clerc, Arthur's court is gathered at Cardigan for the Feast of St John, but Gawain and Ywain do not join in the general merriment:[42]

> Messire Gavains par les dois
> Avoit puis un suen compaingnon,
> Que mesire[s] Yvains ot non;
> Celui amoit de telle amor
> Que onques nus ne vit millor.
> Ainc Acchillés ne Patroclus
> Nul jor ne s'entre'amerent plus
> Com cil doi compaign[on] faisoient.

> [My lord Gawain had taken the hand of a companion of his, namely Yvain, for whom he showed a love as great as ever was seen: the mutual affection of Achilles and Patroclus was at no time greater than that of these two companions.]

This scene is a variation on the opening of Chrétien's *Yvain*, where Gawain and Yvain are in a group listening to Calogrenant's account of his fountain adventure. Owen comments: 'Noticeable in Guillaume's version are the bantering tone and the exclusion of ladies from the scene, the topic of courtly love being replaced by a show of affection between fellow-knights.'[43]

But being compared with Achilles and Patroclus may have been a dubious honour. Achilles is quite often mentioned in medieval literature either as the slayer of Hector or as the lover of Polyxena or Briseis, but Patroclus has a much lower profile. According to Flutre's index of proper names, he is mentioned in only two French romances, one of which is Arthurian.[44] The two heroes do of course have major roles in the *Roman de Troie*, where the nature of their relationship is raised by Hector. When Patroclus is killed, Hector taunts the grieving Achilles about his reasons for wanting vengeance:[45]

---

[42] Guillaume le Clerc, *The Romance of Fergus*, lines 24–31, ed. Wilson Frescoln (Philadelphia, 1983), 31–32; trans. D. D. R. Owen as *Fergus of Galloway* (London, 1991), 1.

[43] *Fergus*, trans. Owen, note on lines 1–43, 114.

[44] Louis-Ferdinand Flutre, *Table des noms propres avec toutes leurs variantes, figurant dans les romans du Moyen Age écrits en français ou en provençal et actuellement publiés ou analysés* (Poitiers, 1962). Comparison with G. D. West, *An Index of Proper Names in French Arthurian Prose Romances* (Toronto, 1978), reveals that Trojan names appear more frequently in prose romances than in verse; this may be linked to the more historical tendencies of some prose romances.

[45] *Roman de Troie*, lines 13181–88, ed. L. Constans and E. Faral, 6 vols, SATF (Paris, 1904–12), II.281–82; trans. Glyn Burgess and Douglas Kelly as *The* Roman de Troie *of Benoît de Saint Maure: A Translation* (Cambridge, 2017), 203.

'E la dolor del compaignon
Dont j'ai fait la desevreison,
Que tantes feiz avez sentu
Entre vos braz tot nu a nu,
Et autres gieus vis e hontos …'

['Including your sorrow for the companion of whom I have
deprived you and whom you have so often felt in your arms,
with both of you naked, as well as other vile, shameful sport …']

Hector goes on to claim that Patroclus's death is the gods' punishment for such outrageous behaviour. According to John Boswell, the classical view of Achilles and Patroclus as lovers was known and alluded to up to the fourteenth century.[46] Would it have been flattering to compare two of the top Arthurian knights with these two Greek heroes, especially when there is so much emphasis on their mutual affection? Is there a hint of more than homosocial fellowship in the *Fergus* passage? Scholars disagree about this. Tony Hunt comments that Guillaume le Clerc is comparing the knights 'loftily' with the Greek heroes, and views the romance as humorous literary pastiche: 'The inherited motifs are inflected with a quizzical zest.'[47] But Michelle Freeman has doubts that I share, describing the mood in this scene as 'highly suspect': she reads the passage as a negative comment about the decadence of the Arthurian court, and even of romance after Chrétien.[48]

Another form of romance allusion to Troy occurs in descriptions of material culture, often with negative connotations. When Lancelot is imprisoned by Morgan, the sight of a man painting murals in her palace depicting the story of Aeneas and his flight from Troy inspires him to ask for paints. He produces murals of his own story, including his love affair with the queen; later, Morgan arranges for Arthur to see them, and thus he becomes aware of the affair.[49] Douglas Kelly has elegantly teased out a number of parallels between Lancelot

---

[46] John Boswell, *Christianity, Social Tolerance and Homosexuality* (Chicago, 1980), 25 n. 44; unfortunately, he gives no references.

[47] Tony Hunt, '*Fergus*: Pastiche or Parody?', in *The Scots and Medieval Arthurian Legend*, ed. Rhiannon Purdie and Nicola Royan (Cambridge, 2005), 59, 63, 69.

[48] Michelle Freeman, '*Fergus*: Parody and the Arthurian Tradition', *French Forum* 8, no. 3 (1983): 199. See also Elizabeth Archibald, 'Questioning Arthurian Ideals', in *The Cambridge Companion to the Arthurian Legend*, ed. Elizabeth Archibald and Ad Putter (Cambridge, 2009), 144–45.

[49] *Lancelot: Roman en prose du XIIIe siècle*, ch. LXXXVI.20–22, ed. A. Micha, Textes littéraires français, 9 vols (Geneva, 1978–83), V.52–54; trans. W. Kibler in *Lancelot-Graal*, ch. 157, gen. ed. Norris J. Lacy, III.218. This is the only reference to Aeneas in the Vulgate Cycle.

and Aeneas suggested in this episode.[50] Lancelot's escape from his prison points not only to Aeneas's flight from Troy but also to his flight from Dido to Italy, where the Trojans are coolly received by their cousins in Latium, just as Lancelot is coolly received by some when he returns to Camelot. The two stories do not match exactly: Kelly sees Guinevere as a sort of Dido, and Lancelot and Arthur as versions of Aeneas and Turnus, noting that whereas Aeneas's marriage to Lavinia resolves the trouble in Latium, the vendetta led by Gawain's brothers leads to the civil war and the fall of Camelot. Nevertheless, he claims that medieval readers would have appreciated the various points of contrast with the Troy story and would have had a similar reaction to the scene a little earlier where three enchantress queens proposition Lancelot in a sort of Judgement of Paris, without divine sanction or an apple (though he is sleeping under an apple tree).[51] Each lady describes to her rivals (but not to Lancelot) her own particular charms, riches, lineage, courtliness, and beauty; he is told he must choose one of them as his lover, but refuses. In the Prose *Lancelot*, the ladies do not recognise him, but they do in Malory's version in 'The Tale of Sir Lancelot', where there are four queens, not three.[52] They say that he must abandon his love for Guinevere (who is not mentioned in the French version) and choose between them, but he refuses and defends the queen as true to Arthur. Is Malory deliberately distancing his version from the Troy story (as discussed earlier in relation to his use of the Alliterative *Morte*) by adding a fourth queen, omitting the rival claims, and alluding explicitly to Guinevere? Or is he presenting her as a fatal Helen, pointing forward to the fall of Camelot?

A chamber painted with Trojan scenes in the castle of Brian des Illes is described at great length in the late thirteenth-century romance *Escanor*, though it seems to be an example of gracious living rather than a pointed reference to any analogy with the Troy story.[53] In the *Didot Perceval*, however, the implications of a Trojan decorative scheme seem more sinister when Arthur gathers his knights to discuss the Roman demands in a room painted with the Judgement of Paris.[54] Baumgartner is surely right that Helen in this fresco is meant to remind us of the fall of Troy and thus hint at the disaster to follow

---

[50] Douglas Kelly, 'Lancelot et Eneas: Une analogie dans le *Lancelot en prose*', in *Lancelot-Lanzelet hier et aujourd'hui*, ed. Danielle Buschinger and Michel Zink (Greifswald, 1995), 227–32.

[51] *Lancelot*, ch. LXXVIII.1–8, ed. Micha, IV.173–78; trans. Kibler, *Lancelot-Grail*, ch. 149, III.155–7.

[52] Malory, 193–94 (VI.3).

[53] Girart d'Amiens, *Escanor, roman Arthurien en verse de la fin du XIIIe siècle*, lines 15592–17748, ed. R. Trachsler, 2 vols, TLF (Geneva, 1994), II.657–62.

[54] *Didot Perceval*, lines 2234–50, ed. Roach, 258; trans. Skeels, 103–4.

in the Arthurian world.[55] Trojan images on artefacts occur in other romances (Enide's saddle in Chrétien has already been mentioned). In *Diu Crône*, an elegant tapestry is sent to Arthur for his Christmas festivities at Tintagel by Guenevere's sister Queen Lenomie of Alexandria; it depicts Helen's escape from Troy, the destruction of the city, and the disastrous consequences for Dido of Aeneas's visit.[56] This seems an ill-omened and pointed gift since it depicts two women from the Trojan past involved in problematic love affairs, as well as the fall of Troy.

There is a more explicit and sinister linking of Trojan and Arthurian themes early in the Vulgate *Mort Artu*, immediately after Arthur's viewing of Lancelot's paintings and Lancelot's rebuff of Elaine of Astolat, when Bors makes a speech about the great men brought low by love and the perfidy of women, addressing Guinevere who has had a quarrel with Lancelot and cold-shouldered him:[57]

> Hestor li preuz et Achilés qui d'armes et de chevalerie orent le los et le pris desus touz les chevaliers de l'encien tens, si en morurent et en furent anbedui ocis et plus de cent mile homes avec eus; et tout ce fut fet par l'acheson d'une fame que Paris pris par force en Gresce. Et a nostre tens meïsmes, n'a pas encore cinc anz que Tristans en morut, li niés au roi Marc, qui si loiaument ama Yseut la blonde que onques en son vivant n'avoit mespris vers lui. Que en diroie ge plus? Onques nus hom ne s'i prist fermement qui n'en moreust.

> [The valiant Hector and Achilles, who won more praise and esteem for feats of arms and chivalry than any knight of antiquity, were both killed, and more than a hundred thousand men with them, and all of that came about because of one woman whom Paris took by force in Greece. And in our own time, it has not yet been five years since the death of Tristan, the nephew of King Mark, who loved Iseut the Fair so faithfully that never in his life did he wrong her. What more can I say? No man ever gave his love to a woman without dying as a result.]

Bors is trying to persuade Guinevere to forgive Lancelot and believe in his faithful love, but this linking of Tristan and Paris seems dangerous, not just in

---

[55] Baumgartner, 'Sainte(s) Hélène(s)', 351.

[56] *Diu Crône*, 520–38, ed. Felder, 14; trans. Thomas, 8.

[57] *La Mort le roi Artu: Roman du XIIIe siècle*, ch. 59, ed. J. Frappier, TLF (Geneva, 1964), 70–1; trans. Norris J. Lacy in *Lancelot-Grail*, ch. 8, IV.109. There is no equivalent speech in Malory. Such lists of male victims of feminine wiles were common in the Middle Ages; but no Trojan men figure in the versions in *SGGK* (lines 2414ff., Gawain to the Green Knight), or in Chaucer's Wife of Bath's Prologue (III.713ff., Jankin's book of wicked wives).

the context of the Tristan/Mark/Isolde triangle but also in the implicit parallel with the Lancelot/Guinevere/Arthur triangle.

I do not know any explicit linking of the Troy story with Guinevere's affair and the end of Camelot in medieval texts, but there are several striking instances in the sixteenth-century Senecan tragedy *The Misfortunes of Arthur* by Thomas Hughes (1587), though the adulterous lover here is Mordred, not Lancelot.[58] At the end of a scene in which Guenevora rebukes him for his plan to usurp the throne, she warns him:

> Looke backe to former *Fates*: *Troy* still had stoode,
> Had not her Prince made light of wedlocks lore.
> The vice, that threw downe *Troy*, doth threat thy Throne:
> Take heede: there *Mordred* stands, whence *Paris* fell.

Mordred accepts and even seems to enjoy this parallel. A little later he comments to the Chorus:

> What though I be a ruine to the Realme,
> And fall my selfe therewith? No better end.
> His last mishaps doe make a man secure.
> Such was King *Priams* ende, who, when he dyed,
> Closde and wrapt up his Kingdome in his death.
> A solemne pompe, and fit for *Mordreds* minde,
> To be a graue and tombe to all his Realme. (II.iv.87–93)

The parallels here are quite explicit, though not linked to Trojan ancestry. Andrew King comments: 'Striking innovations to the received narrative intensify the violence, sexual lust, and fatalism of this Arthurian world, aligning it with the character of Senecan tragedy.'[59]

Some medieval writers found ingenious ways to interweave the stories and characters of Troy and of Arthurian legend more directly. In some manuscripts of Benoit de Sainte-Maure's *Roman de Troie*, reference is made to a horse given to Hector of Troy by Morgan le Fay; presumably as a supernatural being she could have been his contemporary.[60] A more elaborate and ingenious combination occurs in the Italian *Vendetta dei descendenti di Ettore*, probably written about 1400:[61]

---

[58] Thomas Hughes, *The Misfortunes of Arthur: A Critical, Old-Spelling Edition*, I.iv.64–67, ed. Brian Jay Corrigan (London, 1992), 92.

[59] Andrew King, 'Dead Butchers and Fiend-Like Queens: Literary and Political History in *The Misfortunes of Arthur* and *Macbeth*', in *The Scots and Medieval Arthurian Legend*, ed. Purdie and Royan, 123.

[60] R. S. Loomis, *Wales and the Arthurian Legend* (Cardiff, 1956), 106.

[61] These comments are based on the study by Richard Trachsler and Sergio Parussa,

Troiano, a prince of Thessaly, en route to Britain for a tournament, stops at Troy, and decides on vengeance for his ancestors. He goes to Uther's court for help just as a Roman embassy arrives to ask for support against the Greeks. Troiano volunteers to raise troops, and more come from Persia and the Amazon realm of Femenye. But while Uther's men are in the Middle East, the Greeks invade France, and the allied force has to return to deal with them. The Trojans prove to be extremely brutal warriors, torturing their victims and even eating their hearts.

Trachsler and Parussa point out that this text not only abolishes the boundaries, geographical and chronological, between two of the great narrative 'Matters' of the Middle Ages, but also that for the first time British knights are fighting in the East not to free Jerusalem, but to punish and exterminate the Greeks. The brutality of the Trojans links them to the world of epic and *chanson de geste* rather than romance. Troiano does not interact with Arthur but with his father Uther. The vast mid-fourteenth-century French prose romance *Perceforest* takes a similar approach but on a much bigger scale: it describes the prehistory of Britain from Brutus's arrival but adds to Geoffrey's pseudo-history an important Greek element via the arrival of Alexander the Great, who restores order, establishes chivalric practices, and creates a dynasty that will eventually lead to Arthur.[62] There are numerous links with Troy (including inherited objects such as Hector's helmet), and the capital is Troynovant on the Thames.

Perceforest is an extreme example of Rosemary Morris's comment on the Trojan foundation legend that 'Arthur is thus connected, via Brutus, to a whole world of classical knowledge and story. Something of the fame of the antique heroes must surely accrue to the new character, Arthur, the seeds of whose glory are sown at the time of Achilles.'[63] But although knowledge of both legends was clearly widespread, medieval writers seem not to have thought it appropriate to make many direct links and comparisons between them; and as we have seen, allusions are not always positive, or easily interpreted. Writing about Scottish romances, Emily Wingfield comments:[64]

'Un Riflesso della Tradizione Arturiana in Italia: *La Vendetta dei descendenti di Ettore*', *Romanische Forschungen* 114 (2002): 1–26.

[62] The allusions are too numerous to discuss here; see *Perceforest*, ed. Gilles Roussineau, TLF, 13 vols (Geneva, 1987–2015), trans. Nigel Bryant, *Perceforest: The Prehistory of King Arthur's Britain* (Cambridge, 2011); and Sylvia Huot, 'Lest We Forget: The Trojan War as Cultural Matrix', chapter 7 of her *Postcolonial Fictions in the* Roman de Perceforest: *Cultural Identities and Hybridities* (Cambridge, 2007), 161–82.

[63] Rosemary Morris, *The Character of King Arthur in Medieval Literature* (Cambridge, 1982), 14.

[64] Emily Wingfield, *The Trojan Legend in Medieval Scotland* (Cambridge, 2014), 59. The Scots claimed descent not from the Trojans but from an Egyptian princess, Scota.

As in the chronicle tradition, the Trojan legend is aligned with the advice to princes genre and used to reflect on the role of heroes such as Robert I and Alexander the Great. It is also used as a point of positive and negative comparison, both as a means of emphasising a hero's nobility and prowess and as a reminder of the transitory nature of earthly life and power. The Trojan legend and Nine Worthies tradition is thus revealed to be a metaphor fraught with hermeneutical and ideological difficulties.

Many scholars comment on the ambivalence in medieval responses to the Troy legend, sometimes using striking metaphors. For Baswell, 'the Trojan past in Middle English literature is the realm of the undead: it promises imperial (or urban) rebirth, but it also figures inescapable loss, and features the building of both cities and of tombs'.[65] In the light of such comments and the Trojan allusions discussed above, how can the prologue and epilogue of *SGGK* be interpreted?

Much has been made of the reference to treachery in the opening lines, which would no doubt have resonated in every century; Sylvia Federico argues for its relevance in Ricardian England.[66] For her, Arthur has 'a similarly unheroic background' to that of Aeneas, but Moll disagrees:[67]

> Arthur and Aeneas are both historical figures who overcome treacherous beginnings to prove themselves noble in the end. The *Gawain*-poet invokes both Arthur and the story of Troy at the beginning and the end of the poem and thus reminds the reader of these examples of a movement from 'blunder' to 'bliss'. These allusions emphasize the rotation of history and its inevitable return to 'blunder', but they also tell us that Gawain is not wrong to consider his own participation in that pattern.

For Moll cyclic patterns are important. For Malcolm Andrew, the key register is irony, and hindsight is crucial:[68]

> With hindsight, we see what was an essential part of the author's design from the outset: that Arthurian civilisation, which has so much in common with that of Troy – idealism, dynastic associations, the linking of love and conflict – will follow its illustrious example to destruction ... Troy combines the public and the private, love and conflict, nobility and treachery – 'bliss and blunder' ... it is a setting with the potential to generate intense responses to events and searching analysis of conduct, viewed with the retrospective irony which is facilitated by the historical perspective.

---

[65] Baswell, 'England's Antiquities', 234.

[66] Federico, *New Troy*, 35. See also Sylvia Federico, 'The Fourteenth-Century Erotics of Politics: London as Feminine New Troy', *Studies in the Age of Chaucer* 19 (1997): 121–55.

[67] Richard Moll, *Before Malory: Reading Arthur in Later Medieval England* (Toronto, 2003), 154–55.

[68] Malcolm Andrew, 'The Fall of Troy in *Sir Gawain and the Green Knight* and *Troilus and Criseyde*', in *The European Tragedy of Troilus*, ed. Piero Boitani (Oxford, 1989), 92–93.

SGGK is sometimes read as clearly prefiguring the fatal love triangle of Lancelot, Guinevere, and Arthur, and the eventual collapse of the Arthurian world, but I do not find this approach convincing. Medieval accounts of Troy and allusions to it tend to focus on its eventual destruction, but Arthurian writers seem to me more optimistic, or perhaps less explicitly pessimistic; generally they want to dwell on the golden age of Arthurian successes rather than making moralising comments on the inevitable tragedy of the ending. This may be because the Arthurian story is more recent and relevant 'history' for medieval writers and readers, or because the siege context of the Trojan War keeps in the foreground the fact that one side must win and the other lose, whereas chivalric adventures mostly occur extra-temporally, not leading into the final crisis.

According to Tony Davenport, 'it is impossible by the late fifteenth century for any narrative of Arthur to be read in isolation' – context is crucial.[69] It seems to me that the Trojan opening of *SGGK* is deliberately ambiguous as an introduction to keep readers guessing, rather like the spring opening of the *Canterbury Tales*, which might have prefaced a love story or a dream poem, or another kind of story altogether. *Winner and Waster*, another late fourteenth-century alliterative poem, opens like *SGGK* with the fall of Troy, using very similar language:[70]

> Sytthen that Bretayn was biggede*, and Bruyttus it aughte*,
>   [settled; conquered]
> Thurgh the takynge* of Troye with treason with-inn,   [capture]
> There hathe selcouthes* bene sene in seere* kynges tymes,
>   [marvels; various]
> But never so many as nowe by the nyn[d]e dele*.   [ninth part]

The first three lines, with the emphasis on treason and then marvels, could easily lead into a chivalric romance; but what follows is a moral allegory, a debate poem about contemporary social and economic problems. How could the audience/readers of either poem guess from the opening lines what sort of story was to follow? The alliteration might be a clue: Ralph Hanna has argued that alliterative poetry is concerned with 'a troubled penitential self-awareness, a history of power as inevitably futile'.[71] But the form such themes will take in each poem remains unclear for some time. Silverstein argues that the *Gawain*-poet's prologue is an example of the rhetorical device of

---

[69] Tony Davenport, *Medieval Narrative* (Oxford, 2004), 234.

[70] *Wynnere and Wastoure*, 1–4, ed. Stephanie Trigg, EETS o.s. 297 (London, 1990). She comments on the opening (18, note on lines 1–2): 'The theme is given a new twist here, as the poet appeals to Britain's violent origins to account for her present unhappy state.'

[71] Ralph Hanna, 'Alliterative Poetry', in *The Cambridge History of Medieval English Literature*, ed. David Wallace (Cambridge, 1999), 508.

insinuatio, as is the epilogue:[72] 'Like the introduction the epilogue presents to us three faces: as the common medieval trick of quoting apt *auctoritas*, though the story is in fact a new formation; as a sort of proof by likeness of the prologue's sly intention; and as keeping up the poet's straight-faced manner.' Again one thinks of Chaucer: both poets are masters of ambiguity, not least in their attitudes to the Troy story, and leave their readers to use hindsight in attempting to interpret their tales.

In English Arthurian romances, references to Trojan lineage seem to appear more frequently in alliterative poems, perhaps because of links with the chronicle and epic traditions. In French romances, Trojan names appear more frequently in prose than in verse; a renewed interest in Trojan origin legends among both English and continental rulers in the later Middle Ages may have prompted more references at a time when prose romances were increasingly popular. The allusions are muted: Trojan names are given to more minor characters; Camelot does not have the central role of Troy – Arthur's court moves around – and so the collapse of his kingdom does not depend on the fall of a single city.[73] Baswell's comment that 'the Trojan past in Middle English literature is the realm of the undead' seems very apt: the Trojan War and its protagonists are like ghosts in Arthurian romance, significant but present only as shadowy forms (and absent from the indexes of many critical studies). Sometimes they are used to show the superiority of the Arthurian world, sometimes to remind the reader of its inevitable decline and fall. The effect is often ambivalent, and unsettling.

---

[72] Silverstein, '*Sir Gawain*, Dear Brutus', 192.

[73] I am grateful to Professor Sarah Kay for the last point, and to Professor Helen Cooper for comments on an earlier draft.

⊰ 11 ⊱

In Defence of British History: Sir John Prise, King Arthur, and the Tudors

HELEN FULTON

In the wealth of attention given to literary vernacular versions of the Arthurian legends, the Latin material relating to Arthur is often overlooked. While a number of scholars, especially historians, have mined the medieval Latin texts, such as Robert Fletcher's exploration of Arthurian references in the chronicles and John Morris's work on early Latin sources, the work of Siân Echard has been transformative in illuminating the extent and nature of Arthur's presence in medieval and early modern Latin writing.[1] In this chapter, I am using Echard's work as a basis for looking at the post-medieval Latin tradition of Arthur, particularly the sixteenth-century commentaries that aimed to defend Geoffrey of Monmouth's British history and to prove that Arthur was a historical figure.

The main focus of my chapter is Sir John Prise (c. 1502–55), whose defence of British history, *Historiae Britannicae Defensio*, has been less studied than those of his contemporaries, particularly John Leland.[2] With the dissolution of the monasteries, the union of Wales and England, and the break with Rome

---

[1] Echard's work in this field includes *Arthurian Narrative in the Latin Tradition* (Cambridge, 1998), and her edited volume, *The Arthur of Medieval Latin Literature: The Development and Dissemination of the Arthurian Legend in Medieval Latin* (Cardiff, 2011). John Morris edited a series of volumes of Latin Arthurian sources ('Arthurian Period Sources', 9 vols, published by Phillimore in London, 1980–95) that underpinned his major work, *The Age of Arthur: A History of the British Isles from 350 to 650* (London, 1995). An earlier book by Robert H. Fletcher, *The Arthurian Material in the Chronicles, Especially Those of Great Britain and France* (Cambridge, MA, 1906), marked an important step forward in our understanding of the scope and significance of the Latin Arthurian tradition.

[2] Leland and Prise knew each other well through their shared interest in book collecting and in British history. See Caroline Brett, 'John Leland, Wales, and Early British History', *Welsh History Review* 15 (1990): 169–82.

initiated by Henry VIII, the first half of the sixteenth century was a time when history was being rewritten to suit the Tudor agenda of English imperialism. Prise's particular contribution to the debate about British history was his detailed knowledge of early Welsh Arthurian sources. A Welsh-speaking Welshman who worked for Thomas Cromwell at the royal court, and who travelled the country collecting medieval Latin and Welsh manuscripts from the dissolved monastic libraries, Prise marshalled a formidable array of evidence that showed, in his mind, that the Welsh, descendants of the original British inhabitants of the island, were the guardians of the authentic history of Britain. It was in ancient Welsh texts, he was convinced, that the undeniable proof of Arthur's historical existence was to be found.

Prise's *Defensio*, written in his own hand but not published until 1573, after his death, therefore offers a unique argument in support of Geoffrey's version of history and his account of the great King Arthur.[3] In presenting his defence of British history, Prise was supporting, rather than challenging, the Tudor narrative of English history as a continuation of earlier British history. His method was to make a clear and definitive distinction between the popular Arthur of legend and fable and the 'real' historical Arthur whose Trojan origins made him a worthy ancestor of the Tudor kings and justified their rule over what had been Britain and was now the kingdom of England. Prise implicitly acknowledged the popular Arthurian legends, commodified through the medium of romance and exemplified by Thomas Malory's magisterial *Morte Darthur*, published by William Caxton in 1485, and set these aside as the inevitable by-product of fame. It was the political Arthur, the most outstanding of the British kings, whom John Prise was determined to reinstate as the authentic epitome of Tudor kingship.

The Debate about British History

Doubts about the accuracy of Geoffrey of Monmouth's *Historia regum Britanniae*, 'History of the Kings of Britain', completed c. 1138, were raised almost as soon as the work began circulating. William of Malmesbury, whose *Gesta regum Anglorum* of c. 1125 pre-empted Geoffrey's history, positioned Arthur as an ally of Ambrosius fighting against the Saxons, but he made a clear distinction between the historical Arthur as heroic battle leader and the mythical Arthur who appeared in the 'wild tales' and 'false and dreaming

---

[3] Prise's *Defensio* was published in 1573 by one of his sons, Richard, honouring his father's wish, expressed in his will, that the manuscript should be published. See Ceri Davies, ed. and trans., *John Prise: Historiae Britannicae Defensio/A Defence of the British History* (Oxford, 2015), xxxix. All subsequent references to Davies's introduction and notes and to Prise's text are to this edition, abbreviated to *Defensio*.

fable' invented by the British people.[4] Henry of Huntingdon, whose *Historia Anglorum* first appeared in 1129, expressed his amazement that Geoffrey seemed to have found so many sources for early British history, whereas Henry himself had found very few.[5] Alfred of Beverley, writing a history of England in the 1140s, drew heavily on Geoffrey's *Historia* but 'distrusted its veracity and only selected those passages which seemed to him credible'.[6] In the 1180s, Gerald of Wales displayed a markedly ambivalent attitude towards Geoffrey's *Historia*, repeating much of it without acknowledgement in his *Itinerarium Kambriae*, 'Journey through Wales', while also explicitly debunking it. William of Newburgh was even more condemnatory in his opinion of Geoffrey and his history, accusing him of being a liar who gathered together oral tales and 'cloaked them with the honourable name of history by presenting them with the ornaments of the Latin tongue', all in order to deceive his readers and make the British people seem greater than they were.[7] William makes the objection that continued to bedevil later historians, which is why, if Arthur was such a great king, he is not mentioned by either Gildas or Bede.

Despite the doubts and criticisms, Geoffrey's version of British history continued to hold sway throughout the later Middle Ages, institutionalised through various versions of what became known as the 'Brut'. Gaimar's *Estorie des Bretons*, composed in the 1140s, was an early vernacular version, followed by Wace's French verse translation of the *Historia*, called *Roman de Brut*, after the eponymous founder of Britain, written in 1155 for Henry II. Wace's text formed the basis of Layamon's *Brut*, a Middle English alliterative chronicle written c. 1200, and both these texts ensured the continuation of the Brut tradition in Latin, Anglo-Norman, French, and English, mainly in the form of long prose chronicles that appeared in the fourteenth and fifteenth centuries.[8] But still the doubts persisted. Ranulph Higden certainly mentioned Arthur in his *Polychronicon*, but he did not write with the zeal of

---

[4] See Laura Ashe, 'Holinshed and Mythical History', in *The Oxford Handbook of Holinshed's Chronicles*, ed. Pauline Kewes et al. (Oxford, 2012), 153–70, at 155.

[5] See Echard, *Arthurian Narrative*, 75–76; Antonia Gransden, *Historical Writing in England c. 550 to c. 1307* (London, 1974), 200. In general, Henry admired Geoffrey's work, as did Robert of Torigni and Gaimar (Gransden, *Historical Writing*, 212).

[6] Gransden, *Historical Writing*, 212.

[7] William of Newburgh, *Historia rerum Anglicarum* (1196–98). For the Latin text and translation, see *William of Newburgh: The History of English Affairs, Book 1*, ed. and trans. P. G. Walsh and M. J. Kennedy (Warminster, 1988), 'Prooemium', 28. See also Gransden, *Historical Writing*, 264–65.

[8] For a brief account of the development of the *Brut* chronicle in French and English, see Gransden, *Historical Writing*, 73–74. The standard work of reference on the Middle English Prose *Brut* and its Latin and Anglo-Norman analogues is by Lister Matheson, *The Prose* Brut: *The Development of a Middle English Chronicle* (Tempe, AZ, 1998).

the true believer, unlike John Trevisa, the translator of the *Polychronicon*. In Book 5, Higden recounted the history of Britain, based largely on Geoffrey's account, but in chapter 6 of this book he voices doubts about Geoffrey's history, especially the recurrent problem of the silence of Gildas and Bede concerning Arthur.[9] Trevisa, on the other hand, robustly stands behind the factuality of Geoffrey's account because it was based on a 'Brittische book' that earlier historians such as William of Malmesbury had not read, hence their silence or scepticism on the subject of Arthur.[10]

By the late fifteenth century, rumours were circulating that, considering the lacunae in Geoffrey's account, Arthur could not reliably be assumed to be a historical personage. William Caxton, rightly sensing there was nonetheless a solid market for British history, and for legends about Arthur, produced the first printed edition of the Brut chronicle in 1480, which he called *The Cronicles of Englond*, with a second edition appearing in 1482.[11] Eleven other printed texts, including several by Wynkyn de Worde, were produced between 1482 and 1528, indicating the popularity of the Brut and a lively market for British history.[12] Moreover, it was Caxton who published what might be considered the first defence of Arthur. In his preface to his first edition of Sir Thomas Malory's *Le Morte Darthur*, published in 1485, Caxton claims that 'many noble and dyuers gentylmen of thys royame of Englond' asked him to publish the history of the Grail and of King Arthur, 'the moost renomed crysten Kyng'.[13] Caxton uses the cover story of this demanding audience to set out a debate about whether Arthur actually existed, suggesting that some people believe that 'alle suche bookes as been maad of hym ben but fayned and fables'.[14] In reply, 'one in specyal' of his audience, a mouthpiece for Caxton himself, enumerates all the evidence that proved Arthur was in fact a real person. This mock debate allows Caxton to justify the printing of *Le Morte Darthur*, and he concludes comfortably that, given all this evidence, Arthur must have been a real king and the stories about him are therefore worth publishing.

The evidence for Arthur laid out by Caxton is both material and textual. First

---

[9] *Polychronicon Ranulphi Higden Monachi Cestrensis, Vol. V*, ed. Joseph Rawson Lumby (London, 1874), chapter 6, 334–36.

[10] *Polychronicon Ranulphi Higden Monachi Cestrensis, Vol. V*, ed. Lumby, 339, Trevisa's commentary.

[11] STC (2nd edn) 9991 and STC (2nd edn) 9992.

[12] For a list of the printed texts, see Matheson, *The Prose* Brut, 339–48. On the popularity of the *Brut*, in manuscript and print, see Lister M. Matheson, 'Printer and Scribe: Caxton, the *Polychronicon*, and the *Brut*', *Speculum* 60 (1985): 593–614, at 593–94.

[13] W. J. B. Crotch, ed., *The Prologues and Epilogues of William Caxton* (London, 1928), 92. All subsequent references are to this edition.

[14] Crotch, *Prologues and Epilogues*, 93.

there is the grave at Glastonbury, conveniently discovered,[15] and mentioned by that great authority, Higden, in his *Polychronicon*. Boccaccio refers to Arthur in his *De Casu Principum*, and Arthur's life story is told in Geoffrey's 'brutysshe book'.[16] There is the print of Arthur's seal, preserved in red wax at the shrine of St Edward in Westminster Abbey, and various other relics of Arthur and his knights, including the Round Table at Winchester, Gawain's skull at Dover, and Lancelot's sword in some unspecified place. The textual evidence is seemingly overwhelming, with Arthur's deeds recounted in almost every known language and his status as one of the Nine Worthies further proof of his reputation. Finally, the evidence from Wales is incontrovertible, comprising not just texts in Welsh but 'in the toune of Camelot the grete stones & meruayllous werkys of yron lyeng vnder the grounde & ryal vautes [royal vaults] which dyuers now lyuyng hath seen' (p. 94).[17] Caxton's Camelot most likely refers to Caerleon, where the Roman ruins were still huge and impressive, and where Geoffrey of Monmouth located Arthur's great court. The fact that people now living have seen this material evidence of Arthur's presence in Wales clinches the argument as far as Caxton is concerned: 'Thenne al these thynges forsayd aledged I coude not wel denye but that there was suche a noble kyng named Arthur.'[18]

Caxton's elaborate defence of Arthur in his preface to *Le Morte Darthur*, culminating in his apparent conversion to the truth of Arthur's existence, is not only a canny sales pitch that effectively commodified Arthur for the reading public but also an indication that, beyond the world of commercial publishing, the historicity of Arthur continued to be doubted. Even those historians who accepted that Arthur was a historical figure refused, like William of Malmesbury, to accept the romantic stories of his chivalric prowess, while Arthur's supposed conquest of large parts of Europe was simply dismissed as fiction. Summarising Arthur's exploits in Europe in his *Chronicles* of 1587, Raphael Holinshed cuts Arthur's European conquests short, claiming that Arthur had to return to Britain to deal with Mordred before he could reach Rome. He concludes that: 'But for so much as there is not anie approved author who dooth speake of anie such dooings, the Britains are thought to have registred meere fables in sted of true matters, upon a vaine desire to advance more than reason would, this Arthur their noble champion.'[19] Holinshed's contemporary, William Harrison, whose *Description of Britain* was published

---

[15] Echard, *Arthurian Narrative*, 70–75, 121–28; Antonia Gransden, 'The Growth of the Glastonbury Traditions and Legends in the Twelfth Century', in *Glastonbury Abbey and the Arthurian Tradition*, ed. James P. Carley (Cambridge, 2001), 29–53.

[16] Crotch, *Prologues and Epilogues*, 93.

[17] Crotch, *Prologues and Epilogues*, 94.

[18] Crotch, *Prologues and Epilogues*, 94.

[19] Henry Ellis, ed., *Holinshed's Chronicles of England, Scotland and Ireland*,

in 1587, follows a similar line in embracing the figure of Arthur as an important historical king while rejecting the Arthur of romance as a literary fiction, thereby undermining the 'cultural capital' of Arthur's chivalric reputation 'of which Tudor spectacle made such extravagant use'.[20] Edward Hall's descriptions of such spectacles in his chronicle, on the other hand, testify to the enthusiastic embrace of Arthurian costume and armour as an essential element of mercantile pageantry. Hall's lengthy and detailed description of the Field of the Cloth of Gold in 1520 includes a reference to the three 'Christen prynces', Charlemagne, Arthur, and Godfrey de Bouillon, wearing 'long vestures of calendred cloth of golde and purple clothe of gold broched together, with whoddes and cappes of the same, visers and buskyns of grene Damaske'.[21]

The dividing line between what we might call the commercial Arthur, whose deeds were sold to a public eager to consume the popular culture of romance and spectacle, and the political Arthur, the historical king whose rule paved the way for the Tudors, therefore ran from the Brut tradition of the fourteenth century to the post-Reformation retrieval of the medieval past and an emerging engagement with historical truths whose foundations were based on documentary or physical evidence. Even before the Reformation, however, the familiar doubts about the historicity of Arthur had been laid bare for all to see in a new history of England originally designed for the first Tudor monarch, Henry VII. This was Polydore Vergil's *Anglica historia*, and its consequences for the reputation of Arthur were far-reaching. Polydore (c. 1470–1555), who moved from Padua to London in 1502, began writing his history in about 1506–7, but the first manuscript copy did not appear until four years after the death of Henry VII in 1509. Polydore continued to write and revise his history over the next decades, with printed versions appearing in 1534 and 1546, during the reign of Henry VIII, and a third edition, containing an additional book about the reign of Henry VIII, was published in 1555, during Mary's reign.[22]

In his history, Polydore raised significant, if muted, doubts about Geoffrey of Monmouth's version of early British history. While accepting that Arthur was the king who ruled after Uther, Polydore omits all of Geoffrey's long romance of Arthur's life and conquests and reduces the account of Arthur's

---

vol. 1, *England* (London, 1807), 'History of England', Book 5, chapter 12, 576; this is a reprint of the 1587 edition of the *Chronicles*.

[20] Ashe, 'Holinshed and Mythical History', 165.

[21] Janette Dillon, *Performance and Spectacle in Hall's Chronicle* (London, 2002), 94.

[22] These three editions were all published in Basle. Further editions, published in Ghent or Basle, appeared in 1556, 1557, and 1570. See Eugene O. Porter, 'Polydore Vergil: The Forgotten Historian', *Southwestern Social Science Quarterly* 35, no. 1 (1954): 56–63, at 63; Denys Hay, *Polydore Vergil: Renaissance Historian and Man of Letters* (Oxford, 1952), 79.

reign to a few sentences. The figure of Brutus is declared to be fictional, and the discovery of Arthur's grave at Glastonbury is dismissed as unlikely since the monastery had not existed during Arthur's lifetime. Polydore's aim was to report the historical facts and discard all the surrounding myth and legend that had accreted around Arthur, an aim entirely in keeping with the current humanist approach to writing history. Yet because his account put a knife to the heart of 'Britishness', the English belief that they had built an imperial state on the native soil of the island of Britain, founded by Brutus and a line of British kings, the backlash was swift and often vicious. Among many critics, John Bale (1495–1563), who had converted to Protestantism, accused the Catholic Polydore of falsehood and lack of judgement, while John Caius (1510–73) accused him of destroying manuscript evidence that would have proven him wrong.[23]

As James Carley has pointed out, the reason that many of Polydore's critics at the time (and subsequently) were so hostile was because they believed that he was in fact hinting that Arthur himself was a fiction. This was certainly Leland's response to Polydore's dismissal of the Glastonbury burial, claiming that the historian listed Arthur among the British kings 'more to pay lip-service to the custom of our race than because he believes it in his heart'.[24] Yet, as Carley suggests, Polydore was more likely to be following the earlier tradition of scepticism represented by William of Malmesbury, not so much towards Arthur himself but towards Geoffrey of Monmouth's highly coloured account of his reign. What Polydore was hinting at was not that Arthur did not exist, but that Geoffrey 'was not an accurate historian and that the *Historia regum Britanniae* was, in much of its narrative, a work of fiction'.[25]

Polydore's history prompted a number of his contemporaries to mount their own defences of the Galfridian account of Arthur's reign. The best known of these is perhaps the one by John Leland, published under the title *Assertio inclytissimi Arturii regis Britanniae* in 1544.[26] In making his case for the truth of Geoffrey's history, Leland draws on his exceptional knowledge of antiquarian sources, including manuscript and linguistic evidence, oral stories, and place-names, countering Polydore's historical research with his own weight of scholarly learning. Other defences of the Galfridian Arthur came

---

[23] The scholarly backlash against Polydore is described by Henry Ellis, ed., *Three Books of Polydore Vergil's English History* (London, 1844), xx–xxiv.

[24] Cited by James Carley, 'Arthur and the Antiquaries', in *The Arthur of Medieval Latin Literature*, ed. Echard, 156.

[25] James Carley, 'Polydore Vergil and John Leland on King Arthur: The Battle of the Books', *Interpretations* 15, no. 2 (1984): 86.

[26] Leland published an earlier defence of Arthur written in about 1536, much of which was incorporated into the later *Assertio*. Both are discussed by Carley in 'Polydore Vergil and John Leland'.

from Humphrey Llwyd (1527–68), a Welshman from Denbigh, on the March of Wales, who was a leading antiquarian and cartographer known as the first map-maker of England and Wales.[27] Llwyd's *Cronica Walliae* of 1559 was an English adaptation of the major Welsh chronicle *Brut y Tywysogyon* (The Chronicle of the Princes), which subsequently became the standard history of Wales until the modern era.[28] In the *Cronica*, Llwyd criticises Polydore for his lack of understanding of Welsh and early British sources, which prevented him from writing an accurate history of Britain.[29] In a further treatise, published in Latin in 1572 after his death and translated into English in 1573 under the title *The Breviary of Britayne*, Llwyd praises classical historiographers such as Caesar and Tacitus at the expense of non-historians such as Polydore, who had no understanding of the British (that is, the Welsh) people.[30]

What James Carley called 'the battle of the books' was therefore a debate about the very nature of Britain as it was understood in the first half of the sixteenth century. To historians such as Polydore, England was the modern incarnation of what had been Britain, a unified kingdom comprising a number of peoples – English, Welsh, Scottish – but nonetheless a single polity with a shared history. To English antiquarians such as Leland and Bale, the kingdom of England rested on its pre-Saxon British history, personified by that most

---

[27] Llwyd's maps of Wales, and of England and Wales, were produced in 1573 for Abraham Ortelius of Antwerp, whose world atlas, *Theatrum Orbis Terrarum*, appeared in Latin in 1603 and in English in 1606. See R. Brinley Jones, 'Llwyd, Humphrey', in *Oxford Dictionary of National Biography*, published online 2014; https://www.oxforddnb.com (accessed 30 May 2023).

[28] Llwyd's manuscript of the *Cronica* was eventually published by David Powel under the title *Historie of Cambria, Now Called Wales* (London, 1584), STC (2nd edn) 4606. For the modern edition, see Ieuan M. Williams and J. Beverley Smith, eds, *Humphrey Llwyd, Cronica Walliae* (Cardiff, 2016).

[29] Llwyd is incensed by Polydore's error in calling Anglesey by its English name instead of its Welsh name, Môn (Lat. Mona). See *Cronica Walliae*, ed. Williams and Smith, 68.

[30] Llwyd includes Hector Boece and Bede in his condemnation of poor historians who had no understanding of Britain's early history. See Philip Schwyzer, ed., *Humphrey Llwyd, The Breviary of Britain with Selections from The History of Cambria* (London, 2011). The Latin term *Britones* was still being used to signify the Welsh in the early twelfth cntury, with a general shift during the course of the century towards more specific forms such as *Wallenses*, to distinguish the Welsh from other 'British' people such as the Bretons. The Welsh followed Anglo-Norman practice in calling themselves Welsh rather than British in Cambro-Latin documents from the early twelfth century, 'in order to express Welsh identity in terms which would be comprehensible in England and on the Continent'. See Huw Pryce, 'British or Welsh? National Identity in Twelfth-Century Wales', *English Historical Review* 116 (2001): 775–801, at 797.

illustrious British king, Arthur, in all his Galfridian glory. This was the image of British history that animated the early Tudor kings and that led ultimately to the imperial identity articulated by Spenser and Drayton. But to Welshmen such as Humphrey Llwyd and John Prise, British history meant Welsh history, and to doubt the veracity of Geoffrey was to imply that the Welsh had never been a sovereign people with their own kings and their own history. This was the lie of which Polydore Vergil was accused.

Sir John Prise and the *Defensio*

While modern critics have assumed a binary divide between those who supported Polydore's view of history and those who opposed it, there were in fact two separate and slightly different strands of opposition.[31] From the perspective of English antiquarians such as Leland, and indeed Caxton and Thomas Churchyard, whose poem *The Worthines of Wales* (1587) exalted Arthur's court at Caerleon, King Arthur was the ancestor of the Tudor line and founder of a British empire, inherited from the Romans, that spanned the whole island of Britain.[32] Attempts to dismiss Arthur's imperial exploits (as recounted by Geoffrey of Monmouth) as fables or fictions are themselves dismissed as lies or shoddy historiography that ignored the material evidence, as set out by Caxton. But from the point of view of Welsh antiquarians such as Humphrey Llwyd and Sir John Prise, the stakes were higher. Polydore's evident reluctance to endorse the deeds of both the Trojan Brutus and the British Arthur fatally undermined Welsh claims to have held the original sovereignty of Britain.[33] The riposte by Welsh antiquarians to this egregious dereliction of historiographical duty was to accuse Polydore not simply of lying or ignoring the material evidence (though he was accused of both) but of his failure to access some of the most important and irrefutable documentary sources, namely those written in the Welsh language. As Richard Prise said

---

[31] Mary Bateman, for example, treats Leland, Llwyd, and Prise together as a single front of opposition to Polydore's history. See '"The Native Place of that Great Arthur": Foreignness and Nativity in Sixteenth-Century Defences of Arthur', in *Arthurian Literature XXXV*, ed. Elizabeth Archibald and David F. Johnson (Cambridge, 2019), 152–72.

[32] Thomas Churchyard, *The Worthines of Wales* (London, 1587), STC (2nd edn) 5261. For a useful discussion of this text, see Liz Oakley-Brown, 'Writing on the Borderlines: Anglo-Welsh Relations in Thomas Churchyard's *The Worthines of Wales*', in *Writing Wales: From the Renaissance to Romanticism*, ed. Stewart Mottram and Sarah Prescott (Farnham, Surrey, 2012), 39–57.

[33] For an account of the Welsh view of their British (and ultimately Trojan) origins, see Helen Fulton, 'Origins and Introductions: Troy and Rome in Medieval British and Irish Writing', in *Celts, Romans, Britons: Classical and Celtic Influence in the Construction of British Identities*, ed. Francesca Kaminski-Jones and Rhys Kaminski-Jones (Oxford, 2020), 51–78.

in his prefatory letter to his published version of the *Defensio*, the grievous errors made by Polydore in his history arose from the fact that 'the principal records, the ones which contain accounts of [British] origins and achievements of old, are written in the British tongue, a language of which he had no knowledge at all'.[34]

The distinctive contribution made by Sir John Prise to the 'defence of Arthur' tradition was to enumerate and describe the Welsh and Welsh-Latin sources that Polydore had ignored, sources that, according to Prise, proved conclusively that Arthur had lived the life described for him by Geoffrey of Monmouth (though unfortunately overlaid by later fictitious *fabulae*).[35] Prise laid the groundwork for this in Book I of the *Defensio*, where he describes the ancient British language as a model of logic and consistency, whose bards and druids were praised for their arcane knowledge by none other than Lucan, the Roman poet of the first century AD.[36] Using a slightly oblique argument, Prise asserts that, since the ancient Britons were a literate people, there must have been a long tradition of historical writing, now unfortunately lost, that was inherited by later writers of British history. He had already dealt with the issue of why there is no mention of early British heroes (including, it is implied, Arthur) in contemporary Latin histories, arguing, somewhat sweepingly, that Roman authors were mainly focused on writing about the deeds of their own people, and not those of other nations.[37] Nevertheless, he finds opportunities throughout his book to cite examples of classical historians writing approvingly about the heroism of the warlike British people, and to criticise Polydore for watering down such accounts and turning positive descriptions into negative condemnations.[38]

Having established his points that the British language and its early records are very ancient, predating those of the Romans, and that the bardic tradition ensured that the deeds and genealogies of the British people were transmitted down the centuries until they became extant in manuscripts, Prise's next move is to establish the authenticity of Geoffrey's *Historia*. He does this by accepting Geoffrey's own assertion that his history was in a fact a translation from a

---

[34] 'Praecipua monumenta, quibus eorum origines et antiquae res gestae continentur, in lingua Britannica, quam Polydorus penitus ignorauit, sunt conscripta.' *Defensio*, 'Richard Prise's Dedicatory Letter', 12–13.

[35] As Ceri Davies notes, Prise was aware of the problem of 'where to draw the line between history and fable' in Geoffrey's work. See *Defensio*, xlv, II.22, 60–61.

[36] Prise quotes a verse from Lucan in praise of the pagan bards and druids of Britain. See *Defensio*, I.8, 42–43.

[37] *Defensio*, I.1.2, 34–35.

[38] Most of Book X of the *Defensio* is in this vein, with Prise practising some ingenious close reading of the classical sources and comparing them with Polydore's supposedly negative representations of the British people.

'very old book in the British tongue ... into Latin in a rustic style'.[39] Since Prise has previously set out the evidence for a native British tradition of historiography, the likelihood that Geoffrey's claim can be taken at face value, and that he did indeed translate an early history written in Welsh, seems all the more plausible. Prise goes on to mention the various ancient chronicles he has in his possession, some in Latin and some in Welsh, which, he claims, were written before Geoffrey's time and therefore support the history that was translated by Geoffrey. One of these chronicles was a copy of the *Historia Brittonum*, which Prise thought was written by Gildas, even though Leland, 'who saw this book in my house', tried to convince him it was by Nennius.[40] Either way, the text was clearly very old, and it confirmed for Prise that Brutus and Arthur belonged to the historical record.

When Prise finally comes to consider the evidence for Arthur, almost at the end of his treatise, following considerations of Brutus as the eponym of Britain, the etymology of Trinovantum as the early name of London, some early British place-names, and Polydore's deliberate diminishment of the British people, he has already introduced in some form most of the Welsh and Welsh-Latin sources that he believes provide solid evidence of Arthur's historicity. Book XII, entitled *De Arthuro Britonum rege illustrissimo*, 'On Arthur, the Most Illustrious King of the Britons',[41] lays out Prise's trump cards, namely the detailed evidence of early Welsh writing. His first tactic is to confirm the details of Arthur's battles, as set out in *Historia Brittonum*, by quoting from the ancient British bard, Taliesin, who flourished 'tempore Mailgonis', 'in the time of Maelgwn, king of Gwynedd (d. 547): 'Gwae yntwy yr ynvydyon, pan vu waith Vaddon / Arthur benn haelion y lafneu bu gochyon' (Woe to them, the fools, when Badon's battle happened, / red were the blades of Arthur, greatest of lords).[42] These verses seem to prove that Arthur's triumph against the Saxons at the battle of Baddon was known to a sixth-century British poet. Unfortunately, the verses quoted by Prise come from what is usually

---

[39] *Geoffrey of Monmouth: The History of the Kings of Britain*, ed. Michael D. Reeve, trans. Neil Wright (Cambridge, 2007), 'Prologue', chapter 2, 4.

[40] *Defensio*, 65. In Book III, which supports Geoffrey's account of British history, Prise says: 'Is a Leylando, qui hunc librum apud me vidit, Nennius esse existimatur. Sane perantiquum esse, quicunque is fuerit, oportet. Antiquitatem enim tantam tum scriptio ipsa perquam vetusta, tum Britannicae voces tam proprie intersertae expresse redolent' (Leland, who saw this book in my house, thinks that its author is Nennius. Whoever the author was, he must at any rate have been very ancient. Both the handwriting itself, which is very old, and the British words, so correctly added, are distinctly redolent of great antiquity) (*Defensio*, III.25, 64–65). See also Davies's discussion of Prise's certainty that the copy of the *Historia Brittonum* that he owned was by Gildas (*Defensio*, xlvi–xlvii).

[41] *Defensio*, XII.109, 194–95.

[42] Text and translation in *Defensio*, XII.120, 210–11.

referred to as *Ystoria Taliesin*, 'The Legend of Taliesin', or *Hanes Taliesin*, 'The History of Taliesin', a prose tale with verse insertions that recounts the legendary history of the poet as a shape-shifting prophet who comes to the court of Maelgwn Gwynedd and defeats Maelgwn's raucous court poets (as described disapprovingly by Gildas in his *De Excidio*) with his magical powers of versification.[43] The legend of Taliesin survives in its full form only from the sixteenth century, notably in the chronicle of Elis Gruffydd, though there are allusions to this legendary Taliesin (as well as to the 'historical' Taliesin who sang to sixth-century northern British heroes) in the fourteenth-century manuscript known as the Book of Taliesin (Aberystwyth, National Library of Wales MS Peniarth 2), whose contents are much older.[44] So a knowledge of the legendary Taliesin was likely to have been circulating in Wales at least from the early twelfth century, but the verses quoted by Prise are not attested earlier than the sixteenth century.[45]

Prise next turns his attention to the Black Book of Carmarthen (Aberystwyth, National Library of Wales MS Peniarth 1, c. 1260), one of the earliest surviving manuscripts written in Welsh, and the Red Book of Hergest (Oxford, Jesus College MS 111, 1382–c. 1405), both containing versions of a number of early poems that refer to Arthur.[46] Prise had both these manuscripts in his possession

---

[43] The earliest complete text of the legend of Taliesin, taken from Elis Gruffydd's *Chronicle of the Six Ages of the World*, has been edited by Patrick K. Ford, *Ystoria Taliesin* (Cardiff, 1992). Ford also provided a translation of the text in *The Mabinogi and Other Medieval Welsh Tales* (Berkeley, 1979), 162–81.

[44] Elis Gruffydd's vast two-volume universal chronicle was completed around 1552 in Calais, where Gruffydd was then living. It has not yet been fully edited or translated. See T. G. Hunter, 'Taliesin at the Court of Henry VIII: Aspects of the Writings of Elis Gruffydd', *Transactions of the Honourable Society of Cymmrodorion* 10 (2004): 41–56; T. Jones, 'A Welsh Chronicler in Tudor England', *Welsh History Review* 1 (1960–63): 1–17. The editor of the Taliesin poems in the Book of Taliesin, Marged Haycock, does not propose any definite dates for the varied contents of the manuscript. See Haycock, ed. and trans., *Legendary Poems from the Book of Taliesin* (Aberystwyth, 2007), 6.

[45] The poems that form part of the legend of Taliesin are found detached from the prose tale in a large number of manuscripts and were evidently 'not considered an integral part of the tale' (Ford, *Mabinogi*, 162). They are found, for example, in Elis Gruffydd's earlier work, an anthology of Welsh poetry and prose, now Cardiff MS 3.4, and later incorporated by him, with significant changes, into the longer prose tale. See Hunter, 'Taliesin at the Court of Henry VIII', 42–43. Ceri Davies notes that 'Prise's version [of the poems] corresponds closely to none of the earlier witnesses, and he appears to be following a (now) lost source' (*Defensio*, 298, n. 32). Compare the version of the poem cited by Prise in *Ystoria Taliesin*, ed. Ford, 74–75.

[46] The Black Book of Carmarthen has been edited by A. O. H. Jarman, *Llyfr Du Caerfyrddin* (Cardiff, 1982). On the early Welsh poetry that references Arthur, see

for some time and was very familiar with their contents, particularly those of the Red Book, and he draws much of his evidence from these two manuscripts.[47] He quotes, somewhat inconclusively, from the Black Book poem *Ymddiddan Myrddin a Thaliesin*, 'The Conversation of Merlin and Taliesin',[48] a short poetic dialogue in which the two legendary prophets describe battles they have known and are still to come, conjuring up the sixth-century context of Maelgwn Gwynedd and the battle of Arfderydd, near Carlisle, which took place in 573.[49] It was at this battle that Merlin was said to have lost his mind, becoming the legendary 'wild man' of Celyddon Wood. The text has been dated to somewhere between 1000 and 1100 and was a source for Geoffrey's *Vita Merlini*, which includes the story of Myrddin's madness and a dialogue between Telgesinus (Taliesin) and Merlinus (Myrddin). Rather puzzlingly, Prise connects Arthur with Celyddon Wood, where according to the poem 'saith ugein haelion a aethant ygwyllon' (seven score generous noblemen went mad; *Ymddiddan*, ll. 35–38 and *Defensio*, p. 212), including Myrddin himself, but the poem nowhere mentions Arthur, and in fact the connection between Arthur and Myrddin is an invention of Geoffrey himself.

It is the Red Book of Hergest, however, that provides Prise with what he sees as his most conclusive evidence. He cites the elegy to Geraint son of Erbin, king of Dumnonia, where Arthur is mentioned, as proof that Arthur was a pan-British warrior. This elegy, located in the south-west of Britain, evokes a sixth-century context of Britons fighting against Saxons, but the poem is likely to have been composed somewhere between the ninth and twelfth centuries. As Prise is keen to point out, the poem describes Arthur as *ameraudur*, 'emperor', leading Geraint and his army at the battle of Llongborth (modern Langport in Somerset): 'Yn Llongborth lhas y Arthur / Gwyr dewr kymynynt o dur, / Amherowdyr lhywyawdyr lhafur' (In Llongborth Arthur suffered the killing / of brave men who hewed with steel, / sovereign, leader in battle).[50]

Nerys Ann Jones, ed., *Arthur in Early Welsh Poetry* (London, 2019); Helen Fulton, 'The Invention of Arthurian Britain: Arthur in the Early Welsh Literary Tradition', in *The Arthurian World*, ed. Victoria Coldham-Fussell, Miriam Edlich-Muth, and Renée Ward (London, 2022), 35–48.

[47] Prise had possession of the Red Book long enough to number its pages and make numerous marginal annotations. See Helen Fulton, 'Sir John Prise and His Books: Manuscript Culture in the March of Wales', *Welsh History Review* 31, no. 1 (2022): 55–78, at 66–67. It is not known how the Black Book came into Prise's possession nor how long he had access to it. See *Defensio*, xxviii and 300, n. 59.

[48] *Defensio*, 212–13.

[49] The poem has been edited by A. O. H. Jarman, *Ymddiddan Myrddin a Thaliesin*, 2nd edn (Cardiff, 1967). It has been translated by John K. Bollard, 'Myrddin in Early Welsh Tradition', in *The Romance of Merlin: An Anthology*, ed. Peter Goodrich (New York, 1990), 16–19.

[50] Text and translation in *Defensio*, XII.122, 214–15. The poem to Geraint son of Erbin is also found in the Black Book of Carmarthen, giving different readings from

Prise argues that this poem must have been composed by Taliesin in the sixth century and lists some of the other early poems contained in the Red Book of Hergest as further evidence that Taliesin and Arthur were contemporaries. He also refers to two of the triads contained in the Red Book, the collection of narrative themes grouped in threes that is an important source of early Welsh story material. Prise is particularly taken with the triad known as the Three Dishonoured Men of the Island of Britain ('Trywyr Gwarth a vu yn Ynys Prydein'), who are Afarwy son of Lludd son of Beli, the man who invited Caesar to Britain and thus precipitated the Roman occupation; Gwrtheyrn (Vortigern) who invited the Saxons to Britain; and Medrawd (Mordred), 'trydydd, gwaethaf' (the third and worst), who seized power from Arthur and led to Arthur's death.[51] Later, he refers to the triad of the Three Gwenhwyfars (Guinevere) as part of an elaborate attempt to explain why Guinevere was buried with Arthur at Glastonbury.[52] As with the other early Welsh material, the dating of the triads is uncertain, especially as they may have had an oral transmission. However, the earliest manuscript containing some of the triads (Aberystwyth, National Library of Wales MS Peniarth 6) dates from the late thirteenth or early fourteenth century, and the addition of Arthurian material into the triads is clearly influenced by Geoffrey's *Historia*.[53]

As far as Prise is concerned, however, all this literary evidence from the Red Book pre-dates Geoffrey's *Historia*, proving conclusively that Geoffrey was not making anything up but was drawing on early Welsh sources. Prise does not confine himself only to poetry and literary sources but refers as well to Latin and Welsh annals that seem to prove the existence of Arthur in the sixth century. He quotes the beginning of a short Welsh chronicle, known as *O Oes Gwrtheyrn*, 'From the Age of Vortigern', translating it into Latin, 'A tempore Vortigerni' (*Defensio*, XII.122, p. 212), perhaps to add authority to the chronicle.[54] The number of medieval and early modern manuscripts that contain a copy of this short chronicle, with the Red Book and Aberystwyth,

---

those of the Red Book used by Prise, though Prise does not mention this. For the Black Book version, see *Llyfr Du Caerfyrddin*, ed. Jarman, 48–49.

[51] For this Triad, see Rachel Bromwich, ed. and trans., *Trioedd Ynys Prydain, The Triads of the Island of Britain*, 4th edn (Cardiff, 2014), no. 51, 131–39.

[52] *Defensio*, XII.134–35, 230–33. See *Trioedd Ynys Prydein*, no. 56, 154–56. Bromwich's edition of this triad is based on both the Red Book version and that in the White Book of Rhydderch (Aberystwyth, National Library of Wales MS Peniarth 4–5, dating from the middle of the fourteenth century).

[53] Bromwich says of Triad 51 that it is 'the only triad in the [Red Book] collection whose content is drawn entirely from the narrative of Geoffrey of Monmouth' (*Trioedd Ynys Prydein*, 134).

[54] The chronicle has been edited from fifteen medieval and early modern manuscripts by Owain Wyn Jones, '*O Oes Gwrtheyrn*: A Medieval Welsh Chronicle', in *The Chronicles of Medieval Wales and the March*, ed. Ben Guy, Georgia Henley, Owain Wyn Jones, and Rebecca Thomas (Turnhout, 2020), 169–229.

National Library of Wales MS Peniarth 32 (c. 1404) as the earliest witnesses, suggests its popularity among sixteenth-century antiquarians, no doubt because of this opening reference to Arthur. Prise himself copied the chronicle into his personal anthology of British history and genealogies, saying that he copied it 'o hen lyvyr a gaveis gan Ryffydd Hiraethog pan oed oet Christ 1550' (from an old book which I got from Gruffudd Hiraethog in the year of Christ 1550).[55] This 'old book', rather than the Red Book version, is no doubt the source of the opening lines that Prise gives in Latin in the *Defensio*. The Welsh version, in Prise's 'Collections', reads as follows:

> Oes Gwrtheyrn Gwrtheneu hyd weith Vadon yd ymlawd Arthur ar Saesson ag y gorvy Arthur, wyth mlyned ar ugeint a chant. 128. CXXVIII.
> O waith Vadon hyd Gamlan dwy vlyned ar ugeint. 22.[56]

> [The time of Gwrtheyrn Gwrtheneu [Vortigern the Thin] up to the battle of Badon where Arthur fought with the Saxons and Arthur defeated them, 128 years. From the battle of Badon until Camlan, two and twenty years.]

The chronicle, which probably originated from the Cistercian monastery of Aberconwy in Gwynedd, is likely to belong to the second decade of the thirteenth century, so is another example of Prise juxtaposing genuinely early material, such as the 'Gereint' stanzas, with texts that are post-Geoffrey.

Another chronicle cited by Prise is his own copy of charters relating to the diocese of Llandaf, near Cardiff in Glamorgan, part of *Liber Landavensis*, 'Book of Llandaf', made in the 1120s.[57] Prise grandly claims that 'donations made by King Arthur' (*Defensio*, p. 65) are recorded in Latin and Welsh, but although there are references in the Book of Llandaf to a king called 'Noe filius

---

[55] 'Collections of John Prise' (Northampton, Northamptonshire Archives MS Finch-Hatton 7, c. 1540–50), fols 56–8, on fol. 56. Gruffudd Hiraethog (d. 1564) was a trained poet and herald who both collected and wrote manuscripts, some of which survive.

[56] Edited from MS FH 7, fol. 56, with my translation. Ceri Davies says that Prise knew the chronicle from the Red Book, which he certainly would have done, but his Latin version of the opening lines suggests another source, most likely Aberystwyth, National Library of Wales MS Peniarth 135 (1550–64), which is in the hand of Gruffydd Hiraethog and therefore probably the 'old book' that Prise got from him.

[57] The manuscript is London, British Library MS Cotton Vespasian A xiv (c. 1200), which was owned by Prise (*Defensio*, 281, n. 9). It contains copies of some of the materials used to compile *Liber Landavensis* (Aberystwyth, National Library of Wales MS 17110E, 1120–32). The Book of Llandaf is a collection of charters recording donations and payments to the bishops of Llandaf from the sixth to eleventh centuries, with the aim of proving the antiquity and size of the diocese of Llandaf. See Patrick Sims-Williams, *The Book of Llandaf as a Historical Source* (Woodbridge, 2019).

Arthur' who made donations to the cathedral, this is not Geoffrey's Arthur.[58] Prise is further excited by the fact that his Llandaf manuscript includes the life of Dubricius (Dyfrig) by Benedict of Gloucester, assuming that the references to Arthur in this 'Vita Sancti Dubricii' provided a key source for Geoffrey, whereas in fact it was the other way round: Benedict drew on Geoffrey's *Historia* for his Arthurian material.[59] Prise makes the same error with another historical record in his library, an early British annal from St David's Cathedral later conflated with version C of the *Annales Cambriae*.[60] The section quoted by Prise, including Arthur's defeat of the Roman Lucius, Mordred's death at Camlan, and the removal of the wounded Arthur to Avalon, is derived from Geoffrey's *Historia*, rather than the other way around.[61]

Conclusion

These examples of the ways in which Sir John Prise used the evidence available to him indicate his total commitment to a British history that placed the British, later the Welsh, as the sovereign people of Britain before the coming of the Saxons. While William Caxton commodified the great King Arthur and sold him to an English reading public nostalgic for chivalric kingship, Prise recuperated a historical Arthur to prove the antiquity of British kingship, a strategy that happened to work for the benefit of the Tudor monarchs. His detailed knowledge of early Welsh material gave him a unique perspective in the 'battle of the books' and allowed him to re-appropriate Arthur as a British, rather than English, king who could be said to have founded the Tudor line. The fact that he sometimes over-interpreted his sources or was mistaken about their dates of composition, or indeed underestimated the extent to which Geoffrey's *Historia* corrupted later copies of earlier sources (such as the triads), should not diminish the quality and depth of his scholarship. The main limitation on Prise's work was the fact that his primary sources

---

[58] Noe son of Arthur is said to have made a donation to the diocese of Llandaf in the time of Archbishop Dubricius, coincidentally the man who, according to Geoffrey, crowned Arthur as king (*Historia regum Britanniae*, IX.143, 192). See *The Text of the Book of Llan Dav Reproduced from the Gwysaney Manuscript*, ed. J. Gwenogvryn Evans (Oxford, 1893), 77, and also 133.

[59] See Davies's comments in *Defensio*, 300, nn. 54 and 55. The earliest life of the fifth-century Dubricius is found in the Book of Llandaf, probably prompted by the removal of the saint's body to Llandaf in 1120. The claim that Dyfrig was bishop of Llandaf and archbishop of southern Britain (inspiring Geoffrey's association of Dyfrig with Arthur) was a politically strategic move by Llandaf to assert its antiquity.

[60] The manuscript is British Library MS Cotton Domitian A i. On the *Annales Cambriae* and its three main versions, see Huw Pryce, 'Chronicling and Its Contexts in Medieval Wales', in *Chronicles of Medieval Wales*, ed. Guy et al., 1–32.

[61] *Defensio* XII.128, 222–25 and 300, n. 58.

were restricted to those he owned himself, or to which he had access at some stage, a limitation common to many antiquarians before the establishment of large institutional libraries. He relied particularly heavily on the Red Book of Hergest, a volume that he knew well and whose contents he was thoroughly familiar with. It seems that he had less access to the Black Book of Carmarthen, which he may have been able to study only for a short period of time, since he does not make full use of the references to Arthur in this manuscript. Nevertheless, these two anthologies and the other Welsh sources that he had in his possession contained material about Arthur that could not be found anywhere else, giving an authenticity to Prise's arguments that earned the backing of Humphrey Llwyd, among others. Accusing Polydore Vergil of dragging his readers into a 'darke pitte of ignorance', Llwyd recommends 'the apologie of the Britishe historie againste the calumniouse and sclanderouse tauntes of the said Virgile written by Sir John Price Knight where the reader shall see all his erroures confuted at large'.[62]

---

[62] *Cronica Walliae*, ed. Williams and Smith, 66.

12

Boys Gone Wild: Britain's Mythic Tradition in America's Boys' Clubs

MARTIN B. SHICHTMAN AND LAURIE A. FINKE

Writing just after the turn of the century, William Byron Forbush, an American clergyman, educator, and founder of the boys' fraternity, The Knights of King Arthur, opens *The Boy's Round Table* by hailing his readers as medieval knights:

> Fellows! Did you ever wish you were living in the age of chivalry? To ride out in the sunshine of flashing armour in company with brave adventure-seeking comrades, on noble quests, to dash into the tournament and fight for glory, and then to sit at the great Round Table before the splendid throne of the 'Flower of Kings' – those were fine days![1]

The blustery rhetoric of Forbush's interpellation attempts to capture the imaginations of young men desirous for glory as a means of moulding boys into a proper masculinity. It is designed to make young men desire combat, desire to sacrifice their bodies, and, ultimately, their lives, if only imaginatively, not so much for particular causes but rather to belong to a fraternity of elite brother-fighters. This essay explores the Knights of King Arthur as the first fraternal organisation for young boys, placing it in the context of the fraternal movements of the late nineteenth century, the so-called Golden Age of Fraternalism.[2] We examine Forbush's remediation of Arthurian legend, through Tennyson, in a fraternal organisation for boys designed to inculcate particular forms of masculinity through initiation.

Our exploration of Forbush's remediation of Tennyson's *Idylls of the King* (itself a remediation of Malory's *Morte Darthur*) requires our analysis to

---

[1] William Byron Forbush and Frank Lincoln Masseck, *Boy's Round Table*, 8th edn (Detroit, 1910), 5; all references are to this edition unless otherwise noted.
[2] Harriett W. McBride, 'The Golden Age of Fraternalism: 1870–1910', *Heredom* 13 (2005): 1–31.

go beyond simply describing the adaptation of one text to another: it must account for the different affordances of the media involved. Jay David Bolter and Richard Grusin use the term 'remediation' to describe 'the process by which new media technologies improve upon or remedy prior media forms'.[3] Fraternal initiations make texts more transparent by converting them to performances; at the same time, they call attention to themselves through their deployment of ritual words and actions. In the fourth chapter of her 2008 book, *Printing the Middle Ages*, 'Bedtime Chaucer', which investigates adaptations of *The Canterbury Tales* created for children, Siân Echard describes what she calls the 'mark of the medieval' in these books, that is, visual representations of 'the medieval ... in an explicitly pedagogic context'.[4] Forbush encouraged boys not just to read about knights in books but to become them through initiation and participation in the group's chivalric rituals, using material objects – sets, props, and costumes – that evoked the 'mark of the medieval' (see Figure 12.1). Forbush proposes these rituals of the Knights of King Arthur as a solution to the 'boy problem'. They would move boys away from the dangers of the modern world and direct their violence toward more desirable ends.

From the middle of the nineteenth century through the first decades of the twentieth, youth gang violence became an obsession of the British and American press. In the cities of Manchester and Salford alone, journalists reported more than 250 gang-related acts of violence during the thirty years leading up to the turn of the century. Over 90 per cent of these crimes were perpetrated by boys between fourteen and nineteen.[5] While historian Stephen Humphries locates the causes of this violence in economic disparities exacerbated by exponentially increasing degradations to the living conditions of the urban poor and the concomitant increase in wealth and power to those already wealthy and powerful,[6] the popular press of the time was far less generous in its assessment of the 'boy problem'. Anxieties over boys gone wild circulated throughout English communities and, no doubt, inspired the description, in Alfred, Lord Tennyson's *Idylls of the King*, of Cameliard in its time of trouble:

[3] Jay David Bolter and Richard Grusin, *Remediation: Understanding New Media* (Cambridge, 2000), 273.
[4] Siân Echard, *Printing the Middle Ages* (Philadelphia, 2008), 147.
[5] Andrew Davies, 'Youth Gangs, Masculinity and Violence in Late Victorian Manchester and Salford', *Journal of Social History* 32, no. 2 (Winter 1998): 350.
[6] Stephen Humphries, *Hooligans or Rebels? An Oral History of Working-Class Childhood and Youth 1889–1939* (Oxford, 1981), 179.

ROCKRIFT CASTLE, 805, MILFORD, N. H.

Figure 12.1: A boys' club engaging in chivalric rituals
(Forbush, *The Boys Round Table*, 8th edn, p. 32).

> And thus the land of Cameliard was waste,
> Thick with wet woods, and many a beast therein,
> And none or few to scare or chase the beast;
> So that wild dog, and wolf and boar and bear
> Came night and day, and rooted in the fields,
> And wallowed in the gardens of the King.
> And ever and anon the wolf would steal
> The children and devour, but now and then,
> Her own brood lost or dead, lent her fierce teat
> To human sucklings; and the children, housed
> In her foul den, there at their meat would growl,
> And mock their foster-mother on four feet,
> Till, straightened, they grew up to wolf-like men,
> Worse than the wolves.[7]

For Tennyson, fear of social disintegration caused by a growing urban underclass and nervousness about the potential for this underclass to become violent are distilled into the monstrous figure of the feral child, 'the human suckling', telescoped into the alliteration of 'wolf-like men, worse than wolves'. Tennyson's solution to the devolution implied by the emergence of these sub-humans is the coming of Arthur, the representative of a chivalry that will either convert degenerates to proper living or destroy them: 'And Arthur and his knighthood for a space / Were all one will, and thro' that strength the King / Drew in the petty princedoms under him, / Fought, and in twelve great battles overcame / The heathen hordes, and made a realm and reigned.'[8]

Like England, where violence was a 'common feature in the everyday lives of young men in working-class districts'[9], the United States saw an increase in youth gang violence as class disparities associated with the industrial revolution increased. As early as 1849, George W. Matsell, chief of police for the City of New York, would complain to Mayor Caleb S. Woodhull about a 'deplorable and growing evil':

> Constantly increasing numbers of vagrant, idle and vicious children of both sexes, who infest our public thoroughfares, hotels, docks, &c. Children who are growing up in ignorance and profligacy, only destined to a life of misery, shame and crime, and ultimately to a felon's doom. Their numbers are almost incredible, and to those whose business and habits do not permit them a searching scrutiny, the degrading and disgusting practices of these almost infants in the schools of vice, prostitution and rowdyism, would certainly be beyond belief.[10]

---

[7] Alfred, Lord Tennyson, 'The Coming of Arthur', *Idylls of the King* (New York, 1996), ll. 20–33.

[8] Tennyson, 'The Coming of Arthur', ll. 514–18.

[9] Davies, 'Youth Gangs', 356.

[10] Kristin Bates and Richelle S. Swan. *Juvenile Delinquency in a Diverse Society* (Thousand Oaks, 2019), 29–30.

In the United States, conflicts around gangs were aggravated by distinctions among ethnic groups as racism, immigration, and xenophobia reached their turn-of-the-century heights. Many *fin de siècle* discussions of the boy problem in the United States, however, were shaped not by race or class analysis or immigration policy but, as Kenneth B. Kidd has argued, by two distinct and ahistorical discourses: the myth of the feral child and boyology. The myth of the feral child 'dramatizes but also manages the "wildness" of boys', demonstrating that even the most monstrous of children – the most savage – can be redeemed for middle-class respectability – while boyology, which Kidd suggests is a uniquely American phenomenon, encompasses 'descriptive and prescriptive writing on boyhood across a variety of genres'.[11] For *fin de siècle* America, boyhood, considered ahistorically, became a nostalgic locus of contention over what it meant to be an American citizen in a modern world.

Fin de siècle boy workers worried not only about the wildness of boys but also about their feminisation. Kenneth Kidd writes that 'institutional boy work in fact organised itself against the neurasthenia and enervation that ostensibly plagued urban life'.[12] Prominent 'boyologists', like Forbush, bemoaned the feminisation of the three institutions responsible for making men of boys: home, schools, and church. He writes: 'The public school fails in will-training because it gives the will no exercise. ... The home, especially the city home, fails for the same reason. ... The Church fails because it has tried the wrong thing.'[13] While Forbush does not explicitly name women as the cause of these failures, boyologists feared that boys spent too much of their childhood under the tutelage of women. 'The boys should have male ... leaders ... The ideals and capabilities of most women leaders do not point to the highest efficiency with boys of the adolescent period.'[14] The boy problem was producing both the feral child and the 'effeminate babyish boy';[15] both would fail to achieve proper manhood. Forbush's response to the boy problem, as Alan Lupack notes, was 'to translate idyllic notions of knighthood into an American setting'.[16] Eschewing 'the cruder earlier versions' of Arthurian knighthood (like Malory's *Morte Darthur*), Forbush aimed to remediate 'the more spiritualised version of Tennyson's "Idylls of the King"' as a solution to the boy problem, borrowing the poet's recreation of Arthurian chivalry to civilise and masculinise both feral and neurasthenic boys.[17]

---

[11] Kenneth B. Kidd, *Making American Boys: Boyology and the Feral Tale* (Minneapolis, 2004), 1.
[12] Kidd, *Making American Boys*, 18–19.
[13] William Byron Forbush, *The Boy Problem*, 6th edn (Boston, 1907), 26.
[14] Forbush, *Boy Problem*, 47.
[15] Michael Kimmel, *Manhood in America* (New York, 2017), 90.
[16] Alan Lupack, 'Arthurian Youth Groups in America: The Americanization of Knighthood', in *Adapting the Arthurian Legends for Children*, ed. Barbara Tepa Lupack (New York, 2004), 197.
[17] Forbush, *Boys Round Table*, 31.

Forbush founded The Knights of King Arthur in 1893 in Riverside, Rhode Island.[18] He estimates that by 1916 more than three thousand 'castles' had been organised throughout the country, and that more than 125,000 young people 'have been identified with the King Arthur movement'.[19] Forbush notes that he got the idea for this juvenile fraternity from his participation in Casque & Gauntlet, a senior society at Dartmouth founded on Arthurian principles: 'For some time there had been lurking in his mind the memory of a college fraternity to which he had belonged and whose ceremonials, based upon the customs of ancient knighthood, he had had a share in preparing.'[20] Forbush and his imitators – including the Episcopalian Order of Sir Galahad (1896), Perry Edwards Powell's Knights of the Holy Grail (c. 1906), and even Robert Baden-Powell's Boy Scouts (1908) – created a national network of boys' fraternities modelled on Tennyson's vision of King Arthur and his Knights of the Round Table.[21] Their goal was the creation of a 'chivalrous kingdom of knightly-hearted men in the Great Republic' where 'many wrongs will be righted by the hands of lads who wear a tiny white cross above their hearts'.[22]

There is much in Malory that might have challenged Forbush's sunny descriptions of 'brave adventure-seeking comrades', noble quests, and the fight for glory. Episodes such as the rape of Ygraine that results in Arthur's conception; Arthur's out-Heroding Herod by murdering all the children to get rid of his bastard son; the brothers Balin and Balan killing one another; Lancelot and Guinevere's infidelity; and countless violent scenes of senseless slaughter between errant knights would hardly be appropriate moral lessons for children. 'Malory did not write for children', Andrew Lynch remarks, yet 'this largely childless text has been continually produced in children's versions since 1862 when James Knowles, an architect, scholar and friend of Alfred Tennyson, published the first adaptation of the legend for children'.[23]

---

[18] In 1894, he founded the Queens of Avalon, a parallel organisation for girls; see Laurie Finke and Susan Aronstein, 'The Queens of Avalon: William Forbush's Arthurian Antidote', *Arthuriana* 22, no. 3 (2012): 21–40.

[19] Lupack, 'Arthurian Youth Groups', 203.

[20] Forbush, *Boys Round Table*, 15; see also Jonathan Good, '"King Arthur Made New Knights": The Founding of the Casque & Gauntlet', *Dartmouth College Library Bulletin* ns 40 (April 2000).

[21] Baden-Powell's vision of the Boy Scouts included a large dose of medieval chivalry: 'In the old days the Knights were the real Scouts and their rules were very much like the Scout Law which we have now. ... The Knights considered their honour their most sacred possession. They would not do a dishonourable thing, such as telling a lie or stealing. They would rather die than do it. They were always ready to fight and to be killed in upholding their king, or their religion, or their honour.' Robert Baden-Powell, *Scouting for Boys: The Original 1908 Edition* (Dover, 2014), 23.

[22] Forbush, *Boys' Round Table*, 6.

[23] Andrew Lynch, 'Le Morte Darthur for Children: Malory's Third Tradition', in *Adapting the Arthurian Legends for Children*, ed. Barbara Lupack (New York, 2004), 4.

Subsequent editions were produced by Sidney Lanier (1880), Aubrey Beardsley (1893), and Howard Pyle (1903). Forbush, however, mentions Malory only three times in all of his writing on the Knights of King Arthur. Instead, like many *fin de siècle* adapters, 'Arthurian retellings for children often drew on more than just Malory's *Morte Darthur*, and often filtered the many medieval sources through Alfred, Lord Tennyson's Arthurian poetry.'[24] The *Morte Darthur* had to be retained to connect the British nation to an antique past, but it needed cleaning up if it was to serve any pedagogical purpose in the education of the young. Elly McCausland quotes Edward Strachey's preface to the *Morte* of 1868: 'Mr. Tennyson has shown us how we may deal best with this matter for modern uses, in so far as Thomas Malory himself has failed to treat it rightly.'[25] Tennyson's *Idylls of the King*, for the Victorians, becomes a metonymy for the *Morte*, popularising and moralising Malory's tales, sanitising them and providing the material for a children's literature that would bowdlerise Malory even further.[26] Forbush, drawing on Tennyson's *Idylls* – and, no doubt, on its many watered-down knock offs – remediated them from the written page to ritual initiation.

Alan and Barbara Lupack have already asked why 'a legend based on a hierarchical system headed by a monarch' would be attractive in 'a land where such things are alien to our national values'.[27] The feudal ideology that suffuses Arthurian and grail legends would seem unsuited to carry the various meanings associated with the 'Great Republic'; medieval knighthood was a marker of social status, 'an institution created by aristocrats who wanted to glorify their own public service in the face of competition from other elites'.[28] It seems antithetical to the ideals so central to America's view of itself as a democracy in which hard work and perseverance at least ideologically replaced inherited rank and privilege. America as the 'New World' had been founded on the repudiation of the kinds of outmoded medieval hierarchies represented by Arthurian chivalry. In his 1871 'Song of the Exposition', Walt Whitman dismissed the ghostly remains of Arthur, 'Merlin and Lancelot and Galahad'. They were 'all gone dissolv'd utterly', inhabitants of a 'void, inanimate, phantom world' (ll. 48–51); 'ended' he intones with finality, 'the quest of the Holy Graal' (l. 43), replaced by 'a better, fresher, busier sphere – a wide, untried domain' (l. 18). To be sure, the Lupacks are correct to assert that Forbush and his followers succeeded in reinvigorating knighthood as a training ground for boys by removing chivalric hierarchy from the social to the moral realm, by democratising monarchy, and translating the birth equals

[24] Echard, 'Bedtime Chaucer', 127.
[25] Elly McCausland, *Malory's Magic Book: King Arthur in Children's Literature, 1862–1960* (Cambridge, 2019), 21.
[26] McCausland, *Malory's Magic Book*, 18–30.
[27] Alan and Barbara Tepa Lupack, *King Arthur in America* (Cambridge, 1999), 67.
[28] Ruth Mazo Karras, *From Boys to Men: Formations of Masculinity in Late Medieval Europe* (Philadelphia, 2003), 27.

worth ideology of medieval aristocracy to the American ideal of meritocracy and the self-made man. Another answer to this question might be found in the collision and collusion of the boy problem articulated by social commentators during this period with antimodern tendencies that are also finding expression at the same moment in history.

Fraternal organisations for boys like The Knights of King Arthur that responded to the boy problem by nostalgically looking backward to the Old World and the Middle Ages illustrate a growing 'antimodernism' in the United States at the turn of the century, evident especially among the eastern elites, like the Dartmouth-educated Forbush. Antimodernists, Jackson Lears has argued, rejected not only unjust distributions of wealth and power; they began to question 'the modern ethic of instrumental rationality that desanctified the outer world of nature and the inner world of the self – reducing both to manipulable objects. Antimodernists sought alternatives for the banality, feminising influences, and rampant consumerism of the modern world in medieval, Oriental, and other primitive cultures.'[29] Boyhood provided an especially fertile arena for antimodern thought since it offered an ahistorical vision of a timeless childhood that could also shape the future.[30] In *The Coming Generation*, Forbush joins other *fin de siècle* voices in articulating a desire for more intense forms of physical or spiritual experience as a corrective to the utilitarianism of industrial capitalism:

> If we are to have a generation of men who are more than money-grubbers, there must be a long era of free fancy in childhood, and, what with fairies driven out of forests, and the forests themselves cut down, and Santa Claus exiled from the home, and gnomes unknown in the firelight, – because we have no more firelight in our modern houses, – it is a very hard thing to do.[31]

In creating fraternal organisations based on chivalry, Forbush and his imitators embarked on a programmatic effort to translate the political and social hierarchies of feudalism into a new chivalric order, still hierarchical, still authoritarian, but based on 'the fraternal, the emotional, and the intellectual, with a constant emphasis on the spiritual', satisfying a longing for 'authentic' experiences that had been lost to modernity.[32]

---

[29] Jackson Lears, *No Place of Grace: Antimodernism and the Transformation of American Culture 1889–1920* (New York, 1981), xi.

[30] McCausland, *Malory's Magic Book*, 18–52.

[31] William Byron Forbush, *The Coming Generation* (New York, 1913), 20–21.

[32] William Byron and Dascomb Forbush, *The Knights of King Arthur: How to Begin and What to Do* (1915), 21, Camelot Project; https://d.lib.rochester.edu/camelot/text/forbush-knights-of-king-arthur-how-to-begin-and-what-to-do (accessed 21 December 2023).

Forbush targeted the adolescent years between thirteen and eighteen for initiation because, according to psychological theories popular during the period, it represents 'a period of danger and possibility in boy life'.[33] Boyologists of the period drew heavily on the recapitulation theories of psychologists, like G. Stanley Hall, who argued that children recapitulated as they grew up the evolutionary stages of the species, that the various stages of childhood could be mapped on to an evolutionary history.[34] Forbush writes in *The Boys' Round Table*:

> Dr. Hall refers again and again both to the knightly period in boy life and also particularly to this order [Knights of King Arthur]. The theory upon which these words of appreciation were spoken is the now familiar one that children in their progressive development reproduce in a general way the race life. They pass at the dawn of adolescence out of an era which corresponds to that of the outdoor, predatory life of the tribal systems up to a period which has many resemblances, in its delight in fellowship, its exultance in tests of strength, its romantic and imaginative instincts and its yearning for heroism, to the age of chivalry.[35]

G. Stanley Hall asserts that

> the spirit of the pure chivalry of King Arthur and the Knights of the Round Table affords perhaps the very best ideals for youth to be found in history. The value of this material makes it almost biblical for the early and middle teen years. It teaches the highest reverence for womanhood, piety, valour, loyalty, courtesy, munificence, justice, and obedience.[36]

In this way, child psychology was used to manage both normative and perverse forms of boyhood. The middle-class white boy was 'already normative and must simply grow up according to his nature (if with supervision – that's where boy work comes in), whereas the contemporaneous feral boy must be acculturated or recuperated',[37] the feral boy being the stand-in for non-white, non-middle class, non-normative children always in danger, without intervention, of remaining stuck in the period of savagery. Forbush insists on the salience of these 'racial differences'; they 'are quite marked in regions where there are many illiterate

---

[33] Forbush, *Boy Problem,* 39.
[34] Lears, *No Place of Grace*, 147–49; Kidd, *Making American Boys*, 15–18. Forbush was a disciple; Hall contributed an 'Introduction' to the fourth edition (1901) of *The Boy Problem*, 3–4.
[35] Forbush, *The Boys Round Table*, 22.
[36] Granville Stanley Hall, *Adolescence*, vol. 1 (New York, 1969), 532.
[37] Kidd, *Making American Boys*, 15–16.

boys of foreign birth'. Racial differences 'largely determine the special methods of social work with them'; 'them' here referring to

> French Canadians [who] are behind our American-born boys. I am pretty sure that they comprise almost every illiterate boy in Fall River. They are behind the other boys in playing games. They need educating in play and in trustworthiness. They lack the honor sense. I don't see how I could put them upon their honor as we do other [middle-class white] boys – they would hardly know what I mean.[38]

Racial difference also marks Jewish boys, who are argumentative, 'clannish', and read too much, the Irish who 'do not seem capable of rising out of their inborn prejudice of the English', and of course the 'American negro ... has not yet accepted the responsibility for his own life.'[39] These passing references conflate race and class, lumping together French Canadians, Jews, Irish, and Blacks. Forbush's prejudices are typical of his time and elite social standing, but they are difficult to untangle as he is more interested in universalising boys than differentiating them. He boasts that

> Arthurian legends are so simple that they can be told to the most restless boys. ... Successful castles have been conducted among lumber-camp boys, mining boys and street boys, and it is the belief of the authors that results depend more upon the ability of the adult leader than upon any differences of appreciation among different classes of boys.[40]

Boyhood, then, becomes a synecdoche for civilisation and a battleground on which to forge the citizenship of the future.

Fraternal orders for boys like the Knights of King Arthur were designed specifically to capitalise on and redirect the tendencies of adolescent boys to form gangs. Despite 'accounts of the doings of these "gangs," from the comparative innocence of property destruction and hoodlumism to organised theft, assault and murder [that] appear in the daily press continually',[41] Forbush

---

[38] Forbush, *The Boy Problem*, 42–43, quoting Thomas Chew.

[39] Forbush, *The Boy Problem*, 43–44.

[40] Forbush, *The Boys Round Table*, 28. Thomas Edison's 1917 film *The Knights of the Square Table* embodies Forbush's comment that 'the first thing a Castle does is either to break up a bad gang or start a good one' (*The Knights of King Arthur*, 1915), offering parallel stories that follow two groups of boys – a troop of boy scouts and a gang of delinquents, two fraternities, alike in their passion for tales of King Arthur, as they attempt to reclaim masculinity for – and from – the modern world; see Kevin Harty, '*Knights of the Square Table*: The Boy Scouts and Thomas Edison Make an Arthurian Film', *Arthuriana* 4, no. 4 (1994): 315.

[41] Forbush, *The Boy Problem*, 56.

argued that boys needed gangs, needed an outlet for masculine aggression and homosocial bonding, but that these gangs should be controlled by adults and made moral, useful, responsible, and God-fearing. Forbush, along with most boyologists, believed that 'the instincts upon which the activities even of the worst "gang" are built are the innocent and natural ones of adolescence':[42]

> The only place where a boy can learn the brotherhood of man is in the school of the gang. ... Out among his peers God intends that he shall go, to give and take, to mitigate his own selfishness and to gain the masculine standpoint which his mother, his nurse, and his school-teacher cannot give, and to exercise a new power, which is one of the most precious ever given to man, that of making friendships.[43]

Boys had to be weaned both from the feminising influences of home, school, and church, on the one hand, and the 'savagery' of childhood on the other. The task, as boyologists saw it, was to maintain adult control of this 'gang instinct' so that the boy worker could shape this tendency to homosociality, could institutionalise those erotically charged bonds between boys, and contain, constrain, and direct masculine aggression and competition toward socially approved ends – toward the creation of a particular kind of citizenship based on the ideals of fraternity: 'cultivating friendship intensely for a small circle, conscious of representing the corps to others, as gentlemen practising *noblesse oblige*'.[44] Forbush imagined a boy's club, really no more than a gang, but a gang rigidly managed by respectable adults, where American boys could dream themselves socially productive versions of the medieval British aristocracy. He imagined a 'boy's round table' where participants would recognise in each other the qualities of Tennyson's knights, 'Wearing the white flower of a blameless life.'[45]

It should come as no surprise that those seeking to reshape American boys turned to fraternities as a solution. Fraternal organisations for boys, like Forbush's Knights of King Arthur, participated in the proliferation of new fraternal societies during the period between the American Civil War and World War I. Beginning in the last decades of the nineteenth century, American boys and men organised and were organised in unprecedented numbers in fraternal orders that looked to myths of an antique past for models of manhood, appropriating medieval narratives about knighthood and re-imagining mythologies of aristocratic genealogy and privilege. In these fraternal organisations,

---

[42] Forbush, *The Boy Problem*, 47.
[43] Forbush, *The Boy Problem*, 23.
[44] Forbush, *The Boy Problem*, 25.
[45] Forbush, *The Boys Round Table*, 120; quoting from Tennyson's dedication to *Idylls of the King* to Prince Albert, l. 24.

men sought the 'fellowship, friendship and solace that they no doubt otherwise missed' in the pursuit of wealth or even of a living wage in a capitalist world of cutthroat competition.[46] Even as it was happening, journalists and academics were remarking on the efflorescence of fraternal organisations, so much so that the period came to be known as the 'Golden Age of Fraternalism'. As many as one in five men, over 5,400,000, belonged to at least one fraternal society, and many belonged to more than one.[47] The golden age of fraternalism saw the proliferation of collegiate and high school fraternities and sororities that, much to the chagrin of authorities, enabled students to create a youth culture apart from the often stifling control of parents and school. In this context, Forbush's efforts to reassert adult authority and guidance over potentially unruly teens resulted in a 'non-secret boys' fraternity' to counter 'the unfortunate influence of the secret unAmerican high school fraternity'.[48] Children not part of the fraternity were not privy to the ritual secrets of the society, but adults – parents and ministers – would know all.

Members of fraternal orders used fantasies about the Middle Ages to enact certain performances of masculinity as a means of instantiating friendship. Even so-called non-secret children's fraternal orders depended heavily on esoterica and rituals to promote the kinds of heightened experiences sought by the antimodernists. Once again Forbush quotes Hall: 'Every adolescent boy ought to belong to some club or society *marked* by as much secrecy as is compatible with safety. Something esoteric, mysterious, a symbolic badge, countersign, a lodge and its equipment, and perhaps other things owned in common, give a real basis for comradeship.'[49] Children's fraternities, unlike adult fraternities, rarely had a 'room of their own'. During a period when fraternal organisations like the Scottish Rite Freemasons were erecting more and more spectacular temples – complete with auditoriums, stages, and elaborate sets and scenery in which to perform their increasingly theatrical initiations – the Knights of King Arthur usually met in church halls or spaces they shared with other groups.[50] Adult fraternal organisations were wealthy enough to build their own spaces because their membership was well off and paid dues all of their adult lives. Even college fraternities, whose members were active for only three or four years, controlled enough resources

---

[46] Kimmel, *Manhood in America*, 172.

[47] William S. Harwood, 'Secret Societies in America', *The North American Review* 164 (1897): 617.

[48] Forbush, *The Boys Round Table*, 37.

[49] Forbush, *The Boys Round Table*, 24.

[50] On the Scottish Rite building boom, see Lance Brockman, ed., *Theatre of the Fraternity: Staging the Ritual Space of the Scottish Rite of Freemasonry, 1896–1929* (Minneapolis, 1996) and Mark Tabbert, *American Freemasons: Three Centuries of Building Communities* (New York, 2006).

through their alumni networks to be able to build fraternity lodges as early as the mid-nineteenth century and their own houses by the century's end.[51] Members of Forbush's organisation, however, did not control these kinds of resources, and membership costs had to be kept low. Thus, although they adopted much of the ritual and paraphernalia of fraternal organisations, the Knights of King Arthur were always understood as children's clubs, and they remain as ephemeral as most juvenile culture.

The Boys' Round Table describes in detail the set-up of a typical Castle, complete with Round Table and Siege Perilous, even appending a diagram specifically showing how the room should be properly laid out.[52] Knights of the Round Table were organised into 'castles' with names like Avalon, Joyous Gard, or Shalott. Initiates passed through three degrees from Page to Esquire to Knight, through elaborate initiation ceremonies that, like most fraternities of the Golden Age, were largely cribbed from Masonic initiations. Even the set-up of the initiation room mirrored Masonic practice. Upon becoming knights, boys usually took the names of Arthurian knights:

> Give them names of heroes, as far as possible, who had virtues they need to cultivate. Give the name Lancelot to some boy whose chivalric side you desire to develop. Geraint is a good name for an impatient boy. Gareth is a good name for a boy who has a hard struggle.[53]

The adult leader is, however, not the king; he is the Merlin, now diminished from powerful political advisor to pedagogue.[54] There are songs, banners, costumes, badges, countersigns, swords, and other paraphernalia all designed to create a liminal space in which to inculcate very particular social values that could reclaim masculinity for – and from – the modern world.

Any secret society's success depended on creating satisfactory ceremonies. They were what fraternities did; rituals linked members to one another and to other individuals elsewhere who shared the same rituals, symbols, and worldview. All turn-of-the-century fraternal organisations staged highly theatrical rituals that employed elaborate costumes, sets, and props to act out narratives that cast initiates and members as medieval masons or knights and their ladies. Like virtually all fraternities, the Knights of the Round Table emphasised ritual; the initiation into each of the three degrees of membership

---

[51] On fraternal building, see Nicholas L. Syrett, *The Company He Keeps: A History of White College Fraternities* (Chapel Hill, 2009), 161–64.
[52] Forbush, *The Boys Round Table*, see images between 62–63 and 96–97.
[53] Forbush, *The Boys Round Table*, 56.
[54] Stephen Knight, *Merlin: Knowledge and Power through the Ages*, shows how the figure of Merlin shrinks over time from powerful advisor of a world-conquering monarch to children's tutor.

remediates medieval narratives. Each ritual involves the dramatisation of a brief simplified episode from Tennyson. The initiation for the first degree of Page remediates the episode in 'Gareth and Lynette' in which Gareth is allowed to go to Arthur's court but only as a 'fair unknown', who must work as a servant in the kitchen for a year. Like Gareth, and like the medieval squire, the Page must be 'put in a servile position, but only temporarily as part of a life stage'.[55] The second-degree rite to create an Esquire remediates the story of the Sword in the Stone; in this initiation, the candidate must successfully release the sword. The third degree, Knight, is the most elaborate, remediating Tennyson's vision of the Holy Grail and including many of the medieval rituals of knighthood: a purifying bath, a Confession, a vigil ('an hour alone standing in the darkened church with his sword laid upon its altar'), the sacrament, and fasting.[56] Forbush's rites rarely quote Tennyson; they simply borrowed motifs and episodes from the *Idylls* adapted to rites of initiation.

In remediation, these texts are given material substance through the techniques of the theatre; these include a stage, a set, scenery, costumes, props, and most importantly, actors. But unlike the theatre (a different medium), there is no audience because the goal of initiations is transformation rather than catharsis. The candidate, by participating in the ritual and learning the secrets, takes on a new social identity, a new chivalric social skin, created through the collaborative efforts of the fraternity. To effect transformation, the narrative must be shaped by the ritual, not the poetic text; in this case, the rituals are simplified forms of the much more elaborate Masonic initiations. Bayliss J. Camp and Orit Kent isolate four key components of initiation rituals, which are present even in these more simplified remediations: hierarchy and equality, boundedness, hazing, and movement.[57] These are not easily isolated from one another, as they are braided together throughout a ritual that climaxes in an oath and the revelation of secrets. The first-degree initiation – Page – though very short (it runs to only about five pages of text), illustrates these performative elements of initiation that promote bonding. The first mechanism – boundedness – articulates the hierarchies within the fraternity and separates those who occupy the sacred space – the insiders – from the profane and uninitiated. The space of initiation, in this case the Castle, must be physically set apart from mundane spaces. The candidate must be isolated and prepared for the ceremony. Sir Kay, portrayed by one of the initiated boys,[58] blindfolds him, dresses him in ragged clothing, and leads him to the castle gate. Sir Kay performs this

---

[55] Karras, *From Boys to Men*, 30.

[56] Forbush, *The Boy's Round Table*, 94.

[57] Bayliss J. Camp and Orit Kent, '"What a Mighty Power We Can Be": Individual and Collective Identity in African American and White Fraternal Initiation Rituals', *Social Science History* 28, no. 3 (2004): 448–49.

[58] All roles, except Merlin, are played by boys already initiated into the order. The Merlin was always the adult leader of the Castle and usually the only adult taking

role because as Arthur's seneschal, he was the court official responsible for domestic arrangements, including managing strangers (outsiders). Kay vouches for the candidate, indicating his willingness to submit to servitude: 'Grant us to serve among thy kitchen knaves for meat and drink a twelvemonth and a day. Thereafter we will fight.'[59]

These preparations begin the second mechanism, the hazing, which here includes blindfolding and 'testing an initiate's courage or pain threshold'.[60] Hazing was part of Forbush's programme, since 'innocent rioting vents the anarchistic instincts in ways least injurious to the community and makes docility and subordination more easy and natural in their turn'.[61] Hazing not only 'proves' the candidate worthy of membership; it bonds members of the group through a common experience, setting them apart from all others who have not undergone such testing. On their 'journey' towards Arthur's castle, the blindfolded candidate is abandoned by Sir Kay and confronted by a hostile gang of knights (played by one half of the initiated) who threaten him with various punishments including burning him at the stake. He is only rescued when a band of Arthur's knights (played by the other half) arrives just in time. This hazing tests the initiate's courage but also teaches him the loyalty owed to those who have come to his aid. Forbush describes the ritual as 'quite amusing and exciting'.[62]

Movement is the third mechanism of initiation. As Kay and the candidate enter, they march around the room. These circumambulations are ritualistic, distinct from routine movements; they are a frequent component of initiation, often iterating in threes.[63] Camp and Kent note that this movement allows the assembled membership to inspect the initiate and decide whether he is worthy of membership. But more importantly this movement marks 'the liminal moment at which the initiate crosses over from being an outsider to a member'.[64] Only after this ritualistic capture and rescue is the initiate's blindfold removed, while the Merlin intones 'The morning breaks and danger is over.'[65] The initiate is given the secrets of the degree and instructed in its meaning. He swears his oath, a seal is placed on his forehead, and he is given a 'Page's suit'.

---

part in the rituals (the exception being the third degree, Knight, where an adult Lady of the Lake plays a role).

[59] Forbush, *The Boys Round Table*, 82. 'Twelvemonth and a day' is an echo of Tennyson's 'Gareth and Lynette.'

[60] Camp and Kent, 'What a Mighty Power', 447.

[61] Forbush, *The Boys Round Table*, 24.

[62] Forbush, *The Boys Round Table*, 80.

[63] Repetition is another common feature of ritual, which features patterned repetitions of movements, actions, sounds, and speeches.

[64] Camp and Kent, 'What a Mighty Power', 445.

[65] Forbush, *The Boys Round Table*, 77.

Newly created Pages must learn the 'condition of servitude'. However, 'such a condition is not satisfactory and it is not intended that it should be, yet it is most wholesome for a time for the average boy. It prevents a certain self-conscious priggishness in a very decisive fashion.'[66] It also teaches him the hierarchies within the fraternity. Though all are brothers, all are not equal. It is a good example of what Mary Ann Clawson calls the proprietorship model of fraternity, defined as 'an idealised set of relationships involving individual autonomy within a hierarchical order, with the possibility for meritocratic advancement over time in authority and power'.[67] But what kind of masculinity was Forbush's organisation offering its members? Not the rugged masculinity of the frontiersman or the industrial capitalist, which by this time were themselves nostalgic figures of the distant past, and certainly not the masculinity of the medieval warrior. At the same time that Forbush's rituals provided outlets for masculine fantasies of risk taking, aggression, adventure, camaraderie, competition, and prowess, they were also domesticating its members, demanding they embody the 'special virtues of obedience, courage, purity, temperance, reverence, and Christian confession'.[68] The organisation holds these constitutive contradictions in tension. For all its nostalgia for a lost past, for all its attempts to transcend the banality of modern life into a more exciting and romantic world, projects like the Knights of King Arthur ended up serving the ends of a modern rationalised nation state, one in which 'docility and subordination' were more salient virtues than rugged individualism and martial heroism.[69] As Jackson Lears notes, these clubs tended to encourage unquestioning obedience to authority: they 'sought to wean youth away from what one leader called "unwholesome introspection and self-analysis" toward immersion in disciplined group activity'.[70] Under a veneer of medieval romance, these 'paramilitary' organisations reinforced 'adjustment to the regimented, hierarchical organisation of work under corporate capitalism'.[71]

Organisations like the Knights of King Arthur prepared boys to become tools of twentieth-century America's military–industrial complex. With the rise of hyper-nationalist states came the need for a ready and willing military, the boys who would ultimately fight and die in Europe's trenches. Forbush's knights grew up to become the cannon fodder for World War I, perhaps the most misguided war in the history of the planet. The rhetoric Forbush deploys in his vision for the righteous, Christian, chivalric young men who would join his 'Castles' indoctrinated future soldiers who would enthusiastically enlist to

---

[66] Forbush, *The Boys Round Table*, 80.
[67] Camp and Kent, 'What a Mighty Power', 445.
[68] Forbush, *The Boys Round Table*, 29.
[69] Forbush, *The Boys Round Table*, 24.
[70] Lears, *No Place of Grace*, 110.
[71] Lears, *No Place of Grace*, 100.

ARMING THE YOUNG KNIGHT

Figure 12.2: A depiction of a knight being armed (Forbush, *The Boys Round Table*, 5th edn, frontispiece).

fight their nation's wars (unlike, say, the 'feral' gang members of the 1860s who violently resisted serving in the American Civil War). World War I would offer a literal interpretation for the song of the Order of the Knights of King Arthur: 'Comrades, hail the Cross that leads us, / Comrades, hail the Grail that beckons, / Comrades, hail the War that waits us. / Knights of holy chivalry.'[72]

---

[72] Forbush, *The Boys Round Table*, 7.

Forbush envisions

> an American Prince arming himself for the battle of life from crown to foot, his greaves buckled on by a sweet-spirited mother, while a watching sister stands near and breathes a gentle prayer ... He must, he will conquer. In the sign for which he fights, victory is sure. [see Figure 12.2][73]

These same young men would soon be singing George M. Cohan's 'the Yanks are coming, the Yanks are coming, / ... / So prepare, say a prayer, send the word, send the word to be-ware / We'll be over, we're coming over, / And we won't come back 'til it's over, over there!' The song's blustery rhetoric takes up for the modern era Forbush's breezy interpellation of boys with which we began. But, in both cases, the reality was very different. Both songs' rhetoric of exceptionalism created a masculinity that would run headlong into poison gas in Flanders fields.

---

[73] Forbush, *The Boys Round Table*, 6.

ANNOTATED BIBLIOGRAPHY OF SIÂN ECHARD'S PUBLICATIONS

KELSEY MOSKAL AND MAIRI STIRLING HILL

***The Latin Verses in the* Confessio Amantis: *An Annotated Translation.* With Claire Fanger. East Lansing, MI: Colleagues Press, 1991.**

Echard and Fanger here present the first complete translation of the Latin poems in Gower's *Confessio*, thereby making an essential element of the work more accessible to readers and critics. This volume is an invaluable contribution to the Gower recuperation effort of the late twentieth and early twenty-first centuries.

'"Iubiter et Iuno": An Anglo-Latin Mythographic Poem, edited from Oxford, Bodleian Library, MS Digby 64 and British Library MS Cotton Vespasian E.xii.' *Journal of Medieval Latin* 4 (1994): 101–17.

Echard offers an edition of a mythographic poem that she has titled 'Iubiter et Iuno' and that had hitherto been unedited. She notes that the poem 'consistently offers interpretations which are drawn from the realms of etymology, natural science, and what might be called moral psychology' and that its many idiosyncrasies make situating it precisely within a textual lineage especially challenging.

'Map's Metafiction: Author, Narrator and Reader in *De nugis curialium.*' *Exemplaria: A Journal of Theory in Medieval and Renaissance Studies* 8 (1996): 287–314.

Here, Echard suggests that the authorial presence in the *De nugis* functions as 'glue' to hold the collection together, and that this frame requires a reassessment of common critical assumptions about Map's most familiar work. Specifically, Echard argues for a postmodern, metafictional reading of the *De nugis*, as the constructed author-narrator Map simultaneously distances the reader from the narrative and invites the reader to participate in the construction of its meaning.

'Of Parody and Perceval: Middle Welsh and Middle English Manipulations of the Perceval Story.' *Nottingham Medieval Studies* 40 (1996): 63–79.

This piece reframes the Middle Welsh and Middle English versions of the Perceval tale as parody and argues for the appreciation of their exploration of convention as a deliberate alternative to the versions of the Perceval story that follow Chrétien de Troyes' *Conte del Graal* and focus on the grail quest. Echard observes that 'what parody criticizes, it may also cherish', and that by placing *Peredur* and *Sir Perceval of Galles* in such a context we can move away from the historical grudge against them for what they are not and begin to praise them for what they are.

'Pre-texts: Tables of Contents and the Reading of John Gower's *Confessio Amantis.*' *Medium Aevum* 66, no. 2 (1997): 270–87.

Echard argues here for a reassessment of the *Confessio* as lacking in variation across its manuscript witnesses. Leaving aside the text itself, she draws attention to *mise-en-page* and other 'incidental features' – in this case, especially tables of contents – as offering equally valuable evidence of different reading and interpretive experiences.

'Glossing Gower: In Latin, in English, and *in absentia*: The Case of Bodleian Ashmole 35.' In *Re-visioning Gower*, ed. R. F. Yeager, 237–56. Asheville, NC: Pegasus Press, 1998.

Here, Echard argues that the physical framing of Gower's verse by Latin glosses is itself a self-conscious addition to the narrative. The layout on the page evokes readerly assumptions even before one has begun to read. Just as Echard argues elsewhere that Gower's multilingual texts disrupt preconceived ideas about the value, truth, and authority of a text, here she suggests that the presence – or absence – of Gower's Latin framing has a similar effect – one Gower was acutely aware of.

'With Carmen's Help: Latin Authorities in the *Confessio Amantis.*' *Studies in Philology* 95, no. 1 (1998): 1–40.

In this article, Echard argues that the Latin in the *Confessio* offers a valuable inroad into understanding the reception and interpretation of Gower's work. Specifically, she focuses on the way the Latin is treated in different witnesses, and how that treatment produces 'significantly different "readings" of the poem'. In these witnesses, Echard suggests, we see not only evidence of how Gower himself viewed the utility and playfulness of Latin but also the responses of contemporary and post-medieval readers.

Arthurian Narrative in the Latin Tradition. **Cambridge Studies in Medieval Literature 36. Cambridge: Cambridge University Press, 1998.**

This monograph focuses on Latin Arthurian narratives of the twelfth century, produced by the work of 'courtier-clerics' in the court of Henry II. In her introduction, Echard notes that these particular narratives are inextricable from their socio-political context, even as they resist being defined by generic terms commonly in use therein. The texts under consideration include works by familiar names such as Geoffrey of Monmouth, Gerald of Wales, and Walter Map, as well as some perhaps less familiar figures such as Etienne de Rouen and Johannes de Hauvilla.

'Designs for Reading: Some Manuscripts of Gower's *Confessio Amantis.'* **Trivium 31 (1999): 59–72.**

Through case study examples, Echard explores how bibliographic elements such as speech markers, decoration, ink colours, and the presence or absence of Latin glosses might indicate how *Confessio* manuscripts were read – or not – by their initial medieval audiences.

'House Arrest: Modern Archives, Medieval Manuscripts.' *Journal of Medieval and Early Modern Studies* **30, no. 2 (2000): 185–210.**

In this article, Echard explores the role of archival practice in constructing our understanding of the past. Mapping the provenance of two Gower manuscripts from their early owners to current archives, she suggests that the ways in which manuscripts are accessed – or access is limited – and the information provided about them all reflect important ideological stances that become bound up in the object itself.

Anglo-Latin and Its Heritage: Essays in Honour of A. G. Rigg on His 64th Birthday. **With Gernot R. Wieland. Publications of the Journal of Medieval Latin 4. Turnhout: Brepols, 2001.**

This collection explores Anglo-Latin literatures and is offered in honour of George Rigg shortly before his retirement from the University of Toronto. The articles herein cover topics as varied as Rigg's academic interests, and Echard's own chapter – 'Clothes Make the Man: The Importance of Appearance in

Walter Map's *De Gadone milite strenuissimo*' (93–108) – explores how Map's court literature makes use of wordplay and generic and linguistic slippages to invite multivalent interpretations.

'Dialogues and Monologues: Manuscript Representations of the Conversation of the *Confessio Amantis.*' In *Middle English Poetry: Texts and Traditions: Essays in Honour of Derek Pearsall*, ed. A. J. Minnis, 57–75. York Manuscripts Conferences 5. York: York Medieval Press, 2001.

Working from the base understanding that *ordinatio* affects reading and interpretation, Echard focuses in this article on the speech markers in *Confessio* manuscripts, exploring how this feature varies across witnesses and what the reason for, and function and reception of, that variation might have been.

'"Hic est Artur": Reading Latin and Reading Arthur.' In *New Directions in Arthurian Studies*, ed. Alan Lupack, 49–67. Cambridge: D. S. Brewer, 2002.

In this chapter, Echard begins with the familiar, almost playful way Geoffrey of Monmouth troubles the role of Latin as the language of history and truth before moving on to explore how other writers of Arthurian narrative make use of the cultural and historical assumptions embedded in the use of Latin to grant authority and cultural cachet to their works.

'Gower's "Bokes of Latin": Language, Politics and Poetry.' *Studies in the Age of Chaucer* 25 (2003): 123–56.

In this article, Echard proposes a re-examining of modern assumptions about how Gower understood and deployed his own Latinity. She argues that there is a 'doubleness' in Gower's use of Latin in the *Vox clamantis*, one that reflects authority and anxiety, poetry and politics, and the potential for language to be (mis)used in the wrong hands – or voices.

'Last Words: Latin at the End of the *Confessio Amantis.*' In *Interstices: Studies in Late Middle English and Anglo-Latin Texts in Honour of A. G. Rigg*, ed. Richard Firth Green and Linne Mooney, 99–121. Toronto: University of Toronto Press, 2004.

Here, Echard explores the political and personal-poetical implications of the different versions of the Latin *Explicit* and *Quia vnusquisque*, which are the last items in most *Confessio* witnesses. She argues that the treatment of these texts in the Ricardian and Henrician manuscript versions of the *Confessio*, and then again by post-medieval editors, has a significant effect on how readers perceive Gower *and* his works.

***The Book Unbound: Editing and Reading Medieval Manuscripts and Texts.*
With Stephen Partridge. Toronto: University of Toronto Press, 2004.**

A collection of essays based on papers delivered at the 29th Annual Medieval Workshop at the University of British Columbia in September 1999, this volume reflects a pivotal moment in the development of manuscript studies and editorial practice.

***A Companion to Gower.* Cambridge: D. S. Brewer, 2004.**

In her introduction to this volume, Echard argues that 'part of the problem [of Gower's reputation] has to do with a conflict between Gower's own creation of his poetic position, and how later generations have reacted to that position'. As one of few collections at the time devoted to the works of Gower – and not focused almost solely on the *Confessio* – this volume under Echard's editorial guidance (re)introduces Gower through the lenses of early twenty-first-century critical interests. Echard's own essay, 'Gower in Print' (115–35), explores how typeface, page design, and editorial excisions by Gower's early printers influenced perceptions of the poet's reputation and value for post-medieval audiences.

'"For Mortals are Moved by these Conditions": Fate, Fortune and Providence in Geoffrey of Monmouth.' In *The Fortunes of King Arthur*, ed. Norris J. Lacy, 13–28. Arthurian Studies 64. Cambridge: D. S. Brewer, 2005.

This article interrogates the role (or lack thereof) of divine power in the events depicted in Geoffrey's *Historia*. Echard suggests that Geoffrey's invocation of Fate, Fortune, prophecy, and other heavenly interventions is in a state of constant tension: on one side is the belief in a 'providential plan', while on the other is a more chaotic sense of coincidence – to good ends or ill.

'Latin Arthurian Literature.' In *A History of Arthurian Scholarship*, ed. Norris J. Lacy, 62–76. Cambridge: D. S. Brewer, 2006.

This article explores the absent presence of the Latin Arthurian tradition within the field of Arthurian studies more broadly. The first two sections examine how the Latin tradition – particularly the work of Geoffrey of Monmouth – is often considered only for its relation to vernacular works. The third section is a thorough consideration of criticism of the Latin tradition for its own sake. Finally, Echard points in the fourth section to valuable new editions that make Latin texts more accessible to a broader range of scholars.

'"Seldom does anyone listen to a good exemplum": Courts and Kings in *Torec* and *Die Riddere metter Mouwen.' Arthuriana* 17, no. 1 (2007): 79–94.

In this article, Echard reads the figure of the fair unknown, the outsider who proves himself through feats of arms and chivalry and who usually ends up being of worthy lineage. Considering representations of this figure in Latin and Dutch romances, Echard notes commonalities across the disparate traditions as the figurative outsider is a vehicle for larger concerns about courtliness and right rule.

'Of Dragons and Saracens: Guy and Bevis in Early Print Illustration.' In *Guy of Warwick: Icon and Ancestor*, ed. Alison Wiggins and Rosalind Field, 154–68. Studies in Medieval Romance 4. Cambridge: D. S. Brewer, 2007.

In this chapter, Echard uncovers the relationship between the printed illustrations of *Guy of Warwick* and *Bevis of Hampton* from the early prints up to the seventeenth century. Echard suggests that the two texts share an early print history, with generic woodcuts that on multiple occasions appear in both texts. *Bevis of Hampton*, she argues, acquires and retains a 'particular visual identity' much earlier than *Guy of Warwick*, however, whose iconography takes longer to develop.

Printing the Middle Ages. Material Texts. Philadelphia: University of Pennsylvania Press, 2008.

In this monograph, Echard examines the post-medieval printed lives of medieval texts through the lens of visual and material paratexts – illustrations, bindings, layouts, etc. – that create particular reading and aesthetic experiences. At the core of the book is an exploration of the ideological inflections at play in how these post-medieval printings claim authority, authenticity, and – in many cases – Englishness.

'"Whyche thyng semeth not to agree with other histories ...": Rome in Geoffrey of Monmouth and his Early Modern Readers.' In *Arthurian Literature XXVI*, ed. Elizabeth Archibald and David F. Johnson, 109–29. Cambridge: D. S. Brewer, 2009.

This article traces the shifting attitudes to Rome in relation to British history from Geoffrey of Monmouth to the early modern period, especially through Arthur and his Roman exploits. Early modern writers such as John Leland, John Stow, and Richard Grafton move away from Geoffrey's narrative of

British victories over the Romans, a move that Echard argues is partly due to a desire to maintain a historical Arthur in the face of competing Roman histories.

'"But here Geoffrey falls silent": Death, Arthur, and the *Historia regum Britannie.*' In *The Arthurian Way of Death: The English Tradition*, ed. Karen Cherewatuk and K. S. Whetter, 17–32. Arthurian Studies 74. Cambridge: D. S. Brewer, 2009.

Echard examines the varied descriptions of death in Geoffrey of Monmouth's text through the language, setting, and characters involved, and what this means in the Arthuriad setting. Throughout the text, the deaths of good kings are usually briefly described, often followed by an overview of their hereditary legacy. Bad kings often meet more brutal deaths, their violent reign being reflected in their demise. In the Arthuriad portion of Geoffrey's text, the sheer variety of deaths – their descriptions as well as the victims being described – is staggering. As Echard notes, this is partly due to narrative scope, but the notable focus on personal connections and human individuality is also reflective of a move from chronicle to romance tropes.

'BOOM: Seeing *Beowulf* in Pictures and Print.' In *Anglo-Saxon Culture and the Modern Imagination*, ed. David Clark and Nicholas Perkins, 129–46. Medievalism 1. Cambridge: D. S. Brewer, 2010.

Here, Echard considers 'the role of the visual in the *presentation* of *Beowulf*: the ways extra-textual choices both reflect and impose interpretation not only of *Beowulf* itself but of the historical moment in which it was produced and that it claims to represent. Echard traces how cover design, artefactual images, maps, and other visual inclusions create their own narrative alongside the poem.

***The Arthur of Medieval Latin Literature: The Development and Dissemination of the Arthurian Legend in Medieval Latin.* Arthurian Literature in the Middle Ages 6. Cardiff: University of Wales Press, 2011.**

In this edited volume, Echard collects essays that address the unique position of Latin transmissions of Arthurian legends – as opposed to their many vernacular siblings – and the uses to which the idea of Arthur might be put when presented in the language of history, clergy, and the educated elite. Titled simply 'Geoffrey of Monmouth', Echard's own essay in this volume discusses the works of Geoffrey of Monmouth and the tension therein as Arthur is represented as both singular and one among many in the history of the kings of Britain.

'Whose History? Naming Practices in the Transmission of Geoffrey of Monmouth's *Historia regum Britannie.' Arthuriana* **22, no. 4 (2012): 8–24.**

This article explores the naming practices in Geoffrey of Monmouth's *Historia regum Britannie* through composition to transmission. Rather than considering the relationships between individual manuscripts, in this work Echard looks at naming practices as a means of framing texts, and the ways that these practices impact reader expectation and interpretation. Through this, she explores the cultural impact of the *Historia* and its textual tradition.

'Remembering Brutus: Aaron Thompson's *British History* **of 1718.' In** *Arthurian Literature XXX*, **ed. Elizabeth Archibald and David F. Johnson, 141–70. Cambridge: D. S. Brewer, 2013.**

Focused through Thompson's 1718 translation of Geoffrey of Monmouth's *Historia regum Britannie*, Echard traces a lineage of influence – what she calls a 'palimpsest of reception' – back and forth across several centuries. This study, she notes, reminds us of the emphasis on Brutus and the British that begins Geoffrey's work but that is often elided in favour of Arthur in many critical considerations of the *Historia*.

'New Technologies: From Manuscript to Print.' In *A Companion to British Literature*, **ed. Robert DeMaria, Heesok Chang, and Samantha Sacher, 1:403–17. Broadwell Companions to Literature and Culture 84. Oxford: Wiley Blackwell, 2014.**

This chapter offers a helpful introduction to the shift from manuscript to print culture. Echard takes great care to demonstrate that this was hardly an immediate process, and that many of the features common in early printed books were in fact adopted from manuscript culture. Although a brief overview of the transition period, this chapter includes interesting examples to ground what might otherwise be dry procedural information and has extensive references for anyone looking for further information.

'The Long and the Short of It: On Gower's Forms.' In *John Gower in England and Iberia: Manuscripts, Influences, Reception*, **ed. Ana Sáez-Hidalgo and R. F. Yeager, 245–60. Publications of the John Gower Society 10. Cambridge: D. S. Brewer, 2014.**

Focused through a close reading of Gower's short poem 'O Deus immense', this chapter demonstrates how Gower's works 'call forth a certain kind of reading practice' through manipulation of poetic form. While Gower is best known for his long works, Echard argues here that there is equally as much to be learned from his shorter texts.

'Containing the Book: The Institutional Afterlives of Medieval Manuscripts.' In *The Medieval Manuscript Book: Cultural Approaches*, ed. Michael Johnston and Michael van Dussen, 96–118. Cambridge Studies in Medieval Literature 94. Cambridge: Cambridge University Press, 2015.

This article explores how common archival and classification practices such as the format of shelf-marks can have lasting effects on the value assessments of medieval manuscripts and their post-medieval iterations (in, for example, early modern transcripts). Echard examines how institutional structures complicate the tension between the understandable critical desire to reconstruct or locate lost 'originals' and the subsequent erasure of extant post-medieval witnesses as historical objects in and of themselves.

'The Naked Truth: Chaucerian Spectacle in Brian Helgeland's *A Knight's Tale*.' In *Chaucer on Screen: Absence, Presence, and Adapting the Canterbury Tales*, ed. Kathleen Coyne Kelly and Tison Pugh, 169–85. Interventions: New Studies in Medieval Culture. Columbus: The Ohio State University Press, 2016.

In this chapter, Echard reads the 2001 film *A Knight's Tale* alongside the Chaucer's *Knight's Tale*, exploring how director Brian Helgeland's unapologetically anachronistic film intersects with and often offers a more faithful evocation of Chaucer's poem than many more 'authentic' adaptations.

'How Gower Found His Vox: Latin and John Gower's Poetics.' *The Journal of Medieval Latin* 26 (2016): 291–314.

This article explores how Gower's trilingualism is inextricable from his poetics, and how resonances of each language are always at play regardless of the 'main' language of any given work. In particular, Echard examines the development and function of what she calls the 'Gowerian voxative' across especially the Latin and English works.

'Palimpsests of Place and Time in Geoffrey of Monmouth's *Historia regum Britannie*.' In *Teaching and Learning in Medieval Europe: Essays in Honour of Gernot R. Wieland*, ed. Greti Dinkova-Bruun and Tristan Major, 43–59. Publications of the Journal of Medieval Latin 11. Turnhout: Brepols, 2017.

Focusing on moments wherein Geoffrey's Latin juxtaposes past and present, beauty and decay, permanence and change, Echard uncovers a rhetorical tension throughout the *Historia* that is layered further when considered alongside the manuscript record. Geoffrey's 'representation of history', she suggests, can be read as 'a linguistic contest written on both the landscape and the page'.

'Technologies in/of Romance: *De ortu Waluuanii* and *Historia Meriadoci*.' In *Handbook of Arthurian Romance: King Arthur's Court in Medieval European Literature*, ed. Leah Tether and Johnny McFadyen, in collaboration with Keith Busby and Ad Putter, 493–503. Berlin: de Gruyter, 2017.

In this article on two Latin romances, *De ortu Walwanii* and the *Historia Meriadoci*, Echard considers how arguments for dating and authorship proceed through a focus on objects and suggests that this focus on objects and technologies overlooks the significance of the objects themselves.

***The Encyclopedia of Medieval Literature in Britain.* With Robert Rouse. 4 vols. Chichester: Wiley-Blackwell, 2017.**

A crowning achievement project by any definition, the *Encylopedia* brings together more than six hundred entries in a way that Echard and co-editor Robert Rouse hope will 'redefine the study of medieval British literature as the study of the literature *of* medieval Britain'. Echard's individual contributions to the *Encyclopedia* include entries about John Gower, Geoffrey of Monmouth, and Walter Map; *Sir Perceval of Galles*; the Guthlac Roll; and the *Vera historia de morte Arthuri*.

'Part I: The Middle Ages and the Renaissance.' In *The Book in Britain: A Historical Introduction*, ed. Zachary Lesser, 9–133. Chichester: Wiley-Blackwell, 2019.

Echard's contribution to this introduction to British book history surveys the key foundational developments of literary transmission by hand and print. Beginning with the early remediation of oral works to textual forms, this section of the volume combines historical facts with literary exempla to situate readers and the development of early textual culture. Perhaps most significantly, Echard emphasises throughout that this process was neither linear nor stable, and no stage should be understood as having superseded or obliterated the one preceding.

***Historians on John Gower*, ed. Stephen Rigby, with Siân Echard. Publications of the John Gower Society 12. Cambridge: D. S. Brewer, 2019.**

This volume addresses Gower's literary works through the critical specialities of historians. There is particular focus on how the socio-political milieu in which Gower was writing and to which he might have been responding is represented in his works. The hope is that the additional historical focus will help readers bridge the gap between modern and medieval understandings of style, genre, and other features in order not only to make Gower's works more accessible to a variety of readers but to increase appreciation and potential for deeper study.

'Malory in Print.' In *The New Companion to Malory*, ed. Megan G. Leitch and Cory James Rushton, 96–121. Arthurian Studies 87. Cambridge: D. S. Brewer, 2019.

In this chapter, Echard considers the lasting effects of Malory's *Morte Darthur* through its printing and publication history. She discusses what this history can tell us about readership and interpretation and puts each version in conversation with the century in which they were printed. Despite the fact that, until 1934, all versions relied upon the William Caxton edition of the *Morte*, the wide appeal of Malory is made evident through the numerous and varied editions, both popular and scholarly.

'Gower between Manuscript and Print.' In *John Gower in Manuscripts and Early Printed Books*, ed. Martha W. Driver, Derek Pearsall, and R. F. Yeager, 169–88. Publications of the John Gower Society 14. Cambridge: D. S. Brewer, 2020.

In her own words, Echard here 'explore[s] how the unique features of Gower's *oeuvre* were often muted, redirected, or lost entirely, when the medieval poet's work encountered the strictures and expectations of early print'. Differences in layout, script, ink colour, and other features serve Gower's multilingual and often structurally complex work clearly and effectively in manuscript, Echard suggests, in a way that early print simply could not attain.

'The Latin Reception of the *De gestis Britonum*.' In *A Companion to Geoffrey of Monmouth*, ed. Georgia Henley and Joshua Byron Smith, 209–34. Brill's Companions to European History 22. Leiden: Brill, 2020.

This book chapter explores the ways that both medieval and early modern Latin writers interacted with Geoffrey of Monmouth's *De gestis Britonum* through commentary and in-text annotation, through narrative participation and continuation, and through expansion and original creation.

'Charming the Snake: Accessing and Disciplining the Medieval Manuscript.' Written with Andrew Prescott. In *The Cambridge Companion to Medieval British Manuscripts*, ed. Orietta Da Rold and Elaine Treharne, 237–66. Cambridge: Cambridge University Press, 2020.

This chapter explores the institutional structures that mediate our access to medieval manuscripts. In particular, Echard and her co-author Andrew Prescott examine how modes of conservation, cataloguing, acquisition, and other processes are never ideologically neutral, and how our understanding and valuation of medieval manuscripts as cultural objects should always be considered in relation to these structures.

'Rolling with It: Navigating Absence in the Digital Realm.' In *Medieval Manuscripts in the Digital Age*, ed. Benjamin Albritton, Georgia Henley, and Elaine Treharne, 82–90. Digital Research in the Arts and Humanities. London: Routledge, 2021.

This chapter is a rumination on the potential inherent in the digital: manuscripts, once digitised, are opened up to new modes of study. Echard suggests that this is also an opportunity to 'think through how we relate to these objects', that with the flexibility of digital access should come an element of play that is sometimes lost in the strictures and rigours of scholarly structures.

'John Gower.' In *The Routledge Companion to Medieval English Literature*, ed. Raluca Radulescu and Sif Rikhardsdottir, 289–99. Routledge Literature Companions. London: Routledge, 2022.

This chapter offers an introduction to John Gower, using the *Confessio Amantis* as a focal point. Touching on the persistent Englishness of the *Confessio*, themes of universality and localisation, contemporary fourteenth-century socio-political and cultural tensions, and the transhistorical legacy of Gower's work, Echard delivers an incisive overview of key concepts in the study of this trilingual poet.

'Background Noise.' *New Chaucer Studies: Pedagogy and Profession* 3, no. 1 (2022): 111–16.

In this short article, Echard contemplates the ongoing impacts of the COVID-19 pandemic on the medieval studies classroom.

'The Poetic Field, II: Ango-Latin.' In *The Oxford History of Poetry in English*, Vol. 2, *Medieval Poetry 1100–1400*, ed. Helen Cooper and Robert R. Edwards, 88–103. Oxford: Oxford University Press, 2023.

In this chapter, Echard surveys some of the writers of Anglo-Latin poetry of the Middle Ages. Divided by genre, the chapter considers the epic poetry of Joseph of Exeter and Walter of Châtillon, Nigel Whiteacre's satirical *Speculum Stultorum*, the religious writing of Reginald of Canterbury and John of Garland, and interior and exterior space in the poetic works of Henry of Huntingdon and Lawrence of Durham.

'Poetry in Print.' In *The Oxford History of Poetry in English*, Vol. 3, *Medieval Poetry 1400–1500*, ed. Julia Boffey and A. S. G. Edwards, 127–39. Oxford: Oxford University Press, 2023.

In this chapter contribution, Echard discusses the early printers of medieval poetry, what they chose to print, how they chose to present it, and the relationship between the authors' works and their early print editions, and the relationships between different early print editions that drew heavily on one another. Echard writes that the first printers in England helped establish the canon of medieval verse and discusses the 'porous' boundary between manuscript and print in the early period of print in England.

'Elegiac Additions: Marking Arthur's Death in Manuscripts of Geoffrey of Monmouth.' *Arthuriana* **33, no. 2 (2023): 12–26.**

This article considers the marginal responses to Arthur's death in Geoffrey of Monmouth's *Historia Regum Britanniae*. Echard notes the ways that these visual responses to Arthur's death in the manuscripts, be they point of production or interventions by later readers, dictate how the end of Arthur's reign is transmitted and received.

'The Pleasures of Plainness: Ordinary Manuscripts in Extraordinary Traditions.' In *Medieval Manuscripts, Readers and Texts: Essays in Honour of Kathryn Kerby-Fulton***, ed. Misty Schieberle with the assistance of Amanda Bohne, 105–120. York Manuscript and Early Print Studies 7. York: York Medieval Press, 2024.**

Echard's contribution to Katheryn Kerby-Fulton's Festschrift is a reflection on 'plain' medieval manuscripts – ordinary medieval manuscripts that are not the 'best' text of a tradition or especially ornate. Using many such examples from the robust manuscript tradition of Geoffrey of Monmouth's *Historia regime Britannie*, Echard demonstrates how studying ordinary manuscripts of such traditions allows us to recover readerly traditions of medieval texts, document physical features of the manuscripts that would otherwise be overlooked and generally expand our knowledge of both the literary tradition and medieval material culture history.

Facsimile: Making, Likeness, and Medieval Manuscripts. **Philadelphia: University of Pennsylvania Press, 2025.**

Echard's third academic monograph is the first ever cultural history of the tradition of making facsimiles of medieval manuscripts, a tradition which dates back centuries and continues today with powerful digital technologies. Her focus within this tradition, however, is primarily on the eighteenth and nineteenth centuries, a time period when rising interest in medieval studies coincided with a vibrant development of new technologies which came to be applied to the study and reproduction of medieval manuscripts. Focusing on four distinct aspects (Letter, Figure, Colour, and Catastrophe), Echard explores and explains how human hands, eyes, and imaginations incorporated and influenced technology to develop unique, and fascinating medieval-modern hybrid entities.

INDEX

AB Language   67–70, 72–74
Achebe, Chinua   4, 65–66, 85
Achilles   202, 203–4, 206, 208
Aeneas   96, 97, 104, 106–7, 193, 199, 204–5, 209
Aesthetic appeal   94, 107, 109, 113, 131–32, 135
Affect   109, 110, 113, 123, 131
Albertus Magnus   149
Alexander the Great   55, 103 n. 54, 133, 146, 185, 200, 202, 208–9 *see also* Nine Worthies
Alfred of Beverley   214
Alliterative Morte Darthure   197–8, 200–1, 205
Alliterative poetry   196, 210–11
America *see* United States
Anaphora   112, 116, 128, 130, 131–32
Andreas Ammonious   49
Ancrene Wisse   66–67, 72–73
Anglo-Norman *see* French
Anglo-Saxon Chronicle   71
Anglo-Saxons *see* Saxons
Anne of Bohemia   126, 128
Aquinas, Thomas   91
Archetype   177–78
Arnold, Richard
    Arnold's Chronicles   56
Arthur *see under* Arthurian characters
Arthurian characters
    Arthur   9, 10, 18, 201
        Alliterative Morte Darthur   197
        antiquarian interest in   43–46, 50–5, 53–56, 212–28
        Brut y Brenhinedd   18
        Cligés   194–95
        De gestis Britonum   193
        Didot *Perceval*   205
        Diu Crône   206
        Geraint uab Erbin   224–25

Gesta regum Anglorum (William of Malmesbury)   213
Gesta regum Britannie (William of Rennes)   202
Historiae Britannicae Defensio (John Prise)   212–13, 221–27
Idylls of the King (Tennyson)   232
Lancelot-Graal Vulgate Cycle   204
Morte Darthur (Malory)   197, 198, 234
Perceforest   208
Sir Gawain and the Green Knight   196, 209–210
Stanzaic Morte Darthur   197–98
Vulgate *Estoire del Graal*   199–200
Vulgate *Mort Artu*   206
The Worthines of Wales   220
Bors   206
Elaine of Astolat   201, 206
Elaine of Corbenic   201
Galahad   198 n. 22, 201
Gareth   241–42
Gawain   200, 203
Giant of Mont St. Michel   18, 21 n. 61, 201
Guinevere   201, 205–7, 225, 234
Kay   242–43
Lancelot   106, 200–20, 204–5, 206–7, 234, 241
King Mark   200, 206
Merlin/Myrddin   16, 199, 224, 241–43
Mordred/Medrawd   207, 216, 225
Morgan   204, 207
Perceval   202
Taliesin   222–25
Uther   208
Vortigern   16, 20, 23, 225–26
Yvain   203
Arthurian literature

and Latin writing 29–30, 41, 212
  in Wales and Welsh culture, 9–10, 18, 219–28
Astrology/astronomy 137, 146–49
Auctoritas / authorship 77–78, 90–91, 94–98, 100–1, 116
Auden, W.H. 64
Augustine, Bishop of Hippo
  Confessiones 107
  De civitate Dei 107
  Soliloquies 172–73, 184, 185

Bacon, Roger 135
Baden-Powell, Robert 234
Bale, John 56, 218, 219
Beardsley, Aubrey 235
Bede 49, 56, 214, 215, 219 n. 30
Bédier, Joseph 65
Belinus 193
Bell, Idris 181
Benedict of Gloucester 227
Benoit de Sainte-Maure
  Roman de Troie 106, 207
Beowulf 169–201
Berthelette, Thomas 140
Boccaccio, Giovanni 54, 95 n. 18
  De casu principum 43
Boece, Hector 56, 219 n. 30
Boethius 91 n. 7, 111, 115
Books
  Aesthetic appeal 175–77, 185, 186–87
  Archives 139–40, 171, 183
  Collecting 152–53, 159–62, 222–24
  Facsimiles 155, 188–91
  History 27–28, 39–41, 170–92
  Manuscript and book production 31–32, 138, 156–59, 162–65, 182–84
Bors *see* Arthurian characters
Boy Scouts 234, 238 n. 40
The Boy's Round Table (Forbush) 229–46
The Breviary of Britayne 219
Brian des Illes 205
Bristol 71
Britain, foundation and concept of 9–12, 193, 196–98, 213, 219–21, 227
Brut tradition 10–11, 27–28, 42–44, 46–47, 52–53, 55–58, 214–19
Brut y Brenhinedd 10–11, 27–28, 32–35
Brut y Tywysogyon (The Chronicle of the Princes) 219

Brutus 50–51, 193–98, 201, 208, 218, 220, 222, 254

Caius, John 218
Camelot 43, 200, 201, 205, 211, 216
Casque & Gauntlet 234
Catalogues (manuscripts) 126–27, 152, 169, 179–83
Caxton, William 43–46, 52, 54, 56, 140, 215–216, 220, 227, 257
Cerquiglini, Bernard 29 n. 10, 170
The Chandos Herald 108, 120
Charlemagne 55, 217 *see also* Nine Worthies
Chaucer, Geoffrey 60, 74–85, 95, 97, 99–100, 102, 105 n. 65, 130 n. 40, 137 n. 15, 141, 145, 202, 206 n. 57, 211, 255
Children's literature 230, 234–35
Chivalry 194–95, 199, 206, 208, 217, 229–37, 242, 244–46
Chrétien de Troyes 194, 198, 248
Chronicles *see* Historiography (Medieval)
Churchyard, Thomas 220
Cobden-Sanderson, Thomas 176, 177
Cotton Library 26, 37, 38, 139, 172, 175, 176, 178, 180
Cotton, Robert 177, 181, 186
Coveney, Dorothy 178, 179
Craft guilds 127, 128
Cromwell, Thomas 213
Cupid (Roman deity) 95, 96, 97
Cyfranc Lludd a Llyfelys 12, 18

d'Ardenne, S. R. T. O. 66–70
Dares Phrygius
  De Excidio Troiae Historia 106
Davis, Norman 187–90
Debate of Saturn and Solomon 184, 185
Derrida, Jacques 75, 76, 82, 85
Description of Britain
Dibdin, Thomas Frognall 157–58, 161–62
Dictys Cretensis
  Ephemeris belli Troiani 106
Dido 104, 106, 198, 205, 206
Didot 201, 205
Dingestow Manuscript *see under* Manuscripts Aberystwyth, National Library of Wales MS 5266B
Domesday Book 56, 71
Donatus 105
Dream vision 111

Ductus 109, 110, 111, 113, 116, 119, 122, 123, 126, 130, 131

Early English Text Society 164–65, 175–76, 187–88
Edison, Thomas *see The Knights of the Square Table*
Edward (Saint) 216
Edwards, Perry 234
Elaine of Astolat *see* Arthurian characters
Elaine of Corbenic *see* Arthurian characters
England 47, 145, 213, 219–20
English 4, 9–10, 60–86
Episcopalian Order of Sir Galahad 234
Escanor 205

Fabyan, Robert
  New Chronicles of England and France 52
Facsimiles 187, 190, 191, 259
'Feral' children 232, 233, 237, 245
Forbush, William Byron 5, 229–46
Fortune (allegorical figure) 146
Fraternal organizations
Freemasons / Masonic practices 240, 241, 242
French 60–61, 62, 63, 67, 69, 74, 75, 76–78, 79–81, 90
Froissart, Jean 56, 121
Furnivall, F. J. 164, 188

Gaimar
  Estorie des Bretons 214
Galahad *see* Arthurian characters
Gang violence 230, 232, 233, 238, 239, 245
Gareth *see* Arthurian characters
Gawain *see* Arthurian characters, *Sir Gawain and the Green Knight*
Geoffrey of Monmouth 2, 3, 5, 27, 41, 42, 56, 216, 217, 218, 220, 221, 249, 250, 252, 256, 259
  De gestis Britonum (*Historia regum Britanniae*) 9–24, 27–35, 40–44, 212, 213–214, 251, 253, 254, 255, 257, 259
  First Variant Version 24, 28–32, 33, 35, 41
  Vita Merlini 224
Gerald of Wales 25–27, 41, 54, 249

Expugnatio Hiberniae 25–26
Descriptio Kambrie 27, 38 n. 49
History of Llanthony Abbey 39
Itinerarium Kambriae 38, 214
Life of St. David 27, 37–38
Speculum duorum 40
Speculum Ecclesiae 25–26, 39
Topographia Hibernica 25–26, 39
Gesta Regum Anglorum 213
Giant of St. Michel *see* Arthurian characters
Gildas 49–56, 214–15, 222–23
  De Excidio et Conquestu Britanniae 50, 223
Glastonbury 37 n. 45, 43, 51, 54, 216–18
Glissant, Edouard 60, 76–77, 80–82, 85
Gloucester 34, 71
Gnuess, Helmut 183
Gospel of Nicodemus 184–5
Earl Gower *see* Sutherland-Leveson-Gower, George Granville
Gower, John 56, 76, 89–95, 97–107, 111–19, 131–32, 133–37, 140–49, 153
  'Amans' (character) 133, 145, 148
  'centonic' style 104
  Confessio Amantis 90 n. 5, 92–93, 99, 101, 103–4 n. 56, 106, 133–38, 141–51, 247–50, 258
  Cronica Tripertita 98, 104
  'Genius' (character) 92, 145, 147–48
  Mirour de l'Omme 90, 92, 94, 101, 105–6
  Quia unusquisque 101–2, 250
  Trilingualism 90, 100, 152, 250, 255, 258
  Visio Anglie 91–93, 105, 107, 111–16, 121–23, 125–26, 132
  Vox Clamantis 91–94, 98, 101, 103, 111, 250
Grafton, Richard 55, 252
Gregory I (the Great), Pope 90, 172
Guido delle Colonne, *Historia destructionis Troiae* 106
Guillaume le Clerc 202–4
Guinevere *see* Arthurian characters

Hagiography *see* Saint's lives
Hali Meiðhad 63, 66–75, 85
Hall, Edward 55–56
Hall, G. Stanley 237, 240
Harrison, William 217

Havelok the Dane 84
Henry of Huntingdon 45, 54, 258
  Historia Anglorum 214
Headley, Maria Dahvana 170
Hector (also Ector, Antor) 56, 194, 197, 200–8, 219
Hecuba 201
Helen (Helen of Troy and Helen in Arthurian narrative) 201, 205
Hengist 12, 21–22, 143, 194
Hercules 55, 157, 163
Hereford 25–6, 39, 66, 71
Higden, Ranulf 44–46, 51–55, 214–16
Historia Regum Britanniae see *De gestis Britonum*
Historiography 27–29, 39–41, 42–58, 108–11, 122–23, 212–28
The History of Taliesin 222–25
Holand, David 47
Holinshed, Raphael 55–56, 216–17
Holy Grail 198, 215, 234–35, 242, 245, 248
Homer 97
Homily on St Christopher 184
Homily on St Quintin 184
Horace 90
Hughes, Thomas, *The Misfortunes of Arthur* 207

Ireland 14–15, 22, 37–39, 71

James, Richard 178, 184
John of Gaunt 79–82
'Journey through Wales' see *Itinerarium Kambriae*
Judith 184–85
Julius Caesar 219, 225 see also Nine Worthies

Kay see Arthurian characters
Kelmscott Press 186–87
Ker, Neil 180–83
Kings and Queens, English
  Edward I 52
  Edward II 52
  Edward III 52–3, 90, 164
  Edward VI 47
  Elizabeth I 193
  Henry II 214, 249
  Henry III 52
  Henry VII 42, 48, 193, 217

Henry VIII 42, 47–49, 52, 54, 213, 217
  Richard II 144
  Richard III 47
King Mark see Arthurian characters
Knighthood 233–35, 239, 242
Knighton, Henry 108, 120
The Knights of King Arthur (boys' group) 229–30, 234–41, 244–46
The Knights of the Square Table (1917 film) 238 n. 40
Knowles, James 234

Lancelot see Arthurian characters
Langland, William 90
  Piers Plowman 94
Lanier, Sidney 235
Lapidge, Michael 183
Latin literature and language 9–24, 27–29, 32–37, 42–54, 59–62, 66–67, 69, 72, 74–78, 84–85, 119–31, 173, 212–22, 225–27
  Gower's use of 89–92, 98–104, 113–19, 132, 142–44, 146–50
Latini, Brunetto, *Livres dou Trésor* 135, 147
Latinity 59, 74
Layamon 11, 24, 193 n. 2, 214
Leland, John 53–6, 212, 218–20, 222, 252
  Balades and Other Poems by John Gower 152–65
Letter of Alexander to Aristotle 146, 184–5
Lincolnshire 60
Llwyd, Humphrey 219–20, 228
  Cronica Walliae 219
London 12, 49, 52, 78–9, 82, 111, 116, 118, 123–24, 128–30, 163, 169, 189, 217, 232, 247, 248–51, 254–58
  As Troynovaunt/Trinovantum 194–5, 208, 222
London, Tower of 111–17, 120–22
Lucan 97, 100, 221
Lydgate, John 56, 137 n. 15
  Fall of Princes 202

Macaulay, G.C. 92 n. 11, 98 n. 30, 100 n. 38
Madog of Edeirnion, *Strenua Cunctorum* 35–36

INDEX

Maidstone, Richard 102 n. 47, 123–31
Malory, Thomas 43, 46, 54, 200–3, 205, 206 n. 57, 213, 215, 229, 233–35, 257
Manuscripts:
  Aberystwyth, National Library of Wales MS Llanstephan 1 10 n. 4, 19
  Aberystwyth, National Library of Wales MS Peniarth 1 223
  Aberystwyth, National Library of Wales MS Peniarth 2 22
  Aberystwyth, National Library of Wales MS Peniarth 6 225
  Aberystwyth, National Library of Wales MS Peniarth 16 13 n. 18
  Aberystwyth, National Library of Wales MS Peniarth 32 226
  Aberystwyth, National Library of Wales MS Peniarth 44 10–11 n. 4, 18, 19 n. 51, 21, 22 n. 66, 33
  Aberystwyth, National Library of Wales MS Peniarth 135 226 n. 56
  Aberystwyth, National Library of Wales, MS 13210 35
  Aberystwyth, National Library of Wales MS 21608A 47
  Aberystwyth, National Library of Wales MS 5266B 10–24, 33
  Cambridge, Corpus Christi College MS 201 180, 183
  Cambridge, Corpus Christi College MS 303 180
  Cambridge, Corpus Christi College MS 367 180, 183
  Cambridge, Corpus Christi College MS 402 66
  Cambridge, Cambridge University Library MS Ii 1. 33 180
  Cardiff, South Glamorgan Library, MS 2.611 35–6
  Cologny, Cod. Bodmer MS 147 199
  Dublin, Trinity College MS 11500 30
  Lincoln, Lincoln Cathedral MS 149 37
  London, British Library, Cotton MS Julius A. ii 180
  London, British Library, Cotton MS Otho A.xii 139–40
  London, British Library, Cotton MS Tiberius A. iii 180
  London, British Library, Cotton MS Tiberius B. xiii 26 n. 4
  London, British Library, Cotton MS Vespasian A. xiv 36, 226 n. 57
  London, British Library, Cotton MS Vitellius A. xv 172, 175–92
  London, British Library, Cotton MS Vitellius E. vii 38
  London, British Library, MS Add. 59495 (the 'Trentham Manuscript') 153–61, 163–5
  London, British Library, MS Add. 59496 152
  London, British Library, Royal MS 13. C. I 37 n. 45
  London British Library, Royal MS 18. A. LXXV 47, 50 n. 20
  London, Lambeth Palace Library 236 25–6
  Oxford, Bodleian Library, MS Bodley 34 66–7, 70 n. 32
  Oxford, Bodleian Library MS Fairfax 3 99
  Oxford, Bodleian Library, Rawlinson MS B.195 53
  Oxford, Jesus College MS 111 223
  Paris, Bibliothèque Nationale, fr. 794 198
  Paris, BN, fr. 1420 200
  Vatican, Bibliotheca Apostolica Vaticana Cod. Reg. Lat. 470 40
Marvels of the East/Wonders of the East 184–85
Masculinity 118–19 n. 23, 185, 229, 233, 238–41, 244–46
Medievalism 9, 159–64, 186–87, 229–46
Merleau-Ponty, Maurice 171–75
Merlin *see* Arthurian characters
McKenzie, D. F. 171
Middle English Prose Brut 44–47, 52–53, 56–57, 214
Military 106, 116 n. 17, 244
Mordred *see* Arthurian characters
More, Thomas 50
Morgan *see* Arthurian characters
Morris, William 176, 186–87

Narrative 41–45, 109–13, 122–23, 241–43

Nationalism, national identity 45–48, 212–13, 219–28, 235–36, 244
Neckham, Alexander 91
Nine Worthies 200, 202, 209, 216–17 see also Alexander the Great, Arthur, Charlemagne, Hector, Julius Caesar

Ordinatio 109–13, 119, 122–23, 129–32, 250
Orm, *Ormulum* 60
Ovid 89–98, 103–7, 112, 132
   Amores 93, 95–97
   Ars amatoriae 92 n. 11, 93, 98
   Ceux and Alcyon 80–81
   Fasti 93, 143
   Heroides 92, 95–96
   Metamorphoses 92–94, 103 n. 52
   Remedia amoris 93
   Tristia 93, 98, 103 n. 52, 132

Paleography 33–36, 48, 92, 105, 184, 222–23, 226
Paramilitary organizations 244
Parker, Matthew 178, 181
Paris, Matthew 56
Paris (Trojan) 124–25, 201, 205–7
Patroclus 203–4
Peasants/peasantry 4, 78, 93–94, 111–13, 115, 117–22, 129, 131
Peasants' revolt of 1381 4, 78–79, 91, 111–13, 115–16, 121, 123
Perceforest 208
Perceval 201, 204–5, 248
Petrarch, Francesco 95, 99, 102–3, 107
Picts 12–14, 16–18, 20–21
Plenitextuality 139, 170–71, 183
Poetics 60, 63, 76–78, 80, 98, 110, 116, 123, 126, 131, 255
Polychronicon 43–46, 52–53, 56, 215–16
Polydore Vergil 48–58, 217–22, 228
   Anglica Historia 48–56
Postcolonial 4, 61, 63, 66, 69, 76, 85–86
Priam 194, 197, 200, 202
Prise, John 212–13, 220–28
Proba, Faltonia Betitia 104
Prologues 43–46, 91, 104, 144, 148, 150, 198, 209–10, 216
Pyle, Howard 235

Quam cinxere freta (poem of uncertain authorship) 99–102, 105

Race, racial difference 12, 16–19, 64, 74, 218, 233, 237–38
Rastall, John 56
Roland 51, 65
Roman/Rome 14–15, 17–18, 48–49, 51–52, 54, 83, 94, 96–97, 101–2, 106, 193–95, 200, 205, 208, 212, 216, 220–21, 227, 252
Roman d'Eneas 106
Roman de la Rose 84, 90
Roman de Troie 106, 198–200, 203, 207
Romance 106, 110, 180, 194–96
   Arthurian see Arthurian Literature
   English 5, 194–96
   French 5, 194–96, 198
   German 196
   Latin 62
Round Table 200–1, 216, 229, 231, 234, 237, 239, 241
Roxburghe Club 4, 152–55, 157, 159–65
Ruggiero 194

Saint's lives/hagiography 28, 36, 180, 185
   Life of Saint Christopher 185
   Life of Saint Dubricius/Dyfrig 227
   Life of Saint Juliana 68
   Life of Saint Margarete 73
   Life of Saint Patrick 39
   Life of Saint Quintin 185
   Life of Saint Thomas 185
   Life of Saint Wulfstan 71
Sawles Warde 66
Saxons 12–14, 16–24
Science (medieval) 136–37, 145, 147, 149–51, 247
Scotland 13, 15, 51, 208 n. 64
Scribes 13 n. 18
Secretum secretorum 135, 148
Servius 104–6
Shakespeare, William 60, 77, 157, 163
Sir Gawain and the Green Knight 195–96, 209
Sisam, Kenneth 182
Slavery 59, 70–73
Smith, Thomas 178
Speculum Stultorum 92, 112
Spenser, Edmund 77, 220
Soliloquies 172–74, 185
St Albans Chronicle 122
St Columbanus 56
Stanzaic Morte Darthur 197

Statius 97
Strachey, Henry 152–53, 155–56, 158–59
Strode, Ralph 99–102
Sutherland-Leveson-Gower, George Granville, Marquis of Trentham, Earl Gower 4, 152–65

Tacitus 56, 219
Taliesin *see* Arthurian characters
Tedium 137–*38*, 150
Temporal reckoning 145, 149
Tennyson, Alfred Lord 229, 232, 233–35
  Idylls of the King 229–30, 232–33, 235, 242
  Lady of Shalott 201
Thames (River) 94, 144, 208
Thebes 198
Tibullus 96–97
Tite, Colin 181
Tolkien, J.R.R. 64–69, 72, 74
Translations 3, 5, 10–26, 32–35, 37, 40, 44–46, 50 n. 20, 52, 53 n. 29, 54 n. 32, 60, 66, 71, 75, 77, 80, 99–100, 135–36, 141 n. 25, 149, 170, 172, 186, 192, 214–15, 222, 247
Translators 3, 44–46, 71, 125, 170, 176, 215
  Dingestow translator 10–26
Treason/Treachery 14, 16, 22, 195, 209–10
Trentham Manuscript *see under* Manuscripts London, British Library, MS Add. 59495
Trevisa, John 44–46, 215
Tristram and Isolde 106, 207
Trojans 5, 18, 48, 55, 57, 125 n. 35, 193–98, 201–2, 203 n. 44, 205–11, 213, 220
Troy 5, 46, 104, 106, 124–25, 193–211
  New Troy 111, 118
Tudors 4, 42, 46–50, 53–55, 57–58, 213, 217, 220, 227
Tunstall, Cuthbert (bishop of London) 50

United States 5, 174, 229, 232–33, 235–36, 238–40, 244–46
Urbino 48–49

Usk, Thomas 102 n. 47
Uther *see* Arthurian characters

Vendetta dei descendenti di Ettore 207
Vortigern *see* Arthurian characters
Vulgate Cycle 198–99, 201, 204 n. 49

Wace 11, 24, 193 n. 2, 198–99, 201, 214
Wales 11 n. 9, 20, 28, 30, 32–34, 37, 43, 47, 54, 66, 71, 212, 216, 219–20, 223
Wali, Obiajuna 65–66, 77, 85
Walsingham, Thomas 120–23, 131
Warton, Thomas 63–64, 154
Welsh language 3, 9–12, 14, 16–18, 19 n. 51, 20, 22, 24, 28, 32–36, 40, 43, 61, 72–73, 213, 216, 219, 221–22, 225–26
Wharton, Henry 37 n. 45, 38
Whitman, Walt 235
William the Conqueror 70–71
William of Malmesbury 45, 53–54, 71, 213, 215–16, 218
  Gesta regum Anglorum 213
  Life of St Wulfstan 71
William of Newburgh 45–46, 50, 52–53, 55, 214
  Historia Rerum Anglicarum 50, 214
Winchester 43, 184, 216
Winner and Waster 210
Wolsey, Thomas 29
The Worthines of Wales 220

Virgil of Fulgentius 107
Virgil (P. Vergilius Maro) 95–97, 100–7, 228
  Aeneid 96, 101, 104–5, 107, 143
  Eclogues 104–5
  Georgics 101, 104–5
Vernacularity 4, 59–63, 65, 74–75, 85

Ygraine *see* Arthurian characters
Yvain *see* Arthurian characters

Zodiac 140, 148
Zumthor, Paul 170
Zupitza, Julius 175, 187–91

TABULA GRATULATORIA

Ros Allen
Elizabeth Archibald
Dorsey Armstrong
Laura Ashe
Arthur Bahr
Candace Barrington
Mary Bateman
Stephanie L. Batkie and
Matthew W. Irvin
Louise M. Bishop
Winston Black
Julia Boffey
María Bullón-Fernández
Linda Burke
Ardis Butterfield
Siobhain Bly Calkin
Kathy Cawsey
Nicole Clifton
David K. Coley
Margaret Connolly
Chris W. Cullnane II
Orietta Da Rold
Martha W. Driver
Robert R. Edwards
Charlene M. Eska
Susanna Fein
Laurie Finke
Joel Fredell

Helen Fulton
Andrew Galloway
Brian Gastle
Amanda Gerber
Richard Firth Green
William Green
Stephen Guy-Bray
Daniel Helbert
Mairi Stirling Hill
Jonathan Hsy
Michael Johnston
Ashby Kinch
Andrew W. Klein
Roger A. Ladd
Megan Leitch
Molly A. Martin
Julia Marvin
Simon Meecham-Jones
Robert J. Meindl
Robert J. Meyer-Lee
Alastair Minnis
Patrick Moran
Kelsey Moskal
Daniel W. Mosser
Peter Nicholson
Anita Obermeier
Caroline Palmer
Stephen Partridge

Niamh Pattwell
Noëlle Phillips
Raluca L. Radulescu
Jaclyn Rajsic
Stephen R. Reimer
Stephen H. Rigby
Robert Rouse
Paul Russell
Martha Dana Rust
Ana Sáez-Hidalgo
Anne Salamon
Misty Schieberle
Jeffrey Severs
Martin B. Shichtman
Victoria Shirley
Joshua Byron Smith
Andrew Taylor
John Thompson
Elaine Treharne
Michael W. Twomey
Cameron Wachowich
Renée Ward
Lawrence Warner
David Watt
K.S. Whetter
R. F. Yeager

TABULA GRATULATORIA

Ros Allen
Elizabeth Archibald
Dorsey Armstrong
Laura Ashe
Anson Bahr
Candace Barrington
Anne Baseman
Emanuel Bassoden
Marilyn W. Beeler
Carlos M. Bemer
Susan Black
John Bobey
Sean Bullard-Lundin
Linda Burke
Anita Butterfield
Cameron Caslow
Leigh Coate
Neal Coghill
Dawn K. Coley
Margaret Connolly
Chris A. Crichlock II
Lorenzo Cuadrado
Martin W. Davies
Robert P. Fairnttia
Charlene M. Fiehn
Susanna Fein
Laurie Finke
Joel Fredell

Helen Fulton
Andrew Galloway
Brian Gastle
Amanda Gerber
Richard Firth Green
William Green
Stephanos Ittig
David Einson
Mary Suetung Hill
Jonathan Hsu
Michelle John nell
Ashby Kinch
Stacey W. Klein
Roger A. Ladd
Marcel Lofeld
Meg K. Sharon
Rachana
Susan MacDoxe Jones
Robert L. Muneff
Robert J. Meyer-Lee
David Minin
Patrick Moran
Kelsey Moskal
Daniel W. Mosser
Peter Nicholson
Anita Obermeier
Caroline Palmer
Stephen Partridge

Wendi Parsewell
Noelle Phillips
Robert J. Rakatanen
Jaclyn Rajsic
Stephen R. Reimer
Stephen H. Rigby
Esther R. Rose
Paul Rowell
Joanna Choe Royn
Ana Sáez-Hidalgo
Anne Schuman
Meg Schubotz
Jeffrey Severs
Sharon R. Smith
Sherrin Shirley
Susan Byrne Smith
Andrew Snbo
John Thompson
Jason Treharne
Marcel W. Twomey
Lawrence Wade Miro
René, satin
Lawrence Warner
David Watt
K. S. Whetter
R. F. Yeager

Printed and bound by CPI Group (UK) Ltd, Croydon, CR0 4YY
15/12/2024
14612496-0004